FAMILY POLICY

Also by Margaret Wynn

FATHERLESS FAMILIES

MICHAEL JOSEPH BOOKS ON LIVE ISSUES

Series Editors: H. L. Beales, O. R. McGregor

Family Policy

MARGARET WYNN

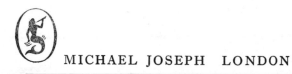

MICHAEL JOSEPH   LONDON

First published in Great Britain by
MICHAEL JOSEPH LTD
52 Bedford Square
London, W.C.1
1970

7181 0745 4

Set and printed in Great Britain by
Unwin Brothers Limited at the Gresham Press, Woking,
in Imprint type, eleven-point leaded, and bound by
James Burn at Esher

Contents

List of Tables

List of Figures

Acknowledgements

I am grateful to many people who helped me in this study of the family. Many of my arguments were inspired not only by colleagues in the United Kingdom but by discussion and correspondence with experts on the family in the U.S.A., Scandinavia and Western Europe and by reading their publications. But I am alone responsible for the emphasis and for the conclusions.

My first debt is to my Editor, Professor O. R. McGregor of Bedford College, University of London, whose advice on sources and reading and whose encouragement and criticism were essential to the conception and completion of the book.

I am indebted to Professor A. R. Ilersic, also of Bedford College, for criticism of those parts of this book relating to taxation and for valuable suggestions.

Dr Gertrude Willoughby, formerly of the London School of Economics, most generously shared with me her knowledge of social legislation in the Common Market countries and allowed me to see books and papers from her library. Dr Willoughby has herself been one of the heirs and successors of Eleanor Rathbone by her work in the British Committee of the International Union of Family Organizations.

Professor Peter Townsend, Professor Brian Abel-Smith and their colleagues in the poverty survey now being financed by the Rowntree Trust, and Mr Tony Lynes and the members of the Child Poverty Action Group have stimulated a wide public discussion of poverty, and have indeed changed the public view of poverty in the United Kingdom. In particular, they have associated poverty with the cost to poor parents of rearing children. The present study is not only concerned with poor families and is not wholly in agreement with the views of the Child Poverty Action Group. I am, however, personally indebted to Mr Tony Lynes and Mr Geoffrey Rankin for comments and discussion in the early stages of my work.

I am indebted to Miss Beti Jones, formerly Children's Officer for Glamorganshire, and now Chief Adviser on Social Work to

Secretary of State, Social Work Services Group of the Scottish Office, for many helpful discussions and for criticism of an early draft. Mr Robin Huws Jones kindly commented on a draft of the early chapters.

I am again indebted to my friend Miss Anne Jackson, who contributed to my book, *Fatherless Families*, from her wide professional experience of family problems. I visited Sweden and Finland with Miss Anne Jackson very early in the conception of this book. Like every writer on family problems, I have been much influenced by the writings of Mrs Alva Myrdal that have, indeed, become part of the thinking of all countries. Miss Britta Hasselroth, of the Swedish Ministry of Social Welfare, gave us every help in studying the family policies of Sweden. Miss Kate Wennerlund, of the Stockholm Child Welfare Board, provided us with many introductions and contributed much from her own knowledge.

The reader will appreciate my debt to Professor Pekka Kuusi of the University of Helsinki, in whose influential book, *Social Policy for the Sixties*, family policy occupies a major part. During a visit which Miss Anne Jackson and I made to Finland we valued the help and advice of Mrs Aune Mäkinen-Ollinen, head of the Department of Welfare and Population in the Ministry of Social Affairs. The Social Welfare Office of Helsinki City Council kindly arranged discussions with officials and visits to day-care centres. We are indebted to Mr Ahti Hailuoto of the Central Union for Child Welfare, to Mr Uusitalo of the Mannerheim League for Child Welfare and to officials of the Population and Family Welfare League for their guidance on measures to help the family, and especially the fatherless family, in Finland.

I am deeply indebted to many people in the U.S.A. whom I have never been privileged to meet. I have, however, been fortunate in having had the guidance on the American scene of Professor Elizabeth Wickenden of the City University of New York on her visits to London and by correspondence.

Everyone who studies the position of the poor and fatherless is indebted to Miss Mollie Orshansky for her papers in the *Social Security Bulletin* published by the United States Department of Health, Education and Welfare. American estimates of family needs at different levels of living, American consumer surveys and census data are more comprehensive than those of any other country. The Community Council of Greater New York provided very detailed information on their surveys and scales of family needs which I have used throughout this book. I have also been influenced by the books and papers of Dr Winifred Bell, Professor James Morgan and his colleagues of the University of Michigan and Dr Alvin Schorr.

The German literature on the family is extensive. The reader will note how frequently I refer to the writings of Professor Helga Schmucker, Director of the Institute of Home Economics of the Justus-Liebig University, Giessen. I am also indebted to Professor Hans Harmsen, Director of the Institute of Public Health, Hamburg, particularly for his publications on the problems of the fatherless family. I am indebted to Dr Ilse Kunz of Weilburg for guidance on the German literature on working women and social security benefits for widows.

I have been particularly influenced by the distinguished papers of Dr Heinz Simon, Head of the German Federal Ministry for Family Affairs, founded in 1953, and especially by his inaugural address on his appointment in 1955. I have also been influenced by Dr Max Wingen of the same Ministry, and particularly by his book on family policy.

I am indebted to several offices of the Federal German Government, and to offices of the provincial Governments, especially the statistical offices of Baden-Württemberg, Nordrhein-Westfalen, Bavaria and Hesse, and to the social office of the City of Stuttgart.

I am indebted for help to a number of German organizations for their bibliographies and advice, including in particular the Central German Institute for Social Questions (Deutsches Zentralinstitut für soziale Fragen), the Society for Social Progress (Gesellschaft für sozialen Fortschritt), and the German Society for Public and Private Social Work (Deutscher Verein für öffentliche und private Fürsorge).

The French monthly journal, *Informations Sociales*, published by l'Union Nationale des Caisses d'Allocations Familiales (UNCAF), (the national union of family allowances offices) is invaluable both in its documentation of a national point of view and in the coverage of the conferences and publications of other countries. Together with the Centre de Recherches et de Documentation sur la Consommation, the family allowance offices published a lengthy report in 1967 entitled 'Les Conditions de Vie des Familles'. Mlle Nicole Tabard and her colleagues who wrote the report have placed students in every country in their debt.

I am indebted to Professor Desabie of the Institut de la Statistique et des Études Economiques for information on the results of consumption surveys. This Institute has published a series of studies on family consumption in its journal *Études et Conjoncture*. Professor Trémolières, of the Nutrition Research Unit of the French Medical Research Institute, kindly allowed me to see his own paper on recommended dietary allowances in France and papers by himself and his colleagues on family budgets and food consumption.

I am indebted to Monsieur Robert Boudet of the International Union of Family Organizations and to Monsieur Vermeire of the European Secretariat for help in studying the publications and conference papers of the International Union, which are a valuable source of material on the position of the family in the modern world.

The Belgian family organizations have a weekly newspaper which reports on the family in Belgium and on the dialogue between the family organizations and the Ministry for the Family. One of the outstanding books published under the influence of the family movement of the last decade was Professor Pedro Beltrão's *Vers une Politique de Bien-être Familial*.

Professor Pierre de Bie kindly gave me information on his own studies of family levels of living. His major work of 1960 was financed by the family organizations of Belgium. I am also indebted to the Secretariat of the Administration for the Family for a copy of the Delpérée report which contains a comprehensive review of Belgian family policy, and for the opportunity to see papers presented to the London conference of ministers concerned with family affairs in 1963.

I am indebted to Dr Meerdink of the Amsterdam Bureau of Statistics for the history of the Amsterdam scale and its earlier use, and to Dr Verstege of the Netherlands Central Bureau of Statistics for information on the use of the scale in recent family expenditure surveys. Dr Mulder of the Netherlands Nutrition Council kindly sent me the Dutch Dietary Allowance scale.

Family expenditure surveys are essential tools in the study of levels of living. We owe the first cross-nation co-ordinated survey to the Director of Social Statistics of the Commission of the European Communities which, in co-operation with the statistical institutions of the six countries, organized the survey of 1963–4.

I thank especially Miss Audrey Moser, Deputy Secretary General of the International Union for Child Welfare, for her help and for the introductions she kindly gave me to many of those whose generous assistance is here gratefully acknowledged.

CHAPTER ONE

Family Responsibilities

The turn of the century is thirty years away. In the United States a 'Commission on the Year 2000' is trying to provide a setting for social policy during these next thirty years. Dr Daniel Bell, one of the members, reported on the way the Commission is thinking to a conference in New York in 1967. By the time we reach the year 2000, Dr Bell reported, society will have come to focus on children if only for the utilitarian reason that the whole progress of large-scale society depends on this human resource and its use:

'If children become, in a sense, a nation's most crucial resource, then one has to pay much more attention to what happens to children and to families with children, and where and why a society loses its resources.'[1]

This imaginative view of the world in thirty years time reflects the growing interest of economists in investment in 'human capital' or 'human resources'. Many readers devote their lives or leisure to the welfare of people because they are people, inspired by compassion or a sense of justice, and not because they are conscious of adding to human capital. The concept of human capital may seem offensive. However, the identification of people, and children in particular, as a *resource*, provides a new justification for devoting *resources* to their development, care and maintenance. As a British economist has said in his own defence:

'Refusal to recognize the investment character of a problem because people are involved may result in people receiving worse treatment than machines.'[2]

Certainly in the world's thinking about education the concept of investment in human capital has come to stay and is being elaborated in an ever-increasing literature from many countries. In the words of an American economist:

[1] Bell, D. (1967), p. 171.
[2] Johnson, H. G. (1964), in Blaug (1968), p. 39.

'It simply is not possible to have the fruits of modern agriculture and the abundance of modern industry without making large investments in human beings. Truly the most distinctive feature of our economic system is the growth in human capital.'[1]

For the first five years, however, of the average child's life the only environment he knows is his home and through most of childhood, school and parents share in his nurture. Both parents and school invest in the child, but the investment by parents is greater and the consequence of under-investment by the parents is more serious. Professor Wiseman concludes his evidence to the Plowden Committee on primary school children:

'We regard two of our findings as being of the first importance: that environmental forces bear most heavily on the brightest of our children; and that factors in the home are overwhelmingly more powerful than those of the neighbourhood and the school.'[2]

In a later chapter we shall give the evidence for the view that the very best schools can compensate for unsatisfactory homes and lack of parental interest. Most of the total investment in human capital is made by parents within the family and depends upon the resources made available to parents for satisfying the needs of their family.

The family environment is the major influence in determining the quality of the next generation and is dependent upon the income, attitudes, education and capacity of parents. The parents' task in bringing up their children depends upon the number of children, every additional child adding to the time, trouble and expense for the parents. The needs of families depend also upon the ages of the children. The extent to which family needs are satisfied also depends upon a great variety of external things including incomes and prices, taxation, social security benefits, the availability of housing at the right prices or at the right rents and upon the amenities of the urban or rural environment.

In the last hundred years the Governments of all developed countries have invested increasingly in the next generation. It has come to be generally understood, at least in the context of educa-

[1] Schultz, T. W. (1961), in Blaug (1968), p. 31.
[2] Wiseman, S. (1967), Plowden Report, vol. 2, Appendix 9, p. 382.

tion, that the future of every country depends upon this investment. It has not, however, yet been so widely accepted in this country that the same logic applies to the whole range of social and insurance services as they affect children and young persons. In Common Market and Scandinavian countries the view is more frequently expressed that not only education but social security and social services have an investment content too, and that this content varies very much from one service to another. The annual report of social security in the Common Market countries said in 1959:

'We have found, since the end of the last war, in the countries of the Common Market, a stirring of the conscience of the public authorities about the specific needs of families and the necessity for measures, both economic and social, designed progressively to spread the cost of family responsibilities over the whole community. In some cases the political reasons for a policy of family support were in origin mainly demographic. But everywhere today the motives have gone beyond the intention to relieve poverty or even beyond considerations of justice: we are now conscious that aid to the next generation is a valuable investment and we are conscious of the exacting cost of giving this aid through education, professional training, employment, help with housing and general economic assistance.'[1]

Two years later, in 1961, another annual report noted that the question of how to share the cost of family responsibilities has no simple or straightforward answer:

'In every country of the Common Market there are completed or in progress studies designed to throw light by scientific methods on the policies of spreading the cost of family responsibilities. Official commissions have been allocated this task.'[2]

There is, then, a growing literature in many countries concerned with the concept of 'social investment'. Expenditure is considered to have a social investment content if it may reasonably be expected to produce a return to the community in terms, for example, of the quality and earning power of the next generation. Expenditure on education is already regarded throughout the world as a social investment. The Newsom Report on the education of pupils of average and less than average ability remarked:

[1] Communauté Économique Européenne, Exposé 1959, p. 275.
[2] Communauté Économique Européenne, Exposé 1961, p. 216.

'We therefore think it essential to state at the outset the economic argument for investment in our pupils. The need is . . . for a generally better educated and intelligently adaptable labour force to meet new demands.'[1]

It is, however, now increasingly recognized that the social investment in education can be frustrated by a poor environment for the child within his family and by a poor environment surrounding his home and family. The quality of the next generation is not only determined by the school but by the family. The Plowden Report of 1966 stated:

'It has been recognized that education is concerned with the whole man; henceforth it must be concerned with the whole family.'[2]

In all developed countries Governments have recognized that the great majority of parents cannot pay for the education of their children; state education paid for by general taxation has become accepted. This is a main investment by Government in the next generation and a country's future.

Indeed, in the context of education, not only the Common Market countries but all countries have accepted that some part of the cost of rearing the next generation must be spread over the community as a whole. Some part of the educational expenditure is frustrated by family misfortune, such as the loss of or prolonged sickness of fathers or mothers, low earning capacity of the father, or serious housing difficulties, and by insurance arrangements that do not adequately reflect family needs. Indeed, a child does not generally do well at school if he lives in a family in difficulties. There is no real separation possible between the educational and family policy, and both must be the concern of Government. If it is expedient to spread some part of the cost of education over the community as a whole, is it not also expedient to spread some part of the other costs of investment in the next generation? The investment content of social policy is discussed in Chapters 9 and 10.

If education has an investment content, so also has expenditure upon children by parents and expenditure upon the family environment. In the course of a lifetime a well-trained man may

---

[1] Newsom (1963), p. 5.
[2] Plowden (1966), p. 48.

add £100,000 or sometimes much more to a country's flow of goods and services. Whether or not he does so does not depend only upon his education but also upon his upbringing from his early childhood. Some men add little to the wealth of the community and some cost the state thousands of pounds. Education is only one factor that decides whether a man becomes an economic asset or a liability.

The family environment is partly determined by family income. The rearing of children requires time, trouble and money. The satisfactory rearing of children may continue to provide its reward for fifty or sixty years. The income of parents, therefore, has a social investment content. The consequences of social expenditure may be short term or long term; the social investment content of the money spent on different services therefore varies widely.

How, then, has the family fared in the development of the social security system during the last thirty years? Is the social investment content of present social security high or low? Does our social security system place emphasis on the community needs in the longer term or upon the satisfaction of short-term needs?

A social policy of meeting needs is too limited, but a policy based upon social investment also has its limitations. How far is money given to, or left in the hands of, parents spent on their children? How much do parents earning £500 or £5,000 a year in fact spend on their children? How far does the useful expenditure on children increase with parental income? Where is the point of diminishing returns? What is the social investment content of the expenditure by the non-parents and the childless? All these are big questions to which this book attempts only to make a contribution.

The quality of the next generation of citizens, work people and parents is mainly the responsibility of families with dependent children in this generation. These family responsibilities are, at any one time, very unevenly spread over a nation's households. Most households do not have any dependent children; the members are unmarried, or childless, or the children have grown up and left home. At any one time most adults have no parental responsibilities. Most earned and unearned incomes are received by adults with no children to support. Most of the nation's wealth flows to non-parents as we shall show in later chapters. We shall ask in the course of this book who benefits from social security allowances and who from the National Health Service. We shall inquire how the tax burden falls on families and on non-families; we shall compare the standard of living of parents and their dependent children with the standard of living of households with no dependent children.

The children are also very unevenly distributed at any one time among the families who have dependent children. Three-quarters of all dependent children are in only 22 per cent of United Kingdom households. Over half of all dependent children are in less than 13 per cent of all households. Rather a small minority of adults are at any one time carrying most of the responsibility for rearing the next generation.

The propagation of the population is also heavily dependent in Western countries on a rather small minority of adults who choose to have three or more children. These families have to compensate for the very large numbers of adults, indeed about half the persons of recent generations, who do not reproduce themselves. There are large numbers of persons who never marry, or marry and have no children, and a similar number of couples who have only one child. The infertility of about half the adult population has to be compensated for by the greater fertility of a minority. At any one time less than 9 per cent of all households in the United Kingdom include three or more children dependent on them; these households are bringing up over 40 per cent of the next generation. Over 40 per cent of all adults alive today were brought up in the minority households of the last generation which contained three or more dependent children.

Any picture of family responsibilities being spread fairly and reasonably across the broad shoulders of most of the country's adults in the prime of life is essentially false. Most of the time, trouble and money expended on rearing the next generation falls on the shoulders of a minority of adults in each age group, in each generation, and on quite a small minority of all adults or earners or taxpayers in the community at any one time. Parents have the care and charge of their children for more of their childhood than have the schools. They feed the child, except for a small contribution from school meals for part only of the year, they clothe him, they provide his leisure pursuits. They nurse him through all illnesses except the most serious requiring hospital care. Above all, it is the parents who lay down the foundations of the child's personality, of his emotional stability and mental health. Parents provide the child's early image of the adult world and of adult behaviour. On the parent's foundations schools build. The school may compensate for parental lack of care or modify the effects of parents' shortcomings, but the school can never entirely replace the role of the parent. In the partnership between parents and school to rear and mould the next generation it is the parents who make the greater contribution in time, trouble and money. It is a part of the ritual of political life to acknowledge the importance of the family. How far does this ritual acceptance extend to parents in their role of the family's managers? In other roles these parents are taxpayers, rate-payers, consumers, or persons receiving social security benefits. How far does a social investment policy require that help should be given to parents in these roles? The life-cycle of family needs is described in Chapter 6.

There are, however, people in every country who accept the relative or absolute impoverishment of families as a means of discouraging an increase in the population. These people believe that human reproduction is motivated by economic circumstances. They believe that there is a deep contradiction between social investment and population control. A reduction in the quality of the next generation should be accepted, so it is implied, to avoid the dire consequences of overpopulation. The final chapter of this book discusses this supposed contradiction between quality and numbers. Do improvements in family life and in the education and well-being of children really increase the reproductive propensities of their parents? Does the impoverishment of families really reduce the birth-rate of these families? It has even been suggested that middle-class parents 'who tend to set standards of family building habits' should be particularly penalized compared with the childless middle class. Do parents in their reproductive tendencies really conform to the image of economic man? Are babies, perhaps, consumer durables?[1] It is suggested in the final chapter that human motivation is indeed much more complicated,

---

[1] 'Are Babies Consumer Durables?' is the title of a recent paper by Judith Blake criticizing the view that reproductive performance is an aspect of economic behaviour. Blake, J. (1968).

and that social investment in the quality of the next generation is not incompatible with population control.

The poorer parents are, the smaller the investment they are able to make in their children, and the more prosperous the parents, the greater is the investment they do, in fact, make on average in their children. While this may be obvious, the implications for taxation and social policy are quite generally disregarded. If taxes on parents are increased the investment in children is reduced, and if parents are helped financially in any way the investment in their children increases in the average case and at all normal income levels.

This concept of investment in human capital and in the next generation is not at all consistent with social policies based upon minimum income, that is, social policies that accept that if a family achieves a certain arbitrary minimum income then it is 'all right', or 'not in need'. Lord Beveridge's recommendations were based upon this concept that the main purpose of social policy was to ensure that people, including families, had at least a minimum income. The notion that help to families should be confined to those below some 'poverty line' would only be acceptable if it could be shown that an increase in parental income above this low level did not result in a useful increase in their expenditure upon their families. It is established, and indeed apparent, that the quality of the next generation depends mainly on investment by parents with incomes above the poverty level, that their investment in the next generation increases as their incomes increase and that it is parents rather than non-parents who make the main investment. The ideal of a minimum income has a long history. Chapter 9 discusses for whom this idea has been superseded and for whom it is still retained.

It is not possible to make the best use of available resources if the needs of families are not understood. The responsibilities of different families vary widely. What, for example, is the cost to parents of boys and girls during their last years at school? The answer to this question is necessary for a national policy on educational maintenance allowances. The estimation of the needs of families in the short term or even over a year or two is necessary for some purposes but it may give quite inadequate emphasis to the investment content of social policy. The investment content of social expenditure is essential as a basis for incomes policy.

This book discusses some part of the problem of assessing needs. The assumption runs through countless statements about social policy that needs can be quantified or assessed.[1] Is it possible to make reasonable assessments of need on which to base social policy? Much current thinking would be seriously upset if it were not possible to do so. It has been assumed that needs can be quantified before any well-based quantitative scale for the assessment of needs has, in fact, been drawn up.

The Beveridge Report of 1942 said:

'The Plan for Social Security starts with consideration of the people and their needs.'[2]

Twenty-six years later, on 17th January, 1968, the Chancellor of the Exchequer said:

'Next year I hope to introduce full selectivity for family allowances and to do it in such a way that people who are not in real need of them do not draw them at all.'[3]

Both the Chancellor today and Lord Beveridge a generation ago, assumed that needs can be assessed, though Professor D. Lees could write quite recently, in an article on 'Poor families and fiscal reform', that a scale of needs does not yet exist:

'Nor is there compelling evidence that supplementary benefits[4] are related to human needs. . . . The very least that is required is a scale of human needs, based on careful and systematic investigation.'[5]

Professors Abel-Smith and Townsend in a book published in 1965 wrote:

'The first aim should be to develop various standards which indicate need or poverty.'[6]

and they throw doubt on the assumption that 'households of different composition living at the national assistance standard have comparable levels of living'.[7]

[1] See, for example, House of Commons Debate, 23rd Feb. 1966: 'Welfare State.' All parties speak of 'meeting needs' as a basic social policy.
[2] Beveridge (1942), par. 310.   [3] House of Commons, 17th Jan. 1968.
[4] National Assistance was replaced by non-contributory benefit (supplementary allowances and supplementary pensions) in 1966.
[5] Lees, D. (1967), p. 7.
[6] Abel-Smith and Townsend (1965), p. 63.
[7] *Idem*, p. 17.

In 1967 the Ministry of Social Security published a report entitled 'Circumstances of Families'. This study was based on the assumption that supplementary benefits do reflect needs, a belief on which Professor Lees throws doubt. There is, indeed, a growing literature in many countries concerned with human needs that suggests that the correspondence between real needs and the supplementary or non-contributory benefit scales of the United Kingdom is unsatisfactory, as is shown later in this book.

The concept of the *standard of living* is closely related to that of *need*. A continuous scale for measuring the standard of living is needed in order to make it possible to advance beyond the primitive and restrictive notion that only a poverty level is required, and that it will suffice for social policy to divide the population into 'the poor' and the 'not poor'.

Recent discussions of social policy have laid stress upon the concept of selectivity. The Chancellor, in the quotation above, used the concept of selectivity to mean selection in favour of those in need and against those not in need. The case for full selectivity in pensions, sick-pay, unemployment pay and other benefits would seem to be very much the same as for the 'full selectivity in family allowances' proposed by the Chancellor. Selectivity applied to all or any of these services assumes, however, that at least rough assessments can be made of the comparative needs of a wide range of family units containing persons of different ages, different sexes, and both with and without dependent children. Chapter 2 discusses methods of assessing family needs and the use of standard budgets and family expenditure surveys. Chapter 3 of this book begins with a simpler question on which there is substantial information: 'What are the comparative needs of children of different ages and of adults?'

In the context of 'selectivity in family allowances' the concept has been used of the 'standard rate taxpayer'.[1] The income

[1] The 'standard rate taxpayer' is any taxpayer who pays tax at the standard rate on increments of income. The 'standard rate taxpaying threshold' defines the lowest income at which a taxpayer pays tax at the standard rate on an increment of income, and this depends upon his 'allowances' for wife and children or other dependants. These 'allowances' are similar to the American 'exemptions' but are lower and more complicated. The 'standard rate' is paid over a range of incomes between the 'reduced rate' level and the surtax level. It is a plateau of tax not found in other tax systems. The gross income levels by family size at which it is paid are given in Appendix 2.

at which a person just begins to pay tax at the standard rate on some small part of his income defines an income level. This concept was used by the Prime Minister in the House of Commons on 16th January 1968, as a threshold of income above which family allowances are not 'needed'. This is an innovation. The community could be divided into those who pay some tax at the standard rate and those who pay no tax at the standard rate. It could then be assumed that the first category, persons paying some tax at the standard rate, all have less urgent needs than those who pay no tax at the standard rate.

How far is this a reasonable assumption? It assumes, of course, that income tax allowances are based on assessments of need. Is this really so? Is it true that at the standard rate taxpaying threshold all families have roughly equivalent standards of living? Or are some families really much better off than others at this level of income? There are many arguments in favour of using the income tax system for assessing need, thus avoiding wasteful and oppressive duplication of means tests. The use of the income tax system in this way could only be justified if income tax allowances were themselves based on careful investigation of the comparative needs of families of different sizes and compositions.

This use of the 'standard rate taxpayer' to define a level of need illustrates again that several levels corresponding to different points on a standard of living scale are necessary. A poverty or subsistence level is important but other levels are required for the guidance of housing policy, educational policy, the payment of family allowances and taxation. Only a standard of living scale can relate these different needs to each other and avoid confusion and inequity. In later chapters of this book the needs both of individuals and of family groups will be discussed and scales of need will be suggested.

In most countries today there are tax allowances for wives and children and special provisions for elderly persons. In the major countries except for the United States, there are also direct money payments to families with children. The distribution of income between different classes of persons is profoundly modified by Governments in all advanced countries both by taxation and by social security payments. Although the first purpose of taxation is to raise revenue, taxation also redistributes wealth. This redistribution cannot achieve a better correspondence between incomes and needs of the population unless there is some way of measuring need. Assessments of need are therefore relevant to taxation and national insurance and all measures that redistribute income deliberately. In the United Kingdom the Ministry of Social Security, the Ministry of Health, the Treasury, the Department of Education and Science, the Ministry of Housing and Local Government, and Local Authorities all make decisions based upon some assessment of the needs of families of different sizes and compositions. These departmental assessments are not all consistent with each other.

Some of these differences between departmental assessments, when they intend to define the same standard of living, seem impossible to justify. The poverty level or minimum income level is one traditional point on a standard of living scale. However, different standards are needed for different purposes. Housing policy cannot, for example, possibly be based on providing housing for persons and families living at the poverty level. Housing standards must look to the future and reflect the expectations of the people. There is an important American concept of a 'modest-but-adequate' standard of living used in this book that is described by a point higher up the standard of living scale than the poverty level, and suitable as a basis of much housing policy. To take one example, the standard for space and amenities in domestic dwellings, known as the Parker-Morris standard, applies only to the 'modest-but-adequate' level of living and above. This is discussed in Chapter 5.

The modest-but-adequate standard of living for families is partly defined by the educational needs of dependent children and the needs of children to participate in the life of the community. Subsistence incomes make no such provision. The traditional right to a minimum income provides an inadequate purpose of social policy seen in the context of educational needs and a community with rising expectations for its children. The modest-but-adequate standard is needed to support education, just as it is needed for planning new housing. The derivation of the modest-but-adequate level and its uses is discussed in Chapter 2.

A social policy based upon sound estimates of need is likely to make better use of resources than many schemes that pay little or no regard to need. For example, the taxation of the estate of a deceased person in the United Kingdom is an extreme case where the needs and resources of the beneficiaries from the estate are largely disregarded. Thus wealth is not spread even though it is taxed.

Again, in most discussion of needs or of the standard of living the emphasis is on short-term needs. Chapter 4 considers needs not only in the very short term but over periods of a year or two. It is emphasized that there is a cumulative element in both prosperity and poverty. A subsistence allowance that is adequate in the short term may not be adequate in the longer term. If a family is dependent on an income over a period of years, how much larger does this income have to be to establish equivalence with an income that only has to support a family for a few weeks? What, also, is the influence on family needs of the season of the year?

The concept of need as something measurable in terms only of current consumption is quickly seen to be too simple. Pensions, benefits and allowances that ignore the duration of dependence upon them are seen not to make the best use of available resources. The very short view of needs leads to wrong conclusions, because some needs that are quite compelling are also cumulative. Considered over still longer periods of time, over a decade or a generation, the concept of short-term needs, even if these are based on careful investigation, is seen to be an even less adequate basis for social policy. It is not enough to satisfy the need to consume in the short term.

The resources available even in advanced countries for satisfying the needs of the people are likely to remain inadequate and limited for a long time. Social policies must be compatible with other policies for promoting economic growth. Social policies placing emphasis upon families with dependent children are growth-oriented in their own right. There is a need to invest in improvements in human standards from one generation to the next; a paper submitted to a conference on social security of the Common Market countries concluded:

'Who does not understand that to provide for the nourishment, the clothing, the education, the training of the younger generation and to prepare them for the tasks of tomorrow, is also to place the European economy at the service of mankind?'[1]

[1] Communautés Européennes, Conference 1962, vol. 2, p. 147.

Family policy must therefore embrace both the future and the present. The family is not only the cradle of our future society but it is also the centre of social life for most people in the present. The working environment is too often impersonal and comfortless. Home and family compensate for deficiencies of many people's working lives. Home and family are at the centre of ambition and self-respect for ordinary men and women. The family provides the supreme comfort and support for persons of all ages. The successful rearing of a family provides the main sense of achievement for most people. Family joys and family griefs are the most keenly felt joys and griefs for most men and women. However successful a man may be in his job, however satisfying his work may be, family life is still important. How often do those who have no children follow with generous interest and find satisfaction in the lives of nephews or nieces, or adopt, or foster, or become 'aunt and uncle' to other people's children? Children are a stake in the future for their parents, and for others who are not their parents.

The family environment is recognized by psychologists as virtually the only environment in which it is safe to bring up children, and they consider that where the natural family does not exist, a substitute family must be found or the family must be substituted by small children's homes reproducing as far as possible the environment of the stable, happy family. The numbers of children who are born into any society are influenced by human motives that quite normally have their origins in family circumstances. The family has great political significance, many of the most strongly held beliefs of men and women being associated with the protection of their homes and children. The support and protection of family life has been a central aim of all denominations of Christianity.

Family policy can only be built upon knowledge and understanding of family problems. Studies of the time, trouble and expense of rearing children are one kind of necessary knowledge. The next chapter discusses the methods of assessing family needs and the purposes of such assessments.

CHAPTER TWO

The Assessment of Family Need

The assessment of human need is difficult; as a United Nations Committee once wrote,

'Human needs and wants range from common biological needs—as for food, water and protection against cold—to culturally defined motivations and wants. Into the picture enters the whole field of desires and values for which man may be striving; desires for particular types of food, drink, housing and clothing appealing to the taste; for access to educational, cultural and recreational facilities.'[1]

However difficult it may be to assess the needs of individuals and families, it must be done if injustice is to be avoided. For if national scales of need are not devised, then rules of thumb and historical remnants will be used; the level of need for particular people will be decided on hunches and guesses. One traditional method has been to draw up a budget with minimum food and clothing requirements and to add a figure for personal spending. Many such budgets have been produced in different countries at different times. The task of producing budget standards for families of different sizes cannot be avoided because in the words of an American writer:

' . . . successful accomplishment of numerous activities in our economy depends on well-defined concepts of adequate living standards. Budget standards are needed to evaluate the adequacy of income of self-supporting families as well as needs for community assistance of various kinds. Estimates of need obtained from such standards provide the basis for broad legislative, economic and social programs.'[2]

The different conceptual levels of adequacy are a major difficulty in the setting of standards. However, two levels of adequacy have emerged in a number of countries as conceptually valuable. There is a 'poverty standard' which has a long history in the United Kingdom and in many other countries. There is also a higher budget standard that is called in America the 'modest-but-adequate standard'. A similar concept is also applied in Sweden for

[1] United Nations (1954, IV, 5), p. 2.
[2] Lamale (1958), p. 297.

the determination of income ceilings above which, for example, rent rebates are not payable to families. The American description 'modest-but-adequate' is used in this book.

The phrase 'a modest-but-adequate standard' was first used to describe the City Worker's Family Budget which was compiled by the Bureau of Labor in 1946 and was revised in 1960 and 1966.[1] It aimed to 'satisfy prevailing standards of what is necessary for health, efficiency, the nurture of children and for participation in community activities'. Hinrichs, one of the men who initiated the work on this budget, said of it:

'It can best be described as a single point on a scale of living patterns that ranges continuously from a mere existence level to levels of luxurious living . . . The point selected for measurement is in general the point where the struggle for more and more things gives way to the desire for better and better quality. Above this level, for example, the average family is likely to be more interested in escaping from an endless round of the cheaper cuts of meat than in increasing the number of pounds of meat that it buys'.[2]

The 'modest-but-adequate' standard of the City Worker's Family Budget generally provides an income that is rather less than double that marking the poverty line, using the poverty

[1] A history of family budgets, an account of the origins of the City Worker's Family Budget and the procedures by which it was compiled is given in: 'Workers Budgets in the United States: City Families and Single Persons, 1946 and 1947', Bulletin No. 927 of Bureau of Labor Statistics, U.S. Department of Labor.

A new set of goods and services and other modifications were included in a revision in 1959: 'The Interim City Worker's Family Budget', by Helen H. Lamale and Margaret S. Stotz, *Monthly Labor Review*, August 1960. Reprint No. 2346.

In 1966-8 the Budget was revised in the light of the Consumer Expenditure Surveys 1960-1: 'City Worker's Family Budget at the Moderate Standard', Autumn 1966: Bulletin No. 1570-1 (1967) of Bureau of Labor Statistics. Alterations in the equivalence scales used are given in: 'Revised Equivalence Scale', Bulletin No. 1570-2 (1968) of Bureau of Labor Statistics. Procedures, pricing and specifications and regional differences are described in 'City Worker's Family Budget: Pricing, Procedures, Specifications and Average Prices', Bulletin No. 1570-3 (1966) of Bureau of Labor Statistics. The Budget is adapted for elderly persons, with explanations in: 'Retired Couples' Budget', Bulletin No. 1570-4 (1968) of Bureau of Labor Statistics. See also Watts (1967); Friedman, M. (1952); Bureau of Labor Statistics, *Monthly Labor Review*, Nov. 1960; Lamale (1963).

[2] Hinrichs (1948), p. 1.

standard more recently developed by the United States Federal Government. It is convenient in transferring these concepts to other countries to regard the 'modest-but-adequate' standard as defined by an income that is *twice* the income regarded in any country as being necessary for minimum subsistence and the avoidance of poverty.

The modest-but-adequate level should be such that a child's education is not seriously prejudiced by those difficulties of the home environment that depend upon family income. The poverty standard, only providing just enough means to avoid malnutrition, still leaves many homes deficient in space or fuel or household equipment or pocket money, deficiencies that will isolate a family from the main-stream of life and prejudice a child's upbringing. At a modest-but-adequate level of housing for example, an adolescent should have to share a room with at most one other family member of the same sex, or have a room of his own. This is usually impossible at the poverty level. At the modest-but-adequate level a family should be able to afford a modest holiday every year; the poor family hardly ever takes a family holiday away from home.

There are many circumstances in which a poverty level is of very little value in making social policy. Thus, in the United Kingdom, when new towns are planned standards of housing have to be set, and these must generally be appropriate to the modest-but-adequate standard and upwards and the rent will then be appropriate to such families. Families near the poverty level cannot afford higher rents. Houses built to let at rents which these poorer families could afford would not be of acceptable new town building standards. The new towns are, in fact, acting as a social sieve accepting the skilled, higher paid persons, providing housing appropriate to them and leaving the unskilled, lower paid workers and their families in the old areas.

In some cases standards of need are being used that are not genuinely related to either a poverty or a modest-but-adequate standard. There are, for example, three different standards of parental need used in the United Kingdom for granting help towards children's education: one for maintenance allowances for children staying on after school-leaving age, another for boarding education for children maintained by local authorities, and a third for maintenance grants for university students.

In the most advanced countries there are many millions of families living above the poverty standard but below the modest-but-adequate standard who may be described as the 'hard-pressed'. The concentration of social policy mainly upon the achievement of a poverty standard is more and more unacceptable; social policy must be concerned also with the hard-pressed.

The National Union of Teachers has published examples of hard-pressed families. A young teacher, Brian Farmer, has two young children; he earns, with an extra job, about the average British wage. His wife wrote:

'My husband left College at 21, and after two months his first monthly salary cheque was £34. We were married with a baby son, and living with in-laws. Financial worries caused us to seek other accommodation, and after several months we had to accept a dilapidated flat at a monthly rent of £18. When our second child was born we were forced to move into a single room at £12 per month. At that time my husband was working every Saturday and every school holiday delivering bread for a local bakery.

'Our marriage was almost ruined by this existence. We were determined to have our own home, and, having no money, we begged £200 from a relative as a deposit on a house. For a year I went out to work as a barmaid, for six evenings a week. The strain was enormous.

'Eventually we obtained a mortgage from the N.U.T. Although the first arm-chairs in our house cost 5/-, we have slowly improved on this and our home is now half furnished. We have had to forgo the "luxury" of a holiday for the last four years, in order to afford the necessities of a home, such as carpets and a cooker. My husband has one suit, which is seven years old, for school and best wear, and I have little more.

'Today, my husband, in addition to his teaching and spare-time bakery job, has two night school classes, which brings his wages to a weekly total of £20. After the standing monthly bills are paid (mortgage and housekeeping, etc.) the £4 left evaporates on bus fares, electricity and gas bills, and the children's clothes. We have an old car, which is necessary for the bakery job, and never used for any other purpose in case it needs repair, which we cannot afford.'[1]

The young teachers in this study who had wives and children were among the hard-pressed. They are, nevertheless, mostly in the category 'not in need' as defined by the Government.

[1] National Union of Teachers (1967), p. 10.

Flat-rate insurance and schemes of public assistance are related to minimum income levels; graduated or wage-related insurance schemes have quite a different objective which is to prevent the standard of living of a wage-earner falling to the minimum income level. Thus, in the United Kingdom, the earnings-related short-term unemployment and sickness benefits and contributions begin at earnings of £9 a week with a ceiling of £30.[1] Nine pounds a week was just over twice the minimum subsistence level of £4[2] which was the flat-rate benefit in 1966. Nine pounds is thus near the modest-but-adequate level in the United Kingdom for a single person.

Ever-increasing numbers of people who are above the poverty level have become interested in achieving the higher modest-but-adequate standard. There has been a 'revolution of expectations' of ordinary people. The achievement of modest-but-adequate standards must therefore be the aim of many measures that will, however, in the event if properly designed, also achieve a further reduction in the numbers of people who are still poor. The development of two standards in the advanced countries is indeed happening apace. Social policies are likely to be concerned increasingly with the hard-pressed as well as with the poor.

In a family with children there is a high national investment content in the family expenditure up to and beyond the modest-but-adequate level; the proportion of their income spent by parents on their children and adolescents at different income levels is discussed in a later chapter.

There are countries even in Europe with large areas where most people are poor, as we shall see, and where the achievement of a modest-but-adequate standard is an unrealistic aim for any but a small minority. However, in other advanced countries the achievement of a higher standard has become a main social purpose. A spokesman from the International Labour Office at a conference of Common Market countries recognized the inadequacy of social policies based only upon the relief of poverty:

'The aims of social security include assuring such a level of benefits as will guarantee a real protection against need and not only afford a

[1] Pensions and National Insurance (1966), Leaflet N.I. 155.
[2] Reasons for the choice of this figure as a minimum subsistence level are given in Chapter 7.

help in poverty . . . the common characteristic of most systems [in the Common Market] is the remarkable effort made to raise benefits to a level sufficient to guarantee the level of life considered appropriate and that is to say adequate.'[1]

The Secretary of the French Trades Union Confederation declared that:

'social security must boldly enable . . . the least favoured groups in society to join those more fortunate without however forbidding the latter to profit by the necessary increase in well-being which an expanding economy permits'.[2]

The French concept of a 'minimum social', the socially acceptable minimum, was described by Professor de Bie, President of the Belgian Council for the Family, to a world conference of sociologists in New York:

'The "minimum social" must include whatever is considered necessary in a given society at a certain state of development. The degree of civilization achieved by a society gives rise to new needs which correspond to the habits of the mass of the population and are part of the culture: when these needs cannot be met by any members of society then these members resent this as a deprivation of something essential to themselves and feel themselves frustrated. Thus, in our societies, the need for food is now sophisticated, there are also the needs for a higher level of hygiene, there are intellectual needs, needs for education and also for leisure which correspond to the "minimum social" . . . This enables us to say that in our countries, the subsistence minimum can no longer be related as an appropriate measure for family allowances. No one any longer thinks that the economic security of families is a matter of procuring for each family the means of keeping their children alive, this would be to limit the economic security of families to minimum assistance levels. . . . The economic security of families is only assured if it enables families whether their responsibilities are large or small to balance their budgets, if it enables children of the family not only to be fed, housed and clothed . . . but to enjoy all those good things, social and cultural which are by right, if not always in practice, available for all children of society.'[3]

The acceptance of at least two bench-marks in codifying

[1] Communautés Européennes Conference (1962), vol. 2, p. 9.
[2] *Ibid.*, vol. 1, p. 197.   [3] de Bie (1960), p. 133.

human needs does not make the assessment of these needs any easier. There are many questions that must be asked and answered about family needs that relate both to poverty and modest-but-adequate standards, and indeed to most families. The research of the last few decades enables us to begin to answer many questions about family needs to which there was no answer even twenty-five years ago.

How far, for example, do the economic needs of a family in the winter time compare with needs in the summer time? How far do the short-term needs of a family differ from the long-term needs? By how much does an income continued for a number of years need to differ from an income continued for only a few months in order to maintain a prescribed standard of living, whether defined as a poverty or a modest-but-adequate level? All these questions are valid for most countries, for although the quantitative answers may be different, it is beyond argument that the economic needs of a family depend both upon the season in all temperate climates and upon the length of time that a family has to subsist upon a low income.

Minimum subsistence incomes are not based upon any absolute assessment of minimum human needs and never can be. They are, indeed, in any country a compromise between what the Government of that country decides it can afford and its wish to spare the least fortunate members of the community from the extreme consequences of poverty and destitution. Public opinion generally has an important influence upon the level of minimum subsistence incomes.

There are many tests that can be applied to minimum subsistence incomes that assist judgement. The adequacy of the diet of the average person living on a minimum income is one basic test. There is now reasonably general agreement between the medical authorities of the leading countries on the minimum nutritional requirements necessary for good health in men, women and children. These generally accepted standards of nutritional requirements provide one basic yardstick for the assessment of poverty in developed countries.

The *poverty standard* is expressed in the United States and sometimes elsewhere as the income that results in the average family avoiding malnutrition. It cannot be too strongly stressed that it is the diet that the people living on this income *choose* to have that is the only test. The diet that they might have if they had expert knowledge of food values and different tastes is generally irrelevant. It has been said that an expert dietician with a thorough knowledge of food values and willing to eat an unpalatable diet could in 1966 keep himself healthy with an expenditure on food of only 7s. a week in the United Kingdom![1] Expert dieticians never have to live on subsistence incomes, but the unfortunate men, women and children who do, have often received an unusually poor education—although this is by no means always so, because extreme poverty can result from the prolonged sickness or loss of the male breadwinner of a family or from infirmity. Among ordinary people, eating habits of long standing decide the cost of an adequate diet. Theoretical low cost budgets cannot be enforced and have little reality. The needs of poor people can only be gauged by what they think, by the way in which they spend their limited resources and by observing the actual consequences in terms of adequate or inadequate nutrition. This must always be so if poverty is to be relieved by the provision of minimum subsistence incomes paid in money.

As the adequacy of the diet of a family living on a minimum income depends to no small extent upon the family and its acquired habits, there will in practice be a substantial spread in nutritional adequacy among any group of families living on the same low income. Some mothers of families will manage quite well while others will spend unwisely or even squander their small incomes. Indeed, on any low income some families manage while others suffer malnutrition and their commonly initial bad health deteriorates further. On a higher income more families would manage and on a lower income more would fail.

No family can spend the whole of its income on food and there is competition for the available resources between food and other demands upon income. Whether or not a family spends enough on food to maintain good health depends not only upon total income but also upon the division of income between food and other demands. This division cannot be predetermined by authority or

[1] Miller, D. S. (1966). The paper was addressed to food technologists in the light of world food shortages. Dr Miller stresses that this is an academic exercise and that men and women eat food, not 'nutrients'.

any abstract listing of a family's needs, but is a question of fact in every community and can only be determined by surveys of family expenditure. The division of income between food and other demands is available from some national family expenditure surveys both for particular income brackets and family composition.

The minimum income necessary in any one country to ensure an adequate expenditure on food by the average family of a particular composition can be determined approximately from some family expenditure surveys. The national family expenditure surveys give details of actual purchases of meat and other proteins, cereals, fats, fruit and so forth. These can be checked against the accepted minimum nutritional requirements and it is then found that these requirements are not met if expenditure falls below a certain level. There is, in fact, in any country a *critical level of expenditure* needed to ensure that nutritional requirements are met. The *critical income* is then the *expenditure* on adequate food multiplied by a factor which is determined by the other demands upon income, and which will always depend upon family composition. *Three* is the factor accepted by the Federal Government of the United States for the definition of the poverty level, so that the minimum income defining the U.S. poverty standard is *three times the cost of a minimum diet*.[1] The factor varies from one country to another. It depends upon climate, customs and social pressures.

There is a well-known law, now more than one hundred years old, known as Engel's law, that said that 'the lower the standard of living the larger is the fraction of that income that must be spent on food'.[2] Engel's law may be used to compare the standard of

[1] Orshansky (1965), Social Security Bulletin, Jan. 1965, pp. 4, 8 and 9 and July 1965, p. 9.

[2] The following translation from Zimmermann (1936) is quoted in *Monthly Labor Review*, Nov. 1960, p. 1198:

'The proportion of the outgo used for food, other things being equal, is the best measure of the material standard of living of a population.'

The 'essential validity' of this law is accepted in the U.S. Bureau of Labor Statistics estimates of comparative family standards of living. The limitation of this law to spendable income, i.e. income remaining after payment of family overheads, is discussed in Chapter 5. See Engel (1857) and (1895). Engel's law was formulated in his paper of 1857 and later reprinted as an appendix to the article of 1895. For a study of Engel's life and work see Berthomieu (1966).

living of countries and of families. The average expenditure on food, for example, is 24 per cent in the United States, 29 per cent in the United Kingdom and 49 per cent in Spain.[1] These percentages provide rough comparisons of the standards of living of these three countries. Again, family expenditure surveys show that the lower the income the higher is the proportion of income spent on food by families of similar size. Family expenditure surveys also show that the more children there are in a family the higher the proportion of total expenditure which must be spent on food. Engel's law measures the increased pressures on the budget of a family as its size increases; as a family gets larger it will become poorer, if the family income remains the same, and will spend a higher and higher proportion of total expenditure on food. This may be illustrated for the United Kingdom:

Table 1a

FOOD IN THE FAMILY BUDGET: EXPENDITURE ON FOOD AS A PERCENTAGE OF TOTAL EXPENDITURE BY FAMILY SIZE: UNITED KINGDOM

1963*

Size of Household	Percentage of Total Expenditure on Food
Single Person	26·5
Couple	27·7
Couple and 1 child	28·4
Couple and 2 children	30·4
Couple and 3 children	33·9
Couple and 4 or more children	37·0

* The Family Expenditure for 1963 was chosen because it gives figures for families with four or more children.

Later United Kingdom surveys enable us to take into account both income and family size: in 1967, for example, families with three or more children and incomes of between £30 and £40 a week spent almost exactly the same proportion (about 30 per cent) of total expenditure on food as did families with incomes of only £10 to £20 a week but having only one dependent child to keep.

[1] Figures from the most recent family expenditure surveys.

The table below shows the effect of family size on expenditure on food at three income levels:

Table 1b

FOOD IN THE FAMILY BUDGET: EXPENDITURE ON FOOD AS A PER-CENTAGE OF TOTAL EXPENDITURE AT THREE INCOME LEVELS: UNITED KINGDOM 1967*

Size of Household	Weekly Income of Household		
	£10–20	£20–30	£30–40
	Percentage of total expenditure on food		
Single person	23·8	17·0 (Income of £20 or more)	
One man and one woman	31·6	27·3	23·3
Couple with one child	29·8	28·6	26·1
Couple with two children	33·1	30·7	27·6
Couple with three or more children	37·9	35·5	30·0

* Agriculture and Fisheries and Food, Ministry of (1967), 'Domestic Food Consumption and Expenditure', Tables 3, 4, 5, 6 and 7.

The reader will notice that as the number of children in a family increases, so does the percentage of total expenditure which goes on food. This is one sign of a fact repeatedly illustrated in this book, the standard of living of parents falls when their children arrive and the standard of living of a family falls as each new baby is added. This simple and obvious fact of life is familiar to anyone who is rearing or has reared a family, but is often ignored in discussions on social policy and is being pushed further into the background at the present time.

The next table shows some examples from several countries of the proportion of family expenditure which goes on food. It will be seen that the proportion varies from country to country and this is a mirror of the general standard of living. The reader will note, for example, that the families of Italian workmen have become more prosperous over the years but that their standard of living is still behind that of families in some other European countries. He will note the contrast between the families in the highest U.S. income bracket spending only 19 per cent on food and those in a low income bracket spending 30 per cent.

Table 1c
FOOD IN THE FAMILY BUDGET: EXAMPLES FROM FAMILY EXPENDITURE
SURVEYS*

Class of Family and Country	Percentage of Total Expenditure on Food
Belgian workmen's families with 3 children 1963–4	41·2
Finnish families with 3 children 1955–6	40
Finnish families with 4 or more children 1955–6	45
Poorest strata of Italian workmen 1953–4	62
Average Italian workman 1953–4	50
Average Italian workman 1963–4	47
Workmen's families with 3 children in Netherlands 1963–4	39
Average family in Spain 1964–5	49
Families in the Spanish province of Lugo with 4·1 people 1964–5	69
Families in Madrid 1964–5	39·5
Average 5-person household in Switzerland 1963	25
Average family in the United Kingdom 1963	29
Average family of 2 adults and 3 children in the United Kingdom 1963	34
Average urban family in U.S.A. 1960–1	26
Average family in all U.S.A. 1960–1	24
Families in U.S.A. with $2,000 to 3,000 a year 1960–1	30
Families in U.S.A. with 3·7 people and over $15,000 a year 1960–1	19

* See Bibliography under country and date.

While the fraction of family expenditure spent on food provides a rough and ready indication of the standard of living, this method of comparison can be misleading. An industrial country sells more food that is industrially prepared or packaged and is consequently more expensive. A poor population that has been poor for generations learns ways and means of making do on a lower income. Countries like the United Kingdom that have forgotten their peasant traditions have also forgotten much of the art of using cheaper foodstuffs. In more advanced countries the pressures to spend on other things are greater. In the United States there is, for example, no alternative to the motor car for many workmen to travel to work.

The poverty standard in a still predominately peasant country can, therefore, be set at an income level that is only twice the necessary expenditure on food, as, for example, in Italy in the nineteen-fifties; while in the United States the poverty standard is set at three times the expenditure on food. These two figures reflect the different stages of development and the different distribution of actual expenditure between food and other things of people living at these levels. Other countries must generally multiply the food expenditure by a number between 2 and 3 to arrive at the correct poverty standard for them. The right poverty standard for the United Kingdom would probably give a factor of nearly 3.

Engel's law, for all its imperfections, was historically the first method of establishing 'equivalent' standards of living, which were assumed to be equivalent if two families or individuals spent the same fraction of their incomes on food. Even today this is still a better method than many other ways of deciding equivalence that are in everyday use.

Of course the advocates of a social investment policy will argue that children are the better investment and should get more than 'fair shares'. Can we give a meaning to the concept of 'fair shares' until there are realistic estimates of the cost of maintaining children and of running families of different sizes and age compositions? In the words of a Committee of the United Kingdom Ministry of Education, can we 'place families on a broadly equal footing'?[1] This concept is discussed in the American literature in terms of 'equivalent needs'. It is the eventual aim of much French and German social policy to 'equalize the family burden' and this has led to many estimates of the economic 'burden' of rearing families of different sizes. 'Equalizing the burden' means to share the cost of rearing the next generation fairly between parents and non-parents at all income levels. 'Equalizing the family burden' is an

---

[1] Weaver (1957), p. 9.

active political phrase that has been influential in Sweden and within the European Community and concerns families at all income levels. The American concept of 'equivalent needs' is closely related but has been mostly used for determining the modest-but-adequate and poverty standards. The same concept has also been used in Germany and other countries for estimating subsistence incomes. 'Placing families on a broadly equal footing' has been used in the United Kingdom in the special context of maintenance allowances for grammar school children and university students.

Most people and nearly all children live in families, so that the concept of equivalent levels of living applies to families rather than to individuals. Two families may be said to be living at equivalent levels if their incomes are commensurate with the size and age distribution of their members, taking any special needs of a kind that can be codified fully into account. Two families where the consumption of all members just reaches the minimum accepted standard, or alternatively, a modest-but-adequate standard, may, for example, be said to be living at equivalent levels.

All attempts to codify human needs must be based upon averages and must ignore the great variability of actual needs. Poor physical or mental health or capacity of one or more members of a family can make it impossible for that family to live upon an income that is satisfactory for the average family. There are, indeed, many other reasons why actual needs may be higher than average.

There will always be special cases requiring the attention of social workers and special services. It can only be the aim of social legislation to reduce the numbers of families in difficulties to manageable proportions. It is impossible in any country to provide the large number of social workers that would be needed to enable every family in need to be treated as a special case. It is essential to avoid detailed and expert examination of the circumstances of families in difficulties wherever possible if only because there is no possibility whatever of enough experts becoming available. The concept of equivalent levels and the codification of minimum needs based upon this concept, indicates how resources can best be distributed to remove as many families as possible from the area of distress. No amount of material support for poor families will, however, remove the need for special public services and private charities to help the families with special problems. Poor people may more readily obtain their rights if these are codified.

The traditional separation in the United Kingdom of the social casework agencies, both statutory and charitable, from the agencies responsible for helping poor persons from public funds has been a very valuable tradition for the social worker and for the client. But social workers had to accept a verdict of the old National Assistance Board that needs were being met, and they had no yardstick of their own to measure the economic situation of their clients. This has not changed. How, for example, is a social worker to measure the adequacy with which a mother budgets if she has no yardstick of need to measure the mother's income? If a mother seems to become less able to cope when her children are in their teens, how is the social worker to know what part economic pressures in the family play, if she, herself, does not know whether the family income which was adequate for toddlers is adequate or inadequate for teenagers? If £1 5s. keeps a child of 2, how much is needed to keep a child of 14? No doubt many families find young children easier to manage; they also find them cheaper. Social work training should include the study of family budgets and family expenditure surveys. The young social worker who has not, herself, had to cope with the growing expense of a family should know in theory how the life-cycle of family expenses will affect her clients. She should know the average expenditure on food, clothing, semi-durables, the comparative cost of clothing children and old people and the food requirements in pregnancy. Without this basic knowledge, verdicts and assessments of family behaviour may lean too heavily on the observation of relationships within the family. Family budgeting and household management and the con-flicting wants of different members are the stuff of life for poorer clients. Existing scales of need based on the historical assistance scales provide a deceptive picture, as we shall show, of poverty and of strains within the family.

The officials of the United Kingdom Ministry of Social Security have a difficult task. One mother concentrates on feeding her family so that clothing remains unbought. She applies to the Ministry for clothing. The next family skimps on feeding and saves up for clothing for children of the same age. Another family finds that fuel takes so much of their income that they apply for an overall weekly increase. From the official's point of view, if one mother can buy clothes, why not the next? If one can afford fuel, why not all? One mother saves up for a cot, others say they cannot afford to do so. One divisional office is lenient on cots, one sympathetic on bedding, another is generous on fuel but tough on unmarried mothers. Practice is erratic and unpredictable. The assessment of need of an individual family requires both professional training and human understanding, and an objectivity difficult for public officials responsible for protecting public funds and tied by tight rules.

The assistance officials have become more and more involved in welfare work. The National Assistance Board embarked on training its staff for the role of welfare workers, while at the same time the Board was required by Parliament to administer a scale of allowances which is historical and is not based on any thorough investigation of family needs or upon present-day available knowledge. The historical relativities have recently been confirmed as the official scale in legislation setting up a Ministry of Social Security in the United Kingdom, and in the Ministry study, 'Circumstances of Families'.[1] The use of this scale to estimate the numbers of poor persons has distorted the picture of poverty in the United Kingdom. Many adults described as poor by the use of this scale are not poor by the same standards as are used to describe children as poor. Or, if higher standards are used and the estimates of poor adults are accepted, then the number of poor children is much larger than has ever been suggested.

Detailed assessments of human and family needs have been made in the United States. One of these scales has been used in this book and is described in the next chapter. However, the official scales of need are more generous than those used in practice in many states and cities. Moreover, the American public assistance programmes for those children and their parents, the old and the handicapped who are not covered by insurance programmes, usually require a detailed assessment of the needs and resources of each applicant and his dependants. Needs are determined by

---

[1] Ministry of Social Security Act, Schedule 2, p. 23, 'Circumstances of Families' (1967). This study applies to families in Great Britain, i.e. Northern Ireland is not included.

the subtraction of the applicant's disclosed resources from the detailed budget laid down by the local or State authorities; these procedures can be generous, but many critics in the United States have emphasized the major interference with the liberty of the subject which has often resulted. American social workers have deplored the dual role of social case-workers and dispensers of public funds which many of them have to carry out. The relation between a social worker and his clients should be similar to the relation between doctor and patient. If the social worker is placed in the position of a custodian of public funds, the doctor and patient relationship is not possible. The client is motivated to tell a convincing story and the social worker to adopt the policeman's role. Confidential information passed to an official of an assistance authority becomes official knowledge. In certain American states the zeal of public officials to protect public funds has led to midnight searches to identify cases of cohabitation, proposals to enforce sterilization as a condition of further support, deliberate enforcement of destitution to punish illegitimacy, and other measures that have little in common with a humane social philosophy, but are not an altogether illogical extension of the policing functions of officials operating a means test system. The United States is a country of extremes and these examples of harsh policies are to be found fully documented by the Federal Government alongside other schemes reflecting great generosity and imagination. Few countries have studied their own social problems with the same honesty and thoroughness as has the United States, as for example in Dr Winifred Bells' study of *Aid to Dependent Children*.[1]

There have been studies in many countries comparing the needs of individuals in different circumstances and families of different sizes and compositions. It is, in fact, possible to compare how countries support their children and how they think children should be supported in comparison with adults. There are also estimates of the needs of families as a whole and by types, introducing the concept of 'family overheads' which are shared by the family group and are in practice less clearly related to the needs of individual members.

The comparative needs of individuals and families of different

[1] Bell, W. (1965).

sizes and compositions show on the whole a remarkable consistency from one country to another. Indeed, whatever the absolute standard of living, the *comparative needs* do not greatly differ. This is not, perhaps, surprising if only because children grow up at roughly the same rate everywhere. The needs of an adult depend upon whether he or she is head of a household or only a dependant, on whether he or she goes out to work or stays at home. Basic needs, if there are children to be looked after, depend upon whether there are two parents or only one, and if there is only one parent, upon whether child-minding has to be paid for. All these factors have been taken into account in assessing basic needs in one country or another.

There is now some agreement among the authorities upon the influence of sex, including pregnancy and lactation, upon food requirements. There is also much evidence of the influence of sex upon total needs, although these are very sensitive to social pressures. They differ, for example, according to whether a boy or girl goes to school or to work and upon the nature of the work. The cost of the minimum essential clothing for a young woman going to college or going out to work, is, for example, found to be substantially higher than the minimum requirements for a housewife.

A growing point in the subject is the study of the needs of adolescents, and it is in the assessment of the comparative needs of adolescents and adults that the biggest differences between countries are to be found. Those differences arise primarily from the continuation of education and dependence of adolescents upon their parents up to widely different ages in different countries; if an adolescent starts work at 13 or 15, the needs of his parents are much lower than if he continues his studies to age 22 or 23. There are also intense social pressures on the adolescent that can, for example, lead him to spend money on clothes at the expense of an adequate diet, or demand money from his parents, to an extent that is not encountered at other ages.

The case of the adolescent who starves himself to look smart illustrates that it is more difficult to be poor in a wealthy country. A subsistence income cannot be determined on abstract grounds but only from analysis of how families at this level of income actually spend their money. Social pressures can substantially increase the income necessary to maintain reasonable health. Children cannot be sent to school without shoes in the United Kingdom today, but there were many children who had no shoes sixty years ago and there still are such children in many other countries. The adequacy of children's footwear is one test of poverty well known to social workers. A Danish family expenditure survey published in 1965[1] showed that the expenditure on footwear was more inelastic and unavoidable than any other expenditure except for fuel and lighting. Footwear together with food, fuel and lighting were shown in this Danish survey to be more necessary than any other main classes of consumption goods.

A French clothing survey[2] also showed that the expenditure per child on shoes for boys and girls aged between 2 and 14 is higher than the expenditure per head on shoes for men and women at all income levels; with one exception, the expenditure on shoes by women in the highest income brackets exceeded that of children in the same income brackets. Children cost more to shoe than adults except for very smart women.

The bare-foot schoolboy is a symbol of the poverty of times past. His shod schoolfellow today is not only a symbol of increasing standards of living but also a symbol of increasing and irresistible social pressures on his parents. School shoes are accepted as necessities, but there are many other items which the teenager especially feels to be equally necessary but which the adult world has not yet entered on its conventional scales of necessities. Scales of needs for children lag ever behind the scales of needs for adults. Dr van Hofsten, now head of the Swedish Central Statistical Office, said in 1954 that:

'It is tempting to add non-essentials to parents' needs, e.g. drink, tobacco, entertainment, but to argue in terms of necessary consumption only for children.'[3]

In the same year Professor Townsend, now in charge of the United Kingdom survey of poverty, said of early estimates of poverty:

'The main fault of the standards used has been the lack of relation to the budgets and customs of life of working people.'

[1] Jørgensen (1965).   [2] Desabie (1965).   [3] van Hofsten (1955).

He proposed that in addition to using adequate nutrition as a basis for the poverty line, the findings should be correlated with 'standards of overcrowding, household amenities, education and so on'.[1]

In his famous paper of 1895, Engel wrote of the value of studying the costs of individuals:

'The study of the "cost of a man" should enable us to reply to the following questions: "What is the level and what are the costs of consumption of persons living and growing from one year to the next in the bosom of the family . . . in relation to the various professional, social, local and other conditions in which the family lives?" . . . Amidst all those topics to the study of which private and public statistical work has been devoted over many years . . . the "cost of a man" occupies indubitably the first place.'[2]

This present study of family needs is based both on 'estimates' and on 'budgets' as found in family expenditure surveys. It begins with the question, 'What are the comparative needs of child and of adult?"

[1] Townsend (1954). This is developed in a later article, Townsend (1962).
[2] Quoted in Berthomieu (1966).

CHAPTER THREE

The Comparative Needs of Children, Young Persons, and Adults

Detailed studies of the needs of children, young persons and adults have been published during the last seventy-five years in Europe and the United States, and during at least the last forty years in Japan. These studies, available from a dozen countries, cover between four and five generations of children in communities at quite different stages of social development. The many pictures of children's needs from different times and places have features in common. Whatever the absolute level of living described in these studies, the comparative subsistence cost of children and adults is one reasonably stable feature of the structure of needs from one country to another.

Unit-consumer scales have been developed in a number of countries to express the needs of children of different ages and of adults. Unit-consumer scales are concerned with comparative needs and are basic to the comparison of standards of living. As we shall discuss in this chapter, the needs of children and adults are often related to a 'standard' adult. There is a limited academic literature using unit-consumer scales and there is a literature comparing the 'cost' or 'needs' of family groups by several different methods.[1] It is, however, mainly of interest to the general reader that the academic studies appear to have had little impact upon social policy in the United Kingdom. Professor Richard Stone of the Department of Applied Economics,

---

[1] A valuable recent study by Clio Presvelou entitled *Sociologie de la Consommation Familiale* gives tables of consumption units from 1882 to 1962 and an account of methods of comparing the cost of families of different sizes developed by authorities in several countries. See in the bibliography to the present book the following: Allen, R. G. D. (1942); Hajnal and Henderson (1950); Henderson (1949) and (1950); Prais and Houthakker (1955); Martin, Y. (1956); Forsyth (1960); Paillat (1960); de Bie (1960) and (1965); Rottier (1963). A bibliography of British studies of consumer wants and expenditure was provided in a paper by Professor Stone to an international conference in 1963. See Stone, R. (1963). For American publications on equivalent needs see footnote to page 34 above.

Cambridge, wrote, in a Preface to a book published in 1955, that:

'The analysis of unit-consumer scales is important in connection with any rational scheme of social security benefits and of tax reliefs in respect of dependants.'

This book, *The Analysis of Family Budgets* by Prais and Houthakker, included a chapter entitled 'Household Composition and Unit Consumer Scales'. The book developed a method for estimating the cost of members of a family from consumer survey data. The method was only applied to the results of rather small, pre-war consumer surveys and only to six classes of foodstuffs. Prais and Houthakker's methods have never been widely used, as far as the author could discover, except in a different context in Denmark.[1] There are papers by Professor R. G. D. Allen (1942), J. L. Nicholson (1949) and many other writers who contribute to the thinking about methods. However, in the United Kingdom these studies have never advanced to the point where acceptable scales have been evaluated of the comparative needs of children, young persons and adults, which is the subject of this chapter. Indeed, in a recent book by Nicholson (1964) the discussion never advances beyond the average child although, of course, the needs of children of different ages vary widely. The very valid excuse of these writers is that United Kingdom consumer survey data are not in any way adequate for such studies to be made.

The present book, therefore, has not attempted to develop new scales from United Kingdom survey data but is based upon official and semi-official scales that are the subject of a large overseas literature. Reliance has been placed on American and German scales in particular, though the scales of other countries have also been used to illustrate particular points. There can be no doubt that the methods of producing scales of comparative needs can be refined as proposed by Prais and Houthakker and others, and that this should be done for the United Kingdom. There is, however, a wide measure of agreement between the scales of different countries and, indeed, in the scales produced in different periods. The author decided to base this study on scales that are in present

---

[1] See Jørgensen (1965). For discussion of Prais and Houthakker see Forsyth (1960).

practical use in social administration, rather than on theoretical scales that have never been used.

The nutritional needs of people of different ages are widely accepted internationally and are not the subject of any major differences of view. In the United Kingdom the British Medical Association produced one of the best known scales of nutritional needs for men, women and children in 1933, which is still used in a revised form.[1] However, there has never been any investigation in the United Kingdom of the *total needs* of children which merits comparison with the quite extensive studies made in a number of countries, notably in the United States and Germany. The Beveridge Report of 1942 was unable to draw on a breakdown of the costs of supporting children such as is to be found today in many publications in other countries, and made no reference at all to items of expenditure now agreed to be essential to a child even on a subsistence income. The Beveridge Report was not based upon any serious analysis of the effect of age upon the subsistence requirements of children and young persons. The conclusions about children's needs of the Beveridge Report are, indeed, no longer tenable in the light of the research undertaken during the twenty-five years that have passed since its publication.

The process of growing up is essentially smooth and continuous. In all countries the cost of maintaining a child increases steadily from a minimum in early childhood to reach the full adult level at about the age of 14. Major discontinuities such as are to be found in some scales of children's allowances and benefits do not reflect the steady growth of the cost of maintaining a child.

The age at which full adult maintenance costs are reached was set at 15 in the United States as early as 1889,[2] and at 14 in Germany, in 1890,[3] and none of the many subsequent investigations has upset these estimates, although the tendency to earlier maturity is likely to reduce to below 14 years the age at which the child costs as much as an adult. The cost scale recommended by the United Nations, which is used in the European Economic Community's co-ordinated family ex-

---

[1] British Medical Association (1961) and Ministry of Agriculture, Fisheries and Food: Domestic Food Consumption and Expenditure: Annual Reports of the National Food Survey Committee: for example, Table 9, p. 91, in Report for 1963.

[2] U.S. Commissioner of Labor (1891–2).   [3] Wörishoffer (1891).

penditure surveys, 1963–64, shows a child reaching adult level at 14.[1]

The most modern American budgets, such as that of the Community Council of Greater New York,[2] also show the cost of a boy in the 13 to 15 age bracket reaching that of a grown man, and the cost of a girl in the same age bracket exceeding that of an adult woman. This family budget standard is based on the City Worker's Family Budget of the Bureau of Labor Statistics, which attempts to describe and measure a modest-but-adequate standard of living.[3] It is not a subsistence budget and is based on very extensive research and Federal Government recommendations. Modern German estimates of the cost of maintaining children also show that costs for both girls and boys reach the cost of maintaining adults at about the age of 14;[4] these German estimates are also based on very thorough study in the different states of Germany and have full official support. The German standards used in this chapter are subsistence standards used for the assessment of need for public assistance or for support costs of illegitimate children. Swedish estimates[5] show that the cost of maintaining a boy reaches that of a man at age 13, and the cost of maintaining a girl reaches that of a woman at age 14 to 15; this conclusion has the authority of the Swedish Central Bureau of Statistics. The Central Bureau of Statistics of the Netherlands uses the Amsterdam scale on which boys reach adult consumption level at age 15. This Dutch scale has been based since 1917 upon the assumption that a boy's needs reach those of a grown man at age 15, and was derived from early German and American studies.[6]

Having reached the level of a man or woman at age 13, 14 or 15, the costs of a young person do not remain there, but rise above the adult level to a maximum in the late teens. The costs of maintaining the young person aged 14 to 21 years are shown to be higher than the cost of maintaining an adult in the more recent

[1] See, for example, volume for Luxembourg No. 1, p. 113, or Belgium No. 2, p. 108.
[2] Community Council of Greater New York (1963).
[3] For the history of the Workers' Budgets in the United States see note, p. 34, Chapter 2.
[4] Baden-Württemberg (1963–4); Bavaria (1962); Nordrhein-Westfalen (1958); Hesse (1961 and 1962).   [5] Van Hofsten and Karlsson (1961).
[6] Netherlands: personal communication from Amsterdam Bureau of Statistics.

studies in several countries. There is a *teenage cost-peak* in any curve of human maintenance costs. Many of the earlier studies found, or assumed, that the cost of a 16- or 17-year-old boy or girl was the same as that for a fully grown man or woman. These studies were concerned with poorer families and 12 or 14 was then the school leaving age. Childhood ended at 12 or 14 and the child thereafter played an adult role as a wage-earner; it was natural to assume that his subsistence requirements were those of an adult. The raising of the normal age of leaving school to above 15 and even to 18 in some countries, notably in the United States of America, and the continuation of dependency to age 21 and above for growing numbers of students and apprentices in all countries, has led to more detailed and objective investigation of the actual cost of maintenance of young persons in the 14 to 21 age bracket. These recent studies show that subsistence costs continue to rise beyond the age of 14 to a maximum well above the adult level in the late teens and then gradually fall during adult life to a second minimum in old age. This is seen in Figure 5.

A part of the subsistence cost of all persons is socially determined, but some of the social pressures on the young person in his teens are especially irresistible. There are standards of dress that the teenager will insist on attaining, if necessary even at the expense of an adequate diet. There are minimum levels of possessions and pocket money that the teenager justifiably needs, and parents are tempted to provide, even at the expense of the well-being of other members of the family.

There are twenty-two official subsistence-level cost scales in Western Germany: they all show higher subsistence costs for the 14- to 18-year-old than for the adult, and range from 106 to 114 per cent of a 'reference man', with an average of about 111.[1] German estimates are for total subsistence cost and include rent, heat, and light components. The Swedish estimate, based on their family expenditure survey, puts the highest cost for a boy at 120 per cent of the 'reference man' between the ages of 16 and 19. The Swedish estimate includes not only food, clothing, education, personal care and recreation but also a share in light, heat, rent, washing and ironing, cleaning the household and family holidays and excursions.[2]

[1] Mayer (1965).   [2] Van Hofsten and Karlsson (1961).

The concept of the 'reference man' was introduced in the United States and Germany in the 1880s to enable the needs of children of different ages, and of adults and elderly persons to be compared in figures, and this concept is still widely used. The needs of the reference man are set at 100 points and the needs of other persons are then equal to, or more than, or less than this. The needs of other persons are, therefore, in effect expressed as percentages of the needs of the reference man, who is generally assumed to be an average adult man. The reference man is not assumed to have to pay the bills which a man may receive by virtue of his position as head of a household; he is in general assumed to incur only his fair share of such costs. We shall see too that there is definable and essential *cost of working*, which includes meals at work, transport, extra clothes and so on, which is not generally included in the essential expenses of the reference man. The reference man may be used for comparing the cost of a child of any age in terms of the total cost of maintenance or subsistence, or in terms of the partial cost, for example of food, or for comparison of the energy or protein requirements of child and adult measured in calories or grammes. It will be seen, as an example, in the table below how children's food costs may be compared with those of the reference man:

Table 2

COMPARATIVE FOOD COSTS OF CHILD AND ADULT: UNITED STATES DEPARTMENT OF AGRICULTURE*

Age of children	Reference man = 100 Boys		Girls
16–19	125		101
13–15	106		100
10–12		94	
7–9		81	
4–6		64	
1–3		57	
Under 1 year		47	

* United States Department of Agriculture (1962) Family Food Plans, Table 9, p. 13. Using the Economy Food Plan. The 'economy' and 'low cost' plans give a higher proportion to children, thus introducing a factor of safety at low income levels.

It will be noticed that Table 2 shows that the cost of food for a child from one to three years is 57 per cent of that of the reference man. The same authority shows the average calorie requirement of a child in the same age bracket as only 43 per cent of that of the reference man. The *cost* of the child's diet, per calorie, is higher than for an adult because children need more protein and particularly of animal origin. Protein is more expensive than calories derived from sugar or starch alone, and animal protein is generally more expensive than vegetable protein. The United Nations recommended that a very young child requires three and a half times as much protein per unit of body weight as an adult.[1] Various authorities make recommendations about the proportion of this protein that should be of animal origin. The Netherlands Nutrition Council, for example, recommends that for children up to 3 years old two-thirds of the quantity of protein should be derived from animal sources, and for all young people from 3 to 20 at least one-half of the protein should be of animal origin.[2]

Recent estimates of nutritional requirements have shown that average physiological needs reach a maximum in the late teens and decline slowly thereafter. These physiological needs can be increased by school activites, especially school games; a boy may expend as much energy in one game of football as in eight hours at rest. Even if the teenager is not still at school his dietetic requirements are greater than at any other time of life. The young person needs both more energy and more protein than the adult. The average needs for male and female throughout life are shown in Figures 1 and 2, *The Energy and Protein Requirements of Men and Women*, which are based on the recommendations of the National Research Council of the United States; they differ only slightly from the recommendations of the United Nations, the British Medical Association and similar recommendations in other countries.

American estimates of food *costs* used in Table 2 are displayed as a curve in Figure 3, *The Rise and Fall of the Cost of Minimum Food Requirements*, which is based on the nutritional requirements shown in Figure 1 and 2 and on American prices. It is seen that

---

[1] United Nations: Food and Agriculture Organization (1957).
[2] Netherlands Nutrition Council: Committee on Dietary Allowances, Sept. 1964–March 1965.

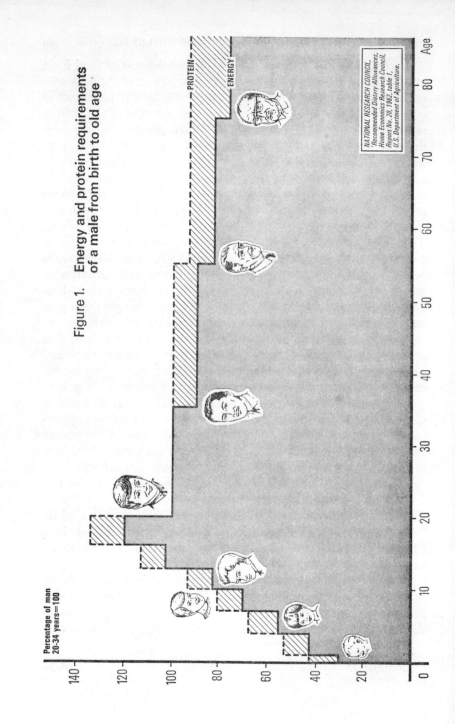

Figure 1.   Energy and protein requirements of a male from birth to old age

Percentage of man 20–34 years=100

PROTEIN

ENERGY

Age

NATIONAL RESEARCH COUNCIL,
"Recommended Dietary Allowances,"
Home Economics Research Council,
Report No. 20, 1962, table 1,
U.S. Department of Agriculture.

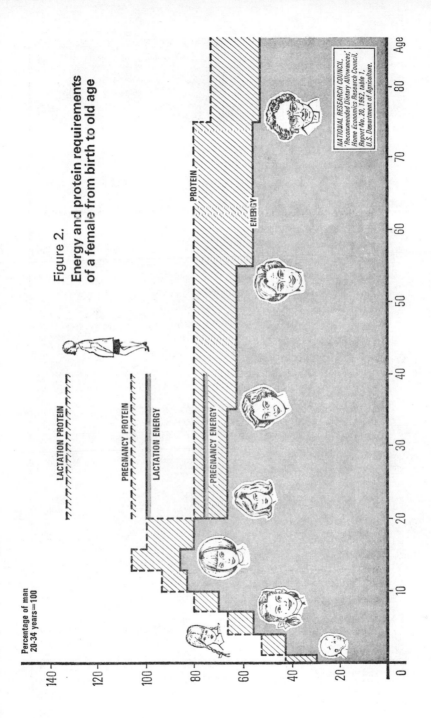

Figure 2.
Energy and protein requirements
of a female from birth to old age

Percentage of man
20-34 years=100

LACTATION PROTEIN

PREGNANCY PROTEIN

LACTATION ENERGY

PREGNANCY ENERGY

PROTEIN

ENERGY

Age

NATIONAL RESEARCH COUNCIL,
'Recommended Dietary Allowances,'
Home Economics Research Council,
Report No. 20, 1962, table 1,
U.S. Department of Agriculture.

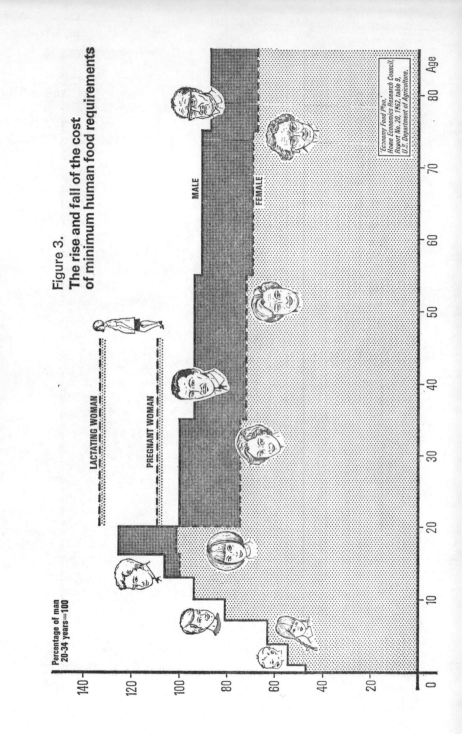

Figure 3.
The rise and fall of the cost of minimum human food requirements

Percentage of man 20-34 years=100

LACTATING WOMAN

PREGNANT WOMAN

MALE

FEMALE

'Economy Food Plan,'
Home Economics Research Council,
Report No. 20, 1962, table 9,
U.S. Department of Agriculture.

Age

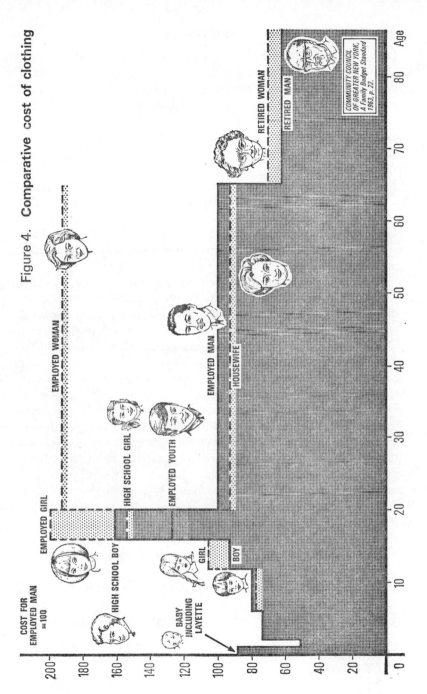

Figure 4. Comparative cost of clothing

the cost of food requirements of a boy, when he is aged 16 to 19, rises to 125 points, and of a girl to 101 points. The absolute cost of food depends upon local prices and in particular on the relative cost of carbohydrates and protein, and the cost of a family diet depends upon what is acceptable to the local population through habit and custom. However, the *comparative* costs of child and adult do not change greatly from one country to another. The curves in Figures 1, 2, 3 compare the needs for food of children and adults living in the same environment, and so eliminate many of the environmental factors determining absolute needs. The shape of the curves is dominated by the rate at which young people grow up physically, which does not differ greatly from one country to another. Figure 3 shows, therefore, a typical *age-need curve for food costs*.

Figure 4 shows an estimate for the comparative cost of clothing children and adults in New York on a modest-but-adequate budget.[1] The dependence of clothing needs upon time is discussed later, and it is enough to note here that the clothing requirements of children on American estimates reach the adult level at about the age of 12. The official German scales show clothing needs reaching adult level at the age of 14 to 15.[2] These estimates of needs are not, of course, based only on the price of garments but include the replacement of clothes because of wear and tear and children's growth. These estimates of clothing needs are based upon family expenditure surveys. Such a survey in France in 1963 showed that the expenditure of young unmarried persons in their teens upon clothing is substantially higher than that of adults or of persons in any other age group. This is particularly true in poor families, both in Germany and France, where parents apparently make great sacrifices to ensure that their young sons and daughters are passably dressed. Thus the 1963 French Government clothing survey[3] showed that young men aged 14 to 20 spent 702·9 francs a year on clothing compared with an average of 548·20 for all men. French girls aged 14 to 20 spent 671 francs on clothing compared with 451·5 for all women. French young women spend not quite as much as French young men on clothing, and teenagers of both

---

[1] Community Council of Greater New York (1963), *Family Budget Standard*.
[2] Baden-Württemberg (1964) and Germany (1965), Child Support Scales.
[3] Desabie (1965).

sexes spend nearly 50 per cent more per head on clothing than their fathers and mothers.

The French expenditure on clothing, shown in Figure 7A, confirmed in 1963 the estimate made in 1959 by the International Union of Family Organisations that the cost of clothing a child of 14 is equal to the cost of clothing an adult.[1]

Clothing the urban family in the United States is shown in Figure 7B. The author of this study[2] showed that clothing expenditure generally increased from the pre-school years to a peak in early adulthood (18 to 24 years of age) and then decreased. Unlike France, in America women and girls spend more on clothing than do men and boys, as the Figure 7B shows. But for both sexes the greatest spurt in clothing expenditure occurred between the 6 to 11 and the 12 to 15 age brackets, at the time of most rapid growth. Footwear costs were highest between 12 and 17 years of age. Only the very wealthiest parents spent more on their own than on their teenage children's clothing. All other families, including the better off, followed the 'well defined age-sex pattern' in their purchases of clothing. Fathers of teenage children will not be surprised to learn that for American men 'the lowest clothing purchases were reported for husbands whose children were all under 18'. In the poorest families mothers spent even less than fathers on their own clothing. Mothers of fatherless families, because of low family income, spent less on average than other mothers.

Estimates of the cost of the *total needs* of children, young persons and adults have been made in many countries,[3] The total cost of a family may be divided into family overheads which are rent, heat, light, furnishings, all of which are shared, and personal

---

[1] International Union of Family Organizations (1959), *Niveaux de Vie et Dimensions de la Famille.*   [2] Erickson (1968), p. 14.

[3] The following are examples:

Belgium: de Bie (1960) and (1965).

France: Int. Union of Family Organizations (1959) *Niveaux de Vie*; Martin, Y. (1956); Paillat (1960) and (1962); Tabah (1951).

Germany: Child support scales (1965); Jessen (1955).

Sweden: Van Hofsten and Karlsson (1961).

United Kingdom: Allen, R. G. D. (1942); Beveridge (1942); Hajnal (1950); Henderson (1949) and (1950); Kemsley (1952); Nicholson (1949); Prais and Houthakker (1955).

U.S.A.: See references in footnote on p. 34.

See also Presvelou (1968) for a number of total cost scales in full.

C

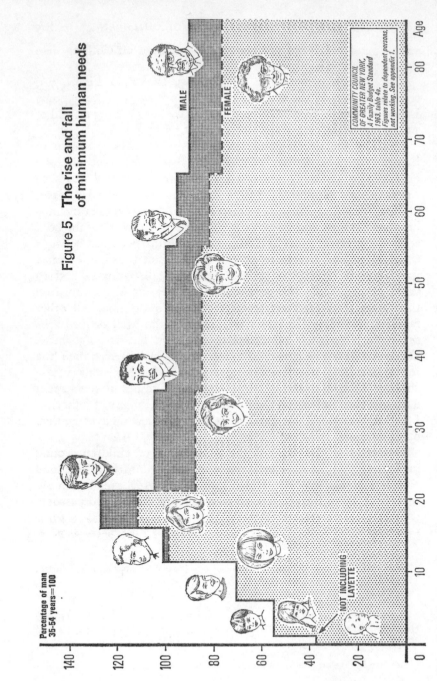

Figure 5. The rise and fall of minimum human needs

Percentage of man 35-54 years=100

MALE

FEMALE

NOT INCLUDING LAYETTE

Age

COMMUNITY COUNCIL OF GREATER NEW YORK, A Family Budget Standard 1963, table 4a. Figures relate to dependent persons, not working. See appendix 1.

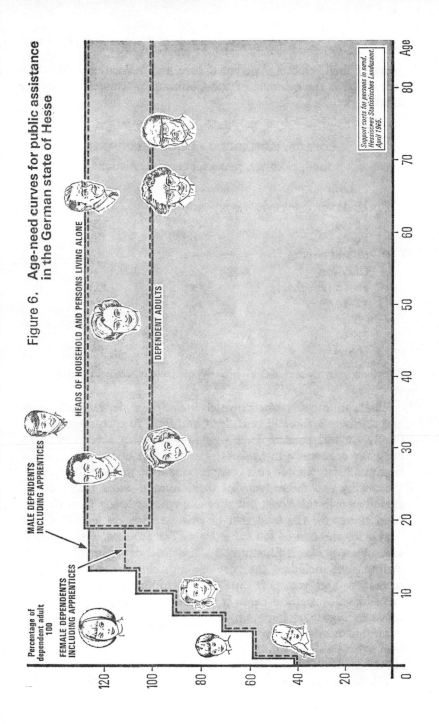

Figure 6. Age-need curves for public assistance in the German state of Hesse

costs of food, clothing, personal care and recreational. Table 3 below shows the estimate of the Community Council of Greater New York:

Table 3

COST OF MAINTAINING FAMILY DEPENDANTS

food, clothing, personal care, recreation*

Adults	Men and Boys	Women and Girls
Under 35	105	87
35–54	100	85
55–64	96	82
65 and over	91	77
Children		
16–19 (at school)	127	111
12–15	101	99
6–11	75	
1–5	55	
Under 1	38	

* Community Council of Greater New York (1963): Family Budget Standard Table 4a, p. 65, adapted in Appendix I of this book.

There are other estimates which include a wider range of needs and attribute a share of rent, heat and light to each member of a family. It will be seen later that families with several children normally economize in overheads at the cost of living space and heat and light. Simple cost comparisons hide many differences in the quality and the urgency of these human needs that are discussed later in this book, but they show nevertheless that the age-need curves for the total cost of maintenance are similar to the curves for the cost of food. Figure 5, *The Rise and Fall of Minimum Human Needs*, illustrates an age-need curve for the cost of maintenance including the cost of food, clothing, personal care, recreation and transport but not including rent, heat, light, furnishings or medical care. It is based on American data. The curve in Figure 5 shows, in effect, the rise and fall of average minimum needs of men and women from birth to death. It is seen to have a shape similar to Figures 1, 2, 3, 4 and 7. An age-need curve based on German data is shown in Figure 6.

Within the limits of accuracy of the curves in Figures 1 to 6 it is

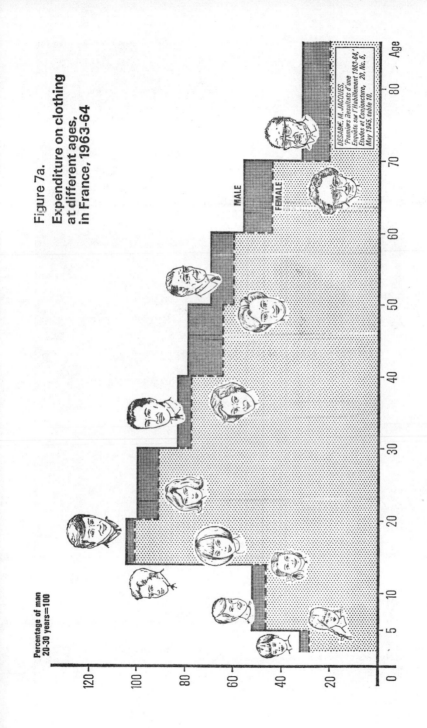

Figure 7a.
Expenditure on clothing
at different ages,
in France, 1963-64

Percentage of man
20-30 years=100

Age

MALE

FEMALE

DESABE. M. JACQUES,
'Premiers Résultats d'une
Enquête sur l'Habillement 1963-64,'
Etudes et Conjoncture, 20, No. 5,
May 1965, table 10.

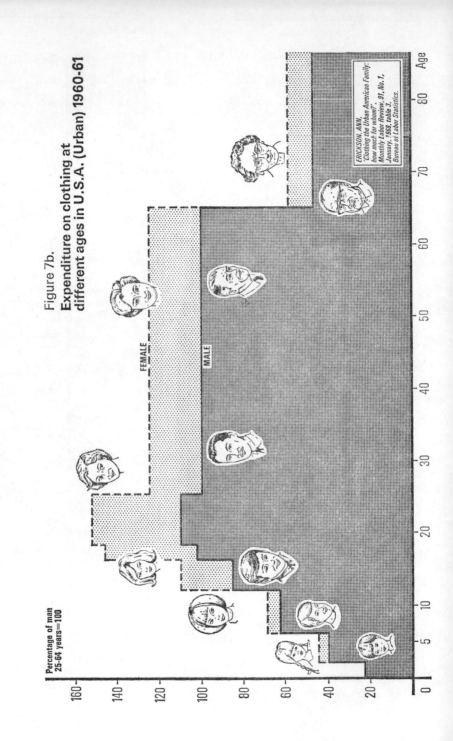

Figure 7b.
Expenditure on clothing at different ages in U.S.A. (Urban) 1960-61

Percentage of man 25-64 years=100

FEMALE

MALE

Age

ERICKSON, ANN,
"Clothing the Urban American Family:
how much for whom?",
Monthly Labor Review, 91, No. 1,
January, 1968, table 3.
Bureau of Labor Statistics.

seen that the cost of the food needs of children increases at about
4·5 points a year, from about 41 points in the first year to 100
points at age 14; and the total needs increase somewhat faster at
5·0 points a year, from about 35 points in the first year to 100 at
age 14. All the more recent and authoritative estimates are very
similar, though only if the figure of 35 points for the infant is not
taken to include a number of special requirements of the first year,
such as a perambulator, cot, mattress and so on, some of which are
purchased for the first child only. These special needs of the baby
require, according to German figures, an increase of at least 20
points in the first year if they are to be included in the index.

At the time of writing the co-ordinated family expenditure
surveys of the Common Market countries have appeared.[1] These
are intended to enable the standard of living of families in the six
countries to be compared and will form a basis for the harmoniz-
ation of social security law in the Common Market. In some of
the tables the concept of units of consumption is used. The adult
male is taken as unity. The scale used begins at 0·2 for a child
under 2, which is lower than the American scales or German
estimates or any modern scale that the author could discover but
rises to 1·0 at the age of 14. A child of 12 has a consumption unit
as high as a man over 60 or as much as a grown woman. The
higher cost of teenagers, and notably the higher cost of clothing
during adolescence, is ignored. The notion that a girl costs the
same at 12 as she does throughout life to 60 years does not accord
with consumer surveys and makes no allowance for working, or
courting expenses. This consumption unit scale is derived from
the United Nations and the Amsterdam scales which are out of date.

The cost of a child begins before he is born. A report on
emergency feeding after the second world war produced by the
United Nations said:

'If a mother is to nourish her child properly in the womb and at the
breast she must herself be well fed. . . . The nutrition of expectant and
nursing mothers is of primary importance.'[2]

Nutritional experts continue to support this view. The food
needs of women and girls throughout life are shown in Figure 2.

[1] Communautés Européennes: Budgets Familiaux, 1963–4 for all Common
Market countries except Germany for which the survey is dated 1962–3.
[2] United Nations: Child Nutrition (1947).

Comparing Figure 1 and Figure 2 it is seen that the pregnant woman requires more protein than a man engaged in active or moderate work. Figure 3, which costs food requirements, shows that the needs of the pregnant woman are surpassed only by those of the teenage boy, and that during lactation a mother's needs outstrip even this high level. The nutritional needs of both the unborn and the suckling child are reflected in the cost of his mother's food. In poor and hard-pressed families there is too much competition between the needs for food, clothing and other necessities for the mother to give herself the high proportion of family food which would be necessary to meet her own needs. The United Kingdom Food Survey for 1961, reporting on a special study of families with a pregnant mother, showed that,

' . . . average consumption of nutrients failed to reach recommended allowances . . . when the mother was pregnant this situation existed even in families with one child; indeed in the largest families with an expectant mother consumption was only four-fifths of that recommended, a lower fraction than that found for any other group identified. . . . It is of interest that families containing three or more children and an expectant mother were those with the lowest income per head.'[1]

Some countries, Finland for example, recognize this danger and include pregnant mothers with certain sick persons in a higher range of assistance allowances.[2] In the United Kingdom and elsewhere there is no general recognition of the dietary needs of pregnancy or lactation in assistance allowances except in provision for cheap or free milk and welfare foods.

After weaning, the child enters on one of his most vulnerable periods of life. Although he requires more protein per pound body weight than at any other period of life, he does not require as much carbohydrate. His diet, therefore, is ideally of different design, and if his appetite is satisfied from the same table as his older brothers and sisters, whose hearty appetites send them back for second helpings, he may be incorrectly fed. The United Nations report commented:

[1] Agriculture, Fisheries and Food, Ministry of, *Domestic Food Consumption and Expenditure*, 1961, pp. 35–6.
[2] Personal communication: Social Welfare Board, Helsinki.

'The pre-school child may not show the ill-effects of an inadequate diet in such an immediate and striking way as the infant so that serious nutritional defects may occur unsuspectedly unless measures are taken to prevent them.'[1]

A later United Nations report repeats this warning and calls the pre-school years 'the dark age of childhood':

'The years between the end of infancy at one year and the entry of the child into school at the age of six or thereabouts are often called the "preschool period". The preschool years have been described as the dark age of childhood and, from the public health point of view, the term is justified . . . it is also justified in the sense that the period is one of great stress in the child's existence. This applies to many aspects of life and very strongly to nutrition. . . . Preschool children are thus even more "vulnerable" in the nutritional sense than children of school age. Both periods of life are characterized by high nutritional needs which often are not, or cannot be, met through family resources.'[2]

The pre-school child needs educational playthings such as pencils and crayons and paper and paints and scissors. The child who does not have access to this kind of material is at a disadvantage when he starts school. The German scales cover these needs by allowing a larger sum for toys and out of school equipment for the preschool child than for the school child. The sum is modest, about 3s. a week, but the need is recognized. The American estimates allow the same annual cost for toys and educational playthings for a baby or child not yet at school as for the recreational and sporting equipment of older children, and this is double the amount recommended for adults for similar purposes.

As a child reaches his middle years in school there is again a period when his nutritional needs may be neglected. A United Nations report describes this period as the 'pre-pubertal spurt':

'There is a relatively short and acute spurt of growth in boys and girls before puberty is reached. . . . The pre-pubertal growth spurt results in increased food requirements at that period, and should be given consideration in estimating requirements."[3]

[1] United Nations: Child Nutrition (1947).
[2] United Nations: Food and Agriculture Organization Nutritional Studies No. 10, 1953: School Feeding and the contribution to Child Nutrition.
[3] United Nations Food and Agriculture Organization (1957). Nutritional Studies No. 16: Protein Requirements.

This period is, of course, well known to the mother of growing children and even finds an echo in dialect and domestic legend; in Sulfolk, for example, a mother will say 'my boy has started to "pack", when the child reaches this stage. Pre-pubertal needs, especially for protein, are not always quantified in scales of nutritional requirements because the age break in these scales comes commonly at 12, and the 12-year-old is bracketed with children from 6 upwards. Figure 8, which is taken from the Plowden reports, shows the rate of growth in height for girls and boys. The pre-pubertal spurt is clearly seen. This is the period of exceptional nutritional needs and lasts for two or three years. It occurs rather earlier in girls. The nutritional requirements at this time are higher than at any other time of life. A child's subsistence allowance, out of which a high proportion will be devoted to food, should take account of these exceptional food requirements.

When a child first goes to school he needs special school clothes even if these are not a uniform. He needs pens and pencils and instruments, all needs which will increase as he gets older. He will also need to pay for extras such as school outings and materials for handwork.[1] The German subsistence scales[2] are generous in the articles allowed to back up the work of the school, and during these years give more to girls than to boys because of the domestic science and housecraft lessons. These are not personal luxuries to be classed with drink, tobacco and cinema-going amongst adults but are the working tools of a school child's life and essential to his mental and social development.

The change from child to man cannot be altered by legislation. 'When I was a child,' wrote St Paul, 'I spoke as a child, I felt as a child, I thought as a child; now that I am become a man, I have put away childish things.' The raising of the school leaving age does not alter this. A boy still at school may find his work satisfying yet long for adult independence. If his family is poor his needs cannot now be satisfied, as we shall see later. The American estimates show that at a modest-but-adequate level of living

[1] For a study of the cost to parents of school 'extras' see Educational Welfare Officers (1968).
[2] See Germany (1965) Child Support Scales. For details see Baden-Württemberg (1964); Bavaria (1962); Hesse (1959) (1961 and 1962); Nordrhein-Westfalen (1961).

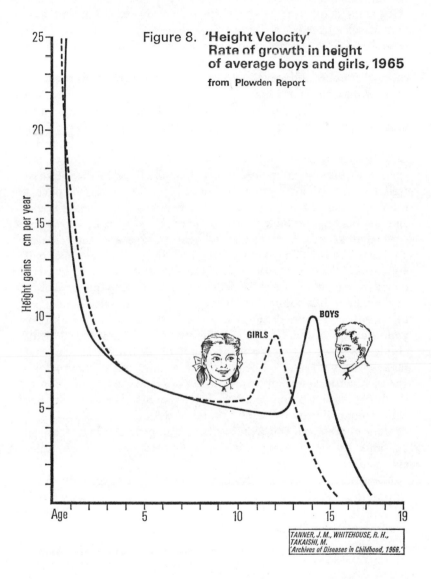

Figure 8. 'Height Velocity'
Rate of growth in height
of average boys and girls, 1965

from Plowden Report

TANNER, J. M., WHITEHOUSE, R. H.,
TAKAISHI, M.
'Archives of Diseases in Childhood, 1966.'

the high school boy needs more clothes than his father at 16, and at 13 costs as much to clothe as his mother if she is not working. Out-of-school needs also increase in the teens. A boy or girl still at school is said to need a sum equal to about half the cost of his clothing for personal expenses, recreation, out-of-school educational supplies and sports, and more than twice the sum required by an adult who is not a householder.

Each birthday is a milestone to a child and his parents, who increase his pocket money and grant him new freedoms. The early teens is the right time to learn the handling of money by making a child responsible for some necessaries as well as casual spending. A study group on the cost of a child by a leading German welfare organization was unanimous on the need for pocket money for school children to include travel to school, cost of books and stationery. The Baden-Württemberg scale for 1964 allows the equivalent of 12s. a month at 13 years of age and increases to £1 7s. at 17 years of age but expects it to cover travel to school and and some other necessaries.[1] Allowances for children as 'dependants' when father is sick or unemployed or receiving assistance rarely take into account that the teenager should not be expected to be entirely 'dependent' in the same way as a toddler or very young child. In the United Kingdom there are few estimates of children's needs so that it is not possible to say whether any pocket money is intended to be provided for a child out of state allowances. Most local authorities provide pocket money in addition to the boarding out money paid to foster parents. For example, one county council provides about 7s. 6d. a week for school children; 14s. for apprentices and working boys and girls of 15; 17s. at age 16, and £1 at 17 years. Similar sums are provided by other authorities.

Magistrates occasionally remark upon a boy's having too much or too little. 'Five shillings is not enough for a boy of 15, he ought to have 10s. a week', said a magistrate in Lancashire.[2] A London headmaster wrote to the author:

[1] Baden-Württemberg (1964), p. 7. It is noteworthy that the breakdown of the price-index of support costs for children shows an increase from 5·2 per cent of child's budget for pocket money and entertainment for the very poorest families to 12·6 per cent for families with medium incomes. All conversions from foreign currency to pounds sterling are at pre-devaluation rates.

[2] *Daily Express*, 13 Jan., 1965.

'Ten shillings per week at 15 years of age, experience tells me, is a reasonable amount for the teenager to expect to be able to handle as independent income. The sum I mentioned should be regarded as an ideal, perhaps, between the two extremes of nothing at all and an unlimited amount. In all walks of life, and at all levels, *desires* become *needs* as incomes increase and I should say that where the family income precludes the giving of any pocket money at all, then allowances (under widows' pensions and other state benefits) should be allocated with this in mind since it is an essential for a balanced outlook on life.'

Pocket money is part of the paraphernalia of growing up. Allowances based on *estimation* of needs usually include such items. Allowances based on the general cost of living without reference to needs specific to childhood are liable to omit them. Children in poor families are then less advantaged in this respect than those in public care. A children's officer gave the following recommendation for the handling of adolescent boys in Residential Homes:

'The adolescent who stays in full-time education, or who undertakes an apprenticeship at a low wage is under a special difficulty, because he cannot so easily keep his inner life private. He will have to ask for the special kinds of clothes which he feels express his personality. Residential staff often have to press the administrators and the committee very hard to get adequate clothing allowances and pocket money for some of their teenagers who are working on a low wage alongside other young people who are treated generously by their own parents.'[1]

The older school child whose needs cannot be met by his family and who feels himself treated like a young child, because his own level of living is only appropriate to a young child, is more likely to want to leave school early.

The benefits or allowances payable for adolescents on all United Kingdom scales show the largest discrepancies between provision and needs for any age group. The study of the needs of adolescents should be one focal point of future social research. The most comprehensive study of the cost of maintaining adolescents so far in the United Kingdom was that of the Weaver Committee in 1957 on educational maintenance allowances paid to poorer children staying at school after school leaving age.[2] Their evidence

[1] Brill, K., *et al.* (1964).
[2] Weaver (1957). See especially Appendix C.

is not available. Taking the National Assistance rate for a dependent adult at that time as 100, the schoolboy of 15 was estimated to cost 136 per cent, the boy of 16 to cost 148 per cent, while the boy of 17 needed 155 per cent of adult costs. This Committee rejected the subsistence or poverty level of National Assistance as a proper basis for assessing need. They had as their aim 'to seek the means of enabling pupils to remain at school and to take full advantage of the educational opportunities provided for them without themselves undergoing hardship and without causing hardship to their parents'. Their figures represent 'a desirable rather than a minimum standard', but they concluded that no items in their budget,

'could be dispensed with or reduced in cost without seriously jeopardising the child's chances of deriving full advantage from full-time education. After a careful re-examination we decided that we could not conscientiously recommend any economies without running the risk of significant loss to the child's education in the broad sense.'[1]

The Weaver Committee said that in calculating clothing costs they considered it necessary to take into account 'not only the running costs, including replacements, of maintaining an adequate wardrobe, but also the costs of repairs to clothing and footwear, and dry cleaning'. They refused to accept the official index weight of 35 per cent of total costs for food and only 11.8 per cent for clothing, and called for an expenditure of 23.9 per cent of total budget on boys' clothing and 27.3 per cent for girls. On pocket money the Weaver Committee said, 'we assume that it is reasonable to expect any adolescent to have a little money of his own which, as part of his education in the broad sense, he is free to spend as he chooses.' The list of pocket money items given includes hobbies, periodicals, clubs and school activities, presents, cinema going, books, games equipment, hairdressing. They allow a modest sum for holidays to include at least one abroad during the senior school years. Finally, they 'take into account the fact that a child of the age in question should, if possible, have the use of a separate room for doing homework and that it is proper to make an allowance for the cost of heating and lighting such a room'.

[1] Weaver (1957), p. 7.

The total cost for a boy of 15 in 1956 came to £128 a year or £3 8s. a week which was more than the *adult* National Assistance rate.[1] The Committee, in deciding on the final cost of children staying on at school, defined a level which is in fact between the poverty and the modest-but-adequate level as being the lowest compatible with full-time schooling for these ages. They accepted the assistance levels of the day as representing only the minimum parental contribution, the difference to be made up in direct grants or other benefits such as meals and clothing. The final estimated cost in round figures was:

Table 4
COST OF SCHOOL CHILD 1956 AND 1966

		at 1955 prices year	at 1966 prices* year	week
Boys and Girls	15 years	£130	£179	£3 8s.
	16 years	£140	£193	£3 14s.
	17 years	£150	£206	£4 0s.

* 137 points, 1955 = 100.

The working party considered, 'It is our firm conviction that maintenance allowances should be regarded as an investment in the nation's future and that no suggestion of charity should attach to them'.[2] Unfortunately this aim was defeated by the level of parental income taken as a basis for payment. The assistance scales plus an addition for rent was the basis for the calculation of net income by family size. It is an illusion that a family at poverty level can continue to keep one member above that level even if funds are provided for this purpose. Apart from help in kind, or where there is a definite article required for school which must be purchased, it is quite unrealistic to expect a family to single out one child for extra food, clothing or pocket money. The whole family must be raised above poverty level if the children are not to be held back. Many parents sacrifice to give to their children, and older brothers and sisters contribute to a younger brother or sister, but public policy cannot be based on such expectations.

[1] Weaver (1957). See Appendix C, p. 19.
[2] *Idem*, p. 12.

In 1967 the non-contributory benefit allowance for a 15-year-old boy was £1 15s.; the Weaver Committee would give him £3 8s. At 16 years the non-contributory benefit allowance was £2 7s.; the Weaver Committee would put his needs at £3 12s. At 17 years the non-contributory benefit was still only £2 7s. but the Weaver Committee would allow £4.[1]

When a young person leaves school and begins to earn, his needs increase, but when he is unemployed he does not return to the needs of a child at school. The American estimates for the recreational needs of young persons at work is that he or she requires for personal spending, recreation and books more than the amount spent on his own clothing and double the personal spending money of adults. On the American modest-but-adequate scale young persons in work are said to need three times as many books as both parents put together, to visit the cinema three times as often as either, to spend about twelve times as much on active sports and nearly five times as much on hobbies, club subscriptions and so forth. This is not merely a response to the commercially created teenage market but is part of the freedom to grow up:

'The child resents interference with his freedom because in many ways it is an interference with his sexual freedom. It involves his right to pass his time with boys and girls of his own age, discussing their common concerns in which sexuality is ever present.'[2]

The working young person learns to spend wisely by making mistakes, freedom to spend small sums foolishly is needed.

In a poem by Auden, Prospero looks back on his own courting days and says to Ariel:

'I am very glad I shall never
Be twenty, and have to go through that business again,
The hours of fuss and fury, the conceit, the expense.'

The expenses of courting days are legitimate expenses. Scales of need recognize them, though allowances to young people who are

---

[1] Allowances before increase October 1967. Non-contributory benefits have been raised since this date, see Annual Report (1967) of Ministry of Social Security, p. 55. Earlier levels of assistance from 1948 and principal Regulations to the winding up of National Assistance in 1966 will be found in Table 32, p. 171 of the Annual Report (1966) of the Ministry of Social Security. As the index of retail prices has risen the value of Weaver Estimates has risen also.

[2] Brill, K., et al. (1964).

dependent usually do not. In 1918 Rowntree suggested that a working girl from his poverty line family needed half as much again as her father for clothes and two-thirds of the entire amount allowed for personal sundries for a family of five with young children. Rowntree recognized 'the fuss and fury, the conceit, the expense':

'A girl rightly demands not only tidy and suitable working clothes but garments which she can wear in the evenings and on Sundays. The question of attractive clothing may seem at first sight of small moment, but a little thought will show that a girl who cannot afford to dress nicely will be seriously handicapped in the matter of marriage. Quite apart from vanity, she rightly and naturally desires to look her best and her admirer or fiancé likes to see her looking nicely dressed. . . . As for clothing, I estimate the cost for a single woman at a higher figure than was allowed for the wife of a worker.'[1]

The recognition of the unmarried working girl's need for dress is shown in American estimates in Figure 4 and in French practice in Figure 7A and in American practice in Figure 7B. Needs for clothing and personal possessions are in great measure socially determined. The high demands of American teenagers are not echoed in all parts of Europe yet, but there is a spreading international similarity of tastes and interests of young people. These similar tastes are not confined to the small minority who are troublesome to the adult world but are found amongst the young people whose education and growing interest in social service, in travel, in youth drama or music draw them together across national boundaries. Estimates of reasonable needs show that our children become men and women earlier than legislators and administrators think they do.

It is desirable for every country with age-related insurance benefits, public assistance, family allowances or taxation allowances to have its own standard age-need curves, and it is desirable to bring these curves up to date from time to time. Variations in prices can affect the adult and child costs in different measure. In Germany it has been felt necessary to have a special cost-of-living index for children distinct from the index for adults because of the different weighting of the child-based index.[2] The scales of support

[1] Rowntree (1918), 1937 reprint, p. 108.
[2] Preisindex, *Wirtschaft und Statistik*, 1962. See Bibliography.

costs for illegitimate children were compiled by the Statistical Offices of the German provinces as a foundation to all attempts to raise the standard of living of these children and to increase support from the father. While a child's cost of living index is a refinement, it does emphasize the trouble taken in some countries to ensure that age-need curves reflect as adequately as possible the comparative basic needs of children, of young persons, and adults of different ages.[1]

The increased needs of a young person when he starts work continue into adult years; it will always be cheaper to stay at home than to work, or to seek work. The cost of working is, indeed, generally so substantial that the use of subsistence scales, such as United Kingdom non-contributory benefit, for the purpose of means tests applied to the income of a family with a working parent or parents, has little validity.

Working men, women and young persons need clothes of the standard required by their jobs. They need to face all weathers and there is a heavier bill for outer clothing, shoes, and greater wear and tear on clothing and shoes. They need travelling money. They eat away from home. They have higher expenses for personal care including hair-cuts and cosmetics. They may have to pay trade union dues and insurance premiums. The cost of working is indeed substantial but will, of course, depend both on the job, on the country and locality.

Table 5 shows an American estimate of maintenance needs for single persons, both men and women, all costs being related to the reference man who is assumed not to work.

Comparison of the standards of living of persons working and not-working can be very misleading if the cost of working is not taken fully into account, and surveys are likely to give inaccurate results in estimating the cost of working because of the difficulties of making a somewhat hypothetical comparison of what would be spent in other circumstances. A typist or secretary must spend very much more on dress and personal care than a housewife, but the difficulty of estimating how much more is liable to lead to

---

[1] Report of the Cost of Living Advisory Committee 1968, Cmnd 3677, rejected the proposal for a special index for children in low-income families, but recommended that special indices of retail prices for one- and two-person pensioner households should be compiled. Pars. 57 and 60.

Table 5

INFLUENCE OF WORKING ON THE COST OF LIVING OF INDIVIDUALS:
EXCLUDING RENT AND OTHER FAMILY OVERHEADS: MAN NOT WORKING
AGE 35 TO 54 = 100*

Men Age	Not working	Working
16–20	127	210
21–34	105	200
35–54	100	184
55–64	96	152
65 and over	91	152

Women Age	Not working	Working
16–20	111	199
21–43	87	192
35–54	85	160
55–65	82	157
65 and over	77	157

* From Table 4a, p. 65, of *Family Budget Standard* (1963), Community Council of Greater New York.

wrong conclusions. The report of the Ministry of Social Security entitled *Circumstances of Families* allowed an additional 5s. a week as an arbitrary allowance for the extra expenses of a mother working over and above the cost of travelling, and other expenses of working put at 10s. per week for a man.[1] The American estimates allocate a cost more than ten times this figure of 5s. and if the American estimates are correct then much doubt is thrown on all quantitative conclusions of the *Circumstances of Families*. More detailed research into the cost of working would appear to be merited. A mother who works has less time in which to make housekeeping economies. The reduced time that she has to spend with her children rightly motivates her to purchase more expensive convenience foods. A mother who works, whether or not she has a husband, will on average spend more on child care than a mother at

[1] Social Security, Ministry of, *Circumstances of Families* (1967), p. 30, par. 71 and p. 31, note.

home; a Swedish scale for this cost of the working mother is given later. It seems likely, indeed, that the much higher American estimates of the cost of working are nearer the mark. Five shillings a week is hardly the cost of extra nylons.

The United Kingdom has an official scale of the comparative needs of children, young persons and adults in the 'rates for basic requirements' used by the Ministry of Social Security.[1] There are two levels of assistance, the 'supplementary allowance' for people below retirement age and short-term cases, and the slightly higher 'supplementary pension' for retired people and those not required to register for employment. At what age does a child reach the cost of a man or woman on this scale? Does it contain a peak of cost for teenagers? What provision is made for the exceptional food requirements around puberty? This United Kingdom scale may be compared with those of other countries.

In Table 6 the United Kingdom scale is compared with that of the Community Council of Greater New York. This American scale was chosen for use in the present book for several reasons: it is a detailed scale and gives many age groups and distinguishes cost by sex; it allows for the cost of both working and not working; it allows for the cost of living alone compared to being dependent; it is based on Federal Government research; it is in practical use; it has been used by Professor James Morgan[2] and others as a scale to compare levels of living of family groups. Finally, it is not dissimilar to the German scales, especially in the treatment of adolescents, a question which the author wishes to emphasize. The key definitions on this scale compare fairly with those of the United Kingdom 'rates for basic requirements'. This particular American scale is not the most generous that may be found amongst the scales in use in American states and cities. The scale is set out in full in Appendix I.

In comparing the two scales it will be seen that the American definition of 'a man seeking work' may fairly be equated with a man 'required to register for employment' in the United Kingdom scale.[3] Again, the 'dependent of head of household' in the American scale corresponds to 'someone living in another person's

---

[1] Social Security, Ministry of, Annual Report (1967), pp. 54 and 55.
[2] Morgan, James, *et al.* (1962), p. 189.
[3] Ministry of Social Security Act, Part II, par. 11, p. 5.

household' of the United Kingdom scale.[1] The reference man, set at 100 per cent in the relativities, has accordingly been chosen on the American scale as a male dependant not working, and on the United Kingdom scale as a male person living in someone else's household, not required to register for employment and therefore receiving the long-term benefit, supplementary pension. In Table 6 all other persons have been given the appropriate relativities from the two scales of money allowances.

It will be seen that a child according to the United Kingdom scale never reaches half the relative cost of an adult; there is no peak of cost for the teens, indeed, adolescents do not even reach the short-term adult benefit level. The difference in the estimation of the cost of adolescents is the main difference between the United Kingdom view and those of the American or main German scales. From Table 6 it is possible to compare estimates of the cost of family groups or of several children. Three young children, for example, aged 1, 4 and 6, would require according to the American scale 168 per cent of the reference adult, but only about 100 per cent according to the United Kingdom scale. Ten years later, when 11, 14 and 16 years of age, the same children would require, according to the American scale, if boys, 303 per cent, and by the United Kingdom scale only 155 per cent. As will be shown later, the non-contributory scale is accepted as the basic scale for means tested applications for help with school meals, clothing and other welfare help, and has influenced the scales for rent, rates, educational maintenance allowances and day nursery charges, and many other similar assessments. There are more generous scales in operation in some places and for some items, but the influence of this scale as the accepted table of relative needs has been very great.

Certain family groups are at a particular disadvantage wherever this scale is used. These are the larger families, families with adolescent children and families with a single parent. A first priority in any review of social security in the United Kingdom should be the reassessment of scales of allowances for older children and adolescents in the light of what is known of their nutritional needs and clothing and other needs, and after study of the estimates and practices of other countries.

---

[1] Social Security, Ministry of, Leaflets (1967), S.P. 1 par. 6, and S.I par. 5.

Table 6

COMPARATIVE NEEDS OF CHILDREN, YOUNG PERSONS AND ADULTS:

A COMPARISON OF UNITED KINGDOM NON-CONTRIBUTORY SCALE OF

BASIC REQUIREMENTS* WITH AN AMERICAN SCALE†

SA = Supplementary Allowance (short term)
SP = Supplementary Pension (long term)

	U.K. Allowances £ s. d.	U.K. Relativities	U.S. Relativities
Single Householder			
SA	4 6 0	107·5	177‡
SP	4 15 0	118·7	100
Wife of applicant	2 5 0	68·7	87
Someone living in another person's house			
Adult SA	3 11 0	88·7	184§
SP	4 0 0	100	100
Young Persons			
18–20 years	2 18 0‖	72·5	127
16–17 years	2 10 0	62·5	127
Children			
11–15 years	1 17 0	46·2	101 (12–15 years)
5–10 years	1 10 0	37·5	75 (6–11 years) 55 (1–5 years)
Under 5	1 5 0	31·2	38 (under 1 year)

* Ministry of Social Security Annual Report 1967, p. 55. Rates from 30 Oct. 1967, plus long term addition to supplementary pension, p. 54, par. 66.

† See Appendix 1. The age of adult used in Table 6 is 35–54 for men, under 35 for wife, and 65 for retired persons.

‡ Includes the cost of working or seeking work. For discussion of this figure see page 82 above. If retired, the U.S. relativity is 100.

§ An adult dependant aged 35–54 if earning is given 184 on the American scale. This includes the cost of working. There is no exact equivalent to supplementary allowance for non-earners.

‖ Where a person 18–20 is the applicant he or she may receive the long term addition making an allowance of £3 7s. 0d. with relativity on this scale of 83·7. Persons 16–17 may not receive this addition. Nor is it received for children.

CHAPTER FOUR

Time and Season in the Assessment of Need

In the temperate climates of Europe and North America the needs of a family are greater in winter than in summer. There is a need for example for fuel and light, that varies with the weather and the length of the night. Estimates of the seasonal variation of family needs are possible.

There are also needs that accumulate with time. Clothing needs provide one important reason for distinguishing between short-term and long-term needs because they accumulate, quickly for the very young, more slowly for the fully grown child and more slowly still for adults, particularly older adults. At all ages the need accumulates. During short spells of sickness, unemployment or low income from any cause lasting for two or three months there may often be no family expenditure whatever on clothes. However, the need grows and becomes increasingly difficult to resist and must be met in the end whatever the family income. Other family needs also accumulate. Household semi-durables such as china, saucepans, sheets must be replaced in the end and broken furniture must be repaired. Family clothing needs are, however, the most inexorable. Winter clothing is more important than summer clothing, especially for young children. Clothing needs are seasonal as well as cumulative and there is a particularly insistent need for expenditure on clothing at the onset of winter. This has to be taken into account when a short-term subsistence income covers the winter months. For a long-term subsistence income a larger percentage increase is needed for clothing than for all the other cumulative needs.

Adults only wear out their clothes. Children grow out of their clothes and do so more quickly than adults wear out theirs. An infant's layette is only useful for about one year and the small child has to be reclothed completely a second time within about one year to eighteen months of birth. Very few clothes that fit the child at the age of two last until he is five; most articles, such as coats, pyjamas, dresses, short trousers and woollies, are out-grown in about one year by children between the ages of 2 and 5, who also need about three pairs of shoes a year. Children continue to grow out of their clothes, notably during the pre-pubertal spurt, until they stop growing at age 15 or 16. The American 'modest-but-adequate' family clothing budget[1] suggests that the average girl of 12 grows out of a winter coat in two years, while her mother can keep a winter coat for four years and her grandmother for seven years. The Americans estimate that at this budget standard, a father may be expected to make his sports jacket last ten years and grandfather to wear his winter jacket for fourteen, but a schoolboy needs three new winter jackets in four years because of wear and tear and growth. Schoolboys up to 15 years are estimated to need three pairs of shoes a year, his father wears out only two pairs a year and grandfather again is said to need a new pair only every other year. Boys are hard on their shoes and need three pairs mended a year from the time they enter school until they are grown up, whereas his mother at home has one outdoor pair mended a year, father two pairs, and grandfather one pair mended every other year.

Poor families have difficulty in saving. They do not generally save enough money to cover the expenditure on clothing which is necessary from time to time. These families sometimes belong to clothing clubs and sometimes save in other ways, but in a poor family there is great competition day-by-day for the available resources, and the greater the competition the smaller the savings. American and British research has shown, indeed, that the level of savings is directly related to family income and family size. Thus the average family with three children saves nothing if its income falls below a certain level, which can be estimated. If the family has only two children the income level at which saving ceases is lower and it is higher for families with four children. Indeed, the initial income level at which all saving ceases has been used to define a poverty line. If income falls below this level the average family runs into debt. However, this critical

---

[1] There are, of course, variations in the detail of clothing estimates. The Family Budget Standard of the Community Council of Greater New York is used here but the City Worker's Budget may be compared. See U.S. Bureau of Labor Bulletins, Nos. 927 and 1570-1.

income level at which all saving by the average family ceases is not a good guide to long-term income needs. Some saving is essential if serious family crises are to be avoided. Some needs accumulate until they must be satisfied, and if there are then no savings and current income is inadequate the family must be given outside support or it will run into debt. A family suddenly afflicted by unemployment or sickness generally hopes for better times and does not save money. The need for new clothing then gradually accumulates and if the better times do not happen there is eventually a crisis. A study of families of sick breadwinners in Bristol showed that:

'With the small margin available after basic necessities had been met there was little possibility for steady weekly saving towards future clothing needs. One purchase of outdoor clothing entered on the budget was sufficient to indicate an alarming excess of expenditure over income. . . . Families agreed that if an item of clothing was urgently needed then all other expenditure had to give way and the deficit was either made up by drawing on savings, or by sharply reducing expenditure in other directions, or by leaving items, e.g. rent, unpaid or by borrowing from relatives.'[1]

Sudden needs for clothing are usually for children who have outgrown or worn out their clothes. A family can usually avoid all expenditure on clothing for three months or even six months depending upon the time of year, but in the end the need for new clothing is inescapable and must be met whatever the indebtedness, deprivation or malnutrition that follows.

The Bristol survey found that 31 per cent of the families with children and a sick father had acknowledged debts, compared with 18 per cent of similar families without children, and that 'liability to indebtedness increased with the number of children'. A case history given in the survey illustrates the difficulty of a mother who relied on a clothing club:

'Some of the difficulties which could beset parents of a growing family are illustrated by the case of a wife, whose husband had been in a mental hospital for some years and who was managing her family affairs not entirely successfully, although she was a good mother with

[1] Shaw, L. E. A. (1958), unpublished. One of the most detailed studies of needs and expenditures in poor families in the United Kingdom. P. 58.

high domestic standards. The youngest child had grown out of all his clothes and she had no immediate hope of replacing them until the present clothing club ticket had been paid off. She was surrounded by relatives who were either pensioners or unskilled workers, but who helped when they could, although they seemed not to realize that there might be pressing difficulties. She was being summoned for a coal bill and was unable to pay the whole of the rent that week. She had had to buy her eldest child aged fourteen some much-needed clothing earlier in the year and she had not "got straight" since then. She had clothing club payments, but no hire purchase.'[1]

There is a crisis of renewal in poorer families at the end of the summer when the children need their first warm winter clothing and mother finds that last year's winter clothing is outgrown, if not worn out. The autumn clothing crisis was described by a mother:

'Our main clothes-buying sessions for children occur twice a year, in spring and autumn. In September we had our usual trying on and measuring up of last winter's things. Everyone had shot up by inches. I could see it was going to be an expensive year. . . . My eldest son's wrists hung nakedly from his gaberdine, his school cap looked silly, and his school shirts would not fasten at the neck. . . . Providing new things for the eldest, who is eight, is maddening when it comes to week-end clothes. His idea of a blissful week-end is climbing trees or excavating someone's pond. He can get through three pairs of dry jeans a day. . . . Our bill will obviously get heavier each year as each larger size costs a little more and the handed down clothes are fewer, because as children get bigger they are harder on their clothes.'[2]

This autumn clothing crisis defines the time-span for the accumulation of clothing needs as about twelve months maximum in a family with children. Heavy demands are certain from October to December for winter clothing; the longer the period of poverty preceding this winter demand the greater will be the difficulty of meeting the family's needs at this time of year. There is a similar but less urgent demand for summer clothing about May.

National family expenditure surveys do not usually show seasonal variations, but smaller surveys have documented the pressure of winter needs in lower income families: the autumn

---

[1] Shaw, L. E. A. (1958), p. 43.
[2] *Guardian*, 3 Nov. 1964, article by Betty Jerman.

clothing crisis, particularly in families with children, the need for
extra fuel and the using up of savings and piling up of debts which
may result.[1] A French survey of families in Marseilles called
October 'the month of debts'.[2] It was shown that poor families
had a peak expenditure for clothing in October when summer
savings were rapidly used up. It was shown that the highest
family expenditure for fuel was in January. Childless couples
showed much higher expenditure on 'sundries' (that is, expenses
other than food, clothes, heating and rent) and high expenditure
in July, the peak French holiday month. Families with three
children spent less than the childless couples on sundries and
July was for them the month of lowest expenditure.

The accumulation of *needs with time* is reinforced by the
pressure of *seasonal needs*, which, in their inexorable return with
the fall of the year, operate to prevent saving against the longer
term replacement and renewals in the home. Winter outfitting
of clothes, winter food purchases, winter illnesses, winter need
for warmth, the Christmas traditional feast and celebration,
however modestly provided, year after year eat into the savings
of the spring and summer. By the time any debts from the winter
period are paid off the remaining months are too short for a poor
family to save for longer term needs. And when these must be
met at last, the result is a period of under-feeding or under-
clothing. The level of living of a family on any particular allowance
depends where they start from. Sickness or unemployment pay
which is adequate for a family normally living on a good wage,
with a home which has been kept in repair and where clothing and
semi-durable needs have been met, will be inadequate for a
family which has been living on a low income for a long time and
whose home already needs repair and replenishing, and whose
clothing needs are pressing.

In a long-term family budget there must be allowance for
clothing alone of between 9 per cent and 14 per cent of total family
expenditure. In an earlier chapter it was seen that the proportion
of total family expenditure spent on food could be used as a

[1] For a detailed study of household consumption by quarter years and by
months, see Wiesbaden Statistisches Bundesamt (1964). December is seen to
be much the most expensive month for these German families.
[2] Carrère (1955).

measure of well-being or standard of living. As the proportion
spent on food falls, that is as families become better off, the
proportion spent on clothing generally rises, though it rises
slowly, and there are many variations in the national surveys
due to national circumstances and climate. There is, however, in
every country an irreduceable clothing minimum. However low
the standard of living, clothing expenditure cannot be reduced
indefinitely. Indeed, in some poor communities at the present time
and in earlier times the proportion of the budget going on clothing
may seem surprisingly high until it is recollected that in money
terms the sums involved may be the minimum for health and
decency. Clothing needs act as a drag on a family's ability to spend
money on food. Social pressures on parents of school children,
especially older school children, operate in more affluent societies
in the same way: it is no longer open to poor families to provide
a good diet at the expense of sending children to school barefoot
and poorly clad. The reader will see in the table *Clothing in the
Family Budget* (pages 93–94) that the percentage of family expenditure on clothing does not vary greatly with time, with size of family
and from high to low income groups.

It will be seen that in Finland, with a prolonged and severe
winter, families spend over 12 per cent of their current expenditure
on clothing, even widow's families, with low average income, spend
13·5 per cent. Figures for Sweden are not very different. The
United Kingdom expenditure on clothing is low in families of
all sizes and incomes and is around 8 per cent, childless couples
having the lowest at 6·8 per cent and families with three children
the highest at 9·5 per cent. This probably is due to both a
milder climate and the lower cost of clothes compared with the
cost of other necessaries. The high cost of house warming in the
United Kingdom may also play a part in limiting expenditure on
clothes. In France amongst workmen's households, clothing
accounts for 9·5 per cent of expenditure of childless couples,
and reaches 10·4 per cent for families with four, five or six
children.

All these figures for family expenditure on clothing are averages
for families of a given size, and do not take fully into account the
much greater clothing demands of children in their teens compared with young children. The social pressures on teenagers to

Table 7

CLOTHING IN THE FAMILY BUDGET* EXAMPLES OF AVERAGE EXPEN-
DITURE ON CLOTHING IN HOUSEHOLDS AND FAMILIES WITH DEPEN-
DENT CHILDREN AS A PERCENTAGE OF TOTAL EXPENDITURE

Country	Survey	Table	Page	Category of Family	Percentage on clothing
Belgium	1963–4	2	162	Workmen, with 1 child	13·1
Belgium	1963–4	2	163	Workmen with 4, 5, 6 children	16·0
Finland	1955–6	3	58	Widows with children	13·5
Finland	1955–6	3	59	All families, with 3 children	12·3
France	1963–4	8	224	All workmen's household—lowest income bracket	7·0
France	1963–4	8	224	All workmen's households—highest income bracket	11·9
France	1963–4	8	224	All employee's and civil servants households—lowest income bracket	8·3
France	1963–4	8	224	All employees and civil servants households—highest income bracket	11·9
Germany	1927–8	—	101	Workmen, with 3 children in lowest income bracket	11·3
Germany	1962–3	B.14.3	224	Workmen all households, highest consumption bracket	11·0
Germany	1962–3	B.13.3	217	Workmen, all households, lowest consumption bracket	10·7
Germany	1962–3	B.35.3	311	Employees and civil servants, all households, highest consumption bracket	10·0
Italy	1953–4	3B	143	Workmen, families with 2, or 3, or 4, or 5, or 6, or 7 people (6 tables)	From 12·1 to 13·6†
Italy	1963–4	7	172	Workmen, with 1 child	9·9
Italy	1963–4	7	172	Workmen, with 3 children	9·3

Table 7 *(contd.)*

Country	Survey	Table	Page	Category of Family	Percentage on clothing
Italy	1963–4	7	172	Workmen, with 4, 5, 6 children	10·5
Netherlands	1955–6	3	16	4-person households	11·5
Netherlands	1956–60	3	16	4-person households	9·7
Netherlands	1963–4	12	228	Workmen's families, 2 children—incomes below 9,250 guilders	11·2
Netherlands	1963–4	13	228	Workmen's families, 2 children—incomes over 9,250 guilders	14·4
Spain	1964–5	1·3	15	Townspeople's households	13·5
Spain	1964–5	1·3	15	Country people's households	9·5
Sweden	1958	3·10		Families with 1 child	11·5
Sweden	1958	3·10		Families with 3 or more children	12·7
Sweden	1958	4·4		Workmen's families with 3 or more children	13·4
Sweden	1958	3·4		Single parents with dependent children and-or adolescents	10·7
United Kingdom	1963	7	50	Families with 3 children	9·5
United Kingdom	1965	13	88	Families with 3 or more children—incomes under £20 a week	7·1
United Kingdom	1965	13	88	Families with 3 or more children—incomes over £25 a week	10·1
United States	1960–1	296	88	5-person households: income $2,000–$3,000‡	10·5
United States	1960–1	296	89	5-person households: income over $15,000— highest bracket given	14·4

* Family Expenditure Surveys are listed under country and date in the Bibliography.

† The highest proportion was in 4-person households.

‡ Not quite the lowest bracket given but is rather below the poverty level for size of family.

dress well are illustrated in Figure 4 which is an *estimate* of clothing needs in Figure 7A which shows what French families actually spend, and in Figure 7B which shows what American urban families spend. At a given income, expenditure on clothing must be greater where there are adolescents as well as children in the family. It is not, in fact, enough to consider family *size* in devising means to help families with cumulative and seasonal clothing needs. The *age needs* of children and special demands of adolescents must be taken into account.

The proportion of family expenditure spent on clothing has remained remarkably stable over the years. In Table 7 the reader will see, for example, what used to be the clothing expenditure of German workers and poorest officials in 1928, at a time when Germany was in economic crisis and wages were low, and families must have had the strongest reasons for clothing economy. Yet they spent 11.3 per cent of total family expenditure on clothing. The co-ordinated survey of the Common Market countries, shows that workers' families in Germany in 1962–3 were spending 11·0 per cent on clothing; and the table of support costs for illegitimate children prepared by the statistical department of the provincial governments estimates about 15 per cent of the total allowance for clothing.

In one of the surveys of poverty in the United Kingdom between the world wars, M'Gonigle and Kirby[1] compared two groups—of unemployed and employed families—in the North of England. They wished to show what could be left for food. They found an average expenditure of 10 per cent on clothing; the amount of money was above the Poor Law Authorities' standard for destitute children. Nevertheless the authors commented that careful consideration did not reveal any means of reducing this proportion.

There are other similar human needs that make it desirable to have a greater difference between long-term and short-term incomes. Expenditure on household semi-durable goods, including repairs, can be deferred for weeks or months but not for years; the time comes when furniture or heating appliances must be repaired and china or glass or blankets or sheets must eventually be purchased.[2] A broken kettle or burnt out electric light bulb

---

[1] M'Gonigle and Kirby (1936).
[2] Illustrated in Shaw, L. E. A. (1958), pp. 62–3 and 88.

must be replaced quickly and usually is bought instead of an item of food, but the purchase of more expensive items such as blankets or sheets will be deferred until there is a crisis such as an illness in the family. Cumulative poverty eventually shows in the lack of the customary household furniture and appliances. The German budget survey of the twenties showed that even the poorest workmen spent 3 to 4 per cent on replacing semi-durables and household repairs, the poorest clerks 3·2 per cent, while the best paid officials spent 6·7 per cent.[1] In 1961 Belgian workmen's families with two children spent about 4 per cent of their family expenditure on bedding, semi-durable household replacements and upkeep of the house and of clothing when the father only was working; if the mother also worked the proportion devoted to these expenses doubled.[2] If other European family expenditure surveys are examined, it is seen that the expenditure on household semi-durable goods generally lies between 4 and 5 per cent of household income and even in the poorest families rarely falls below 4 per cent. This expenditure, expressed as a percentage, remains very constant from one country to another.[3]

Most families with children have established homes. The national surveys of family expenditure are based on samples of families, sometimes many thousands of families, most of whom have established homes. There are, however, families who do not have established homes and their needs are not mirrored in the national surveys, for example the young couple who have not yet got a home together is grouped with the couple whose children have grown up. The family that loses its home, perhaps because it loses the father, or the family that moves late in family building into unfurnished accommodation, needs the initial capital outlay on essential furniture and household goods. An addition of 4 or 5 per cent added to a subsistence income to meet replacement of semi-durables and repairs would not meet the needs of these families. If families without an established home are not given special help, then the furniture and household goods will be bought at the expense of food or clothing, or by incurring debts

---

[1] Germany: Family Expenditure Survey, 1927–8.
[2] Belgium: Family Expenditure Survey, 1961, vol. 2, Table I.
[3] See Consumer Behaviour (1955), vol. 2, 'The Life-cycle and Consumer Behaviour', especially paper by Lansing, J. B.

through hire-purchase, or the furniture will not be purchased and the family will be living below the standard of comfort of its neighbours. A mother who lost her matrimonial home on the breakup of her marriage described her struggles over 10 years, from 1956 to 1966 in letters to the author:

'I finally left on 22nd March 1956 with 3 children one 6-year-old boy, a 5-year-old girl, a baby 10 months, bringing only their clothes, pram, cot and toys. . . . My father-in-law gave me £50 which secured the cottage I now have, similar to what you describe in your book, old, damp, poor locality, no bathroom etc. The home I left was *new*, *modern*, with gardens front and back. We had a car and were on the 'phone. Next was the problem of furniture. I was then getting £4 12s National Assistance. They provided us with a double bed, in which 3 of us slept. I had baby's cot. They sent 2 old chairs and I got a table for 3s. We were provided with 2 blankets, 2 sheets and made do in winter with coats, but many are the times when we had not enough to eat and no coal. If we had a shilling we had a warm round the gas cooker and all went to bed together about 7 to 7.30 p.m. . . .

'As the years have passed I have tried to make a home. The old bed the National Assistance gave us in 1956 dropped through. I got a cheap camp bed for my daughter, one for my son, and for 6 months I myself slept on an old mattress on the bare boards of the bedroom floor. The National Assistance had increased, and then I got about £6 8s. (I am not exactly sure of the figures over the years), but I had the house to pay, 18s., rates 10s., coal 10s. if possible, gas, electric, feed 4 of us, shoe repairs, socks, undies. I took on H.P. two cheap beds for the boys, and the girl and I now have the camp beds. I have done cleaning for the 30s. the National Assistance allow us to make and bought paper and paints and tried to make a home of a kind. I was a shorthand typist when I met my husband. . . . I have pulled out window frames, put new cords in myself, painted the place on the outside myself, done bricklaying and, cementing. I have waited weeks to afford another tin of paint and so on and I have today, after 10 years of this struggle, still only 2 chairs, small carpet 2' × 3½', 1 settee and 2 boy's beds—none of them paid for. The rest of my home is sheer junk.'

Milestones of childhood are passed only once. As a child develops there are certain needs which are age-related but do not return in the way in which seasonal needs return year by year. When a child is born he must have waiting for him a suitable cradle, mattress and coverings and a baby's layette. He will

D

inevitably grow out of his cradle and in most countries of Europe and North America will need the traditional cot and later a bed, each with its covers. When he enters school there is usually a need for school clothes, different in type even if not a uniform. He may need clothes to protect him on the journey and stouter footwear. A few needs are firmly traditional and so are necessary additions even to a subsistence budget, as, for example, a pram for the young baby living in a town and his toilet articles, or the French school pinafore and the English school blazer or cap. Sometimes parents can improvise without damage to the child, sometimes they cannot and should not be required to do so. These milestone needs of childhood are not always sufficiently recognized. In one area in the United Kingdom mothers can obtain money to purchase a cot from the local office of the Ministry of Social Security, but not a pram, in others a pram is more likely to be considered a necessity than a cot. A bed is sometimes granted and usually bedding. Discretion remains with the officials, yet the child cannot choose but grow up in his due time.

The scale of support costs for an illegitimate child in the German province of Baden-Württemberg includes two milestones for bedding, first a cot with its mattress, pillow, quilt and blankets at one year, and a bed with mattress and covers between 7 and 8 years.[1] Leather trousers are traditional but expensive; they are provided at 7 and 11. Bathing things are allowed at 7, and an athletic tracksuit at 11 or 12. The boy's first suit is allowed at 9. These milestone needs are distinguished from the regular items of clothing as, for example, an anorak every two years starting from the age of 3.

The coldest months of the year add the need for extra fuel to the budget of a family. Table 8 shows some typical family expenditure for fuel and light as a percentage of average expenditure.

For typical families the expenditure on fuel varies between 4 and 7 per cent of total income. Fuel is weighted at 6·6 per cent in the United Kingdom Index of retail prices. Fuel is a very inflexible family need and as income falls the percentage spent on fuel increases. In the United Kingdom the very poorest families spent as much as 13·6 per cent on fuel, twice the estimate of the Index of retail prices, and families in the £10 to £15 a week

[1] Baden-Württemberg (1964).

Table 8

HEATING AND LIGHTING IN THE FAMILY BUDGET: EXAMPLES FROM
FAMILY EXPENDITURE SURVEYS*

Country	Survey	Table	Page	Category of Family	Percentage on heat and light
France	1963–4	B.75	130	Workmen's families with 2 children	6·4
Finland	1955–6	3	59	Poorest households	5·2
				Wealthiest Households	3·5
Italy	1963–4	B.14	98	Workmen's Households	5·7
Netherlands	1963–4	B.34	107	Workmen's Households	6·9
Norway	1958 Vol. 1	3	7	Workmen's families with 3 children under 15 years	4·0
Spain	1964–5	1·3	15	Townspeople's households	3·4
Sweden	1958	3·4	114	All households	4·0
United Kingdom	1965	1	25	All households	6·3
United Kingdom	1965	8	65	Head of household over 65. Income £5 10s.	11·0
United States	1960–1	290	30	Urban families—2 or more persons	4·5

* Family Expenditure Surveys given under country and date in the Bibliography.

income bracket spent 9 per cent in 1965. The poorest Italian families spend 8·9 per cent. Swedish fatherless families spend 7·7 per cent.

Fuel and light are also a very seasonal requirement. A poor British family may spend very little on fuel and light in the summer but spend 20 per cent of the weekly income during some winter weeks. It is better to economize even quite severely on food rather than be cold.

The seasonal swing in expenditure on fuel and light often depends upon the method of payment. Many families on the European continent live in flats and the cost of central heating is spread over the year. In the United Kingdom solid fuel for consumption in the winter may be purchased in the summer when it is generally cheaper, although this is a form of saving least practised by the poorest families. The biggest bills for electricity and gas may be payable about May of each year, but where prepayment meters are used the biggest costs are in January and February.

In general the amount of fuel and light purchased in the winter time by a very large number of families is just enough to heat and light one room and provide heat for cooking. Thus in 1967 in the United Kingdom the average household spent 29s. 3d. a week on fuel, light and power. This only varied from 24s. 3d. for households with incomes in the £8 to £10 a week bracket to 32s. 8d. for families in the £35 to £40 a week range. The Family Expenditure Survey for 1967 showed that the expenditure on fuel only varied from 26s. 5d. for a childless couple to 33s. 4d. for a couple with three or more children. After subtracting the cost of light and of gas for cooking, the sum remaining will barely pay for heating one average room. One warm room is everywhere considered an essential, but whether a family contains two or seven persons one warm room is still the ration. Warm bedrooms *and a* warm kitchen *and a* warm sitting room is reserved for a minority in the upper income brackets in most countries, and unless they live in centrally heated flats the poorest families have great difficulty in warming even one room. The surveys of family expenditure also suggest, as would be expected, that the demand for heat and light in the warmer countries like Spain and Italy is less insistent than in, say, Scandinavia.

Better information is needed on the seasonal distribution of expenditure by poorer families upon heat and light. If, however, a poor family spends from 8 to 10 per cent of the annual family expenditure on heat and light, then the summer figures may well be below 5 per cent and the winter figure above 15 per cent. In the absence of adequate survey data on seasonal spending, these figures are no more than guesses.

There is also a small seasonal swing in expenditure on food.

German survey data show,[1] for example, that the highest expenditure for food every year is in the fourth quarter, although the increase in expenditure in the fourth quarter is much more marked for clothing than for food. A French survey[2] showed a substantial increase in food consumption in the winter months in families with dependent children; the increase was almost as marked for food as for clothes but it was not so marked in households of adults only. Children particularly need more food in the winter.

In families well above subsistence level the higher cost of living in the winter is matched by the cost of holidays in the summer; indeed, for the well-to-do family, expenditure peaks in the summer time. Poor families with dependent children cannot afford holidays and the cost of living, notably of clothing, fuel and light, and food, especially for the children, peaks in the fourth quarter of the year and reaches a low point in the main holiday month. More research is needed to throw light on the extent of the seasonal swing, and a careful investigation for all countries to relate family needs to season and month. The continental data suggest, however, that the increase in total basic needs in the third quarter when the clothing peak is reached, and in the fourth quarter when food and light bills increase, is at least 25 per cent for a family with dependent children, or 15 per cent if clothing is not included as being a longer term requirement.

Table 9

BASIC NEEDS BY TIME AND SEASON

	Summer	Winter
Short term	100	115
Longer term	120	135

Twenty-five per cent should be accepted as a reasonable estimate pending proper investigation of the increase in basic family needs during the winter months commencing in October.

Family needs, therefore, depend on time and on season. It was shown earlier in this chapter that the cost of clothing, consumer durables, semi-durables and repairs add up to a supplementary need of at least 20 per cent. Table 9 shows a simple presentation

[1] Baden-Württemberg (1963) and (1965) and Wiesbaden, Statistisches Bundesamt (1964).
[2] Carrère (1955), p. 710.

of the main conclusions. In this table the expenditure on clothing is only included in the longer term need.

The table suggests strongly that the great variety of state-maintained incomes which are the same winter and summer and which are the same for short-term and long-term dependence could be revised with advantage, although better figures are needed to show just how they might best be revised to satisfy winter needs, and long-term needs, with greater efficiency.

Estimates of need and family expenditure surveys show that retired persons have smaller requirements for food and clothing than younger adults, teenagers or many children. They are, however, dependent long-term on their pensions. The pensioners' need, therefore, is to have incomes at least 20 per cent above that of an elderly adult who is not a pensioner but is temporarily sick or unemployed for a short period. A fatherless family dependent upon assistance needs an income at least 20 per cent higher than the dependants allowances for the same family with the breadwinner temporarily unemployed, solely because of the duration of the dependency.

For countries that cannot afford reasonable state-maintained incomes necessary to meet basic needs, there is the cheaper alternative that has been used in Germany in particular for many years, namely help in kind and special grants for poor persons for winter fuel, winter clothing, or Christmas presents for children. Similar help is given by charities in most countries. Such remedies are often said to be damaging to parental pride and to the status of the father, and the introduction of such grants into assistance schemes of central government has been strongly opposed by the French family organizations and the British Labour Movement. If, however, state-maintained or state-supplemented incomes are inadequate for the support of families with dependent children either long-term or in the winter months, it can be argued that the interests of the children are more important than parental pride or paternal status.

In Germany the autumn help, *Herbstbeihilfe*, and Christmas help, *Weihnachtsbeihilfe*, and money for Christmas presents, *Weihnachtsgabe*, acknowledge the seasonal needs of the family. Such special grants, made at times of year when poor families have been found to be in special difficulty, are one way of meeting seasonal and cumulative needs. There are variations in payment and regulations in different parts of the Federal Republic. In Frankfurt-on-Main, for example, a special winter fuel allowance is paid at the onset of cold weather.[1] One or two person households received about £13 in 1966, and three or more person households about £17. The allowance is normally paid in cash. 'Christmas help' to poor persons in the same German city was over £5 for single persons and heads of households, and over £2 10s. for a child; a family of parents and four children therefore received nearly £20 for Christmas expenses.

The city of Stuttgart authorities[2] used both 'autumn help' and 'Christmas help', a total of about £40, in 1960–1 as one means of assisting lower paid employees with several children. The report on the housing difficulties of these families is described in the next chapter. When studied in 1960 they were living on incomes which, owing to the numbers of their children, were below 110 per cent of the local assistance scale (which includes allowances by age for children). The families were already receiving family allowances.

One year later a report to the city council stated that all their employees now had family incomes over 110 per cent of the assistance scales by family size. 'Winter help' and 'Christmas help' were part of the method used. These German families did not enjoy a high standard of living, but it should be remembered that in the United Kingdom there is no administrative device for helping large poor families with employed breadwinners to reach even assistance level. Help for seasonal needs by some administrative device merits study in the United Kingdom, especially as the wage-stop has been confirmed as official policy in 1966.[3] Objections which may be made to seasonal help for families with employed fathers could not apply to seasonal increases to the long-term allowances received by families with a chronically sick father, a handicapped member, a child subject to winter

---

[1] I am grateful to the Deutscher Verein für öffentliche und private Fürsorge for details of the special help in Frankfurt-on-Main at this time.

[2] I am grateful to the Sozialamt of the City of Stuttgart for copies of papers on the standard of living of the city's employees and papers on methods of helping the poorer and larger families amongst them. See page 114 of the present book.

[3] Ministry of Social Security Act, 1966.

sickness, a sick mother or those who are fatherless or motherless. Such seasonal help could be a most effective means of helping such families at a time of greatest need. Small increases in allowances have been made in winter, for example old people have received a few shillings extra for fuel. Such small sums are not commensurate with the differences between winter and summer needs at subsistence levels, nor were they given to all the households which need seasonal help.

There is nothing absolute about a family's need for heat and light. There is only a harsh, inescapable minimum. Above this minimum the additional needs are both psychological, expressing the family's wish for something more than the minimum comfort, and they are also medical. There is, indeed, growing evidence in the medical literature that in particular circumstances much more than the inescapable minimum of heat and light is necessary for the maintenance of good health and even recovery from illness at all. The effect of normal childhood illness in the budgets of poor families has been neglected.

There are also family needs that are neither essential nor inescapable but are increasingly regarded as socially necessary. A family holiday is such a need. The great majority of families have for long survived without a summer holiday. A holiday is a seasonal need which is not part of the basic needs of families but is an essential part of the modest-but-adequate standard of living. This is discussed in the next chapter.

Detailed classification of family needs into short, medium and long-term has been made in Germany. The Table 10 opposite shows recent German estimates based on a 1962–3 consumer survey.

In this survey shoes and clothing are classified as semi-durables and comprise most of this category; the balance is mainly household semi-durables some of which have to be renewed every year, for example some towels, sheets and electric light bulbs. The consumer durables are mainly furniture and household appliances, including radio. The durables also include some personal equipment such as hair brushes, combs, razors, school bags, child's sports equipment and writing pens. The semi-durables are predominantly annual purchases and include the autumn and winter clothing purchases and therefore also largely seasonal. The need for consumer durables generally accumulates over a

Table 10
DISTRIBUTION OF GERMAN FAMILY EXPENDITURE 1962–3 BETWEEN
SHORT, MEDIUM AND LONG-TERM REQUIREMENTS*

Expenditure Type	All households	Poorest 12 per cent of households
Total expenditure: Average household	729·7 DM per month	308·9 DM per month
Short Term Expenditure: Percentage on current consumption including services	74·4	81·8
Medium Term Expenditure: Percentage on semi-durable goods, or long life goods of low value	18·3	14·9
Long Term Expenditure: Percentage on consumer durables of long life	7·3	3·3
Total	100·0	100·0

* Euler (1965), Table 6, p. 494.

longer period than a year.[1] The figures in Table 10 relate to all households or all poor households and will, of course, depend upon the family composition; German families with several children spend, for example, a higher percentage on shoes and clothing than the average family and thus spend, by this classification, a higher proportion of income on semi-durables.

The United Kingdom Minister of Social Security has given recognition for the first time to the need for a supplement to the allowance 'for those who require such a benefit over a long period.'[2] The amount given is 9s.; it is received by the applicant only. The quantum of the allowance is about 10·5 per cent for a single householder, 6·4 per cent for a married couple, 12·7 per cent for a

[1] David, M. H. (1962), examines family purchases of consumer durables. See also Rottier (1963), and Tabard (1967).
[2] House of Commons 23 May and 24 May, 1966. See also Ministry of Social Security Annual Report 1967, pp. 54 and 55, and Ministry of Social Security Act Schedule 2, Part II par. 11 and 12: Rates from Oct. 1967.

non-householder aged 21 or over, 15·5 per cent for the 18 to 20-year-old who is the applicant and *zero per cent for all young persons under 18 including all children*. There is a delay in entitlement to the award for two whole years after the commencement of dependence on assistance. The two whole years is too long and the quantum is too small. While the recognition of long-term needs for the first time is a welcome development, the form and amount of the extra allowance ignores what is known about the effect of time and season upon family needs. Needs accumulate most rapidly precisely in families with dependent children and least rapidly in retired persons' households. Parents are not entitled to any long-term supplementary allowance at all for a dependent child under 18, so that this long-term supplement is almost an extreme case of bias against families with dependent children for the greater benefit of non-parents.

The cumulative character of poverty and the need for a larger family income in the longer term than in the short term is relevant to all attempts to increase the social investment content of benefits and allowances. However, children are directly dependent upon the fortunes of their families for at least fifteen years, and under-investment in children, with all its very long-term social consequences, depends upon the family fortunes for the whole of this period. It must be doubted whether short-term spells of hardship, for example while the father is changing jobs, have social consequences in any way comparable with a low standard of living continuing for years because the parents have a low earning capacity through chronic sickness, poor education, or low skill, or because one parent is missing. The simple figures of income requirements in the long term may therefore well underestimate the emphasis that is desirable on reducing the longer term, continuing poverty.

CHAPTER FIVE

Expenses and Economies of the Family Group

An architect planning a new town or housing estate might be expected to study the distribution in size of the families likely to occupy the new houses. There are certain to be some childless couples who will look for small labour-saving flats, and some families with several small children who will seek a house and garden. There will be families with older boys and girls anxious for rooms of their own. Needs vary from family to family, and the perfect new town would reflect these family needs. 'Homes for Family Needs'[1] would seem to offer the right framework for a national policy on housing.

Unfortunately the implementation of any such policy is subject to the restriction that families with several dependants cannot on average afford to spend any more on housing than childless couples. Whether there are zero, one, two, three, four, five or six dependent children and whatever their ages it cannot be assumed that the larger family with the greater need for housing space can afford to spend any more at all than the smaller family. The needs of families would only be met if the rent or mortgage interest on the labour-saving flat for the non-parents and the house for the family with four children were the same.

The evidence from consumer surveys is convincing; in most of the countries of Western Europe and North America, expenditure on housing is almost independent of family size. The published data suggest that this is equally true of the poorer countries like Italy and the wealthier countries like Sweden and the United States. Belgium and Germany are exceptions in that expenditure on rent increases somewhat with the size of the family. These two countries are discussed later in this chapter.

The French family expenditure survey of 1956[2] showed a

---

[1] 'Homes for Family Needs' is the title of Chapter 2 of the Parker-Morris report (1961).
[2] *Consommation* (1960), Nos. 2 and 3.

slight fall in expenditure on rent with increase in size of the family, and this in spite of family housing allowances. The French volume of the co-ordinated family surveys of the Common Market showed virtually the same pattern.[1] The special survey of French families with dependent children only, published in 1967,[2] showed that in both the poorest, middle income and highest income groups there was a decrease rather than an increase in expenditure on housing by the largest families. In the United Kingdom, family expenditure surveys have usually not given adequate information on expenditure in relation to family size. However, in the report 'Circumstances of Families'[3] it was shown that whereas 32 per cent of families with only two children could afford to pay £4 a week or more for rent, only 15 per cent of families with six children could afford this sum.

In Table 11 no attempt has been made to compare country with country.[4] By reading across the columns, following the name of each country, the reader will see how the amount paid in rent varies little, and even falls in some cases, as families get larger.

The incomes or earnings of family heads are not, of course, generally related to their family responsibilities. It is not surprising to find that expenditure on housing is related to family income and is virtually independent of family size. As families become larger the pressure upon family resources increases to meet demands for food, clothing and other necessaries. There is *less* rather than more money available to pay rent or mortgage interest in the larger family.[5]

This is not only a problem of poor families. Thus if, for example, we take the highest income bracket in the 1961 United States family expenditure survey[6] with family income over $15,000 a year, then the annual expenditure on housing by families of six or more persons was $4,118, while that of families of two persons was $4,559. This is about the wealthiest 3 per cent of families and

---

[1] Communauté's Européennes (1963–4), Office Statistique, vol. 6.

[2] Tabard (1967), Families with 2–6 children, urban areas, p. 366.

[3] Social Security, Ministry of (1967), Table VI–11.

[4] For comparison of housing in E.E.C., see vol. 7 of *Budgets Familiaux*, 1963–4, Communautés Européennes. See also Vernholes (1967).

[5] David, M. H. (1962), pp. 74 ff.

[6] U.S. Bureau of Labor Statistics Consumer Expenditures and Income: Urban United States. Table 29c, Item 'Housing: Shelter'.

shows perhaps the highest expenditure on housing of any social class in the world; we still find that the greater the need the lower is the family expenditure. The social inefficiency is carried right through into this prosperous social class indicating under-taxation of non-parents. Of course, little hardship of any kind will be found in this upper middle-class American society. It is, however, still noteworthy that in this high income bracket of over $15,000 a year, the small non-parent household spends over $2,000 per head on housing; while in the same high income bracket the largest families spend less than $700 per head which is only about the same as childless couples in the $4,000 to $5,000 a year income bracket, who in general belong to a quite different social class.

At very low income levels the contrast is similar but of greater social consequence. Thus, again in the United States, two-person families in the $1,000 to $1,999 annual income bracket spent $703 on housing, while families of 6 or more persons in the same income bracket spent $576. Once more we find the greater the need the less the expenditure on housing. All persons in this income bracket with even one dependant are poor by Federal Government standards. Expenditure on housing in the larger families at this level is curtailed to buy food and other necessaries.

It does not always follow that the health of a family with dependent children will improve following rehousing, because the amount of money available for food and clothing may be less when a higher rent has to be paid. Surveys of particular towns and housing estates have shown that in addition to a higher rent a move to new housing can create new overheads as, for example, expensive travel to work for a wage-earner who previously had only a short distance to travel. New heating appliances and the temptation to use more space, and so to have to heat it in winter, increases the proportion of total family expenditure spent on fuel. The very natural desire for new clothes and other means of keeping up with the new neighbourhood's standards sharpens the conflict between the food budget and the clothing budget. In Newcastle a group of one thousand children was followed in a survey started by Sir James Spence in 1947. When the children were 5, the second volume of the survey noted the effect of a move to new council houses:[1]

[1] Miller, F. J. W., et al. (1960), p. 33, Plates VI and VII.

Table

VARIATIONS IN RENT* WITH SIZE OF FAMILY:

Country	Survey		Category of Family (§)	Expenditure
Finland	1955–6	Table 3	All families	finmarks per year
France	1956	Table 26	All families	new francs per year
France	1963–4†		Workmen's families	new francs per year
Italy	1963–4†		Workmen's families	lire per year
Luxembourg	1963–4†		Workmen's families	francs per year
Netherlands	1963–4†		Workmen's families	florins per year
Norway	1958	Vol. 2 Table 1 p. 14, 24	Wage and salary earners families	kroner per year
Sweden	1958	Table 3.9	All families	kroner per year
Sweden	1958	Table 4.3	Workmen's families	kroner per year (including heat, light, maintenance)
United Kingdom	1963	Table 7	All families	shillings per week
Italy‡	1953–4	Table 3A	All families	lire per month
Italy‡	1953–4	Table 3B	Workmen's families	lire per month
Netherlands‡	1951	Table 2 p. 22	Lower paid employees' and civil servants' families	gilders per month
Netherlands‡	1951	Table 1 p. 10	Workmen's families ¶	gilders per month
United States‡	1960–1	Tables 29D to 29H	All urban families	dollars per year

* Rent excludes heat, light, water, housing charges and repairs wherever this was available in the survey.

† Co-ordinated surveys of Communautés Européennes: Tables 54, 64, 74, 84, 94.

‡ No division by age of members of family unit is given in this survey.

II

SOME EXAMPLES FROM FAMILY EXPENDITURES SURVEY

1 man and 1 woman	1 man 1 woman 1 child	1 man 1 woman 2 children	1 man 1 woman 3 children	1 man 1 woman 4 children	
51,930	52,680	70,800	66,760	61,820	4 or more children
475	460	436	433 3 or more children		
326	509	432	521	499	4, 5 or 6 children
81,727	91,356	84,270	78,907	68,688	
31,851	15,002	14,712	—	—	
448	452	578	514	565	
1,058	1,014 / 914‖	1,756	1,072	—	
725	910	809	683	—	
1,372	1,777	1,678	1,694	—	
32s. 7d.	34s. 8d.	33s. 9d.	37s. od.	33s. 2d.	
3,928	3,884	3,807	4,008	4,000	3,776 7 persons
2,884	3,172	2,890		2,895	2,687 7 persons
282	301	336	309	331	285 7 persons
253	274	280	285	272	284
688	832	872	873	809	6 persons or more

§ In this table 'family' includes childless couples.
‖ Norway: Rent in one-child families is given for child under 10 and child 10 to 15.
¶ Confined to income bracket 3,000 to 4,000 gilders per year, the lowest given.

222222222222222222222222222222222222222222222222222222222 vs22222222222222222222222222222222222222222222222222222222222222222222222

'The great delight of the families with their new houses, the ensuing improvements in the standards of family and personal hygiene and the increased happiness and vigour of the children on the new housing estates were often very obvious.'

But there was a minority too poor to benefit. One photograph illustrating the book shows a lane between backs of old houses; yard doors set in a high continuous wall open on to a narrow pavement. A group of children share the lane with lines of washing. The caption runs:

'Young children playing in a lane. Despite poor housing they are of good physique and well turned out.'

The next picture shows a council estate with gardens and hedges lining the road. The caption runs:

'Another group of children on the pavement outside their houses. Although the houses are good and there is no over-crowding, the families are poor and the children are neither so robust nor so well cared for as those in the (previous picture).'

In February 1966 the Liverpool Personal Service Society described the difficulties of rehoused families in a memorandum to the Minister of Housing:

'Our district offices on new estates have dealt with a wide range of problems but a noticeable feature of the work has been the extent to which we have helped families who have fallen into serious debt within a few months of being rehoused. Some of the most common reasons for this are as follows, but we have not listed them in order of importance:

Rent—This is usually much higher on a new estate than in the older areas.

Travel—The cost of travelling to work, to school, to shops, to places of entertainment and to relatives is usually much higher on a new estate.

Furniture—Initial expense, due to the new dwelling being larger and because the rooms are of a different shape and size, can be considerable.

Electricity—There is often a complete failure to understand how to economize. Tenants are sometimes experiencing under-floor heating, water heating or electric cooking for the first time. The bill may be six times as high as in their previous dwelling and hire purchase charges may increase the bill still further. No doubt other sources of power would present similar problems.

Door-to-Door Salesmen—The first week of a new tenancy appears to be a critical period. The housewife is anxious to create a comfortable new home and she may feel that her furniture and equipment, which was perfectly adequate in her old home, now looks old-fashioned and shabby. If at the same time she is feeling lonely and homesick she is likely to be very susceptible to the persuasions of door-to-door salesmen.'[1]

Council tenants who are rehoused from a local authority waiting list are more likely to have several children and so to have incomes which have no slack with which to stand an added strain of higher rent or greater overheads. If rent is taking 15 per cent and other overheads another 15 per cent of family income, then the family cannot afford a further increase without suffering in food or clothing. It is possible to predict that these items will be sacrificed by examining the family income and the ages of the children in the light of the proposed move. Parents who fail to improve domestic standards and disappoint housing managers (or social workers) by 'inadequate' response to a new home may simply be facing the task of filling a quart pot from a pint jug.

In 1965 the *Economist* newspaper[2] criticized the Scottish housing authorities for building too many houses with only 'two bedrooms and one modest living-room', and for charging only 'one-third of an economic rent for its houses', and advocated the construction of homes with 'more space *inside* their houses'. The *Economist* did not, however, attempt any analysis of real family needs and resources. There are large numbers of families with children, in Scotland and elsewhere, who can only afford either old and dilapidated property or new houses that are really too small; they can afford neither more space nor economic rents. The *Economist* was particularly wide of the mark in suggesting that houses with more than four bedrooms should be built for the '20 per cent of Catholics' in East Kilbride.

Families may come to the notice of authority because they do not pay their rent. A study of 'bad rent-payers' in Southampton in 1964[3] showed that such families had more than average numbers of children and that 78 per cent were living at or below National Assistance level. If a realistic scale of comparative needs had been used a much greater deficit of needs over income would have been revealed. Families of the same size and income who succeeded in paying their rent can only have done so at the

---

[1] Taken from the Memorandum by kind permission of the Society.
[2] *Economist*, 6 Nov. 1965.   [3] Harbert (1965).

expense of food or clothing. Such parents have a difficult choice.

In 1960 the City Council of Stuttgart in Germany arranged for the city social security office to study the living standards of lower paid employees' families with four and more dependent children; the families were selected by the city personnel department.[1] It was found that thirty-six out of seventy-one families investigated were living below the public assistance level. The average rent of 70 DM paid by these families was 13 per cent of the average monthly income of 534 DM. However, the rent varied between 30 and over 100 DM a month and, as the report to the City Council explained

'. . . the level of rent paid was one of the determining factors as to whether the family was above or below subsistence level. . . . The investigation establishes that most of the poor families are in accommodation which in no way corresponds to the numbers in their family.'

The investigating committee estimated the cost of increasing the accommodation to an adequate level. Stuttgart did not at that time build publicly owned flats with over four rooms. Using, therefore, fictitious costs and fictitious plans and allowing notional increased rent for an increased number of rooms, the committee was able to show that if adequate accommodation had been provided the families would not have been able to pay for it. Some families would have fallen below public assistance level, assessed on income left after payment of rent, other families would have been below the 110 per cent of assistance level which was the 'welfare level' used in the study; finally, all the families with more than four children would have needed public assistance if they could have been rehoused. The Stuttgart committee commented that 'families can, in fact, only keep above public assistance level by putting up with overcrowding'. The Stuttgart City Council was subsequently able to supplement the income of all the lower-paid employees to raise their level of living above public asisstance level, as described in Chapter 4.

One of London's central boroughs has surveyed its housing and housing demands. A study published in 1968 shows that families cannot afford the dwellings they need even when there are enough such dwellings:

[1] See note (2) page 103

'In the private sector it is the maldistribution of the larger dwellings, with five or more rooms, which is especially serious. There is no net shortage of such homes. On the contrary: there are *more* dwellings of that size than there are households of equivalent size (with five or more persons). But few of such dwellings are occupied by the households who need them most. So there is, in fact, a persistent shortage of large homes for larger families with limited incomes.'

The 'large family' of the study was two parents and three children as well as families with four or more children. They made up more than half the overcrowded households. The poorer the families were, the higher was the proportion of income spent on rent or mortgages. The local authority's own housing had not succeeded in removing 'the undue share of disadvantages' suffered by families with children, because council housing had fewer children than private housing and more elderly, and one- and two-person households.[1]

London, like all major cities, has a most difficult housing problem. But the inability of families with several children to afford the housing they need is not confined to the largest cities. The United Kingdom report on families showed that in 1966 the larger the family the greater was the chance of overcrowding. Five per cent only of families with two children and a full-time working father were overcrowded, but this rose to 62 per cent if there were six children. The report commented that overcrowding is one of the 'distinctive housing characteristics of larger families.'[2]

American estimates of family costs recognize that crowding is the economy which is enforced on the family group. The New York modest-but-adequate scale allows an increased sum for housing between two- and ten-person households only at two points, with the addition of the third person, and the addition of the sixth. The Community Council were indeed baffled by the problem of matching scales of support to family housing needs.[3]

Table 12 shows that in Germany, and also in Belgium, both the average total family expenditure and the average expenditure on rent do increase with the size of the household. This relationship is partly attributable to differential fertility, the more prosperous

[1] Centre for Urban Studies for the Camden Borough Council (1968) (mimeographed, to be published).
[2] Social Security, Ministry of, *Circumstances of Families* (1967), p. 61.
[3] Community Council of Greater New York (1963), p. 32.

Table 12

AVERAGE FAMILY EXPENDITURE ON RENT: BY SIZE OF THE FAMILY
IN GERMANY 1962–3 AND BELGIUM 1961

GERMANY*
(Monthly figures in marks)

Size of Household	Total Expenditure	Expenditure on Rent	Rent as Percentage of Total Expenditure
1	385·5	65·6	17·0
2	627·5	72·9	11·6
3	824·8	87·3	10·5
4	912·1	90·6	10·0
5 or more	1,049·8	99·2	9·4

* Euler (1965), Table 3, p. 490.

BELGIUM†
(Annual figures in francs)

Number of Children	Total Expenditure	Expenditure on Rent	Rent as Percentage of Total Expenditure
Workmen			
0	76,559	10,064	13·1
1	92,846	11,552	12·4
2	97,403	10,536	10·8
3	106,686	10,739	10·1
4 or more	126,707	11,777	9·3
Employees			
0	118,599	16,200	13·6
1	132,050	17,404	13·1
2	135,136	17,889	13·1
3	156,108	19,884	12·6
4 or more	201,919	24,903	12·3

† Belgium: *Enquête sur les Budgets* (1961), vol. 2, pp. 12–13 and 36–7.

families having the larger numbers of children,[1] and is partly also a consequence of taxation policy and of social policy, including family allowances which favour the family. The achievement of a positive correlation between family income and family size in these two countries is notable. Table 12 shows family size, expenditure and rents in Germany and Belgium.

[1] See Epilogue to this book and references, p. 284.

The general picture of the population of most countries suggests that an average family begins and increases in size without any increase in accommodation, the members of the family gradually filling up and then sharing the available rooms. Dr Alvin Schorr, of the United States Department of Health, Education and Welfare, has shown in a study of American and British housing problems that families in higher income brackets often move to older, roomier and more dilapidated property with a lower rent per unit area of floor space as the family increases in size.[1] The great bulk of families in the medium and lower income brackets, however, either stay in their original home or, if they move, move to accommodation very similar in size to the home in which they began. The Milner–Holland Report on Housing in Greater London (1965) notes that overcrowding is largely confined to families with young children and adds:

'. . . we find that in three-quarters of the cases there was no over-crowding when the family moved in: it is increasing numbers of children since, which have produced the overcrowded conditions.'[2]

The 1951 Census of England and Wales showed that:

'. . . the private households of Great Britain were much more heavily pressed for rooms in their dwellings the larger the number of children they contained.'[3]

Table 13 shows the average number of rooms per person in different sized households in England and Wales and France.

The larger households containing all the dependent children are seen to have very much less accommodation per head than the small households consisting almost entirely of non-parents. The larger the family the greater the crowding. The main change in the distribution between 1921 and 1951 in the United Kingdom was an increase from 2·9 to 3·3 in the number of rooms in single-person households. Between 1951 and 1961 there was an increase of between 7 and 8 per cent in the number of rooms per person overall, but again the biggest increase, of about 10 per cent, was for one- and two-person households. Overcrowding and housing

[1] Schorr (1964), p. 80. See also David, M. H. (1962).
[2] Milner–Holland (1965), p. 321.
[3] General Register Office: Census 1951, *Housing Report*, p. cxxiii.

Table 13

ROOMS PER PERSON IN HOUSEHOLDS OF DIFFERENT SIZE: FRANCE

AND ENGLAND AND WALES

		Number of rooms per person	
Persons in	France*	England and Wales	
Household	1956	1951†	1961‡
1	2·50	3·30	3·6
2	1·55	2·06	2·2
3	1·13	1·45	1·56
4	0·90	1·15	1·23
5	0·80	0·97	1·04
6	0·70 }	0·80	0·89
7	0·64 }		0·78
8	0·56 }	0·63	0·70
9	}		0·63

* *Consommation* (1962), No. 3.

† General Register Office: Census 1951, *Housing Report, England and Wales*, Table 2, p. 12.

‡ General Register Office: Census 1961, *Household Composition Tables England and Wales*, Table 2, p. 2.

difficulties reflect the inability of many larger families with three or more children to pay for the accommodation they need; and the capacity of many persons with no family responsibilities to cover their requirements more than adequately.

Rent is part of the cost of living of a family group as a whole. In this sense it contrasts with food and clothing, which may be more easily estimated in terms of personal, individual costs. Rent may, indeed, be regarded as a part of the "family overheads", which also include solid fuel, gas, electricity and other costs of running the household such as linen, furniture and cleaning materials.

The poorest German families in the 1962–63[1] survey spent 16·9 per cent of their total budget on rent, and 16·0 per cent on all the other overheads falling under the heading of electricity, gas, fuel and household management, but not including food, clothing, personal care, health, transport, or communications, such as telephone or newspapers. Family overheads defined in this way for these poor German families were therefore almost 33 per cent of the total budget. The percentage of income spent on overheads is generally higher for the poorer families; the

[1] Euler (1965), Table 5, p. 492.

average for all German families is about 27 per cent and there is no great variation between income levels except for this increase among poorer families, who generally spend a higher proportion of their income on both rent and fuel.

In the United Kingdom these family overheads average about 24 per cent for all families and are also higher for poor families at about 27 per cent.[1] In the United States the average family overhead expenditure for all families is about 26·5 per cent, while American families of very modest incomes in the $3,000 to $3,999 bracket spend 31 per cent of income on 'housing', which is the United States family survey classification for 'overheads'. 'Housing' in the American survey includes heat, light, household furnishing and management. The very poorest American family units, below the official poverty line, spend over 40 per cent of their budgets on overheads.

The family expenditure surveys of different countries have a structure differing in detail so that the estimates of family overheads are only broadly comparable. The concept of family overheads has some value in assessing family needs and in discussing the difficult concept of 'equivalence of need' between families of different sizes and compositions. It is, indeed, possible to estimate the total personal needs of all members of a family for food, clothing, personal care and other personal needs and to add a fixed percentage to the aggregated personal needs of the family as family overheads. A split of the overall family budget between 70 per cent personal needs and 30 per cent on family overheads for the average family is often appropriate to poorer families.

The relationship between family size and maintenance cost was investigated in the United States during and after the 1940–45 World War.[2] Some of the studies showed how far families of different sizes were able to afford an adequate diet. Other studies showed that families of different sizes had different levels of savings or overspending of income.[3] For a 'reference family' of a given size it is possible to find the income at which an adequate diet is, in fact, purchased, as shown by nutritional analysis of surveys of family expenditure. In drawing up the City Worker's

---

[1] See Chapter 7 where 25 per cent is used. U.K. Family Expenditure surveys do not always give the same breakdown by family size.

[2] For history of these studies see note 1, p. 34. See also Lamale (1958).

[3] For early studies in U.S. see Brady, D. (1951).

Family Budget the reference family was four persons, a mother and father, boy and girl. Other families of other sizes and ages of children were then shown to need higher or lower incomes to achieve the same nutritional level. Similarly, the point at which a reference family began to save, or ceased to acquire debts, was determined in other studies, and other families were shown to need higher or lower incomes to achieve the same savings level. Both these methods of arriving at 'equivalent' standards of living produced similar results, which are shown in Table 14:

Almost the same results as were obtained by these quite

Table 14

FAMILY INCOMES PROVIDING THE SAME LEVEL OF WELL-BEING AMONG AMERICAN FAMILIES OF DIFFERENT SIZES RELATIVE TO INCOMES OF 4-PERSON FAMILIES*

Size of family Number of persons	Relatives based on	
	Adequacy of Diets	Amount of Savings
1	—	46·0
2	65·1	66·4
3	83·7	84·4
4 (reference family)	100·0	100·0
5	114·8	114·1
6	128·6	127·0

* Brady, D. (1948), p. 51.

elaborate American surveys follow from the simple assumption that 65 per cent of income is spent on personal needs and depends upon the family size and composition, and the remaining 35 per cent is independent of family size and represents the family overheads. In the United States the average family living near the minimum subsistence income or 'Poverty standard' does, in fact, spend roughly 35 per cent of income on overheads.

These definitions of *equivalence*, based as they are on equivalent nutritional standards, or equivalent saving propensity, have some value, but are in no sense true equivalents of well-being. They assume, in practice, roughly the same expenditure by a single person or a childless couple as by a larger family on rent, heat, light and household management. There is no equivalence in comfort or privacy. The overcrowded home is also the home where accidents are most likely to happen.

True equivalence of need cannot be estimated simply by adding a fixed overhead expenditure in money to the aggregated personal needs of the members of a family, if it is accepted that the amount of heated and furnished living space should depend upon the size of the family. The fixed overhead method and techniques based on equivalent nutrition or equivalent saving propensity overestimate the economy of numbers and ignore needs for space, privacy, and safety.

It is, however, useful on occasion in assessing need to estimate, say, 65 per cent of necessary income by aggregating personal needs of the members of a family, and to estimate the remaining 35 per cent of overheads separately from quite other considerations. The split between 65 and 35 is perhaps reasonable for the United States in estimating minimum income requirements, but will vary from one country to another and needs to be decided upon separately for each country. Thus in France, for example, the expenditure on housing is low and on food is high by custom and tradition, and a split of 75 and 25 may be much more in accordance with French life. However, in large cities such as London and Paris, the family overheads are very much higher than in small provincial towns, though without personal needs being higher to the same extent. Estimates of family overheads can only be based upon expert judgement of actual need, or upon housing standards. Most countries have, in fact, laid down acceptable standards of accommodation and have defined overcrowding.

Possibly the worst kind of overcrowding is the overcrowding of adolescents. Children's progress at school is greatly affected by overcrowded homes which provide insufficient privacy and space for study because the family has too few rooms or, in winter time, because only one room can be heated on the family budget. A written contribution from the International Union of Family Organisations to the Common Market conference on Social Security in 1962 stated that rent subsidy should be part of social security:

'For the family the cost of a dwelling is problem number one, for it is the base of all stable family life, and of all chance of education and instruction for future generations.'[1]

Surveys in the United Kingdom also support this view. Similar

[1] Communautés Européennes Conference (1962), Vol. II, p. 146.

evidence has been collected in other countries. A French study showed that overcrowding due to larger families in small apartments affects the school performance of children.[1] A French social administrator addressing a national conference declared: 'We could say of education what M. Sand once said of morality, "It is a question of square metres".'[2] In the United Kingdom a committee on maintenance grants for school children in their teens said that if a child is to take full advantage of full-time education 'he should, if possible, have the use of a separate room for doing homework and it is proper to make an allowance for the cost of heating and lighting such a room'.[3]

Rowntree commented in 1918 on the needs of adolescents for privacy and decency:

'Even when there are only two children, if they are a boy and girl, the need for three bedrooms will arise as soon as they come to a certain age . . . It cannot seriously be argued that for a family of five or more, physical efficiency can be secured along with common decency if less than three bedrooms are provided.'[4]

Young children can share a room. Older children, adolescents and young bachelors and spinsters need a room of their own. Not only, therefore, do such young persons have higher needs on average for food and clothing than most people either older or younger, but they also have special demands on the family overheads. The overcrowding of young persons has many unfortunate social consequences. A children's officer said to the author:

'. . . the overcrowded home makes for too early marriage. If you have to share a bedroom with many brothers or sisters, and the living room with all the family, then one room with one other person is luxury. Many young people marry before they are ready for marriage to escape from two overcrowded homes.'

Local authorities in London were praised in the Milner–Holland report[5] for their attempts to fit house size to family size. Many provincial authorities have done the same in their housing. However, the adaptation of housing to families of different sizes is only beginning and seems likely to take a very long time to com-

[1] Magierska (1961).   [2] Desmottes (1955).
[3] Weaver (1957), pp. 5 and 21.   [4] Rowntree (1918), 1937 edition, p. 87.
[5] Milner–Holland (1965), Chapter 6.

plete. It seems doubtful, indeed, whether it can ever be completed until there is a better correspondence between family income and family size. Belgium and Germany seem to be the first countries to have achieved some correspondence between the average family income and family size, but they also have a very long way to go before housing is adapted to the needs of families of different composition. The greater overcrowding of families with dependent children is found in every country.

Direct assistance with families' housing costs is a major feature of the Swedish social security system. Home purchase is assisted by loans to householders and by Government help for co-operative housing projects. A rent rebate scheme had its origin in the attempt to make newer and larger dwellings available to families:

'It was decided that a part of the rents which families [with several children] would have to pay in new quarters, should be rebated or subsidized in order to enable them, rather than the relatively more affluent childless couples and single individuals, to move into the lion's share of the newly built accommodation.'[1]

At a gross income of about £1,300 a family with two children receives a rent allowance of up to £45. Families with about half this income receive about double the rent subsidy. The ceiling for the granting of rent rebates is set in Sweden not at the poverty level but at approximately twice that level, that is at the modest-but-adequate level, so that both poor and hard-pressed families benefit. Although the poorest receive the largest sums in rent subsidy, application does not depend on categorization of the family as poor.

'These taxable income ceilings are sufficiently high so that the families of most manual workers . . . and those of a great number of white collar workers qualify for these rebates.'[2]

Were similar arrangements in force in the United Kingdom, a comparable gross income below which families with two children would qualify for rent rebates would be about £25 a week.

Two forms of housing subsidy have recently been sponsored in the United Kingdom by the Ministry of Housing.[3] *Rate* rebates

[1] Uhr (1966), p. 22.   [2] *Idem*, p. 15.
[3] Housing and Local Government, Ministry of (1967 and 1968), *Rent Rebate Schemes*, Circular 46/67, Rate Rebates Leaflet (1968).

suggested by the Ministry set the ceiling at £15 a week for a couple with two children. This allows £2 to be set against income for each dependent child. An even lower level of £10 for a family of two children, with an allowance against income of only £1 per child, is recommended to local authorities in assessing *rent* rebates. This child allowance is below subsistence for a child of 5. These levels are below any recognized poverty level for older children and adolescents. If, as a family's income rises above these very low levels of £15 or £10 a week, more must be paid in rates or rent, the result is to keep families in poverty. The Swedish system enables families to become better-off up to the skilled industrial worker's level of earnings before rent subsidy is lost.

Every country attempts in one way or another to fill the gap between family housing needs and family incomes, at least for some of their families. However, economy on housing at the expense of the space and comfort of family members remains the main economy of family size.

It is generally believed that there is some economy in numbers in expenditure on food. The U.S. Department of Agriculture have published their estimates of this economy and suggest, in effect, a reduction of 5 per cent in expenditure per head for each additional member of the family up to the sixth member or fourth child.[1] There is undoubtedly some economy to be achieved in fuel needed for the preparation of food and in purchases in larger quantities. However, recent official American papers suggest that the evidence for the extent of any 'economy of numbers' in family spending on food or clothing is not reliable. Indeed, Miss Orshansky of the U.S. Department of Health, Education and Welfare writes:

'It thus appears that what passes for 'economy of scale' in the larger family may in part reflect a lowering of dietary standards enforced by insufficient funds.'[2]

The U.S. Department of Agriculture's 5 per cent was only intended as a rough estimate and cannot, indeed, be right as an estimate of need, if only because it assumes, for example, that the economy achieved by adding a fourth child is greater than when

[1] U.S. Dept. of Agriculture, *Family Food Plans* (1962), Appendix B.
[2] Orshansky, (Jan. 1965), p. 8.

adding the second, which is most improbable. Any economy in numbers in food is certainly small, must remain difficult to estimate, and is probably best ignored.

In practice in every country the larger families have a more economical diet and malnutrition is to be found largely in families with three or more children, but this is, of course, the consequence of spreading limited resources over a larger number of persons.[1] A study of the detail of food purchases by families from the family expenditure surveys of any country will confirm this trend to dilution of diet with the cheapest items available. Dr Lambert examined the United Kingdom Food Surveys over a decade from 1950 to 1960 and found:

'In the last decade family size had more influence on the nutritional value of the diet than social class or income. Throughout the decade there has been a sharp downward gradient in the value of the diet as the size of the family increases such that the diet of childless couples in Class A, C and D are closer to each other in nutritional value than they are to the diets of large families in their own class . . . it is clear that, on average, the larger families in all classes, and also those families containing both adolescents and children, constitute the most vulnerable groups nutritionally.'[2]

The Domestic Food Consumption Surveys in the sixties confirm Lambert's finding of the earlier date:

'Younger childless couples devoted a greater proportion of their expenditure to meat, butter, green vegetables and fruit; in contrast, families with four or more children were more dependent on the cheaper sources of energy such as bread, potatoes and margarine . . . The two nutrients whose average consumption failed to reach the recommended allowances were *protein* in the larger families containing adolescents with or without children, and *calcium* in the families containing three or more children, (or) children and adolescents.'[3]

---

[1] Drion (1961) in a study of Dutch families showed that 'the qualitative differentiation in the diet according to age prescribed by nutritionists is not made by the general population.' French studies of consumption of articles of food by family size and socio-economic group: Trémolières (1951) and (1953) and Vinit (1962).

[2] Lambert (1964), p. 13.

[3] Agriculture, Fisheries and Food, Ministry of (1961), *Domestic Food Consumption and Expenditure*, pp. 24 and 29.

Most family budgets suggest that it costs more for a man or woman to be head of a household than to be a dependant. For example, the family budget standard of the Community Council of Greater New York shows the cost of a male head of household under 65 years of age to be 13 per cent and of a female head of household 16 per cent higher than for a dependent adult:

Table 15

RATIO OF COST OF HEAD OF HOUSEHOLD TO DEPENDENT MALE*

Dependent Male = 100

Age	Male Head	Female Head
Under 35	113	116
35–54	113	116
55–64	114	116
65-over	107	109

* Community Council of Greater New York (1963), *Family Budget Standard*, p. 65.

These American figures include payment for semi-durables which have to be replaced, such as sheets, linen, cooking utensils, electric light bulbs, and for cleaning material and laundry and household repairs. A small sum is also added towards the eventual cost of replacing durable goods and furnishings. There are also minor current items which a householder pays for, such as television and radio, newspapers and some entertaining. This notion, that the head of a household has a higher cost of living than the remaining members, may sometimes be useful but can cause confusion. The head of the household usually pays *all* the family overheads including rent, light, heat, repairs and so on. The head of the household may also have to pay all the other bills for food or clothing. It will usually be better in estimating family needs to estimate in terms of personal needs and overheads separately, rather than to show the head of the household as having arbitrary or inflated personal living costs. Of course, as discussed in an earlier chapter, the head of household or any other member of a household who goes out to work will have a special supplementary cost of working.

Estimation of the needs of a whole family must also take into account the inflexibility of many needs particularly of the need to pay rent. It is useless to tell a family that it ought not to spend more than 15 per cent of its budget on rent if it is, in fact, spending 25 per cent. Expenditure on food or clothing can be adjusted to some extent from week to week, but rent or mortgage interest is likely to be unchangeable and has to be paid before other expenses are met. Electricity, gas and solid fuel bills are also not easily changed. The poorer a family, too, the more difficult it is for it to move. Poverty reduces geographical mobility. It is in housing needs that there is the greatest difference between what ought to be and what is. It is, therefore, in this particular area that theoretical budgets and statements of family need have least practical value. There is much to be said for schemes of social security and assistance that recognize that rents are an essential overhead that must be paid, and that the viability of a family often depends upon this being done.

Some domestic appliances have already moved from the category of luxuries to that of necessities. Using the words of the economists, the demand for them is becoming less 'elastic' in the same way as the demand for school shoes has become 'inelastic'. In a study of the consumption of families in France, Dr Rottier in 1963 contrasted family expenditure on housing and on domestic equipment. He explained that families with children have a greater need for domestic equipment such as washing machines, vacuum cleaners and refrigerators than households without children; families even economize on housing and consumable goods to buy these things.[1]

The French survey of families published in 1967 showed that these domestic appliances are purchased at an early stage in family building by families of comparatively modest means and at the sacrifice of expenditure on current consumable goods.[2] The cost is often spread by credit over a period of years so that payment competes with other items in the budget. Domestic appliances are becoming a necessity. One result is that poor families who cannot afford to equip their houses become conspicuously different from their neighbours in their habits.

The same French survey showed that as the income of a

---

[1] Rottier (1963).
[2] Tabard (1967), Part IV. See also David, M. H. (1962), *Consumption*, Chapter 4.

French family rises up to and beyond the modest-but-adequate level, the greatest rates of increase in outlay are for holidays, sport, amusements including the cinema, reading matter and all other things that meet the needs of the mind rather than basic physical needs. If income falls, it is these things that suffer the first economies. Indeed, incomes even substantially above the poverty level may be adequate to meet physical requirements but leave the environment of the family and the environment of its children poor in every means of satisfying mental curiosity and stimulation. Poverty or near-poverty is dull and retards the mental development of children.

An annual holiday away from home is a touchstone of increased standard of living. The lower standard of living of families with dependent children compared with the rest of the community may be seen from the holiday statistics. In any particular year only about 40 per cent of British households with dependent children have a holiday, defined as four nights or more away from home.[1] About 60 per cent of households with dependent children have no such holiday with the children. In contrast, 72 per cent of adult households with no dependants have a holiday. Of all holiday parties only 27 per cent include one or more children.

Substantially less than 40 per cent of children in the United Kingdom have an annual holiday as, of course, the larger the family the less usual it is to have a holiday away from home; only about 18 per cent of families with four children, for example, have a holiday.

Rather more than 10 per cent of households afford a holiday abroad. However, of all the parties taking holidays abroad only about one in nine includes one or more children. Indeed, the more expensive the holiday the smaller is the proportion of holiday parties that include a child.[1]

Family expenditure surveys show that in most countries the amount spent on average per household on holidays increases with income but decreases with the size of the family. The amount spent per *head* therefore decreases sharply as numbers in the family increase. The French statistical department publishes

[1] These figures have been based upon the unpublished national survey undertaken for the British Travel Association by Social Surveys (Gallup Poll) Ltd. and have also used the Census 1961 Household Composition Tables.

very detailed figures on holidays.[1] From 1961 to 1964 there was an increased tendency for adult households and adults in small families to take holidays but this was not true of larger families. The number of fathers of large families who could afford to take a holiday did not increase in the same way. The report comments:

'It is probable that, when the number of children increases, the income of the household is not enough in many cases to pay for a holiday for the whole family, and often not even enough to pay for the children.'[2]

In contrast to the United Kingdom, many children in France spend their holidays away from their families in subsidized holiday centres or camps. This ensures that, notably in the poorer and larger families, a substantial proportion of the children have a holiday. However, the average amount spent per head in French families by persons taking a holiday fell from 658 francs for a single person to 311 a head, which included holiday allowances, for six-person families in the same year.

The French survey of families of 1967 devoted a long chapter[3] entirely to the influence of family income and family responsibilities on holiday-going, and showed that the number of families in which everyone took a holiday more than doubled between the poorest and best-off families, but that the larger the family the less chance there was of parents going with their children even amongst the better off:

'The larger the number of children the less frequent are holidays in the family. At the same income (but let us recall that this does *not* mean at the same standard of living) the effect of the number of children is even more apparent, even at higher income levels where the consideration of expense would be expected to become less . . . As the number of children increases it is less possible for a family to put aside the considerable sums required for a holiday because of the increased volume of "necessary expenses".'[4]

There has been a pattern in the development of holiday-going in France.[5] At the lowest income levels and especially amongst

[1] *Études et Conjoncture*. A paper on holiday-going in France has appeared in several recent years, for example, June 1965, May 1966.
[2] *Ibid.*, June 1965.   [3] Tabard (1967), Part VII.
[4] *Idem.*, p. 278.   [5] *Idem*, p. 275.

E

larger families no member of the family has a holiday. This is still true of one French family in four. The first step forward has been the holiday for children alone. A great many French families of modest means are still at this stage, a holiday all together is still a luxury. But the survey questionnaire asked the families what they wished, and 90 per cent insisted that a holiday with their children was what they really wanted. The larger the family the less these wishes could be realized.

The co-ordinated family expenditure surveys (1963–4) of the Common Market countries enable us to compare the amount spent on holidays by incomes and family size. From the details of family expenditure the special expenses for holidays may be extracted, omitting food and clothing but including hotels, travel, incidental expenses, sport and camping equipment and week-end holidays.[1]

Workmen's households of couples without children in the Netherlands spend on average nearly three times as much as workmen's families with four or more children, who spend so little that clearly a holiday is a rare luxury in this social group. Amongst employees and civil servants, a couple with three children spends only rather more than half the money spent on holidays by a childless couple, and this is true both of average families and for those in the highest income group given.

In Italy the difference between the family and the childless couple is even more striking. Amongst workmen the childless couple spends five times as much on hotels and lodgings as the three-child family, and twenty-two times as much as the large family with four or more children. On total holiday expenses the childless spend more than ten times as much as the three-child families.

In France, on the other hand, the difference between the family with and without children is much less marked. Childless couples amongst workmen's families spend less than twice the amount spent by families with four or more children. The sums *per head* are small, however, and show that in large families the whole family cannot take a holiday but on average only some member. This would be expected from the surveys described above. Amongst salaried employees in France the family with three

---

[1] The code numbers used here are 60·12; 72·01; 72·02; 74·05; 74·10; 74·99; 82·00.

children spends very slightly more on average than the childless couple. The effect of holiday allowances and high family allowances in France is seen in these results.

Amongst German workmen's families, the larger families with four or more children spend about a quarter of the money on holidays spent by childless couples, and one-sixth of the amount on hotels or lodgings. In fact, in Germany also a holiday is a rarity for large working-class families. In the families of salaried employees and civil servants a childless couple spends on average over three times as much per head as a family with three children.

The difference between families and the childless is more marked, in the amount they can afford on holidays, amongst workmen's families than amongst salaried employees' families. This is not only due to higher incomes but to a different salary structure. Among employees a father earns a higher wage than a younger man. Even so, the difference between the childless family and the family with children is clearly shown in the holiday expenditure of the salaried employees.

In the discussions on raising family allowances in the United Kingdom it is often suggested that families would use these allowances to pay for school meals or for other specific purposes. One of the objectives of the French survey of 1967 was 'to foresee how families would alter their consumption patterns if family allowances were to be increased'. It was learned that the allowances were not, in fact, spent on any particular items but contributed to the taking of the next step in family well-being appropriate to the family's own level of living:

'The difficulty of foreseeing on what family allowances would be spent in the future, in particular their economic effect should they be raised, arises precisely from the fact that the allowances mirror exactly the evolution of the way of living of families. At the present time family allowances seem to reinforce the tendency to spend money on equipping the home or on the future schooling of children because these are the preoccupations which dominate families at the present time: in the near future, doubtless (and probably at the present time for many families) priority will be given to the need for educationally valuable leisure occupations for children, then to holidays for which expenditure is already in fact stimulated by a "designated allowance". . . . . It is an illustration of this that the two special grants which are most frequently applied for by families should be the grants for maintenance at the beginning of the school year and holiday allowances.'[1]

Family allowances, in short, increase the standard of living of the family group in exactly the same way as any other addition to family income.

[1] Tabard (1967), pp. 144–5 and note 1, p. 145.

CHAPTER SIX

The Life-Cycle of Family Needs

The standard of living of a man (or woman) is inseparable from that of the family to which he belongs at different times during his life history. Only persons who live alone have a standard of living that is independent of other people and that reflects their spendable income independent of family circumstances. Among persons who live in families there are two main factors influencing their standard of living, namely the family income and the extent of the family's responsibilities, notably the number of non-earning dependants.

The family income and family responsibilities rarely keep in step. A man's earned income rises to a maximum at some point between his twenties and his sixties, according to his occupation. In general, the peak in earnings increases with age with the level of skill and education required in the particular occupation. If a man marries and has children his family responsibilities also rise and fall but follow a very different curve.

The lack of correspondence between income and responsibilities is enhanced today by the pattern of women's working lives. As family responsibilities increase, women give up their jobs. The greater the family responsibilities, the less in general is the wife's contribution to the family income. This is one main reason why the average income of households with dependent children is lower than that of households without dependent children.

Studies of the standard of living will therefore be not only incomplete but will be misleading if confined to studies of individuals isolated from the family, or even to families at any one point of time. A typical family household is created, expands and develops and then eventually declines and disappears. There is, indeed, a family cycle.[1] The standard of living of a family depends upon the family cycle, but in the average case of a family with children, in ways that are not very socially desirable.

Rowntree, in his classic studies of poverty,[2] showed that the

---

[1] For studies of consumption over the life cycle, see Lansing (1955); Fisher, Janet H. (1952) (1955); Lydall (1955); David, M. H. (1962).
[2] Rowntree (1901), (1918, (1941), (1951).

income of the typical working class family does not expand and contract in step with family responsibilities. He noted that there are two periods of relative prosperity in the life-cycle of a typical family. Rowntree presented this life-cycle as a diagram, which is printed below together with his comment on the poor family of his day:

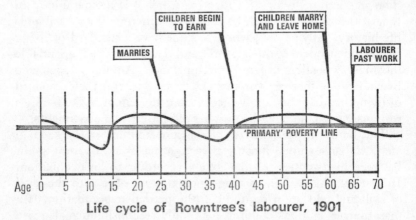

Life cycle of Rowntree's labourer, 1901

'The life of a labourer is marked by five alternating periods of want and comparative plenty. During early childhood, unless his father is a skilled worker, he probably will be in poverty; this will last until he, or some of his brothers or sisters, begin to earn money and thus augment their father's wage sufficiently to raise the family above the poverty line. Then follows the period during which he is earning money and living under his parents' roof; for some portion of this period he will be earning more money than is required for lodging, food and clothes. This is his chance to save money. If he has saved enough to pay for furnishing a cottage, this period of comparative prosperity may continue after marriage until he has two or three children, when poverty will again overtake him. This period of poverty will last perhaps for ten years, i.e. until the first child is fourteen years old and begins to earn wages; but if there are more than three children it may last longer. While the children are earning, and before they leave the home to marry, the man enjoys another period of prosperity—possibly, however, only to sink back again into poverty when his children have married and left him and he himself is too old to work, for his income has never permitted his saving enough for him and his wife to live upon for more than a very short time.[1]

---

[1] Rowntree (1901), p. 171 (2nd Edition, 1902, p. 137). Adapted by kind permission of the Joseph Rowntree Charitable Trust.

The same pattern is repeated at other income levels, at other times and, indeed, in families throughout most of the world. The standard of living has, of course, risen since the 1890s when Rowntree was writing. It is still true, however, that the income of the typical family does not expand and contract in step with family responsibilities, and that there are two periods of relative prosperity in the life of the average family.

The family life-cycle has been the subject of recent studies in many countries. *The Life-Cycle of Family Needs* shown in Figure 9 is taken from Professor Helga Schmucker's study of 1961 and is based on official Bavarian statistics.[1] The life-cycle is seen to include two peaks and a 'trough' or depression in between. The two periods of relative prosperity during the life of a family noted by Rowntree at the beginning of this century are shown clearly in this figure for a Bavarian industrial worker's family with two children. The first period of prosperity is in early married life while the father is still in his twenties and the mother, who is a few years younger than the father, continues to work. The couple at this time have two incomes and their domestic responsibilities are small. This first period of the family life-cycle is one of relative prosperity, which comes to an abrupt end when the arrival of children results in the mother giving up her job and staying at home. Figure 9 shows this sudden drop in the family standard of living happening when the father is 30 years of age. Today this sudden drop in the family standard of living when children arrive and the mother ceases work generally happens when the father is below the age of 30.

This short period of comparative prosperity of the young married couple is a period of family life when it is possible and normal for the young people to accumulate savings, household goods and other property. It is often possible, indeed, for the young couple to furnish and equip a home, to take out insurance policies and to accumulate some savings, and, if the man's wages are high enough, to start buying a house through a building society. Very few young couples today in the United Kingdom are poor when both are earning and before any children arrive.

Of course, this period of saving and accumulation often begins in anticipation of marriage. Possessions are accumulated in a

[1] Schmucker (1961), p. 30. See also Lansing (1955).

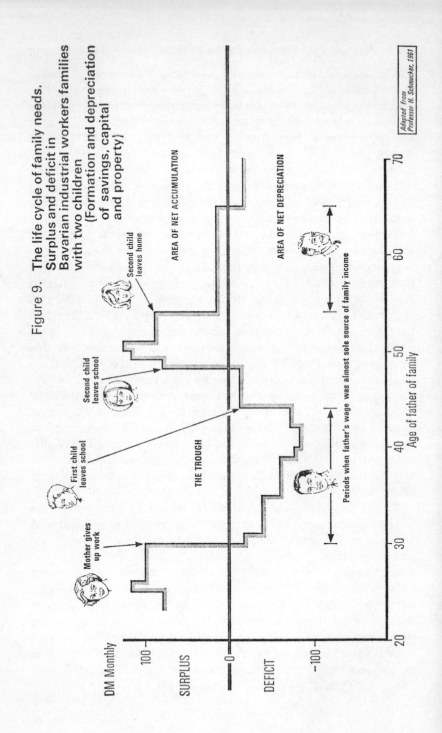

Figure 9. The life cycle of family needs.
Surplus and deficit in
Bavarian industrial workers families
with two children
(Formation and depreciation
of savings, capital
and property)

DM Monthly

100 —

SURPLUS

0

DEFICIT

-100 —

20   30   40   50   60   70

Age of father of family

Mother gives up work

First child leaves school

Second child leaves school

Second child leaves home

THE TROUGH

AREA OF NET ACCUMULATION

AREA OF NET DEPRECIATION

Periods when father's wage was almost sole source of family income

Adapted from
Professor H. Schmucker, 1961

'bottom drawer' and wedding presents contribute to the possessions of the young couple. The extent of the home-building during
these early years has an important influence upon family stability
and childhood environment later on. Failure of a young couple to
acquire a house, or savings towards a house, or household goods
and equipment before the arrival of children must generally
increase family overheads during the years when they can least be
afforded. Premature or early marriage or the very early conception
of children resulting in the shortening of the period of home-
building is likely to increase family difficulties when the children
are growing up. Housing costs may be too heavy for the young
couple to carry except on two incomes. The moment the wife
leaves work the proportion of income spent on housing becomes
too great. Professor Alfred Sauvy gives this picture of the effect
on young households of the increasing age span of the population:

'In traditional society young persons were part of the family and were,
in some measure, supported by the family because of family solidarity
and the effect of death. A young person of twenty-five had one chance in
two of being an orphan. Today young people form a horizontal group
which feels above them the weight of two generations. The adults have
the jobs and the old people have the wealth. Many a young household is
devoting thirty per cent of its meagre income to its small dwelling
whilst their parents only devote five per cent. It is true that the economy
is not an exercise in altruism and political economy is the science of
sordid motives. But in our splendid collection of egoisms and social
cruelties the most inhuman and also the most discretely focused are
those blows which fall upon the young. Every reproach which we can
find to make against the young comes from this . . .'[1]

Professor Donnison gives a similar picture of the young household
in Britain in a book published in the same year as Professor
Sauvy's paper:

'. . . the student who is willing . . . to rent a flat for a quarter of the
income he and his wife earn together, may be unable to afford more than
a tenth of his income for the larger house they require to shelter a
growing family. Later their rent-paying capacity may rise again for
fifteen or twenty years to fall once more in old age.'[2]

[1] Sauvy, A. (1967), 'Cinquante Millions, Part II, La Bataille de la Jeunesse',
Le Monde, 7 Sept. 1967.
[2] Donnison (1967), pp. 67–8.

The British television play *Cathy Come Home* was a moving illustration of just these pressures of housing costs on a young couple of modest means, from their wedding day to the break-up of the family unit of parents and children.

Young couples frequently fail to anticipate the fall in standard of living that they will have to suffer when the children begin to arrive. In all too many cases the young couple while still childless enter into hire purchase commitments that cannot be afforded when the wife ceases work and there are children to pay for. Excessive hire purchase commitments, entered into during the short period of prosperity subsequent to marriage, later deepen the trough in the family cycle and are a cause of much distress in families with dependent children.

Figure 9 shows that, in these German families, once the mother gave up work because of the arrival of children there was virtually no further net accumulation of property for eighteen years. In effect, the various family possessions, including furniture, household equipment and so on, all depreciated until the eldest child left home or began to earn for the first time.

Of course Figure 9 is based on the circumstances in a particular country at a particular time. A certain minimum income is necessary, depending upon the size of family, before there is any net accumulation of savings or possessions. Figure 9 shows that Bavarian wages were above this critical level for single persons or childless couples, but below it for families with two children. The position of the zero accumulation line changes with time and place and, indeed, from family to family.

The average income below which there is no net savings and no accumulation of property has, as we have seen in Chapter 5, been used to define the poverty line. However, the income level at which a particular family saves depends in practice upon its past history. The family that failed to accumulate enough blankets before the children arrived has to purchase blankets after their arrival. Two families may have identical incomes and numbers of children, but one will be forced to purchase household durables while the other will be able to live without many further purchases for years.

The trough in Figure 9 is not dependent upon absolute standards of living and is characteristic of all families. Figure 9 is for a family of parents and two children. The trough is wider and deeper for families of three, four or five children. The trough is also wider the longer the period of education is extended, and the depth is then much increased because the years added by raising the school leaving age are most expensive years of dependence.

Every facility enabling mothers to work makes the trough shallower. A mother going out to work can help to lift a family out of the trough and many families only escape poverty by the mother working. There is considerable literature discussing the consequences to the family of mothers working and the consequential problems of day-care and child-minding.

Rowntree showed that the poorest sections of the community were families with dependent children and old people. Figure 9 shows the same picture, and also shows that the maximum economic pressure on these Bavarian families occurred when the father of the family was between 40 and 44. The years of maximum family difficulty were those immediately before the eldest child left school. The study in an earlier chapter of the comparative costs of children, adolescents and adults provides the explanations; an adolescent boy costs as much or more than a man to keep, and an adolescent girl as much as a woman.

This coincidence of maximum economic stress in the typical family with the adolescence of the children has many unfortunate consequences. These are the years when children are beginning to think of freedom and independence, and when they begin to see where their own family stands in our competitive society. If relations between parents and children are good then the economic difficulties of the family can be explained to the children who will understand. If relations between parents and children are not so good then the economic stress can be disruptive. Disputes develop between parents and children about money. Adolescents have to learn about money and to experiment with it to form their scales of value. Such experimentation appears to hard-pressed parents to be irresponsible extravagance. Such disputes lead to loss of parental influence and control. If the parents have not built very good relations with their children, the father in particular, in a hard-pressed family, is liable to lose the respect of his teenage children just because of his inadequate earning capacity. Dependent children too often blame the father if they are unable to maintain the standards of their peers.

The conflict is aggravated by the great contrast between the standard of living of families with children who are still dependent and families with children who go out to earn their living. The contrast obviously creates strong incentives for children to leave school, and, indeed, for children to leave home, particularly if the parental home is overcrowded. Federal government studies in the United States showed that poor homes had *less* than their expected number of adolescents.[1] Poverty had the effect of driving some young people from home, sometimes into early marriage, and sometimes to independent living. A voluntary society reported in 1967 in the United Kingdom that it was believed that an additional ten thousand teenage boys were in need of lodgings every year.[2] The full extent of the problem in the United Kingdom is not known. In France[3] the family allowance regional organizations have begun to provide hostels for young working boys living apart from their families because they have entered big cities in search of work or have left over-crowded homes.[4]

In Figure 9 the second period of relative family prosperity is initiated by the eldest child leaving school and going out to work and so contributing to the family income. There are strong incentives in families of modest means to solve their problem of poverty in this way. A boy's or girl's decision to leave school in order to help the parents' family is generally a decision taken at the expense of the young person's own eventual earning power; it is a decision to help the last generation at the expense of the next generation and the next but one. In this typical Bavarian family the second period of relative prosperity lasts for only six years, when the father is between 48 and 54 years of age. The children then leave home, and for another eleven years the father's wage has only himself and his wife to maintain and provides a modest surplus.

Economic pressure on the family with dependent teenagers leads too often to early marriage being used as an escape route from the exigencies of a poor or hard-pressed family. There are many social objections to early marriage and many reasons for

[1] Orshansky (July 1965), p. 6.
[2] Report of St Christopher's Fellowship (1967).
[3] The Missoffe Report (1967) estimates 207,000 'jeunes isolés', see p. 49.
[4] Orshansky (July 1965), p. 6.

encouraging young persons to defer marriage at least until they reach their majority. There is also much to be said in the average case for keeping families together and for deferring the day when children either leave home or get married or terminate their education. Social arrangements are in need of reform if they subject families with dependent adolescents to greater economic stress than is suffered by any other type of normal family. Social insurance arrangements that are strongly biased against these families with dependent adolescents are also inconsistent with public preoccupation with juvenile delinquency. No country has adjusted its social security benefits to reflect the true costs of adolescents.

Some countries, notably France and Belgium, have family allowances and tax concessions generous enough to make the trough of the family life cycle shallower. The worker mother, nevertheless, has done more than governments to raise the standard of living of her family. A French expert declared:

'The mother of two children must perform 48 hours of paid employment outside the home to compensate for the presence of the children, even supposing that her own needs are not greater than those of a mother staying at home.'[1]

The pattern of women's lives is changing, and the age structure of gainfully employed women is changing.[2] A United Kingdom government report gives this picture of three generations:

'In many instances the children were cared for (or were expected to be cared for) by their grandmothers, who themselves had worked little, if at all, since their marriages.'[3]

In grandmother's day the labour force consisted largely of unmarried women, mostly young, but including older spinsters, widows and deserted wives of all ages. Today two-thirds of the women's labour force in the United Kingdom is made up of married women. Even in Belgium, which has amongst the lowest proportion of married women working in Europe, they are the majority of women workers.[4]

[1] Paillat (1960), p. 780. Her needs include the cost of working, as discussed in Chapter 3.
[2] Hunt, A. P. (1968); Klein (1965); Chester, T. E. (1962); Laurent (1961); (Guelaud-Leridon) (1964 and 1967, Part II).
[3] Hunt, A. P. (1968).   [4] Gubbels (1966), p. 63 ff.

Women are least able to work when they have young children under school age. In the United Kingdom the number of women working is at a minimum between 25 and 29 years of age. Of the mothers who work, most work part-time.[1]

When the children all go to school, and as the older children reach the more expensive years, more mothers return to work and more work full-time. In the United States the years of life when women are least likely to work are from 25 to 34 years.[2]

In France the minimum working age is rather older, between 30 and 35.[3]

However, this general tendency for mothers to go back to work when their children are at school is spreading in every industrial country. It helps to make the trough of the family life cycle shallower and so to offset the cost to parents of prolonged schooling. The co-ordinated family expenditure surveys of the Common Market countries include the working wife as an 'indicator of level of living' together with consumer goods such as cars, television sets and refrigerators.

Table 16

PERCENTAGE OF HOUSEHOLDS IN WHICH THE WIFE OF HEAD OF HOUSEHOLD HAS PAID EMPLOYMENT: IN E.E.C. 1963–4*

	Germany†	France	Italy	Nether-lands	Belgium	Luxem-bourg
All workmen's families	23·46	26·19	13·21	10·96	20·60	3·33
All employees' and civil servants' families	15·94	28·70	13·69	9·17	22·89	2·97

* Communautés Européennes, *Budgets Familiaux* (1963–4), vol. 7, Tables A1 and A2, Section D, pp. 6* and 7*.

† Germany, 1962–3.

However, the benefit of a mother's working is less than appears from a simple addition of parental incomes. For a given net family income the standard of living enjoyed if both parents are working is

[1] Hunt, A. P. (1968).

[2] American literature on the working mother is extensive. Three recent papers of note are Waldman, E. (1967) and (1968) and Perrella, V. (1968).

[3] For studies of women's work in France see Guelaud-Leridon (1964); *Études et Conjoncture*, Dec. 1964 and Feb. 1967; *Informations Sociales*, June 1968; Isambert-Jamati (1960) (1960) (1961); Legoux (1962).

less than if the income were all earned by one parent. Personal 'expenses of working' for two people must be deducted and there are, in addition, what might be called 'the home expenses of the working mother', such as convenience foods and articles bought because there is not time to make do and mend.[1] Above all, there is the loss of leisure, the loss of time spent on homemaking by the mother and the loss of her hours of play and activity with children and husband which must now be devoted to catching up on the household tasks.[2]

The pattern of life of the unsupported mother is quite different from that of the working mother in a complete family. Indeed, from the time she is alone, it will follow the pattern of the single woman's life. Not for her the years off work devoted to young children nor the half-way house of part-time work in their early school days. Not for her the liberty to give up a job when the children have a bad winter of childish ailments. She must work when they are infants, when they are sick, in school holidays. Her only alternative is a poverty level subsistence income provided by the state (and that only if she lives in a country which, like the United Kingdom and most States in the U.S.A., allows her this choice; many countries do not).

Figure 10 contrasts the percentages of single women and married women working at different ages in France in 1962. The 'single women' include widows and divorced women. The married women in general earn less per woman working than a single woman. It will be seen from the figures that married women with a husband earn less than half as much over a life-time as single women.[3]

A paper on the employment of women and mothers in Germany

---

[1] Lamale (1963).

[2] Morgan, J. N. (1962) discusses the sacrifice of leisure for the purchase of things: 'Most important of all are differences in the leisure available to different families. Indeed perhaps the major practical and conceptual difficulty in discussing welfare is the problem of how to trade leisure for other kinds of real income . . . How many of the families who appear well-off are actually sacrificing leisure for other things that surveys find it easy to measure.' See also Morgan, J. N., et al. (1962), Chapter 21.

[3] Guelaud-Leridon (1964), pp. 18–21. See also Études et Conjoncture, Dec. (1964); Informations Sociales, Apr. (1960), Jan. (1966), June (1968); International Union of Family Organisations (1963); Le Travail Professionel des Femmes Mariées; Laurent (1961).

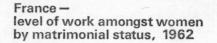

Figure 10.

**France —
level of work amongst women
by matrimonial status, 1962**

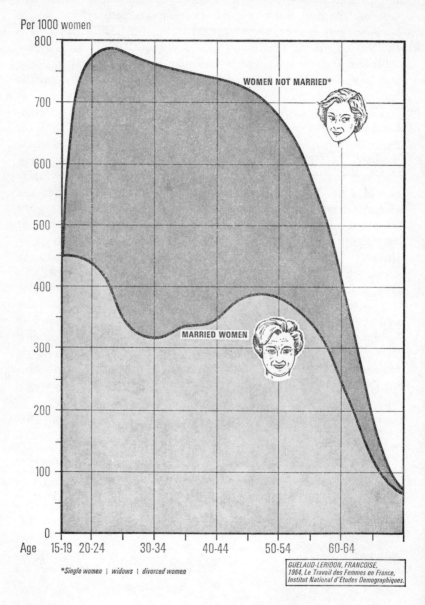

Per 1000 women

WOMEN NOT MARRIED*

MARRIED WOMEN

Age   15-19 20-24   30-34   40-44   50-54   60-64

*Single women ¦ widows ¦ divorced women

GUELAUD-LERIDON, FRANCOISE,
1964, Le Travail des Femmes en France,
Institut National d'Etudes Demographiques.

gives figures from the micro-census of 1962 showing the difference between mothers with husbands and those without:

Table 17

WORKING MOTHERS IN GERMANY BY MARITAL STATUS, ALL WITH
DEPENDENT CHILDREN UNDER 14, 1962*

Marital Status of Mother	Percentage of that marital status which is gainfully employed
Married (husband present)	33·1
Widowed	40·2
Divorced	75·1
Unmarried	84·1

* Germany: Employment of women and mothers and child minding. Wirtschaft und Statistik, No. 8 (1964), table, p. 445 (rearranged), Statistisches Bundesamt Wiesbaden.

Dr Heinz Simon, permanent head of the German Ministry for the Family, gave a moving picture of the plight of unsupported mothers in a paper to a national conference on public health:

'Even (for the widow) there are great hardships . . . However, the most essential means of livelihood are guaranteed to the widowed mother and her children . . . However, this is not true of the separated, divorced and unmarried mothers. Here there is not a guaranteed basic minimum income and this is the explanation of the 3, 4, or even 5 times increase in the proportion of mothers going out to work as against the normal number from complete families. And in fact extreme poverty reigns.'[1]

Dr. Simon stressed the dual standard which society has towards the working mother in complete and broken families. He described the medical opinion against mothers of young children going out to work and the public support for this view, and continued:

'However, the situation is quite different for mothers of fatherless families, here the public accepts that of course the mother must go out to work if she hasn't enough money. . . .

The mother in a complete family earns her right to a livelihood, in all justice, by housekeeping and looking after the children. She has no duty to go out to work if the income of her husband is adequate. It is not easy to see why the situation must be different in principle in the case of the unsupported mother. Her children particularly need her, and more

[1] Simon, H. (1963), p. 106.

urgently than in the complete family where the mother does not have to carry all the worries and all the burdens alone.'[1]

The years of greatest hardship in the fatherless family are also the years when children are in their teens and at their most expensive. In a complete family this is the time when mother, working full-time, may be a great help; there is no second wage-earner in the fatherless family.

The life cycle of family needs is not by any means only relevant to the elimination of poverty. The main investment in the next generation is made in developed countries by parents living above subsistence levels. Most families in Western Europe have a standard of living above the poverty level but below the modest-but-adequate level. A rise in the standard of living of these families increases the investment in the children, and a fall in standard of living reduces the investment. The average expenditure on a child within a family ordinarily increases almost proportionately to the family income. Expenditure on a child also increases with the child's age. At a given income level the standard of living falls with the number of children in the family, and also falls as the children grow older, as long as they are dependent. Benefits that do not reflect the higher cost of older children and adolescents not only result in a lower standard of living of the adolescent, but of the whole family, including any younger children. The typical distribution of expenditure within families is, indeed, important to an understanding of the consequences of different levels of benefit under any scheme. Families living on sick pay in the United Kingdom do not actually spend £1 8s.[2] (the benefit for a child) on each child, but spend very much more in the great majority of cases, depending on the age of the child and the total sick pay of the family unit.

A few surveys have studied the allocation of expenditure within families. Parents of modest means have been shown by these studies to make great sacrifices to ensure that their sons and daughters are well fed and well dressed. For example, the French survey of 1963-4 showed that, in all the lower income brackets,

[1] Simon, H. (1963), p. 107.

[2] January 1968. Increased Family Allowance for second and later children was followed by deduction from dependants allowances, so that all children receive the same total sum. See House of Commons Debate, 23 May 1968, and Leaflet N.I. 147, Ministry of Social Security.

the expenditure per head on clothing and footwear for older children and adolescents is substantially higher than the expenditure per head by parents on themselves. This was shown in Figure 7A.

The Statistical Office of the German Government undertook a budget survey in 1950–1 of 10,600 families that included a study of the allocation of expenditure within the families to the different members. This study showed that the actual expenditure attributable to a child of a particular age was approximately proportional to income over the modest range of incomes covered by the study. If the total family income doubled, then the expenditure on a child almost doubled too. If the total family income halved, then the expenditure on a child almost halved too. If a child was added to a family, he was paid for by a proportionate economy in the expenditure on behalf of all the other members.

This German survey classified family incomes into four income brackets. The lowest bracket included families with an annual income of less than 2,500 DM a year, and the highest bracket included families with more than 5,100 DM a year. This sample was representative of all families living around or between the poverty and the modest-but-adequate levels, whenever there were two or more dependent children. The survey showed that the expenditure on children throughout these income classes was roughly proportional to family income for a family of given composition. The implication is that families spend a high proportion of their income on their children up to and beyond the modest-but-adequate level of income:

Table 18

PERCENTAGE OF FAMILY INCOME SPENT ON A CHILD AT DIFFERENT

AGES IN 4-PERSON HOUSEHOLDS

GERMANY, 1950–1*

Household income bracket DM per year	1–6	Age bracket of dependent child 6–10	10–14	14–19	over 19
2,500–3,600	12·6	17·0	20·1	26·7	33·4
3,600–5,100	12·0	16·1	20·1	24·7	33·0
Over 5,100	12·0	15·2	19·6	23·8	31·6

* Germany, Expenditure on children within Families, Wirtschaft und Statistik (Sept. 1955), Table 3, p. 452, Statistisches Bundesamt, Wiesbaden.

Table 18, taken from the German survey, shows the actual proportion of family income spent upon a child in a particular age-bracket in four-person households. The figures are difficult to interpret as the other three persons may have been adults or may have included one or even two children. It is notable, however, that in all five columns of figures the percentage spent on a child diminishes slightly from top to bottom; thus, in the first column, the percentage of family income spent on a child in the 1 to 6 age bracket diminishes from 12·6 to 12·0 per cent, with the increase in income and in the last column for the dependent child over 19 years of age from 33.4 to 31.6 per cent. While these are small differences, it is apparent that as family income increases the percentage spent on dependent children declines very slightly and is likely, indeed, to decline more still at higher income levels outside the scope of this German survey.

It was an important conclusion from this German survey that typical parents of modest means spend their incomes reasonably and fairly for the benefit of all members of their families. Every social worker knows that this does not invariably happen, but it does happen in the great majority of families, and for the average figures for a large sample of families. It is also apparent, and very understandable, that as parents become better off they become slightly, but only slightly, more self-indulgent and spend a slightly ower proportion of their incomes on their children, but apparently to such a small extent up to and beyond a modest-but-adequate level that no practical conclusion follows. The distribution of family expenditure within families at higher income levels has not, to the author's knowledge, been studied.

In many European countries, and especially within the Common Market, the policy of *compensation des charges familiales*, in German *Familienlastenausgleich*, is now a long-term aim of governments. This concept might be translated as 'sharing the cost of family responsibilities', that is spreading the cost of rearing the next generation over the whole community. This aim can only be realized by an understanding of the actual cost of dependent children, and this can only be estimated from family budgets that make it possible to allocate expenditure to the individual members of the family.

The German survey only shows that the proportional allocation is roughly constant over a narrow band of modest incomes. This provides no basis, for example, for income tax allowances aimed at sharing the cost of family responsibilities at higher income levels which must rest on other considerations. The survey does show that the family with dependent children may be overtaxed at the lower income levels if the proportion of family income *actually* spent on the children is not taken into account.

Recent official estimates have also been made in Sweden of the proportion of family expenditure attributable to dependent children.[1] These show, for example, that in a Swedish family with three children of average age and a net income after tax equivalent to about £900 a year in 1960, about one-half of the total family expenditure, including family allowances, was attributable to the children; this is consistent with the earlier German survey data that suggest roughly the same result. Both Swedish and German estimates show that much more than half the income of a family of modest means would be attributable to three adolescent dependants, and a family with £900 a year to spend and three such dependants would be in real difficulty.

The eighteen year long trough in Figure 9 reflects the falling standard of living in the family as children arrive and grow up. There is, of course, no such trough in the economic life of the bachelor, spinster or of the childless couple. The filling-in of the trough by one means and another is necessary to reduce poverty which is concentrated in families with dependent children. The filling-in of the trough is also necessary to increase the social investment in the next generation, if only because the main investment is made by parents. The quality of the next generation depends in a high degree upon the money expended by parents upon their children. Indeed, the elimination of child poverty is not enough, and the quality of the next generation will be improved further by raising families with dependent children to the modest-but-adequate level and above.

It has never, of course, been the aim of trade unions to seek wages for their members that bear any relation to differing family responsibilities. However, some of the more old-fashioned systems of wage-payment show a quite unnecessary disregard of the normal demands of the family cycle—those wage agreements that provide

[1] Van Hofsten and Karlsson (1961).

for a maximum wage at age 21 or 25, without provision for further increments throughout a working life, being particularly inefficent socially. There is, indeed, much to be said for wage and salary scales that increase until the earner is at least 40 years old, because the father of a family is likely to face his maximum expenses when he is about 40 to 45 years of age. Scales that reach a maximum at age 21 are also said to be quite inappropriate for rewarding skilled and educated workmen who are most unlikely to merit as much money at 21 as at age 40. It would seem that the trade unions could do something to promote a better relationship between age and reward, a relationship that is already much more satisfactory for salary earners than for workmen earning a weekly wage.

Once children grow up and begin to earn they quickly become independent of their parents, and in the average case the parents do not generally need their children's help for another ten or fifteen years. The father or mother may fall sick or die and throw a responsibility on the children, but given good health the father of a family can generally continue to earn until his eldest child is 35 or 40. It therefore happens not infrequently that grandparents are in need of help from their children at about the time when the father of a family is under the greatest pressure from his own children.[1] In the absence of adequate pensions, responsibility for grandparents can deepen the trough in the family cycle still further.

The role of grandparents while still earning is, however, of much consequence in many families. The endowment of children by their parents is of many kinds and does not necessarily end when the children marry in their turn. Many parents help their children to build their homes by contributing household possessions, loans, presents to the grandchildren and in many other ways. Young parents are often helped by legacies. Many grandmothers mind children while the mother earns.

However, parents who have reared three or four children are in general much less able to save for their own old age than are the bachelors, spinsters and the childless.[2] During the trough of the family life cycle savings are used up so that in families of modest means little is left to help the children when they marry.

The passing of possessions from one generation of a family to

[1] Townsend, et al. (1968), *Old People in Three Industrial Societies*.
[2] Acton Trust (1959).

the next and to the next but one can strengthen the family and help fill the trough. However, as many writers have shown, inheritance concentrates wealth in the hands of the less fertile, creates positions of privilege increasingly unacceptable in the modern world, and provides little help at all for the great majority. Death duties should be revised with the interests of the family in mind. There is little to be said for taxing an estate in exactly the same way whether it is left to a childless widow or other childless relative, or is left to a widow with dependent children, or to adult children with young families of their own. It is socially expedient that the wealth of one generation should be spread more widely among the members of the succeeding generations. It is socially inefficient to tax the estate of a testator in the same way whether it is left to one successor or to a dozen. Death duties are generally progressive and increase with the size of the estate, and tax is paid by executors or administrators. A change of system has been suggested so that tax is paid by beneficiaries and the amount of tax paid is made to depend upon the family responsibilities of the recipient, his income, and the amount left to him. There is the same case for death duties being made to depend upon the family responsibilities of beneficiaries as there is for income and surtax being made similarly dependent.

A legacy that ensures a family of children a holiday every year or just raises a family's standards of living to the modest-but-adequate level is very different in its social implications from a legacy that guarantees a family life-long affluence. Absolute as well as comparative standards need to be defined in taxing the beneficiaries. The whole system of death duties is in need of reform as part of a national family policy.

In France, Germany, Sweden and, indeed, in most countries tax is levied on money inherited in the hands of the beneficiaries and depends upon the amount that each beneficiary receives. A reform of the British system by introducing a tax graduated according to the amount received by a beneficiary was prepared by Lord Randolph Churchill as long ago as 1886. It has been advocated over all the intervening years and recently by the *Economist*[1] and the Institute of Economic Affairs.[2]

[1] *Economist*, 20 March 1965.
[2] Sandford (1967).

The life cycle of family prosperity is common to both rich and poor families. However, the arrival of three or four children can result in the standard of living of one family sinking from well above the modest-but-adequate level to the poverty line, while in another family three or four children will never depress the standard of living even to the modest-but-adequate level. The trough represents malnutrition and social isolation for the first family and only a little tight budgeting for the second. The American concept of the 'welfare ratio' which is called the 'prosperity number' in this book, provides a scale for measuring the relative prosperity of families of different sizes. The prosperity number scale is discussed in the next chapter.

CHAPTER SEVEN

Prosperity Numbers

The phrase 'standard of living' is used widely in every developed country. The concept of standard of living is, however, meaningless unless it can be quantified at least approximately. A statement that the standard of living of one person is higher than that of another, or of one city is higher than that of another city, implies that there is at least some single scale that may be used for measuring the standard of living.

It is, of course, apparent that there are components of any standard of living that cannot be measured, such as differences in climate, or proximity to alpine scenery or bathing beaches. The merits of the total environment of man can never be aggregated on a single scale. However, a single approximate scale for measuring the standard of living can be devised for that component of the standard of living which is dependent upon money incomes and is purchased.

The standard of living of any family unit increases with its money income. The standard of living also depends upon the general level of prices of the goods and services purchased by the family unit. The standard of living also depends upon the size of the family unit dependent upon the family income; a family unit of, say, six persons obviously enjoys a very much lower standard of living than a single person living on the same income.

Money incomes by themselves have become an increasingly unsatisfactory basis for generalization about standard of living as society has become more egalitarian. For the great majority of the population, the spread of money incomes after taxation is now less than the spread of family responsibilities. Three-quarters of the working population today have take-home pay within the bracket £500 to £2,000 a year. This is a range of four to one. The cost of maintaining a family at its most expensive stage of the life cycle, when a man and wife are maintaining, say, four adolescent children, is substantially more than six times the cost of maintaining a single elderly person. The influence of family responsibilities on the standard of living is seen to be as important as that of take-home pay for the great majority of people. A scale for measuring the standard of living must therefore take into account both real income and family responsibilities.

This chapter discusses a scale that may be used to measure the standard of living of any family group. The standard of living is measured in units called *prosperity numbers*. Single persons, childless couples and families of different sizes are presumed to have the same standard of living if they have the same prosperity number.

A 'prosperity number' is essentially the same concept as the 'welfare ratio' of Professor James Morgan[1] and other American writers. However, the words 'welfare ratio' imply too close an association with public welfare and its clients. The words 'prosperity numbers' are, therefore, used here instead of 'welfare ratios' as being more appropriate to indicate the points on a scale measuring standards of living and extending from poverty to affluence. PN is used as shorthand for prosperity number.

Figure 11 shows the prosperty scale in outline. Only three points on this scale are named. The poverty level, also called the poverty threshold or poverty standard, has a PN of unity. PN less than unity indicate different degrees of poverty. The modest-but-adequate level has a PN of 2, following the assumption in Chapter 2 that the income at the modest-but-adequate level should be accepted as twice that at the poverty level for families similar in size and composition.

A PN of 5 is taken as the threshold of affluence. The choice of a prosperity number of 5—that is, an income five times that at the poverty level for families of similar size and composition—is, of course, a matter of opinion. This is discussed later.

How, then, is such a scale to be related to incomes in money terms? The first difficulty is that any such scale must have a basic monetary reference point to which the standard of living of every family unit can be related. Professor Morgan used the budget requirement in dollars of families in the U.S.A. prepared by the Community Council of Greater New York to define his poverty level. Following this procedure, a PN of unity is made to correspond to the poverty level. The levels in dollars used by Professor Morgan are not useful in the circumstances in the United Kingdom.

[1] Morgan, J. L., *et al.* (1962).

Figure 11. The prosperity number scale
measuring the standard of living

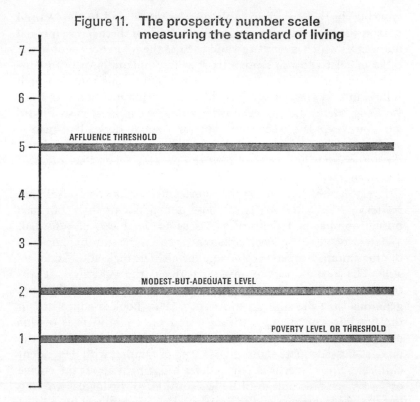

and it is necessary to choose as a reference point an income in pounds sterling appropriate to the United Kingdom in order to establish a useful scale.

The author chose, in 1967,[1] an income of £4 a week plus rent for a single man as the basic reference point defining the poverty level. At that time £4 (plus one shilling) was the sum allowed under supplementary allowance for the single householder. The single dependant's allowance was slightly less. The retirement pension was then also £4. Since that time rates have risen slightly, and the long-term or guaranteed level for a dependent male, defined as 'someone living in another person's household', is now £4 (1968). This corresponds closely with the 'male dependant of head not

[1] Changes in scales for basic requirements of the Supplementary Benefits Commission are given in the annual reports of the Ministry of Social Security; see, for example, Report 1967, p. 55.

working' in the American table of relativities, and to the 'retired person aged 65 and over, living alone'. Both of these have an equal allowance, which is set at 100 and used as the reference point in the table of relativities in Appendix I, where dollars have been converted to percentages of this reference point. The figures which follow in this chapter are based on this reference point and the very slight later increases for elderly people can be seen in Figure 14. Four pounds a week plus rent for a single dependent man is similar to the allowances under sickness, unemployment and short-term non-contributory benefit at the present time. These figures are, of course, revised from time to time.

Every nation has an official subsistence or poverty level that reflects not only the needs of those dependent upon it, but also public opinion and political views as to what can be afforded. Whether or not £4 a week plus rent is the right sum to choose as the minimum or reference income for a single male adult is debatable. The author does not imply that this is the right sum. It was the sum given to such an applicant in 1968 and was slightly more generous than the sum given in 1967. This book is concerned in the first place with the *relativities*, and the consequences of this choice of a reference point in assessing the poverty level and the modest-but-adequate standard of living of families with dependent children. The reader is asked to defer judgement about the choice of £4 a week plus rent until he has considered the logical working out of the assumption and the presentation in graphical form. The use of a reference point higher or lower than £4 a week for a single man would only diminish or increase the PN proportionately for all other families.

In order to generalize from this basic reference income of £4 a week plus rent to the standard of living of ordinary families, it is necessary to make some assumption about rent, and also about overheads other than rent. In the following pages it is generally assumed that rent, or its equivalent in mortgage interest and rates, is 12 per cent of total expenditure. This is the same figure as used in the cost-of-living index.

The PN for a particular family may be calculated using the rent actually paid, or, if the rent is not known, by assuming that 12 per cent of income is spent on rent. Of course, the estimate of standard of living or PN is likely to be more accurate if based upon actual rent rather than an assumed average rent. Elderly retired persons living alone, for example, generally spend a higher percentage of their incomes on rent or its equivalent: 18 per cent, rather than 12 per cent, would be a reasonable assumption for elderly persons living alone.[1] Again, rents are generally higher in London than in the North of England. The accuracy of estimated PNs, like that of any other measure, depends upon the accuracy of the assumptions, which depend in turn upon the accuracy of detailed knowledge about a particular household or class of households for which estimates are to be made!

The relativities used by the author, based upon the family budget standards of the Community Council of Greater New York, relate only directly to those goods and services that vary with family status, age, sex and work status.[2] The PN scale is based on disposable income after payment of tax and rent.

It is assumed by the author that, in the average case, these relativities relate in the United Kingdom to about 75 per cent of a family's total expenditure. The figure of 25 per cent[3] of expenditure on overheads, that is housing, heat, light and consumer durables, is low for the United States, but high for most Continental countries. As noted in Chapter 5, overheads in most countries are a remarkably constant percentage of income, and show very little relation to family size. The error in estimating PN on the assumption of constant overhead percentages is generally small. Table 19 (page 158) shows the American, French, United Kingdom and Swedish figures for overhead percentages at a large number of income levels.

Only the United Kingdom figures show a marked tendency for the percentage of these overheads to fall as income rises. In general, they are very constant at all income levels and all family sizes for a particular country. Our basic reference income of £4 a week for a dependent man not seeking work is, therefore, assumed to include his share of overheads other than rent. The same assumption is made for other family members.

The Family Budget of the Community Council of Greater

---

[1] 18 per cent of expenditure on rent for single-pensioners households is given in Lynes (1962) based on Allen, R. G. D. (1958).

[2] See Appendix I.

[3] See Table 19, p. 158.

Table 19

OVERHEADS IN THE FAMILY BUDGET

Examples from family expenditure surveys showing expenditure on housing, heat, light and consumer durables as a percentage of total expenditure

UNITED STATES (1961)*

All urban families; 8 income brackets extending from $2,000 to over $15,000 per year: Urban U.S. Table 29A.

1	2	3	4	5	6	7	8
37·9	36·0	34·6	35·0	34·7	33·1	32·4	35·1

FRANCE (1963–4)*

18 income brackets extending from under 6,000 *FF* to over 30,000 *FF* per year: Table 9.

1	2	3	4	5	6	7	8	9
19·2	19·2	19·4	19·4	19·0	20·1	19·4	19·0	19·3

10	11	12	13	14	15	16	17	18
18·6	18·8	19·0	19·2	18·3	18·7	18·7	18·3	19·6

UNITED KINGDOM (1965)†

7 income brackets extending from £10–£15 a week to over £50 a week: Table 2.

1	2	3	4	5	6	7
32·2	25·9	24·7	21·2	21·6	20·6	21·1

SWEDEN (1958)*

8 Income brackets extending from under 5,000 to over 40,000 kroner per year: Table 3·8.

1	2	3	4	5	6	7	8
26·5	24·5	24·9	25·2	24·3	22·7	21·2	21·3

---

* Family Expenditure Surveys are listed under Country and date in the Bibliography. Dates here given refer to the survey not publication date. 'Family' here includes childless households.

† Labour, Ministry of (1965).

New York makes rather different assumptions about overheads.[1]
It has made overheads, as a matter of desirable policy, a function
of family size so that, for example, rent increases by a factor of
50 per cent and house furnishings by a factor of 500 per cent as the
numbers in a family increase from one to ten. The author has
not followed these figures that introduce a somewhat arbitrary
value judgement, and has preferred to base overheads on consumer survey data. In fact, at all income levels the percentage
of income spent on overheads varies very little with family size,
as shown in the following table.

Table 20

VARIATION IN PERCENTAGE OF EXPENDITURE SPENT ON OVERHEADS
WITH SIZE OF FAMILY: UNITED KINGDOM: 1963 AND 1965

Number of children in family	0	1	2	3	4 or more
Percentage of expenditure spent on overheads: 1963*	26·5	23·2	23·2	22·8	25·5
1965†	27·9	25·1	22·7	23·2	not given

* Labour, Ministry of, *Family Expenditure Survey* (1963), Table 7.
† Labour, Ministry of, *Family Expenditure Survey* (1965), Tables 9 to 13.

The differences here are comparable with the sampling errors
in the United Kingdom survey. The author has, therefore,
assumed that overheads both with and without rent are a percentage of total expenditure. This is an approximation that can
be improved upon whenever the necessary information is available.

The sum chosen for a PN of unity, or the poverty level, does
not include the cost of working or of seeking work. In order to be
applicable to a man in work the cost of working must be added.[2]
Unfortunately there are no reliable figures for the cost of a man
working in the United Kingdom. The cost of working is certainly
very much higher than the 10s. for a man and 15s. for a woman,
which is assumed in the Ministry of Social Security report
entitled 'Circumstances of Families'.[3] The cost of working
includes the cost of transport to and from work, the extra cost of

[1] Community Council (1963), p. 31 ff.
[2] See Chapter 3, p. 83.
[3] See p. 82, and p. 83, note 1.

the midday meal, the extra cost of clothing including extra
expense to maintain the standard needed for the job and extra wear
and tear, laundry, extra cost for personal care, trade union and
other dues associated with the job and a reduced contribution to
the household economy, for example, to do-it-yourself maintenance;
there are small off-setting economies such as reduced heat and
light expenditure.

In the absence of good United Kingdom survey data, American
percentages are used. The budget of the Community Council of
Greater New York assumes the cost of working, based on survey
data, to require a 49 per cent increase in the personal budget of a man
not working and aged between 35 and 54 when he goes out to work.

It is noteworthy that, according to American estimates, it is
cheaper to maintain a woman, for example a housewife, at home
than to maintain a dependent man at home, but the cost of the
woman working is somewhat higher than for a man. Thus, taking
the maintenance cost of a man as 100 not working, and 149
working, the corresponding figures for a woman are 87 not
working and 152 working.[1] The woman, in fact, has somewhat
higher costs than the man for working clothes and personal care
if she goes out to work. In fact, on the American relativities, the
necessary personal expenditure of a wife who goes out to work is
almost double that of a housewife who stays at home. The cost of
working is of special social importance for women who are heads
of households, especially if they have dependent children.[2]
The cost of working may then also have to include the cost of
child-minding or of attendance at a nursery school, costs that are
not included in the relativities in Appendix I. This merits further
study, but it is apparent that at low income levels the cost of
working for the lone mother may be higher than the whole cost of
maintenance if she stays at home. This is currently ignored in
social provisions, including means-tested benefits: for example,
day nursery fees and school maintenance allowances.

Comparisons between the standards of living of persons working
and not working can be wholly deceptive if the cost of working is

[1] See Chap. 3, p. 83
[2] Erickson (1968), note 12. Clothing costs were higher for women heads
of families than for other women in the same income group because women
heads were likely to be working.

not taken fully into account. The cost of working is a very substantial part of living costs for individuals at all normal income levels. The cost of working merits much further investigation in the United Kingdom to provide an adequate basis for tax and other allowances.

Children also have a cost of going to school, analogous to the cost of working. This is an item also meriting much further study, but it is assumed in this chapter that the relativities for children take account of the cost of going to school. All children and young persons either go to school or work, and if they work the cost of working must be added.

The income needed to maintain any individual member of a family may be calculated by using a table of relativities. The cost of maintaining the whole family may then be obtained by adding together the cost of maintaining the individual members. The American table of relativities also includes the work status of the family members. The full table is given in Appendix I.

If overheads are assumed to be a fixed percentage of income, the relativities apply to all expenditure. If the relativities are used in this way caution is, of course, needed in applying the results to individual families. A family may, for example, be paying a rent in excess of the average percentage assumed and its standard of living may then be lower than suggested by the calculation. There is no great difficulty in arriving at the PN of any particular family, taking into account the rent paid and allowing for other special overhead expenditure. PNs are calculated less tax and national insurance contributions, that is, they are based on 'take-home pay'. Corrections may be made for a whole class of families. The problem is then similar to that of providing a special cost of living index for families living in, say, London or Scotland or for families at a particular income level. The official cost of living Index[1] also assumes fixed percentages of expenditure on particular items, and only provides an approximate indication of the cost of living in particular areas or for particular social classes.[2]

---

[1] The official title is 'Index of Retail Prices', Ministry of Labour (1964).

[2] A special index for pensioners is proposed but not for children. An index for low-income families with children may be reconsidered: see Employment and Productivity, Department of (1968).

F

Figure 12, entitled *Prosperity Numbers of Young Families*, illustrates the use of the relativities to calculate PNs for families of different sizes. It is assumed that the father works but not the mother and that all children are over 6 and under 12. It relates, therefore, only to a special class of families. This figure includes overheads other than rent and assumes that they are a percentage of income. It indicates PNs for different incomes and sizes of young families. The assumption that relativities are indepen-dent of income results in straight-line relationships. More adequate data and detailed study might change the straight lines to curves.

German research[1] on the allocation of expenditure suggests that, at least for modest incomes, the percentage allocation of expenditure between the members of a family is similar at all levels; all family members benefit, indeed, proportionately from an increase in family income. In the United Kingdom, however, but not in most other countries, the allocation of family income to overheads appears to decline as income rises. If full account were taken of this change in overhead allocation the lines on Figure 12 would become slightly curved. The author is concerned, however, to indicate method and approximate relationships. Much more research is needed to add precision, by research workers better supported by computational facilities and better consumer survey data for the United Kingdom.

Other figures may be drawn, similar to Figure 12, for children outside the 6 to 12 age bracket; or to provide for the mother working as well as the father; or alternatively PNs may be calculated directly, using the relativities in Appendix I.

Figure 13, *Prosperity Numbers of Families with Adolescents*, shows another case, giving the highest family costs, where all the children are adolescent and the woman of the household does go out to work full time. This is the most expensive class of household!

The incomes necessary to achieve both a poverty standard of living and the modest-but-adequate level may now be seen from these charts for the family types shown and for single persons and childless couples. It will be seen from *Prosperity Numbers of Young Families*, Figure 12, that a family of two adults and two children (over 6 and under 12) needs £15 15s. a week *after tax*

[1] See Chapter 6, p. 147.

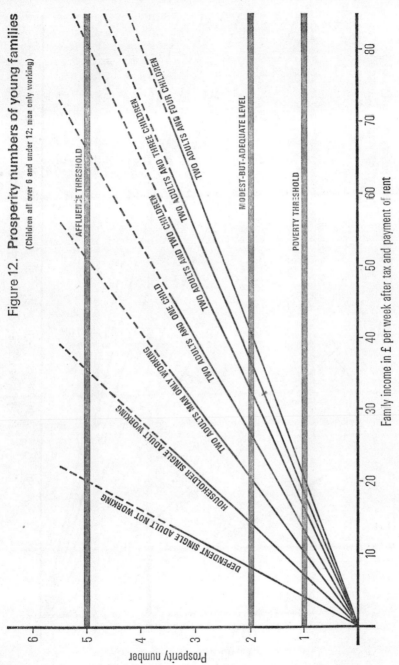

Figure 12. Prosperity numbers of young families

(Children all over 6 and under 12; man only working)

AFFLUENCE THRESHOLD

TWO ADULTS AND FOUR CHILDREN

TWO ADULTS AND THREE CHILDREN

TWO ADULTS AND TWO CHILDREN

TWO ADULTS AND ONE CHILD

TWO ADULTS MAN ONLY WORKING

HOUSEHOLDER SINGLE ADULT WORKING

DEPENDENT SINGLE ADULT NOT WORKING

MODEST-BUT-ADEQUATE LEVEL

POVERTY THRESHOLD

Prosperity number

Family income in £ per week after tax and payment of rent

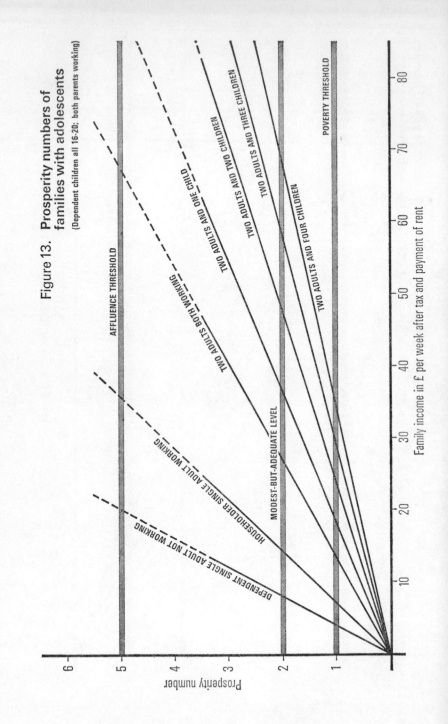

Figure 13. **Prosperity numbers of families with adolescents**
(Dependent children all 16-20; both parents working)

AFFLUENCE THRESHOLD

TWO ADULTS BOTH WORKING

DEPENDENT SINGLE ADULT NOT WORKING

HOUSEHOLDER SINGLE ADULT WORKING

TWO ADULTS AND ONE CHILD

TWO ADULTS AND TWO CHILDREN

TWO ADULTS AND THREE CHILDREN

MODEST-BUT-ADEQUATE LEVEL

TWO ADULTS AND FOUR CHILDREN

POVERTY THRESHOLD

Prosperity number

Family income in £ per week after tax and payment of rent

and payment of rent at the poverty level, and £32 a week to reach a modest-but-adequate level.

Figure 13, *Prosperity Numbers of Families with Adolescents*, shows that the same family will need £23 5s. a week *after payment of rent and tax,* when the children are over 12 and under 19 to reach the poverty level, and £47 a week to achieve a modest-but-adequate level. It will also be seen from Figure 13 that while a single working person achieves the modest-but-adequate level on an income of £14 a week after payment of rent and tax, a family consisting of two adults and two adolescent children requires £47 a week to achieve the same modest-but-adequate standard of living with a prosperity number of 2, and that a family with four adolescent children would require no less than £67 a week.

These figures for weekly income, both for the poverty level and for the modest-but-adequate level, may seem high to many readers both in relation to the weekly earnings of most families and in relation to the conventional concepts of the poverty level or a modest-but-adequate standard. The reader was asked to defer judgement about £4 a week plus rent for the single man not working as the poverty level and basic reference point for all these scales. The calculations really only depend upon this basic assumption and upon the relativities which, if not exact, are reasonable approximations in the light of existing knowledge.

The reader who considers that the poverty level for families in general resulting from the author's calculations is too high, must logically challenge the £4 a week plus rent for the single man as being too high. He may also challenge the relativities and produce alternatives, but this would require expensive research, which is indeed merited but would only be likely to produce relativities different in detail, comparable to the differences already apparent between, for example, the research results of Germany, France and the U.S.A.

Difficulties of accepting soundly based standards of a poverty or a modest-but-adequate level, that is, a true level at which all families enjoy an approximately equivalent standard of living, are substantial. These difficulties arise from a traditional under-estimation of long standing of the cost of maintaining and rearing a family of children or family of dependants generally. This underestimation of the cost of family responsibilities has been quite general in taxation and legislation involving monetary allowances of every kind. Taxation affecting the family, including recent proposals for 'selectivity', are examined in the next chapter.

Figure 14 gives *Examples of the Prosperity Number Scale applied to United Kingdom Non-Contributory Benefits* (1967–8).[1] The reference point again is the £4 a week for a single dependent male aged 35 to 54. The standard of living of persons and families wholly dependent on non-contributory benefit, or supplemented up to this level, is seen. The long- and short-term benefit levels are marked. Non-contributory benefit, of course, replaced National Assistance in 1966. It will be seen that the prosperity numbers achieved diminish with the size of the family. A family with three children aged 5 to 10 has a PN of only 0·66 on the short-term supplementary allowance and 0·71 on the long-term supplementary pension or guaranteed level, compared with the single person's PNs of 1·06 and 1·18. The discrimination against families is seen to be greater in the long-term, officially defined as over two years, because a supplementary pension is only paid to pensioners or to adults dependent on non-contributory benefit for over two years, and there is no long-term supplement for dependent children at all! It was a notable contribution of the Ministry of Social Security Act, 1966, that it officially recognized the difference between short- and long-term poverty for the first time. The supplementary pension, or guaranteed level for long-term dependence, is seen in Figure 14 to be not yet adequate, notably again for the families with dependent children. Indeed, the actual supplement is the same regardless of the family responsibilities of the recipients. This is, of course, a feature of present United Kingdom arrangements that could be corrected before there is any further advance in the benefits for the single person.

Prosperity numbers can be used to examine any group of families at any social level. An individual family has, of course, a PN life curve showing the PNs achieved throughout the life-cycle. Figure 15, *Prosperity Numbers in the Life Cycle of a Family of Modest Means*, gives a picture of the family life-cycle curve drawn using prosperity numbers. The father of the family is

[1] Rates of benefit are given in the Annual Report of the Ministry of Social Security, 1967, and in the leaflets S.I. and S.P.I.

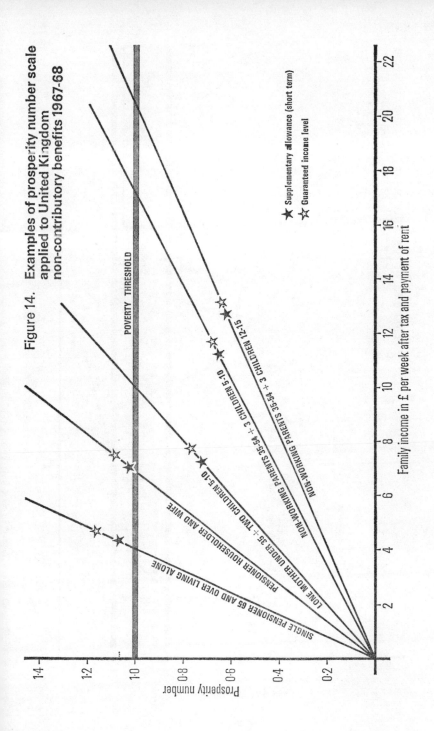

Figure 14. Examples of prosperity number scale applied to United Kingdom non-contributory benefits 1967-68

POVERTY THRESHOLD

NON-WORKING PARENTS 35-54 + 3 CHILDREN 12-15

NON-WORKING PARENTS 35-54 + 3 CHILDREN 5-10

LONE MOTHER UNDER 35 + TWO CHILDREN 5-10

PENSIONER HOUSEHOLDER AND WIFE

SINGLE PENSIONER 65 AND OVER LIVING ALONE

★ Supplementary allowance (short term)
☆ Guaranteed income level

Family income in £ per week after tax and payment of rent

Prosperity number

1·4 1·2 1·0 0·8 0·6 0·4 0·2

2 4 6 8 10 12 14 16 18 20 22

Figure 15. Prosperity numbers in the life cycle of a family of modest means

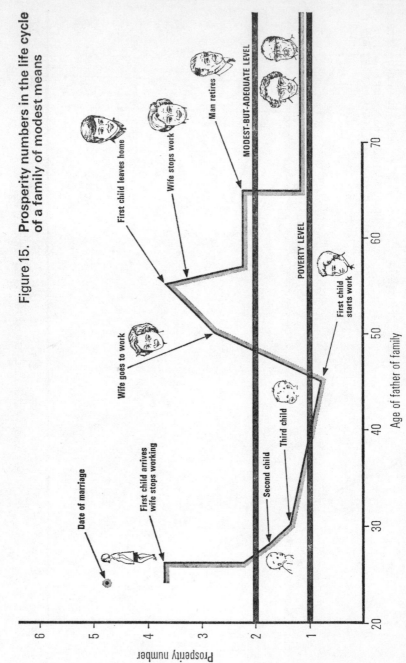

Date of marriage

First child arrives
wife stops working

Wife goes to work

First child leaves home

Wife stops work

Man retires

MODEST-BUT-ADEQUATE LEVEL

POVERTY LEVEL

First child
starts work

Third child

Second child

Prosperity number

6

5

4

3

2

1

Age of father of family

20

30

40

50

60

70

assumed to earn the average British man's wage and his wife the average woman's wage until the arrival of the first child. After marriage the young couple have a prosperity number of 3·7. During this period the young couple are among the better-off although they never achieve affluence. With both of them working they can live comfortably and can afford to save or to acquire household goods. Just before the first child arrives the wife gives up work, the family's disposable income drops and their PN falls to 2·2. The second child reduces the PN to 1·8, below the modest-but-adequate level. The third child, and the increasing expense of the first two, eventually reduce the family to below the poverty level when the children approach adolescence. If the mother worked part-time and earned half an average woman's wage, the family would then be lifted somewhat above the poverty level. Even if the mother worked full-time and earned her old wage, the family would still be well below the modest-but-adequate level when the children were in their teens.

When the three children leave school, and begin to earn, the family become better off once again. Even when the children leave home the couple, who only have themselves to support, just pass the modest-but-adequate level, with PN of 2·2. Only if the wife continued to work full-time could they again achieve the relative prosperity of their early married life. When the couple are both retired their standard of living falls again to only slightly above the poverty level. Having had three children at this income level this couple has no appreciable personal savings, unless they were accumulated in their latter years after the children left school.

The three levels marked on the PN figures are *points* on a scale. Families will, of course, fall into the *areas* between. Below the poverty threshold families may be described as *poor*, between the poverty level and the modest-but-adequate level they are *hard-pressed*, and above the threshold of affluence they may be described as the *affluent*.

The plight of poor families has been often described. Failure, *in practice*, to purchase an adequate diet is one characteristic. Inadequate and especially overcrowded housing is another, particularly in urban areas. Lack of income for participation in the life of the community and in social activities is another test. Figures 12, 13 and 14 show the disposable incomes required to raise families of different sizes up to and beyond the poverty level. The standard of living of the average family falls as the children grow older. Only a minority of families with a working father of exceptional earning capacity who is regularly promoted in his thirties and forties will advance *up* the PN scale; the average family moves *down* the PN scale until the children leave home. In contrast, the average non-parent moves slowly up the scale.

In the area between the poverty level and the modest-but-adequate level, that is in families which have been described as hard-pressed, there is still competition amongst the many demands on the family budget for the basic purchases of food, clothing, fuel and household expenses; but as incomes approach the modest-but-adequate level for family size and composition, careful budgeting enables these demands to be met, and also makes possible a modest expenditure on things which are not basic physical needs but are necessary for a satisfactory life and rearing of children, such as holidays, visits to the country at week-ends, reading matter and so on. As income rises, an increasing proportion is spent on satisfying psychological rather than basic physical needs; the modest-but-adequate level is a threshold at which there is a modest part of the income available for satisfying non-physical needs. Below the poverty level even the basic physical needs cannot be met in spite of careful budgeting. At the modest-but-adequate level the home should contain the essential furnishing and space for relaxation and social activities, and sleeping arrangements adequate for privacy and rest. At the poverty level there is no provision for any family holiday, but at the modest-but-adequate level a modest holiday every year should be possible.

The affluent level is assumed to provide the income at which all the reasonable economic requirements of a family can be met. It is assumed that the members of a family, and notably dependent children, continue to benefit as the income increases above the modest-but-adequate level to a prosperity number of about 5. Benefit is partly subjective and therefore a matter of personal opinion, but benefit is also partly objective because, for example, expenditure on the environment of childhood has an important investment content. The suggestion here is that if the prosperity number of a family with dependent children is increased from

2 to 5, the childhood environment may generally also be improved
with benefit to the quality of the next generation.

The French survey of families, 1967,[1] classifies their expenditure
into three groups, first is 'consumption in the classic sense,
universal, almost routine expenses, allied to subsistence . . . such
as food, housing, heating, health'; then comes the expenditure
on the *cadre de vie*, the setting of daily life, such as furniture,
decorations, appliances, things which make for comfort; lastly
come the expenses arising from 'the activity of individuals, the way
they spend their time'. These *expenses of aspiration* include leisure
activities, sport, culture, adult education, amusements, holidays.

German research suggests, as we have seen in Chapter 6, that
typical parents continue to increase the amount of money they
spend on their children in proportion to family income up to and
beyond the modest-but-adequate level, although there was seen
to be a small decline in the proportion of income spent on children
as income increases. Figures 12 and 13 imply that they may
continue to do so up to prosperity numbers of 5 or thereabouts,
although this is a matter of opinion rather than fact, as there is
no available study to the author's knowledge. Above this level
the proportion of family expenditure that is spent on children
probably diminishes, and at the same time the value of the expenditure to the children becomes increasingly questionable.
Only a very small minority of families in any country have
prosperity numbers in excess of 5. The author is not aware of any
serious research into the expenditure of affluent families that
would throw light on the extent that children benefit from a very
high standard of living. The number of families involved is so
small that the consequences of real affluence upon the family are
of very marginal interest. Certainly the law of diminishing returns
is likely to apply with greater force to a prosperity number scale
than to an income scale.

The efficient working of families and rearing of children is
also not, of course, the only purpose of incomes. The subjective
benefit or utility of incomes affects people's incentives to work,
to save money, to contribute to charity and is, indeed, intimately
concerned with problems of human motivation that are outside
the scope of this book.

[1] Tabard (1967), p. 202.

How are families distributed on the prosperity number scale? Germany and the United States provide some studies. Professor Helga Schmucker, writing in 1961, analysed the Bavarian wage-tax statistics for 1955.[1] She used three poverty levels at an average annual income per head, corrected for family size and composition, of 1,000 DM, 900 DM and 800 DM. The statistics cover all persons in full-time employment aged between 20 and 65 and earning more than 1,837 DM a year gross. Assuming that Professor Schmucker's intermediate poverty level of 900 DM per head defines a PN of unity, then some distributions of families may be estimated roughly from her tables as follows:

Table 21

DEPENDENCE OF PROSPERITY NUMBERS ON FAMILY SIZE: BAVARIA,

1955*

Number of children	Prosperity Number
0	2·4
1	1·8
2	1·4
3	1·2
4	1·0
5	0·9

* Schmucker (1961), adapted from Table 2, p. 23.

There has, of course, been a substantial increase in the Bavarian standard of living since 1955, and family allowances introduced since that date will have provided assistance, especially to the larger families. Professor Helga Schmucker shows (opposite) the percentage of families of different sizes living below her intermediate poverty level at that time.

While, on average, the larger the family the lower is its standard of living, the conclusion should not be drawn that the main problem of poverty is that of the very large family. This is not so. Professor Schmucker showed that the largest number of poor children were to be found in families with three dependent children. This was so at all three levels of poverty that she used. At the 900 DM level, for example, which is taken as the poverty level with a prosperity number of 1 in Table 22, 31 per cent of all

[1] Schmucker (1961), Chapter 3.

Table 22

PERCENTAGE OF FAMILIES OF DIFFERENT SIZES LIVING IN POVERTY:
BAVARIA, 1955*

Number of Children	Percentage of families in poverty
1	2·1
2	10·8
3	31·2
4	53·2
5	72·4
6	76·5
7	78·5
8 or more	85·8
Average number of families in poverty	11·5
Average number of children in poverty	19·9

* Schmucker (1961), Table 3, p. 25.

poor children were in families with three dependent children. The American poverty surveys[1] have shown that the size of the family with the largest total number of poor children is the family with three or four dependent children. American poor children are, indeed, less concentrated in the three-child families than the German. The United Kingdom report entitled *Circumstances of Families* suggested that the largest numbers of poor children were in two- and three-child families.[2]

The three-child family is, of course, of great social importance. The reproduction of any population is dependent upon a minority of marriages producing three or more children, to compensate for those who do not marry and those who marry but have no children or only one child. In particular, the contribution of marriages producing three and four children is critical if a population is not to decline. On German figures about one-third of all marriages produce two-thirds of the next generation; these are the marriages producing three or more children. On Professor Schmucker's figures rather more than one-half of all poor children are also in these families with three and four children.[3]

[1] Orshansky (1968), Table 4, p. 7.
[2] Social Security, Ministry of (1967), Table II, 3, 4 and 6.
[3] Schmucker (1961), Table 14, p. 92.

It is, therefore, a delusion that there is any solution to the problem of child poverty solely through limitation of the size of families or by paying attention exclusively to the problems of very large families. In no country is child poverty restricted to the very large, very poor families but is spread among families of all sizes. The greatest problem is to be found in families with three and four dependent children, and there must always be many families of this size in any population that is not declining. In the United Kingdom there are about 1·2 per cent of the households at any one time with five or more dependent children. These very lage families are, indeed, more likely to be poor than smaller families and their poverty is often deeper; the problems of child poverty are not, however, concentrated in these large families. In Germany[1] the large families contribute 12 per cent to the numbers of poor households and 23 per cent to the numbers of poor children. American figures show, in contrast, that 43 per cent of poor American families have five or more children compared with the 12 per cent of German and 18 per cent of United Kingdom families.[2] The large poor family is a much more serious social problem in the U.S.A. than in the United Kingdom, Scandinavia or Common Market countries.

The American Federal Government have studied the income deficiencies of their lower income groups with greater thoroughness than any other country. Miss Mollie Orshansky described the poverty index of the Social Security Administration and used it to analyse the low income population in an outstanding series of articles in the official journal during recent years.[3] She answers many questions about the American poor which cannot be answered for the poor of most other countries. The prosperity number scale may be applied to some of Miss Orshansky's findings; for example, the percentage of all American families with prosperity numbers less than unity and between unity and 1·3 can be calculated approximately.

Table 23 shows that the percentage of American families in poverty, that is with prosperity numbers less than unity, increases as the number of dependent children increases beyond two. The

---

[1] Schmucker (1961), Tables 14 and 15, p. 92.
[2] *Circumstances of Families* (1967), pp. 15 and 20.
[3] See Bibliography for a list of her main contributions.

Table 23

PERCENTAGE OF AMERICAN FAMILIES WITH PROSPERITY NUMBERS
LESS THAN I AND ABOVE I·3*

Prosperity Number	\multicolumn{6}{c}{Number of Children}
	1	2	3	4	5	6 or more
Above 1·3	82·3	82·5	73·2	65·2	47·0	36·5
Between 1 and 1·3	5·6	6·2	9·4	12·0	17·0	14·2
Below 1	12·1	11·3	17·4	22·8	33·8	49·3

* *Social Security Bulletin*, Jan. 1965, 28, No. 1, p. 19, adapted to P.N. scale.

percentage of American families with prosperity numbers over
1·3 declines from over 80 per cent to only 36·5 per cent as family
size increases. The 34·6 million persons identified as poor in the
United States had an average prosperity number of 0·6.[1]

Some such technique as that suggested tentatively in this
chapter, using prosperity numbers, is essential not only in
enumerating the poor, but for introducing a sense of proportion
and equity into social policy and the quantitative determination
of benefits and allowances of all kinds. The development of
wholly satisfactory criteria for the United Kingdom requires
more than the resources of the author. In particular, as pointed
out by Prais and Houthakker,[2] a satisfactory scale for measuring
standards of living must be based on consumer survey data, and
the United Kingdom surveys have not hitherto been adequate for
this purpose. Professor Townsend wrote in 1954: 'A yardstick for the
measuring of poverty can only be devised in the light of knowledge
about family budgets.' A survey of the condition of life of all families
along the lines of the French survey published in 1967 is needed.

[1] The count of poor persons in the United States shows that non-white
persons are more likely to be poor. In 'The Shape of Poverty in 1966', Miss
Orshansky says: 'The total with low incomes included from 12 to 19 per cent
of the white population and from 41 to 54 per cent of the non-white' (*Social
Security Bulletin* 31, No. 3, March 1968, p. 4).

This difference is associated with the higher number of fatherless families
amongst non-white populations and 'in 1966 households headed by a woman
accounted for nearly one-half of all units tagged poor'. Lower earnings and
larger families and the clustering of non-white families in poor areas of cities
and in the South are also associated factors. Miss Orshansky stresses that 'of
the total in poverty, however, 2 out of 3 were white and among the near poor
4 out of 5 were white . . . for the nation as a whole, the white poor outnumber
the non-white even in the central cities.' (*Ibid.*, pp. 4 and 14).

[2] Prais and Houthakker (1955); see also Nicholson (1949).

The preliminary report of the United Kingdom Poverty Survey, entitled, 'The Poor and the Poorest' (1965), may be said to have put the problem of the poor family with an earning father on to the agenda of political parties and of public discussions of social problems. The preliminary report did not produce a new identification of poverty but accepted as an interim standard the National Assistance scale for the years under review. The authors state that:

'In using it we do not intend to imply that we, ourselves, consider either that this level of living is an appropriate measure or that the households of different composition living at the National Assistance standard have comparable levels of living.'[1]

The 'households of different composition' living at the National Assistance standard do *not* have comparable levels of living, as shown in this and earlier chapters. The Ministry of Social Security, in the report *Circumstances of Families*, also used the minimum requirements of a family under the National Assistance Acts for estimating the circumstances of families. The results can only be misleading.

A sound technique for determining which families achieve a PN of unity and which families fail to do so, i.e., a technique for enumerating the poor, is manifestly needed. However, there are very large numbers of families with dependent children living at PNs between 1 and 1·5, only somewhat above poverty level. The average family in Western Europe with three or more children does not achieve a PN of 1·5. It would be a limited and artificial family policy indeed that was only concerned with the minority that failed to reach a PN of unity.

Government policies of many kinds influence the distribution of income, thereby altering the standard of living of families including that of the majority in Western society with PNs between 1 and 2 who fail to achieve the modest-but-adequate standard of living. The continued use of an historical scale which lacks any basic justification and is unsound must distort policy and judgement.

A university department may lack the resources for producing

[1] Abel-Smith and Townsend (1965), p. 17.

the basic criteria for estimating prosperity numbers. Governments, however, have the resources. Hundreds of millions of pounds are spent each year in the United Kingdom and every other major country on benefits and allowances. It is worth spending a few hundreds of thousands of pounds each year to ensure that these large sums are distributed in the most efficient way to meet the needs of the people.

In the United Kingdom the political parties have recently declared themselves in favour of 'selectivity in the social service', and many schemes have been put forward. The Government has begun to apply selectivity by using the concept of the standard rate tax-payer. In the next chapter we shall discuss the distribution of single persons, childless couples and families with dependent children on the PN scale. We shall ask who are to be found above the modest-but-adequate and the affluent levels. We shall reinterpret the notion of the standard rate tax-payer in PN terms and suggest conclusions.

The social security system inherited from the Beveridge Report of the early forties has been and still is under review, and a reformed system is promised in the coming years. In a later chapter we shall examine the needs and costs of misfortune, and then discuss the investment content of social policies. Before, however, these more constructive possibilities can be discussed it is necessary to look somewhat critically at the present tax structure as it affects families, and at the new proposals to use the existing tax structure more directly than hitherto as a means of implementing a more selective policy.

CHAPTER EIGHT

The Taxable Surplus[1]

It has long been a principle of taxation that direct taxes should only be levied upon the 'surplus' income that is left after subsistence requirements have been met. The direct taxation of the poor has been accepted as undesirable. In 1830 Paley wrote, 'We should tax what can be spared'. Marshall said that 'the whole of a very small family income is put to good use, and should make little or no contribution to the revenue'.[2]

Many other writers down to the present day have discussed the application of this principle in the form of tax-free allowances or similar devices, or exemptions for families of different sizes. Most systems of direct taxation of income in the world now have special tax allowances for the head of the household, for a wife, usually for children and frequently also for other dependents belonging to the household or dependent upon the family income. Generally, it is intended that the level of allowances, or income left untaxed, shall approximate to that part of the tax-payer's income necessary for subsistence, and that only the surplus over and above the subsistence income shall be taxed.

For long, however, this theory, although accepted in principle, was difficult to apply for there was insufficient understanding of subsistence incomes. It has always been understood that the subsistence income of a childless couple, for example, was lower than for a family of two parents and four children, and that the childless couple had therefore a larger taxable surplus than the family. Tax-free allowances, can, however, only observe the principle that the poor should not be taxed and that only the surplus over and above a subsistence income is taxable, provided that there is an accepted means of determining the subsistence income for single persons or for families of all sizes and compositions. The prosperity number scale described in the last chapter illustrates the kind of calculations that are necessary.

[1] Figures in this chapter are taken from the Report of the Commissioners of Inland Revenue for the year ended 31 March 1965, Cmnd 2876, unless otherwise stated.   [2] Stamp, Josiah (1929), p. 49.

Men and women have a tax lifetime. During their working lives the number of people dependent on their earnings varies. Taxation appropriate to one period of life will be too harsh at another period of a man's tax-lifetime unless his dependants are taken into account. This is the individual wage-earner's point of view. Society has another interest: over the tax-lifetime of a man the social value of the expenditure of a man's earnings also varies. When a man spends his money on rearing children it will generally be spent to better purpose from the community's point of view than when it is spent upon a single person. Revenue must be raised for many purposes and the tax man must seek out areas of taxable surplus which, he can argue, should bear a higher rate of tax. No one likes taxes, but the fairer a system of taxation is, and the more it appears to the individual to be fair over his tax-lifetime, the more likely the system is to be understood and accepted. A man should feel that his tax-lifetime fits his life-cycle. Taxation can then be seen to be in part a transfer of the tax burden within one man's lifetime from his childless to the child-rearing years as well as being related to his level of earnings. Such a policy can be seen to be reasonable.

Figure 16 illustrates the *profile of incomes* within the community as a whole, before tax and after tax.[1] It will be seen that over 95 per cent of tax-payers had incomes less than £2,000 a year before tax, and over 97 per cent had less than £2,000 a year after tax. Furthermore, only ½ per cent of tax-payers were left with more than £4,000 a year after tax. The percentage of persons with even moderately high incomes is very small. It follows that in terms of *social policy* the persons receiving more than £2,000 to £3,000 a year are of quite secondary interest.

In 1964–5 the average income of tax-payers was very close to £1,000 a year; in 1968–9, this increased to slightly over £1,100 a year. 'Average income' gives a misleading impression of the resources of most households. It will be noted from the tax

---

[1] It has been suggested by Professor Titmuss that the tables provided by the Commissioners of Inland Revenue do not give an accurate picture for the higher income brackets. This may be so, but the number of people in these brackets is small and no correction of the numbers in the higher income brackets would affect the conclusions of this chapter, which is concerned mainly with the great bulk of taxpayers earning less than £2,000 to £3,000 a year. Titmuss, R. (1962), *Income Distribution and Social Change.*

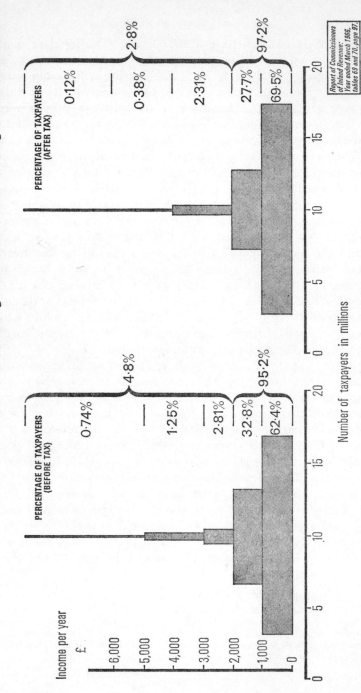

Figure 16. Number of taxpayers: Profiles of income 1964-65, including income from both earnings and investment

Income per year £

Number of taxpayers in millions

PERCENTAGE OF TAXPAYERS (BEFORE TAX)

0·74%
4·8%
1·25%
2·81%
32·8%
95·2%
62·4%

PERCENTAGE OF TAXPAYERS (AFTER TAX)

0·12%
2·8%
0·38%
2·31%
27·7%
97·2%
69·5%

Report of Commissioners of Inland Revenue: Year ended March 1966, tables 69 and 70, page 97.

profiles that the majority of tax-payers, in fact about 62 per cent before tax and 69 per cent after tax, have incomes *less than the average income*. The 'average' is raised by the higher incomes above the median or 'typical' income. Although the average income in 1964–5 was close to £1,000 a year, there were about as many people taking home less than £800 a year as were taking home more than this sum.

The tax profile emphasizes that the spread of incomes within the community is such that most of the revenue from income tax has to come from people of modest means. In 1964–5, 47 per cent of all tax-payers took home more than £500 and less than £1,000 a year, and 97 per cent of all tax-payers took home more than £275 and less than £2,000 a year.

The tax profile, however, throws little light on the *distribution of the standard of living* within the community. A typical income of, say, £900 a year in 1968–9 may support only a single person or a family of six or more persons belonging to two or three generations. The spread in the standard of living of different family units is caused more by differences in family responsibilities than by differences in earnings or measured income. It is, indeed, an illusion that inequalities in our society are only due to differences in incomes. In truth, differences in family responsibilities or, put in another way, the differences in the number of persons dependent upon an income, are as important as differences in incomes for the great majority of the population. Moreover, the inequalities attributable to family responsibilities are socially of particular importance because it is the households with children that are generally underprivileged compared with the households without children. The majority of households have no dependent children and three-quarters of all dependent children are being brought up in only 22 per cent of households. This 22 per cent of households have two or more children and it is in these households that the standard of living is most reduced by family responsibilities.

The last chapter suggested a scale of need based on prosperity numbers. It is possible, however, to show broadly where the taxable surplus in the community lies by simple calculations without using prosperity numbers. The tax tables do not show the ages of children entitled to tax allowances, so that only averages for large classes of families can be estimated, without using the refinement of a prosperity number scale. In Figure 17, entitled *Taxable Surplus*, income per head in the United Kingdom is shown on the horizontal line. This income per head is calculated counting a man or a woman as 1·0 consumer unit and a child as 0·67 of a consumer unit. Only two groups are shown on the diagram, childless couples with the wife earning and three-child families with the mother at home. On the vertical line the numbers of households are shown. The reader will see that almost all the families are poorer than almost all the childless couples. If a verticle line is drawn at, say, £600 per year per unit consumer, it will leave half the childless couples above the level, but an insignificant number of the families have a higher income per unit consumer than this. It will be seen also that the largest number of families are contained in the £200 to £250 per year income group (per unit consumer), and the largest number of childless couples in the £500 to £600 per year income group. The very great majority of families have an income (per unit consumer) less than £350, and the very great majority of childless couples an income above £350 per year.

Similar diagrams could be drawn for bachelors, spinsters, and families of other sizes with wives earning and not earning. A diagram for single men, for example, would not be dissimilar from that for childless couples with the wife earning, but would show a larger number over £600. Families with one and two children would give diagrams intermediate between the two in the figure. Larger families would show an even lower standard of living. The total number of families is given by the *area* under the diagrams, and there were, in fact, 2,468,000 childless couples with the wife earning and only 731,000 families with three children and the wife not earning, as shown in the diagram *Taxable Surplus*. Tax-payers with three dependent children and a wife not earning are only 3·5 per cent of all tax-payers, but their households include 2·19 million children and are of particular importance for the next generation. It has been pointed out in the commentary to the Swedish Family Expenditure Survey, 1958,[1] that retirement pensioners now receive a higher income on average per head than is available for the average member of a

[1] Sweden (1958), *Household Consumption*, Diagram 3.3, p. 77.

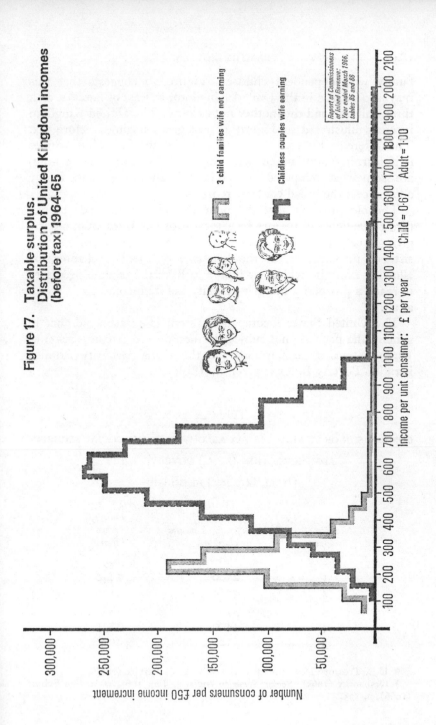

Figure 17. Taxable surplus. Distribution of United Kingdom incomes (before tax) 1964-65

3 child families wife not earning

Childless couples wife earning

Report of Commissioners of Inland Revenue: Year ended March 1966, tables 85 and 86

Income per unit consumer: £ per year   Child = 0·67   Adult = 1·00

Number of consumers per £50 income increment

300,000

250,000

200,000

150,000

100,000

50,000

100 200 300 400 500 600 700 800 900 1000 1100 1200 1300 1400 1500 1600 1700 1800 1900 2000 2100

family with dependent children. Figure 17 suggests that this may also be true in the United Kingdom, at least of families with three children and the mother not earning. The United Kingdom incomes illustrated in Figure 17 are gross incomes before tax. The difference between the standard of living of childless couples (wife earning) and families with three children (wife not earning) are somewhat tempered by child tax allowances and family allowances; the broad contrast remains.

The old principle that the poor should not be made to pay direct taxation can be met in a variety of ways, for example, by giving everyone income tax-free allowances equivalent to subsistence incomes; or, in the language of the last chapter, by allowing every individual or family to have the income necessary to reach a prosperity number of unity before income tax is levied at all.

The United States income tax system is so arranged that in general the poor are not subject to income tax. A comparison of United States tax exemptions and the Social Security Administration Poverty Index is given in Table 24.

Table 24

COMPARISON OF U.S. INCOME TAX ALLOWANCES AND SOCIAL SECURITY

ADMINISTRATION (S.S.A.) POVERTY INDEX

Urban families, in dollars*

Number of children	Income tax-free* allowance (exemptions for 2 adults plus children)	S.S.A.† Poverty Index Income
0	1600	1990
1	2300	2440
2	3000	3130
3	3700	3685
4	4400	4135
5	5100	4600

* U.S. Treasury Department, Internal Revenue Service (1965).

† Orshansky (1965), *Social Security Bulletin*, Jan. 1965, p. 9. See Schorr (1966), p. 135.

The relativity and level of these allowances show a reasonable correspondence with subsistence incomes in the average case and, in particular, for children of average age. The number of children in American families with incomes below the level at which income tax was paid was 15·7 millions. The number of poor children estimated, using the poverty index of the Social Security Administration, was 15·6 millions. To a large extent the 15·7 and 15·6 millions were the same children, though not entirely. Where there are dependent adolescents in the family the American tax exemption is rather too low, so that poor families with dependent adolescents are liable to pay a small sum in income tax. It would be necessary to make the tax-free allowance for children age-related, or to increase this allowance to avoid altogether taxing poor families with older and more expensive children, notably high school or college students.

This principle that persons below a defined poverty line should not pay income tax is applied not only in America but widely throughout the Western world although there are many exceptions in detail. In the United Kingdom, for example, the tax-free allowance of £40 for 'a daughter who lives with you because you are, or your wife is, old or infirm' is less than one-fifth of the corresponding American allowance and is much below any poverty standard; indeed, United Kingdom tax allowances for dependent adults, other than members of the nuclear family, fail to observe the general principle of not taxing the poor. It is amongst poorer families and hard-pressed families that elderly parents are least likely to have independent means. This principle is one application of the more general principle of *family equity*, which, in the context of taxation, requires that all families enjoying the *same standard of living* receive parity of treatment from the tax man. Applied to lower incomes, the principle of family equity requires that all individuals and families should be allowed to achieve a certain minimum standard of living before having to pay income tax, and this minimum standard should, as far as possible, be the same for all families.

The principle of *family equity* is quite inconsistent with the concept of *individual equity* as discussed in the older literature. In its extreme form this old individualist principle held that every individual with the same income should be treated alike. Whether the individual, according to this principle, spends his income on maintaining a wife and raising a family, or stamp-collecting, or breeding rabbits is irrelevant. Professor Titmuss notes that the more individual needs and dependencies are recognized, the more the principle of individual equity may fall into disrepute.[1] The discredited principle of individual equity ignored equity between husband and wife, and between parents and children, and applied only to equity between wage-earners or the receivers of incomes. The broadening of the tax base to wage-earners of modest wages and the introduction of the Pay-As-You-Earn method of collection made it necessary to take account of family responsibilities, the second division of income. Individual equity ignores dependants or treats them like any other of a man's 'possessions'; family equity treats dependants as part-sharers in a man's income. The principle of individual equity ignores the social consequences, both short-term and long-term, of taxation or of income distribution on the family life cycle.

In social security arrangements the provisions accord here and there more with the old principle of 'individual equity' than with the newer principles of 'family equity'. The 'earnings stop' principle, that lays down that a man's unemployment or sickness benefit may not exceed 85 per cent of his earnings, is a lingering application of individual equity;[2] it treats wage-earners, and not families, alike, providing, as it does, exactly the same income ceiling whatever the number of children.

The 'wage-stop' under the non-contributory benefit scheme is also an application of 'individual equity'. A man's normal wage is taken into account and his allowance is reduced below the level of his wage however many children he supports and whatever the resulting gap between the supplementary allowance and the official scale of his children's needs.

The individual equity principle lingers, too, in social security contributions which are really a form of tax, and notably in the United Kingdom. Flat-rate benefits and flat-rate contributions add up to very regressive financing. The move first to a graduated pension scheme and then to graduated unemployment and sickness

[1] Titmuss (1958), p. 49.
[2] Pensions and National Insurance, Ministry of (1966), Guide to the New Earnings-related Short Term Benefits Scheme, Leaflet N.I. 155.

insurance have been early moves away from this regressive financing, but the graduated proportion of contributions is still very small. The continental system, with contributions generally calculated as a percentage of income, is also less inflationary than the British system, as contributions rise with increasing income, while in the British system the real value of the contributions is continually falling.

The United Kingdom flat-rate social insurance contributions reflect a curious egalitarianism; the poor, hard-pressed, better-off, and affluent pay the same actual contribution per week disregarding altogether capacity to pay. The non-parents pay the same as the parents, the effect of dependent children on the capacity to pay being ignored. A flat-rate or a graduated contribution system based on earnings only, flouts modern views of family equity; the father of three children earning £20 a week pays the same contribution as a bachelor earning £20 a week,[1] and more than a spinster earning any salary.

In order to give the wage earner who is below the threshold at which tax is paid the benefit of family equity, his insurance contribution (the only direct tax he will pay) should be adjusted to his ability to pay in view of his family responsibilities.

In the United Kingdom income tax system the principle of individual equity also survives in the taxation of the *taxable income* left after deduction of allowances. All *individuals* with the same *taxable income* are treated alike and pay the same tax. Countries differ widely as to how the balance of income, left after deduction of tax-free allowances, is taxed.[2] In France the rate of tax on this balance is much lower for the father of a family than for the childless couple or the bachelor. In the United Kingdom the balance is taxed in essentially the same way whether the income is that of a single person or of the father of a large family. A balance of income, after deduction of tax-free allowances, that is spent for the benefit of six people is likely to be socially more beneficial than the same balance spent for the benefit of a single person. The taxable balance, after deduction of tax-free

---

[1] Pensions and National Insurance, Ministry of (1966), Guide to the New Earnings-related Short Term Benefits Scheme, N.I. 155.

[2] In Sweden the lower rate, the 'family tax scale', applies also to couples without children.

allowances, may be, for example, £20 a week; in the United Kingdom the income tax paid on this sum is the same whether the income after tax is spent by the taxpayer for himself, on his wife, four children and two grandparents, or is spent by a bachelor or spinster on themselves. The French, however, consider that the income that is used for the benefit of a family group is used to better social purpose. This is the principle underlying the French system and not acknowledged in the United Kingdom system. The French income tax system applied the principle of family equity. In the United Kingdom as the level of income increases the old principles of individual equity take over, with consequences that put the family at a great disadvantage.

Indeed, in the United Kingdom at a *given standard of living* above the tax threshold, the larger the family the more income tax has to be paid. Thus, at the modest-but-adequate level, a single person earning £1,000 a year (from the 1965–6 tax tables) pays £186 in income tax, leaving £814 to spend. A family with parents and three children (two under 11, and one over 11, but not over 16) earning £2,500 a year pays £465 in tax, leaving £2,035 to spend. Both the single person and the family will have approximately the same standard of living with a PN of about 2, or the modest-but-adequate standard, but the family with children pays more than twice as much tax as the single person.[1]

The available information does not allow very accurate estimates of the proportions of taxpayers in different categories who achieve different standards of living. The age of any dependants affects the income at which, say, the modest-but-adequate level is reached; but the Inland Revenue reports do not give information on the ages of dependent children. It is also impossible from the tax tables to distinguish between the taxpayer who is working and the one who is not (though working and not working wives are given) in the same tables which show the number of children in the family. The classification of taxpayers according to ranges of net income in the official tables also reduces the accuracy of any estimate.

The purpose of using the PN scale to analyse all personal income is to find out who needs help and who has a surplus. A

[1] Report of the Commissioners of Inland Revenue, year ended 31 March 1966, Table 24, p. 39.

single author has not the computational resources to make this analysis. It is clear, however, from the figure entitled *The Taxable Surplus* that such an analysis is needed as a basis for tax reform. Such an analysis of all personal incomes is also needed as a basis for social policy to show who are the poor and hard-pressed families, who should be helped in the interests of a policy of investing in children, and where taxable surplus is to be found for this and for other social purposes.

The PN scale can, however, be used readily for individual families or, given assumptions on rent and on ages of children, to show the standard of living at a particular tax level. Thus it is possible to show the standard of living, as measured on the PN scale, of families of different sizes at the standard rate tax-paying level. This level is now being used not only as a taxation device but as a sociological measure of 'need'. The level at which families begin to pay the standard rate is now regarded as a level of income above which increases in family allowance are not needed. This definition was introduced into tax law in 1968 when increases in family allowances were first deducted in full from fathers who are standard rate taxpayers, through reductions in child tax allowances, with proportionate deductions from those paying the reduced rates of tax. Table 25 shows the standard of living for different taxpayers at the level of income at which the standard rate is first paid:[1]

Table 25

STANDARD OF LIVING AT THE STANDARD RATE TAX-PAYING THRESHOLD

(Single earned income; wife not earning)

Family Unit	Prosperity Number
Single person	1·33
Married couple, no dependants	1·17
Two parents	
One child	1·13
Two children	1·11
Three children	1·09
Four children	1·08
Five children	1·07

[1] The levels of gross income at which standard rate is first paid (in 1968) are given in Appendix 2.

It is assumed in this table that the children have an average age of over 12 and under 15. The PNs for families in this table would be somewhat lower if the children were older, and higher if the children were younger. It is assumed that there is only one earner in the couples and families, and his cost of working is included in estimating PNs.

It is apparent that the standard rate tax-paying threshold is such that, at this threshold, the larger the number of dependants *the lower is the standard of living.* The single person is privileged and so to a lesser extent is the couple with no dependants. The use of the standard-rate threshold for the purposes of social policy introduced a bias against the family, and particularly against the larger family.

This does not, of course, invalidate the idea of using a tax threshold for the purposes of social policy. It does, however, indicate that the standard-rate threshold does not correspond to a standard of living at all, and that the single person, and to a less extent the married couple with no dependants, are undertaxed compared with families with dependent children. The disparity is not so great that it could not be remedied.

It is noteworthy that the standard-rate threshold is not so much above the *poverty level*, particularly for the larger families. It will be remembered that the poverty level with PN 1 is defined in terms of the £4 a week plus rent for a single dependent man not earning. The income tax allowance for a child used in the above table is £140 or £2 15s. a week; this is low compared with £4 a week plus rent for a man; it is particularly low for older children, so that as the number of children increases the PN must gradually fall to the poverty level. A working man paying tax at the standard rate, and paying a London rent and London costs of travelling to work, and paying his National Insurance contributions, may have less money left to feed and clothe his family than a man living on supplementary benefit. At the standard-rate threshold, a taxpayer pays £80 a year in income tax and a further sum for National Insurance contributions (£44 for a single man and £55 a year for families with dependent children).[1]

There is a range of income over which a *reduced rate* of tax is paid. This range is independent of family responsibilities,

[1] After April 1965 Budget: Financial Statement 1965–6, Table h, p. 25.

thus introducing a bias against families into the total tax system. Thus, the 'first £100 of your taxable income will be taxed at 4s. in the £', says the P.A.Y.E. Coding Guide; this £100 is the same whether you are a single person or the head of a family with four children. 'The next £200 is taxed at 6s.'; again the £200 bears no relation at all to family responsibilities. This generous concession to all taxpayers is worth between zero and £43 15s. a year, and is dependent upon income[1] and not upon whether you have a wife, children or other dependants. It introduced, therefore, a bias against the family *before* the standard rate taxpaying level is reached, and indeed, at all other levels. The larger the family the greater the bias.

The single elderly person living on investment income, or investment income plus standard National Retirement Pension, first pays tax at the standard rate on an income of £663.[2] Such a person does not pay National Insurance contributions and does not incur the costs of working. Making a very generous allowance of 20 per cent for rent,[3] instead of the 12 per cent average for all households, the PN of an elderly person at the standard-rate threshold is still about 2·25. The elderly retired person is only paying tax at the standard rate when a standard of living above the modest-but-adequate level is reached. The elderly person is, indeed, much more generously treated in terms of income-tax allowances than all families with dependent children or even single persons and childless couples.

Small income relief in the United Kingdom provides an allowance of two-ninths of any unearned income if total income does not exceed £450, and a smaller allowance if total income is less than £704. This relief is wholly non-family, non-child oriented, the amount of relief being the same for a bachelor, complete family or fatherless family.

The use of the standard rate taxpaying threshold as a component of social policy is being associated with the 'clawback' principle. This principle has been described by Ministers as taking back the

---

[1] 4s. 3d. a year is saved on the first £100 and 2s. 3d. a year on the next £200 in comparison with tax at the full rate of 8s. 3d. in the pound.

[2] Feb. 1968. See Appendix 2. In the budget of March 1968 the Chancellor raised the age exemption for elderly single persons by £14 and for elderly couples by £22.

[3] See Chapter 7, p. 157; Lynes (1962) suggests 18 per cent.

increase from those who did not need it through tax, and has only been applied so far to an increase of 10s. in family allowances.[1]

This 'claw-back' principle' is language used by politicians, and the principle has received a measure of support from both Government and Opposition. Whoever invented this language cannot have wished this curious innovation well, because it conjures up the image of the Government using claws upon large numbers of Her Majesty's more humble subjects.

The 'claws' are, indeed, only used on parents. There is no 'claw-back' for non-parents. Retirement pensions are not 'clawed back' from retired persons whatever their incomes. The selectivity is selective at the expense of parents only. In more old-fashioned language, the claw-back principle is a 100 per cent tax on this increase in family allowances at incomes above the standard rate tax-paying level. The increase in family allowances has, in fact, been made subject to a higher rate of tax than any other component of income even of a wealthy person. The claw-back is a highly progressive tax rising from zero at the tax threshold to 100 per cent at the standard rate tax-paying level. The claw-back is indeed applied to very large numbers of people who have very modest incomes or are living below the poverty level, depending upon their rent and cost of working.

This innovation also has the new feature that money is clawed back from the husband's pay-packet if he is a taxpayer, and is paid in the form of family allowances to his wife. Whatever may be said in favour of this innovation it is, as might be expected, unpopular. The Labour Party guide for their speakers, entitled 'Talking Points', remarked:

'It must be admitted that the decision to "claw-back" the increases in family allowances from tax-payers has provoked a hostile reaction. Inland Revenue staff have been overworked in answering complaints from angry husbands who did not know that their wives were receiving an increased family allowance. Others have found the administration of the system very difficult to understand.'[2]

---

[1] The 10s. increase was given in two stages of 7s. and 3s. For debates on selectivity and the claw-back see, for example, House of Commons, 16, 17 and 18 Jan. 1968, 26 Feb. 1968, 23 May 1968; and House of Lords, 20 March and 21 June 1968.

[2] *Talking Points*, No. 9, July 1968

Of course, the use of the tax system for the purpose of social policy is not only defensible but is as unavoidable as the social consequences of taxation. However, once family allowances, retirement benefits, school maintenance allowances and other social benefits are integrated with the tax system a review of the tax system itself can hardly be avoided. Is it not better for a country's future that an income of £1,000, £2,000 or £3,000 a year should be spent on rearing a family of children, than upon a childless household? Is it not socially undesirable that the childless on average enjoy a substantially higher standard of living than the families with dependent children? Even if this is inevitable for a long time, the decision as to how severely parents should be taxed compared with non-parents cannot be avoided.

The use of the standard-rate threshold as a test of need would not be defensible even if it corresponded to a standard of living which we have seen it does not. Income tax in most countries is progressive. The higher the income the higher is the percentage of income paid in tax. It has been assumed that the utility of each increment of income diminishes as income increases. Or, in other words, that needs are increasingly satisfied as income increases. Needs are assumed to diminish progressively as income increases and not to be discontinuous and stop suddenly at a particular income level. The same logic applies to single persons and to families of any size. There can be no logic or justice in any scheme that taxes family allowances at a higher rate of progression than, say, the unearned income of a bachelor or spinster at any level of income.

A soundly conceived progressive tax system would relate the tax paid to the standard of living of the taxpayer. Such a system can never be based on a primitive division of taxpayers into those 'in need', the poor sheep and the 'better-off' goats. It is a basic assumption of a progressive tax system that needs only diminish quite slowly but continuously from poverty to affluence. Indeed, not only the claw-back but the fixed ceiling to the child tax allowance contradicts the basic logic of progressive taxation, lowering the standard of living of families with dependent children compared with the rest.

The majority of taxpayers with earnings of £2,000 a year have no dependent children, the percentage of the childless is about

G

55 per cent. The large numbers of single men and even larger
numbers of single women with no dependants and over £2,000
a year still enjoy affluence with PNs of over 5. Most of the smaller
number of families with earnings over £2,000 a year and three
or four children do not reach the modest-but-adequate level.
The modest-but-adequate level requires an income after tax of
over £2,000 a year for a family of two adults and three children.
A rough calculation suggests that more than 80 per cent of all
persons achieving a modest-but-adequate standard of living with
a PN of 2 or more have no dependent children.

The bias against the family in these higher income ranges is of
much less social consequence than at the lower income levels.
The importance of these calculations is that they indicate where
taxable surplus is to be found. There are more than 400,000
single men, single women and married couples with no dependants, with earnings of over £2,000, who all enjoy a standard of
living well above the modest-but-adequate level with PNs greater
than 2. There are probably less than 100,000 families with
dependent children achieving the same standard of living, and
about half of these families have only one dependent child.

The great majority of persons reaching any high standard of
living have, in fact, no dependent children. Thus 60 per cent of
taxpayers with incomes over £5,000 a year have no children, and
this rises to 75 per cent if parents with only one child are included
with the childless. Indeed, a rough calculation, and this is all
that is possible from the tax tables, suggests that at least 90 per cent
of persons reaching a PN of 5 are non-parents, that is childless
couples, single men and women. The affluent are overwhelmingly
childless.

In an earlier chapter on the life cycle of family needs, it was
suggested that the working mother has done more than either
tax allowances or family allowances to raise her family's level of
living. The working wife who has not the present care of children
will also, of course, add to her own and her husband's level of
living. But it is easier for a married women to work if she has only
a husband to look after and a home for two adults to keep, than
if she has children also. The most prosperous people in the
community are the couples with no dependants and both husband
and wife working, although the most numerous class of persons

achieving the modest-but-adequate level, or better, are the couples with no dependants and the wife staying at home.[1] The following table shows that the more responsibilities a woman has the less likely she is to work outside her home. Whether or not the mother of a family goes out to work also has a substantial effect on the percentage of families with children that achieve a satisfactory standard of living.

Table 26

PERCENTAGE OF WIVES WORKING: UNITED KINGDOM, 1965*

(excluding Pensioners)

Married couples with no dependants	42
one child	36
two children	28
three children	22
four or more children	19

* Commissioners of Inland Revenue (1965), Tables 68 and 69.

This table illustrates one reason why families with dependent children are less prosperous. The larger the number of children the less inclined is the mother to work and supplement the family income, quite apart from taxation. One outstanding way, indeed, for many families to achieve a satisfactory standard of living is for the wife to earn, and this becomes less and less possible as the size of the family increases. The taxman only makes the situation worse, above PNs of about 1·5, by imposing more taxation the larger the family *at a given standard of living.*

The GNP can vary by hundreds of £ millions a year according to the numbers of married women who work. In 1963–4[1] there were over 8 million married women who earned nothing and about 4·6 million who earned. Of over 8 million married women who did not work, over 3·3 million had no dependants at all, either adults or children. Table 27 shows that the higher the husband's income in the brackets above £2,000 a year, the less work his wife is likely to do. Indeed, in the bracket between

[1] Titmuss (1958) comments on the favoured childless groups: 'a higher proportion of the national income is being received by those without dependent children', p. 31.

£1,000 and £2,000 a year over two-thirds of the wives work, while in the highest income bracket, over £5,000 a year, only a third of the wives work:

This table implies that there are large numbers of married women with no dependants who would work if the economic incentives to do so were stronger. It also suggests that the incentives for childless, dependantless women to work become weaker as the husband's income rises above £2,000 a year. It might have been expected that, because of the contribution from the wife's income, more couples with the wife working would be found in the upper income brackets. This is, however, far more than offset by the tendency of wives not to work as the husband's income rises. It is arguable that these many thousands of women who do not work and have no dependants are the most under-employed section of our society today, although there are many who make a contribution to voluntary work.

Table 27

PERCENTAGE OF MARRIED WOMEN WITHOUT DEPENDANTS WHO WORK:

UNITED KINGDOM, 1965*

Annual income of Married Couple	Percentage of wives working
Between £1,000 and £2,000	68
£2,000 and £2,500	54
£2,500 and £3,000	50
£3,000 and £4,000	46
£4,000 and £5,000	44
Over £5,000	34

* Commissioners of Inland Revenue (1965), Tables 68 and 69.

It is arguable that the tax system could produce a substantial increase by altering the incentives for these larger numbers of women to go out to work. The tax relief given to husbands in respect of wives who neither earn nor look after dependent children is very expensive, comparable in cost to the sum total of all child tax allowances, and is a disincentive to work for married women with no dependent children. Whether or not married women with no dependants are encouraged to work or not is a matter of tax and economic policy rather than family policy.

There is an unused reserve of resources at this point that might be put to good use. Any policy for the transfer of resources from non-parents to parents should aim at the better use of this reserve.

The number of taxpayers in the higher tax brackets is, however, small compared with the millions of taxpayers. The average disposable income is still very much too low to provide a modest-but-adequate standard of living for the great majority of people. An increase in total national wealth must remain for a long time a dominant objective of national policy.

Table 25 has indicated the low PNs corresponding to the standard-rate threshold. It will be seen from the tax tables that the majority of families with dependent children do not achieve even these low standards of living. The median income for parents is substantially lower than for married couples without dependent children. In 1961–2[1] there were, indeed, 5·53 million married couples with no dependent children and a median income in the £1,000–£1,499 bracket, while the median income of the families with dependent children was in the £800–£999 bracket. The median income for the fatherless families with dependent children was in the £400–£499 tax bracket, that is £8 to £10 a week.[2]

Families with dependent children are at a disadvantage in another respect. In what we have called the 'trough' of the family cycle the standard of living of most families is heavily depressed. Greater prosperity precedes marriage, and couples are relatively prosperous both before any children arrive and when the children have grown up and left home. The minority who never marry, or never have any children, are also more prosperous on average than the parents throughout most of their lives. It was noted that there is no trough in the life cycle of those who have no children.

There is a curious doctrine to be found in the literature to the effect that 'tax forgone is as much a welfare payment as if the families had received it as a cash payment'.[3] Tax relief for children is then said to cost about £500 millions a year and suggestions follow as to how this £500 millions might be better spent.

[1] Commissioners of Inland Revenue (1963), Table 70, p. 77.
[2] 413,000 tax returns for 1961–2 related to fatherless or motherless families.
[3] Aydon (1967).

That 'tax forgone is a welfare payment' is logical enough assuming only that words are given rather special meanings. The doctrine is, however, rarely extended by those who use it beyond the tax forgone in favour of parents of dependent children. There is also 'tax forgone' in personal allowances in favour of couples with no dependent children, which amounts to another sum substantially in excess of £500 millions a year in these personal allowances for a man and his wife, whether earning or not earning. We have noted that there are 3·3 million married women with no children or dependants who do not work. There is also tax forgone in favour of bachelors, childless widowers, spinsters and childless widows in personal allowances amounting to about another £500 million a year. Suggestions could also be made as to how these further 'welfare payments', amounting to over £1,000 million a year, might be redistributed, more particularly as they are 'paid' to very much larger numbers of people with a satisfactory standard of living. The earned income allowances are also distributed mainly to taxpayers with no dependent children and could be counted as 'welfare payments' too. The value of this doctrine that 'tax forgone is a welfare payment' is doubtful. It seems generally to be used to support arguments for levelling down the standard of living of most families in favour of poor families. Our studies have shown that families are 'levelled down' to a high degree already. It is also used to support the view that only a lesser contribution for the support of poorer families should come from the childless at any income level.[1]

Together with the argument that child tax allowances are a welfare payment is coupled the view that family allowances go not only to the poor but to wealthier families who do not need them. The very great majority of the beneficiaries from both family allowances and child income tax allowances do not achieve the modest-but-adequate level. Of all categories of the population the families with children are already 'levelled down' most by taxation, and the 5·7 million married couples with no dependent

---

[1] This is usually referred to as 'a small additional burden on the exchequer'. Child Poverty Action Group memorandum to the Chancellor of the Exchequer, reprinted in *Poverty*, Spring 1967; see also Abel-Smith (1968), pp. 117–18: 'The necessary increases in family allowances could be paid for by cuts in tax allowances for children, leaving only a modest amount of extra taxation to be levied primarily on single people and married couples.'

children have been 'levelled down' least. This subject is discussed again in the next chapter in the more basic context of social investment.

Individual taxpayers and families of all sizes at PNs much above 1 pay more in taxes, including indirect taxes and social insurance contributions, than the total value of the benefits received, including the cost of education. Only individuals and families well below the poverty line receive any net advantage from social benefits less tax. A family with a man and wife and two children aged between 6 and 11 has a PN below 1 at an income of £681 a year. According to the official journal *Economic Trends*,[1] even at this income the value of all benefits received, including the cost of education of the two children, is less than the taxes paid by this family. In 1964 the typical family with this income paid about £237 a year in taxes, largely indirect, and social insurance contributions. The total cost of all benefits received, including family allowances and the cost of education for the two children, was £199 for a family in the same bracket which is below the poverty level for a family of this composition. Of course, taxation has to pay for many things other than social benefits. Many families with dependent children at or not far above the poverty line are making a net contribution, after deducting the cost of all benefits received, to the cost of those other things that do not benefit their standard of living directly at all.

The official journal *Economic Trends* is also using 'social benefits' in a different sense from the writers who talk about 'tax forgone' as a 'social benefit'. Is expenditure on children's education really in the same class as family allowances or tax forgone?[2] Family allowances and tax-exemptions increase a family's standard of living; education and the raising of the school leaving age lower a family's standard of living in the short term. Most families would be better off in the short term if the children, particularly adolescents, went out to work. Education is a social investment to which parents, as discussed in the next chapter, make a *larger* contribution than the state and from which

---

[1] Central Statistical Office (Aug. 1966).
[2] Nicholson, J. L. (1964), includes 'the average expenditure per child by public authorities on all State Schools combined' amongst his list of Direct Benefits to families.

they benefit very little in a material sense. Indeed one might say that *children's earnings forgone by parents* is a benefit provided by parents to the state (and a 'welfare payment' to those non-parents who are dependent on other people's children in their old age). There is, indeed, much writing on this subject that is special pleading and apologetics.

Discussion of family allowances sometimes seems to imply that all persons and families who are not poor are necessarily 'quite well-off'.[1] In fact, of course, there are degrees of poverty and prosperity. It is certainly a serious misuse of language to suggest that more than a very small minority of families with dependent children are 'well-off' in the sense that they achieve a high prosperity number, or that their standard of living is in the area of great taxable surplus. The great majority of families are hard-pressed, if not poor. However, if we take any satisfactory standard of living whatever, with PNs of 2 or 3 or more, then the great majority of people who achieve it are not parents at all but men and women with no dependent children. Only a small fraction of people who achieve these satisfactory standards are parents of two or more dependent children; indeed, most of the nation's wealth flows to non-parents. There is a very poor correspondence between family responsibility and income, which any increase whatever in the taxation of parents with dependent children can only make worse.

[1] A selection of debates in which definitions of 'the poor' and 'the better off' are discussed, and debates on selectivity in family allowances, is given in the Bibliography under House of Commons and House of Lords.

CHAPTER NINE

The Cost of Misfortune[1]

It is one of the main roles of parents, and especially of the father, to earn an income to support the family. Both private and social insurance have been concerned with protecting the individual and the family against loss of income due to a variety of causes, and notably as a consequence of sickness. In the United Kingdom, between 5 and 6 per cent of the working population is away from work because of sickness at any one time. More than one-third of the whole working population has a spell of absence because of sickness every year.[2]

When a man takes on the responsibility of a wife and children the risk of not being able to earn takes on a new seriousness. He is the breadwinner for others as well as for himself. It is an inconvenience for a single man to be sick. If he has children dependent on him it could be a misfortune if he were not insured. Loss of income due to sickness or unemployment of the bread-winner is more harmful to a family with children than to a household of adults. The time scale of a child is shorter than the time scale of an adult. As we have seen in an earlier chapter, time and season operate inexorably on the needs of a growing child. An adult can make do with his clothes for a time; a young child may not be able to squeeze into last winter's clothing. On a lower income, as where normal earnings are replaced by insurance or assistance payment, there is a risk that food purchased will be less nutritious. A young child may be damaged by a poor diet for a

[1] Social Security Benefits in the E.E.C. countries, as in the United Kingdom, are raised from time to time. Comparisons of levels of benefits at any one point of time are necessarily out of date when published. The figures in this chapter are taken from official publications of the E.E.C. (Communauté Économique Européenne) and especially: Étude Comparée des Prestations de Sécurité Sociale dans Les Pays de la C.E.E.: Série Politique Sociale, No. 4 (1962), and companion volume No. 3. See also Tableaux Comparatif des Régimes de Sécurité Sociale, No. 1. Régime Général, published by the Communauté Européenne du Charbon et de l'Acier (1964). Use has also been made of the annual volume: Exposé sur l'Evolution de la Situation Sociale dans la Communauté, for the years 1959 to 1966, published by the Commission of the E.E.C.

[2] Office of Health Economics (1965), p. 1, and Table A, p. 8.

period, an adult will recover. Pressures on a family budget are more varied and parents find it more difficult to save. In times of misfortune parents have less to fall back on than they had when they were non-parents. It is easier for them to fall into debt. The different time scale of family needs is not fully recognized in the insurance schemes or the assistance schemes of any country. Misfortune strikes hardest on those who are most vulnerable.

Insurance against loss of income during a spell of sickness has spread rapidly during the twentieth century in every developed country and is still extending. In most of the countries of Western Europe today, the sickness benefit is adequate to provide the single wage-earner with no dependants with at least a subsistence income and, with the help of graduated supplements, the standard of the single wage-earner may be maintained at, or well above, the modest-but-adequate level during sickness. Under recent legislation this is also true in the United Kingdom.

In some countries only, is the amount of sickness benefit also made to depend upon the extent of the family responsibilities of the sick person. Sickness benefit is on the one hand wage-related or earnings-related and depends upon the normal wage or earning of the sick person, and is on the other hand need-related and depends upon the extent of the sick person's responsibilities. The outcome is a compromise, generally unsatisfactory to the family, that varies from country to country.

The social forces that have led to social security systems have been immensely complicated. Many social security schemes have been vote-related, in the sense that politicians have sought to meet the wishes of large numbers of voters. Excellent services have nevertheless been developed in many countries to help minorities, such as the spastics and the blind, under pressure of public opinion. Other services, notably the British National Health Service, were designed as need-related services; everyone pays broadly the same contribution but receives a service according to his need. Then in many countries, and recently in the United Kingdom, services have developed that are contribution-related and apply insurance principles in such a way that the benefits received depend in part upon contributions.

There is much to be said in favour of need-related and of

contribution-related schemes. These two principles, however, are generally incompatible with each other; the man on the lowest wage will, it can be argued, generally have a greater need when he is sick than a man on a high wage who has been able to save, but he will, of course, receive less sickness benefit under a contribution-related scheme. The greater the need, the lower is generally the benefit in contribution-related schemes. However, given a substantial spread in the distribution of incomes, it is logical to have a similar spread in pensions and benefits. It is reasonable enough to expect a man, or even to compel a man, to save more and pay higher insurance premiums the higher his income; it will, indeed, raise the general standards of the community to do so. There is nothing to be said for holding pensions or benefits down to the poverty level, or even to the modest-but-adequate level.

The Common Market countries and Scandinavia have largely graduated or contribution-related schemes for their main public insurance programmes. In the words of an I.L.O. spokesman, 'the aim of social security is to provide such a level of benefits that they guarantee a protection in need and are not solely a help in poverty'.[1]

All the arguments in favour of need-related and contribution-related schemes are, however, in danger of ignoring the great spread in the investment content of different schemes. There is a danger of both kinds of scheme taking too short a view. There is a danger that too much may be spent on passing ephemeral needs and too little on meeting needs that, if satisfied, will pay big long-term dividends.

There is in general a poor correspondence between earnings and family responsibilities and this is largely reflected in sickness benefits. Sickness insurance had its origins in sick clubs, voluntary societies and in the concept of mutuality. It developed in close association with the trade union movement which was essentially wage-oriented. Sick pay was a substitute for wages, and regular insurance contributions were a means by which workmen, who were considered essentially as wage-earners, might help each other. In one country after another this early voluntary movement has been either regulated or superseded by legislation and has

[1] Communautés Européennes, Conference 1962, vol. 2, p. 9.

reached a degree of maturity in the sense that most workmen are now entitled to varying percentages of their wages as sick pay. There is a 'ceiling' for the collection of contributions and for the calculation of benefits. The Netherlands sickness benefit is 80 per cent of earnings up to the ceiling. This is the highest of any country. West German sickness benefit is 65 per cent of earnings after the first six weeks; Belgian benefit is 60 per cent; French and Italian benefit is 50 per cent and so on. These are all basic figures for sickness benefit payable to all insured wage-earners within the limits.[1]

The notion that the amount of sickness benefit ought to depend upon the extent of the recipient's family responsibilities is new and largely a development of the years since 1945. It has gradually come to be realized that purely wage-related sickness insurance can only ever go some way towards eliminating the poverty in families resulting from sickness of a breadwinner. In all societies hitherto it has been impossible to pay every wage-earner when sick as much as would be required if he had a wife and a large family, whether or not he has a family. Even in the wealthiest society it would never be an efficient, even if feasible, use of resources to pay every man when sick a sum of money adequate to support a large family, regardless of his actual responsibilities.

Most countries, therefore, now make some concession to family needs in their sick-pay schemes, but the concessions are small and nowhere comparable to the actual spread of family responsibilities.[2] In Germany sickness benefit is increased by 4 per cent for one dependant and 3 per cent for each subsequent dependant (and employers must make up the difference between benefit and wages for the first six weeks). In France there are no family supplements to sick pay unless there are three or more children, when the sickness benefit is increased from 50 to $66\frac{2}{3}$ per cent after thirty days. The Netherlands, Italy and Belgium still pay no sickness benefit supplements for wives or children; the bachelor and the father of a large family receive the same benefit.

The sickness insurance schemes in Germany, France, Luxembourg and the Netherlands, although wage-related, all have ceilings to the sickness benefit expressed in terms of the maximum wage to which the sickness benefit can be related. In all these countries

[1] Communauté Économique Européenne, Études, Serie Politique Sociale, No. 4, Chapter 2.   [2] *Ibid.*

the ceiling operates at very much lower *standards of living* for the
family than for the single person, while the larger the family the
less adequate is the ceiling. The very small regard paid to family
responsibilities in all continental countries in sickness insurance is
however, ameliorated by the payment of family allowances whether
or not the breadwinner is sick.

The United Kingdom sickness insurance scheme pays more
regard to family responsibilities than the continental schemes and
the ceiling is also higher than on the Continent.[1] On the other
hand family allowances are lower, and if these are included the
total cash benefits received by a family with a sick breadwinner
are rather similar in the United Kingdom and these continental
countries as shown in the following table:

Table 28

TOTAL SICKNESS BENEFIT RECEIVED BY A FAMILY WITH AN AVERAGE

WAGE OF HUSBAND, WIFE AND TWO CHILDREN, INCLUDING FAMILY

ALLOWANCES, 1962: IN E.E.C.* AND UNITED KINGDOM†

	(U.S. Dollars)	
	4 weeks	26 weeks
United Kingdom	71·66	465·76
Germany	75·46	427·26
France	62·31	430·10
Italy	55·28	382·64
Luxembourg	80·64	524·16
Holland	69·09	495·39

* Communauté Économique Européenne (1962), Études, Serie Politique
Sociale. 4, Table 16, p. 38.
† Sickness Benefit, 1962.

However, in all these countries the total effect of these complicated
sickness insurance schemes is that the larger the family the greater
is the hardship. Most of the families in Western Europe with
dependent children are not yet effectively covered against sickness
of the breadwinner. Only persons without family responsibilities
are reasonably well covered. In all these countries the sickness
benefit supplements for wives and children are well below the
country's own recognized bare subsistence levels. The United

[1] Ceilings were raised in Germany in 1968.

Kingdom supplement for a wife of £2 16s. a week is the best in
Europe, but is fixed and not wage-related and is less than is
necessary to support a wife at poverty level. The present sum of
£1 8s. for a first child, and the 10s. plus 18s. family allowances
for a second child, and the sum of 8s.[1] plus 20s. family allowance
for subsequent children is not the best in Europe, and is below
the cost of maintaining even a young child at poverty level. This
United Kingdom sickness benefit supplement for a child is
independent of the child's age and is almost derisory as a supplement for a dependent adolescent.

The adolescent is particularly at a disadvantage under the
United Kingdom Social Security Scheme. In an earlier chapter it
was suggested that the cost of a young person reached that of an
adult man at about 14 years, and rose above the adult level in
the later teens to about 120 per cent of adult costs, excluding for
either the cost of working. Benefits paid to young persons are,
however, much below adult level.[2] Thus, under the most generous
scheme for Industrial Injury, an adult receives £7 5s., a boy of
15 to 17 years only £4, and £5 1s. 3d. at ages 17 to 18. If a schoolboy is injured while working part-time, for example as a paper-
boy, he receives only the dependent child's allowance of £1 8s.[2]
If he is employed and under 18 and falls sick he receives £2 10s.,
a lower sum than the dependent wife of a sick adult. If he is
dependent on his father because, for example, he is still at school,
and his father is sick, the sum of £1 8s. is considered enough for
his needs; whereas insured adults receive £4 10s. If a dependent
adolescent is in a family receiving non-contributory benefit his
allowance is £2 13s. from 16 to 17 years, and £3 1s. from 18 to
20 years. If the father is dead he receives £2 5s. 6d. From these
small sums parents must provide food, clothing and personal care
to an adolescent. What can be left for pocket money? Yet a sick
adult in hospital or an old person in a Home is allowed to retain
some benefit for pocket money. Adolescents have a grievance.

The chief criticism which may be made of purely earnings-

---

[1] April 1968. Social Security, Ministry of, Annual Report (1967), Table 54,
p. 132, altered at 8 Oct. 1968 as above.

[2] Social Security, Ministry of, Leaflet No. N.I. 149 (May 1968), FAM 29
(June 1968), S.I. (October 1968), N.I. 151 (August 1967), and N.I. 152 (August
1967), For earlier rates see Annual Report of Ministry of Social Security 1967,
Tables 54 and 55, pp. 132 and 133.

related insurance is that it has a low social investment content. Sickness absence for both men and women increases with age. Most of the sick pay in wage-related schemes is in consequence paid to persons over 50 who have no dependent children in the great majority of cases. Most parents of dependent children are under 50 years of age. In 1966–7 only 27 per cent of all sick-pay recipients were fathers with one or more dependent children; 73 per cent of all sick-pay recipients were non-parents.[1]

Sick-pay allowances in respect of dependent children may be estimated as likely to constitute only about 5 per cent of all sick-pay benefit paid, although dependent children are nearer 25 per cent of all persons. The national cost of sick-pay allowances in respect of dependent children is so low both because parents are much less often sick than non-parents, and because of the sub-poverty standard level of the flat-rate benefits for dependent children. The children's allowances under National Assistance were, of course, substantially higher for older children than under these new insurance schemes; nevertheless, only about 7 per cent of the National Assistance Board's resources were paid on behalf of dependent children. The non-contributory benefits that replaced National Assistance in the autumn of 1966 kept the relativities that are disadvantageous to children.

Earnings-related sickness insurance results, therefore, in a very substantial transfer of resources from parents to non-parents. Parents of families would, indeed, be very much better off if they had their own sickness insurance for the benefit of parents only, although this might be a clumsy way of increasing the social investment content of sickness insurance.

The transfer of wealth from parents to non-parents is revealed in a study of a particular group of households in the United Kingdom published in 1967. This group of households consisted largely of men and women of working age, chiefly parents, with only a quarter of those over retirement age, and a larger number of young children when compared to the population as a whole. It was found that these younger households, largely with children, made less demands on insurance and assistance schemes than the population as a whole. It was shown that: 'In 1961–2 more than sixty per cent of total national insurance and assistance benefit

[1] Social Security, Ministry of, Annual Report (1967), Table 9.

went to the old and by 1965 the proportion was even greater. Benefits totalled some £13–£15 per head for those under 65 but £160 per head for those of pensionable age.'[1]

At the same time the households in childbearing and rearing years paid per head more insurance contributions because, even allowing for the children, they contained fewer non-contributors. The younger households made smaller demands on social services, even taking those for children fully into account. In 1961–2 health and welfare expenditure was £20 per head for the under 14s, £14 per head for adults of 15 to 64, and £39 for the old. This particular group of young households were immigrant families, but what is true of them is true of families with children as a whole. The effect of the age structure of immigrant families outweighed the few special demands on services which they made; they too suffer in the transfer of wealth from parents to non-parents. Immigrant families were said in this paper to provide a 'once and for all gain for some 30 years'. Their age-composition will eventually be that of the rest of the population. But parents of children at any point of time are always net contributors. The main transfer through insurance schemes is to the old who take over 60 per cent of all benefits in the United Kingdom. This is true of other countries; a study by the Statistical Department of the Common Market Commission in 1967 showed that:

'Chief place amongst social security benefits is, without any doubt and in all countries, taken by benefits to retired persons which are about a third (France and Italy) and nearly a half (Germany and Luxembourg) of the sum total of benefits.'[2]

This transfer of resources from parents to non-parents involved in earnings-related insurance schemes is not, of course, the primary reason for their low investment content. It is more fundamental that these schemes are not intended to protect the family as a first consideration, so that the larger the family or the older the dependent children the less adequate is the sick pay. However, the larger the family and the older the dependent children the greater is the investment content of the family's expenditure, whether out of the father's wages or out of social security benefits.

[1] Jones, K. (1967), p. 34.   [2] Murcier (1967).

Earnings-related[1] insurance has led the way historically. Further extensions of earnings-related insurance seem likely, however, to yield diminishing returns in reducing the social problems that still remain, although in Europe there are still some categories of the working population waiting to be covered. Earnings-related insurance has achieved much in reducing hardship and poverty, but greater family-orientation of social insurance is now necessary. A change of direction is needed in the further extension of sickness insurance.

This change of direction should first of all establish parity between children and adults at the minimum level. This minimum is likely to remain part of any social security system for a long time to come. A minimum subsistence income for all was a great ideal to Sidney Webb[2] writing in the first decade of the century. The ideal was realized in Beveridge's Scheme of 1942.[3] However, Beveridge used relativities for the cost of a child compared to an adult which were already out of date. Although he gave a child aged 10 to 14 years the same sum for food as an adult, when he drew up total costs for a child he left no 'margin', as allowed for adults and retired persons, he made the child's need for 'fuel, light and sundries' only 10 per cent of those for an adult (not including rent).[4] The final result was that his cost for a child of 14 to 15 was only 72 per cent of that for an adult (not including rent), and for the 'average' child only 56 per cent of that for a man. Thus there came about an underestimation of the cost of a child in Beveridge's own calculations. When his plan passed into law the scales were further weighted against children. In the legislation on national assistance adults were given slightly more than the Beveridge minimums (at 1948 prices) but children were given yet less again. When Insurance rates were fixed, adults were given 20 per cent below the Beveridge level but children were given *40 per cent below*. Family allowances were fixed lower still, less than half of Beveridge's minimum. His strong plea for age relation in child allowances was ignored except for the assist-

[1] In the United Kingdom graduated schemes are related to earnings. In some countries the contributions are calculated on wage or salary.
[2] Webb, S. (1909).
[3] Beveridge (1942).
[4] Hemmings (1965), p. 48, contains a discussion of the child's levels under Beveridge's Scheme and subsequent legislation.

ance rates. Over the years there has been a slight improvement in
the relativities for children. A radical reassessment of children's
needs is required as part of the change of direction in social
security.

A second change of direction should be to allow children (and
their mothers) to move away from the minimum subsistence
income concept to the newer concept now increasingly accepted
for wage-earning men and women and for non-working retired
persons. There is no reason in equity why mothers and children
should be left to suffer from a philosophy which is regarded as
out of date for the elderly and the childless.

The extension of the graduation concept to supplements for
wives and dependent children would achieve a better correspondence between sick pay and family needs. This can be achieved
by making the supplements for wives and dependent children a
percentage increase on the basic pension or allowance in place
of the present fixed minimum allowances for dependants provided
in the United Kingdom. There are precedents for percentage
increases in benefits for dependants. In Sweden, 'survivor' benefits,
that is widows' benefits and their children's allowances, include
percentage increases on the graduated portion. Small percentage
increases for wives and children are given under sick-pay schemes
in Germany, and under invalidity benefit in Belgium, Germany
and Italy. In the United Kingdom, widows, but not their children,
receive graduated additions for six months.

It is the children's allowances under nearly all sickness insurance
that are particularly low in relation to needs, and it is the families
with several children, and notably older children, that suffer
particular hardship from the sickness of the breadwinner. The
extension of the graduation principle to sick-pay supplements for
children should be a priority in any further extension of sick-pay
schemes. The higher cost of older children should be taken into
account by making the percentage increase in basic sick pay for
a child dependent on his age. This would concentrate help where
it is needed most.

An extension of the graduation principle to mothers in charge
of dependent children should also be considered. It would,
however, achieve less in helping families than an extension of
graduation to supplements for children, because it would not be

related either to the numbers or the ages of the children. An extension of the graduation principle to mothers would, nevertheless, achieve more in reducing hardship and poverty of families and in increasing the social investment content of sickness insurance than any further general increases in sick pay.

The small flat-rate supplements for wives and children do not automatically benefit from increasing prosperity and their real value falls with any inflation of the economy. The graduation of the supplements by making them a percentage of the basic sick pay would enable families in misfortune to share more automatically in any general advance in living standards.

However, the graduation of sick pay supplements for mothers and dependent children is no more than one change of direction that is needed. What can be achieved by these means is limited by the adequacy of earnings of fathers, and by the 'earnings-stop' that limits sick pay in the United Kingdom to not more than 85 per cent of earnings. A single man or woman earning £12 a week is entitled to a graduated supplement of £1 per week in the United Kingdom; a married man with four children on the same wage is, however, only entitled to 8s. per week, and if he has five children he will not be entitled to any graduated supplement at all.[1] The graduation of the supplements for mothers and children would not benefit such poor families because their sick pay is limited by the earnings-stop, inhibiting any increase. Maximum sick pay in other countries is also limited to maximum percentages of earnings.

In the United Kingdom, both employers' organizations and trade unions have advocated and supported the earnings-stop on the grounds that a man—and in practice this means a father—must have a financial incentive to work. The 85 per cent rule implies that a man must be able to increase his earnings by at least 15 per cent by working. The extent to which the level of sick pay does in practice influence fathers' inclinations to work is possibly debatable. The degree to which work-incentives should have priority over family needs is also open to question. Certainly the retention within insurance schemes of the earnings-stop must perpetuate family poverty, in families in which the father has a

---

[1] Social Security, Ministry of (1967), Leaflet N.I. 155, Guide to the New Earnings-related short-term Benefit Scheme.

record of much sickness, from one generation to the next. In families in which the father has a good work record but low earnings, even normal periods of sickness will increase family poverty. Means both outside and inside the framework of insurance must be found to help families with low earnings.

There is, of course, a variety of ways of helping such families. Family allowances are not open to the objection that they reduce work incentives. Lord Beveridge underlined twenty-four years ago that family poverty could only be alleviated without influencing work incentives by increasing family income, whether the father was working or not, by some such device as family allowances.

The earnings-stop would limit or altogether prevent substantial numbers of families from benefiting from the graduation of insurance supplements for mothers and children. Graduation of these supplements would, however, help many families with modest incomes by reducing hardship and poverty during sickness of the breadwinner, and would reduce the numbers of families in distress. There is little to be said for the present egalitarianism, reflected in the fixed supplements for mothers and children, that levels families down to a low standard. There is nothing to be said for a poverty level egalitarianism applied only to dependent women and children, but not to single wage-earners. The graduation of the supplements for mothers and children would make it easier for very many families to escape from poverty during sickness of the breadwinner.

There is both a ceiling and a floor for sickness and unemployment benefit. Families are disadvantaged by the ceilings; the larger the family the lower is the standard of living that can be achieved under the scheme at all. The maximum sickness benefit for a single man under the United Kingdom scheme is £11 per week, payable if he was paying graduated contributions on £30 per week. The maximum total benefit payable to a man with a wife and four children is £16 16s. a week. These are the ceilings laid down in the scheme. The standard of living of a single man on £11 per week will be altogether higher than that of a man, wife and four children on £16 16s. a week.

The family is similarly disadvantaged by the floor of £9 a week before graduated contributions are paid. The single person is allowed to achieve a much higher standard of living than the family before he has to pay graduated contributions. Furthermore, it is almost always the larger family whose sick pay is restricted by the earnings-stop. The father, however, still has to pay his full graduated contributions to the sick pay scheme even though he may be debarred from receiving any graduated supplement or receives only a reduced supplement.

In one respect the family in the United Kingdom is more fortunate than families in other countries. The National Health Service has *taken medical care outside the family budget*. There are defects in the National Health Service, for example, more is spent per head in some other countries, but over the greater part of Europe and North America medical care must be included in the family budget, and must there compete with the need for food, clothing, warmth and other things. There is all the difference for families of poor or modest means between a system in which there is *no cash transaction* in seeking medical or hospital care, and a system in which the family pays at the time of sickness in part, or in whole, and must await *reimbursement later*. If medical care has to be paid for, then families must either budget long-term by private insurance, as in the United States for those families unable, or unwilling, to qualify as 'medically indigent', or they must set aside cash, lest sickness befall, from money urgently needed for current expenses, as in the Common Market countries and Scandinavia. Of course, the schemes of some large firms in the United States and Europe offer the same sick care, free of immediate payment, as the British National Health Service, but this is available only to the employees of the firm and their families. If medical care is part of the family budget, parents are tempted not to seek medical advice, at least for themselves, for fear of the expense, and also from experience of the vexations of applying for reimbursement. The nuisance of form-filling, letter writing, collecting signed chits for visits or for medicines purchased, is a grievance for users of those health services which have reimbursement schemes. A child's need for medical care not only competes with his need for food, clothes and other necessaries, but may be at the mercy of his parents' forethought to budget, or their facility in dealing with paper work. Dr Gertrude Willoughby, an authority on the social security system of the Common Market countries, gives this description of the French system in 1966:

'While in the other Common Market Countries the doctors have agreed to fees being paid through a third party, in France and Belgium the patient is expected to arrive at the surgery with the doctor's fee in his hand, a proportion of the fee will ultimately be refunded through the social security agencies. . . . A patient consulting a doctor in Paris, where the conventional fees are higher than in other areas, will be expected to pay 19s. for each visit he makes to the doctor's surgery; should the doctor be asked to pay a home visit the fee will be £1 9s. and the average prescription charge is much the same as here, about 10s., so that, relating the cost of prescriptions and consultation to average wages in France, the worker will have to find an initial sum equal to about six hours' work. He will ultimately be reimbursed about 80 per cent of his outlay.'[1]

It is not surprising to find that the amount spent per head on medical care amongst families decreases as families increase in size. Dr Willoughby continues:

'a report published by a research group of the University of Paris analyses the effect of this direct payment by the patient on his recourse to medical care. About 39 per cent of the people interviewed claimed that at one time or another they had been unable to consult their doctor, or had had to postpone their visit for lack of money to pay the doctor's fees . . . the report notes the disquieting fact that the more children there are in the family the less is the recourse to medical care.'

This is fully confirmed by the latest French national research survey on the condition of families (1967). The larger the family the smaller is the expenditure per head on medical care, although the needs of the larger family are certainly not less than those of the smaller family. The average expenditure per head on medical care of families with two children was 143 N.F., with three children 113 N.F. and with four children only 96 N.F., and for still larger families was lower still.[2] The French system does not work from the family point of view. The British Health Service is better. It merits the description of an Archbishop addressing doctors:

'Let us be balanced in our judgement. Many as are the faults of welfare state medicine it has lifted an insufferable burden from many anxious parents worrying about children or their spouses.

[1] Willoughby (1966).   [2] Tabard (1967), Table 2 E.P., p. 355.

'In these days of personal stress and worry one can say that the state itself, by reason of the legislation, has been a good physician.'[1]

In the United Kingdom, unemployment and sickness benefit are essentially a part of the same scheme. Families with an unemployed breadwinner are at a severe disadvantage compared with the single wage-earner in the same way as are families with a sick breadwinner. The incidence of unemployment also increases with age. In 1966–7, 64 per cent of the recipients of unemployment pay were non-parents.[2] In unemployment insurance there is also on average a transfer of resources from parents to non-parents.

In countries of the European Community, unemployment insurance differs both from country to country and from sickness insurance in each country.[3] In general, family allowances are payable during unemployment of the breadwinner and in Belgium, France, Germany and Italy there are family supplements to unemployment pay. There is an earnings rule in Germany limiting unemployment pay to 90 per cent of wages at the lowest level and to 70 per cent at the ceiling. In France the limit is 85 per cent for families and 80 per cent for single persons. Unemployment pay is generally earnings-related but family supplements are fixed sums.[3]

Among all the sick and the unemployed there is one particular class of family that suffers the greatest privation. This is the large family with dependent children who have to live for long periods upon sickness or unemployment pay. In the United Kingdom, graduated additions to unemployment and sick pay terminate at the end of six months and a family becomes dependent on flat-rate benefits and finally on non-contributory benefits. Income declines at a time when needs are increasing, as explained in Chapter 4, in which the dependence of need on time and season was discussed.

In Italy graduated sick pay continues for 180 working days; in Holland for 312 working days; in France for six months with extensions to a year or even three years for a prolonged illness;

---

[1] Archbishop Murphy, Meeting of the British Medical Association, *Catholic Herald*, 16 July 1965.

[2] Social Security, Ministry of, Annual Report (1967), Table 9.

[3] Communauté Économique Européenne: Études, Serie Politique Sociale, No. 4, Chapter 10.

in Germany sick pay is *increased* at the end of six months for the following six months or more if there is a reasonable chance of recovery sufficient to enable a return to work. In the Common Market countries sick pay may be followed by invalidity pay, generally if the recipient is certified as being more than two-thirds or fifty per cent incapacitated. Invalidity pay is sometimes higher and sometimes lower than sick pay. The continental family allowances continue irrespective of sick or invalidity pay. In general there is no sudden fall in sick pay at the end of the six months as in the United Kingdom. However, the benefits for the wives and children of sick breadwinners are so low in most countries that such families suffer great privation when the sickness continues for long periods. The most generous provisions are probably Swedish, by which, under the new graduated scheme, invalidity pay includes both fixed family benefits and graduated supplements for a dependent wife and children, as though the invalid were a pensioner with dependants.

The breadwinners who are sick for prolonged periods, or disabled with dependent wives and children, are a very small minority. The consequences to the children of such families, in the absence of adequate support, may be serious and long-lasting. The mother, in such a family, is liable to suffer from great strain, both emotional and economic, because of the insistent and competing demands of the sick father and the children. The sickness of the father often makes it difficult or impossible for the mother to work and increases the expenses of the family for fuel to warm a sick-room and for special foods.

There is no insurance cover specifically designed to cover the risk of long-term civil disability in the United Kingdom. Holland in 1963 combined civil and industrial injury insurance in one scheme. The report of the Common Market Commission commented:

'Clearly we have here a radical innovation in respect of existing legislation in the six countries. The Dutch Minister for Social Affairs was clearly conscious of this and was at pains to make this point in explaining that "the fact that no country in the European Community has a similar system to that which we propose, is not a valid reason to prevent Holland becoming a pioneer". . . . The Dutch proposal will incontestably be a progressive step in aligning the system of (civil) invalidity with the more favoured system of industrial injury. But more than this, we may well foresee that the solution proposed in Holland will be the solution of the future, towards which the other countries will come when they are able to, without prejudice to the actual advantages contained in legislation on industrial accidents and diseases. We cannot see how, in the long term, a discrimination can be maintained in the relief of invalidity according to whether it is of industrial origin or not. The insurance cover for road accidents has already made this distinction artificial when we consider the law suits which they result in and the overall problem of traffic accidents.'[1]

Where there are young children, the illness of the mother can well be more disruptive of family life and more expensive than the illness of the father. Indeed, many a father of several children would rather be ill in bed himself for two or three weeks than have to cope while his wife was confined to a sick-bed for the same period. The bread-winning, child-caring and housekeeping roles of parents are generally distinguished. The sickness of the mother may result in some failure in all these roles. If the mother is earning then there is a loss of family income, but, depending upon the ages of the children, the failure of the mother to be able to care for the children or participate in housekeeping may be more serious.

The loss of a mother's services through illness is an insurable risk but is generally not covered in the insurance schemes of countries outside Scandinavia. Indeed, today most families have some insurance against sickness of the father but very few against sickness of the mother. In Sweden,[2] mothers who are not employed outside their own homes are insured against sickness and are entitled to sick benefit at the adult flat-rate of 5 kroner per day (£2 8s. 4d. per week) plus a child supplement of not less than 2 kroner per day (19s. 3d. per week) if there are children under the age of 10 living with her. She is also eligible for a disability pension for partial or total incapacity to perform her household tasks and care for the children. The Swedish Insurance Act, 1962, states that in calculating disability pensions 'the value of household work performed in the home shall be equated to a reasonable

---

[1] Communauté Économique Européenne, Exposé (1963), p. 184.

[2] Sweden (1966), *Social Benefits in Sweden.* Mothers must be members of the Sick Fund. £1 = 14·5 kroner.

extent with income from work'. A mother who is employed in Sweden receives the same graduated sick pay as a man in the same circumstances. In contrast, in the United Kingdom, even if a mother pays full women's rate insurance contributions she receives only £3 2s. sick pay on normal earnings of less than £9 a week (the flat-rate benefit), whereas the adult man and single woman receives £4 10s. in flat-rate sick pay.[1] The insurance cover in the United Kingdom for the loss of the mother's contribution to the family is less satisfactory than for a father, or a bachelor or other male non-parent. There is even an earnings rule of a particularly harsh kind on the earnings of the working wife of a disabled man. If she earns anything over the dependants' allowance received by her sick husband for her the whole of that allowance ceases. Part-time work, which may very well be all that is possible or desirable for a woman who cares for a sick husband, is therefore likely to result in loss of benefit.

Insurance cover for invalidity from any cause will not be complete if it omits the mother of a family. The father should be covered against the loss of her services in the home whether or not she was working outside the home. In a paper on the cost of a child, Dr Van Hofsten in 1954 estimated the minimum number of hours of attention and direct handling required by children of different ages:

Table 29

MINIMUM HOURS OF HANDLING AND ATTENTION NEEDED BY CHILDREN
OF DIFFERENT AGES: SWEDISH ESTIMATE*

Age	Hours per year:
1	1,200
2	1,100
5	475
11	90

* Van Hofsten (1955).

These hours are essential minimum woman-hours that must be expended in handling and care of dependent children. If the mother is sick then they must be expended by a substitute who will today quite normally have to be paid for. Dr van Hofsten

[1] Social Security, Ministry of (Aug. 1967), Leaflet N.I. 151.

suggested that if the care of a child is transferred from a mother's unpaid services to paid services of a mother substitute, then 'the value of the work of a busy housewife equals the average wage paid to a female worker'. These hours of child-handling do not include the time spent in shopping or normal housework, which will, in addition, have to be done by the father, or someone else, if the mother is sick.

In 1961 Dr van Hofsten published an article on the cost of children's care, consumption and education and showed the value of care and supervision by ages. Sterling equivalents have been added:

Table 30

VALUE OF CARE AND SUPERVISION OF CHILDREN IN THEIR OWN HOMES IN SWEDEN 1961*

Age in years	Value of care Kroner per child per year	In sterling 1 Kr. = 1s. 5d. per week		
0–2	3,300	4	10	0
3–6	2,800	3	16	0
7–10	2,300	3	3	0
11–13	1,800	2	9	0
14–16	1,300	1	16	0

* Van Hofsten and Karlsson (1961).

The insurance of the family against the sickness of the mother, which has been pioneered in Sweden, is one extension of sickness insurance that is required in every country to help the family. The minimum woman-hours that must be expended caring for dependent children should be taken fully into account.

A man who loses the mother of his children is in great difficulty. In the United Kingdom and, indeed, in most countries a father, unlike a mother, is not usually allowed to stay at home indefinitely to look after his children and to live on non-contributory benefit. A father has either to find someone to look after his home and children or place the children in the care of the local authority, or a voluntary society or a foster home. In fact, the loss of the mother very greatly increases the risk of a child being placed in care and so becoming, in effect, a complete orphan. It nearly always costs a father money to find someone to look after his home and children even when a relation is willing to help. The free services of the mother of the family are virtually impossible to replace except at substantial cost to the father.

This risk is recognized by the payment of a small pension for the motherless child in Finland, Germany, Italy, Sweden and elsewhere. No country pays the widower an allowance on the loss of his wife if he is in work. The motherless child remains uncovered in the United Kingdom even if his mother was fully insured. Numerically the number of motherless children is small; a motherless child allowance would reduce the risk of children being taken into care, often at public expense, would be a good social investment and should have priority over other extensions of insurance schemes of lower investment content, for example wage-related insurance. The number of motherless children is over 95,000 in the United Kingdom. An official publication of the Federal Government puts the number in the United States at 850,000 maternal orphans under 18, not entitled to insurance benefit and living with their father, plus a further 100,000 entitled under their deceased mother's work record. This report comments

'Perhaps the economic loss to a family caused by the death of a non-working mother has been underestimated. A survey of maternal orphans living with their unremarried father could answer many questions.'[1]

This economic loss to families should be investigated in all western countries.

The widow with dependent children has to fulfil all three parental roles—namely breadwinning, child-caring and house-keeping—with the support, however, in most cases of a widow's pension and allowances for children. In the United Kingdom, a graduated supplement is only paid for the first six months of widowhood and there are no graduated additions for fatherless children. In the Common Market and Scandinavian countries, the widow's pension and allowances for the widow's children generally include graduated additions up to the pension level attained by the deceased father.

It is an argument in favour of graduated additions to old-age pensions that retirement should not result in too great a fall in

[1] Palmore (1966), p. 67.

standard of living and that pensions should, therefore, bear some relation to previous earnings. The same argument is made in favour of graduated additions to sickness and unemployment pay. The widow, including the widowed mother and her children are, however, expected to adjust themselves to a minimum standard of living in the United Kingdom after six months of widowhood, regardless of the previous level of living when the father was alive. The bereaved children receive only a flat-rate allowance, regardless of age, which for older children is below the subsistence level of non-contributory benefit. The pensioner is given a more privileged position than the widowed mother and her children. A family policy placing emphasis on social investment would not accept this low status of widowed mothers and bereaved children.

Wage-related pensions for widowed mothers and fatherless children would still leave great poverty amongst minorities unless there were provision for an acceptable minimum for the families where the deceased father had low earnings, below or not much over the lower graduation limit, or where the father had only been insured for a short-time, or was not an insured person. Most countries have such minima but they are generally very low, resulting in the great poverty of large numbers of widows with dependent children. In Italy, which has the lowest minimum of the Common Market countries, the pension and allowances of a widow with dependent children may be barely adequate to ensure survival if the father had only been insured for a few years at a low wage.

In the United Kingdom the widowed mother's pension plus children's allowances does provide a minimum that is reasonable compared with the minimum of most countries. The abolition of the earnings rule has also enabled many widows to raise their standards above the minimum by working. The most urgent need is to increase the allowances for the older children of widows and make them age-related. While graduated supplements to widows' and old-age pensions are desirable, if they can be afforded, the guaranteed minimum for older children must come first and the widows' children's allowances should be a priority. Children who have lost their father are more often older children, frequently in their teens; the flat-rate widowed mother's allowance for teenage boys and girls is not commensurate with their needs.

A widow's children are, of course, at a great disadvantage compared with the children of a normal family. There is only one parent to fulfil all the parental roles; the love and discipline of the father is not replaced by insurance benefit. The position of these families, however, is made worse by many anomalies, reflecting their underprivileged position in the insurance schemes of all countries. In the United States, to take an example, under the survivors' insurance scheme there is a 'maximum family benefit limitation' on the cash payable to the widowed mother's family.[1] Once the limit is reached, there is nothing for younger children whatever the father's contribution record may have been. Later-born children are in effect less favoured, contrary to the spirit if not the letter of the U.S.A. constitution, which guarantees equal rights for its citizens. The pensions for widowed mothers and their children in the U.S.A. are, in effect, wage-stopped by the 'maximum family benefit limitation', although the purpose of a wage-stop has always been to maintain the father's incentive to work. A wage-stop is irrelevant to a deceased father. Other countries also have rules for maximum benefit, either in money or by a maximum percentage of the 'father's presumed pension' on which the widow's allowance is calculated. There is no such disallowance of later-born children in the United Kingdom. The anomalies which deepen the poverty of widows and their children would fill many pages of comparative study. No country is guiltless in the treatment of the widowed and fatherless.

Widows and their children are, however, only a minority of fatherless families in all countries. They are outnumbered by the deserted, divorced, separated and unmarried mothers with dependent children. These families are on average younger and the period of fatherlessness in the children's lives is, therefore, longer. In Western Europe and North America there are roughly 12 million children who are being brought up in homes in which there is no male breadwinner and where the mother is the sole parent. Studies in many countries have shown fatherlessness to be a main cause of child poverty. About 7 per cent of all children are fatherless children in the United Kingdom,[2] but the Ministry of Social Security in its study, *Circumstances of Families*, showed that roughly 30 per cent of the poorest children were fatherless,

[1] Palmore (1966), p. 21.   [2] Wynn (1964).

although the standard of poverty used was itself harsher for the fatherless family than for families with two parents. A lone mother with three children receiving £7 19s. a week (the standard taken) would have a lower standard of living than a man, wife and two children of the same age receiving £9 6s. Again, a lone mother and teenage son have needs equal to a man and wife, but the poverty line was set at £5 9s. 6d. in this report for the mother and son, and at £6 5s. 6d. for the couple.[1] The report underestimates poverty amongst households with children.

In the U.S.A. almost half the child poverty is amongst fatherless families, and of the fatherless children the poorest are those whose homes are broken by separation, divorce or unmarried parents. Because of the large numbers of children affected and the long-term social consequences, the fatherless family must provide one of the most important chapters of any family policy. Lord Beveridge proposed that women should be insured against break-up of marriage and the loss of a husband by causes other than death.[2] This recommendation did not find its way into subsequent legislation. Sweden has, in effect, provided such an insurance for families fatherless by desertion by providing a state guarantee of a minimum level of maintenance allowance called the 'advance of maintenance'. The sum received is equal to the Swedish flat-rate allowance for widows' children (who will, however, be increasingly eligible for graduated additions as discussed above). This Swedish advance of maintenance allowance is less than the United Kingdom child's maximum under a magistrate's court order or affiliation order. However, in Sweden 90 per cent of mothers receive at least this for their child,[3] whereas in the United Kingdom many children are awarded less,[4] and others receive in the event nothing from their fathers.

Those countries with family allowances do, of course, continue to pay them to fatherless families. The higher level of family allowances in Western Europe is a great help to the fatherless.[5] However, the aim must be to raise the standards of all lone

[1] Social Security, Ministry of (1967), *Circumstances of Families*, p. 3.
[2] Beveridge (1942) par. 7.
[3] Sweden: Ensamstående Mödrars (1957), Tables 17 and 22. This figure includes 10 per cent of mothers supported by cohabitation.
[4] Graham-Hall (1967), par. 105, Table 16, p. 49.
[5] See Appendix 3.

mothers and their children at least to the modest level of the widows: a failure to do so will perpetuate many social problems. In the United Kingdom about a third of all fatherless families are being helped by the Ministry of Social Security, generally with non-contributory benefit.[1] Indeed, the Ministry is preventing the worst consequences of fatherlessness. However, unlike the widows' pension, non-contributory benefit is subject to an earnings rule making it much more difficult for the lone mother, not a widow, to lift herself above the minimum by her own efforts. The lone mother can only earn £2, regardless of the number of her children, before her benefit is reduced. The extension of disregard of earning to a disregard for each child would be no charge on public funds. An elderly couple may each have £2 of earnings disregarded, a total of £4, when receiving the supplementary pension with its long-term additions.[2]

Fatherlessness is one of the main roads into poverty. But the poverty need not perpetuate itself in the next generation, and social policy should give every chance to the family to escape from poverty by using the mother's earning power, her zeal, ambition and ability to the full. The folly of assistance given as a ceiling over which the mother can only rise by earning a high wage, rather than as a floor under her feet above which all her earnings raise her family up, is that it closes the road out of poverty. Assistance tied to not working is not appropriate for able-bodied mothers with children above infancy. The children of a widowed mother who can earn above her pension are encouraged to be upwardly mobile; the children of a mother dependent for long periods on non-contributory benefits are discouraged from upward mobility.

There are difficulties in raising the standard of living of fatherless families that arise from the identification of the fatherless family and from the danger of the establishment of wrong incentives. These difficulties are underlined by the long experience of Aid to Families with Dependent Children in the U.S.A. Adults may be

---

[1] Social Security, Ministry of (1967), *Circumstances of Families*, p. 51.

[2] Leaflet S.I., par. 2c, and S.P.I. par. 2c, Ministry of Social Security Act 1966, Schedule 2, Part II, par. 11 and 12, and Part III, par. 23. The earnings disregard of £4 per couple applies to supplementary pensions and long-term supplementary allowance. Where a man is liable to register for employment he may have £1 only disregarded—a total of £3 for man and wife.

divided into those with responsibility for dependent children and those without dependent children; there are adults who exercise parental responsibility and those who do not do so. This is a useful classification for many purposes. There are, however, also men who beget children and women who give birth to children who subsequently do not exercise the normal parental responsibility which should be theirs. When natural parents, generally men but sometimes women, do not exercise normal parental responsibility it is very costly to every society. Most of the children in public care have natural parents or at least one parent living. Most of the fatherless families are a consequence of desertion rather than death. All the worst social problems are aggravated by natural parents not exercising their parental responsibility.

The break-up of marriages is associated with low educational levels[1] and low incomes.[2] The Graham-Hall Committee on Statutory Maintenance Limits in the United Kingdom showed that deserting fathers are overwhelmingly poor men. The following table is adapted from the report:

Table 31

INCOME OF FATHERS OF FATHERLESS FAMILIES: (DEFENDANTS' INCOME AT DATE OF ORDER FOR A SAMPLE OF ORDERS LIVE ON 1ST JANUARY, 1966)*

Weekly Income	Matrimonial and guardianship orders percentage		Affiliation orders percentage	
Under £10	43	} 87	51	} 93
£10 but under £16	44		42	
£16 and over	13		7	
	100		100	
Numbers	743		300	

* Graham-Hall (1967), Table 7, p. 39.

Generally a mother who is deserted has a right in civil law to an action against the father for maintenance. This civil right of the mother has, in one country after another, proved to be a quite inadequate safeguard for the lone mother and her children.

[1] Carter and Plateris (1963); Martz, H. (1963).
[2] Kaplan, S. (1960).

H

Much poverty and hardship has resulted from a failure of the processes of the civil law to secure either adequate maintenance for a mother and children or even maintenance at all. A father can, in consequence, quite normally improve his own personal standard of living by deserting his wife and family. Family bonds in the stable family are very much stronger than these financial incentives, but there can be no doubt that where the family bonds are not very strong, and the family is struggling with economic and other difficulties, the temptation for the father to contract out is reinforced by the knowledge that he can also improve his personal standard of living by doing so. If the state is willing to step into the father's shoes without pursuing the father, then fathers may have less compunction about desertion and mothers may be more inclined to encourage not very satisfactory fathers to desert.

If the interests of the children come first, then the family which is fatherless by desertion or divorce must receive the same help as the family of the widow. Many social problems arise, indeed, from the failure to protect children from the sins of their parents, and there is nothing to be said for arrangements that penalize children deliberately because of the anti-social behaviour of their parents. However, wrong incentives tending to encourage marriage break-down must result unless the desertion of children by fathers and mothers is made unprofitable and expensive, rather than profitable and cheap as it is in most countries today.

The Graham-Hall Committee proposed the removal of limits on maintenance allowances but made no proposals for the collection of money from the fathers or for the extension of help to fatherless families. This they regarded as a task for central government, and they added:

'We understand that the needs of the fatherless families are included in the Government's review of the social services at the present time.'

They looked to a 'new perspective of state and personal obligations to "fatherless families" and a far-reaching evolution of the maintenance system within the next decade or so.'[1] Government and public opinion have to come to terms with this question: how

[1] Graham-Hall (1967), p. 77.

are we to support the children in fatherless families, which means in practice supporting the mother also, without increasing incentives for the break-up of marriage? Mother and child must look to the state for support as they do now under the non-contributory benefit scheme. Fathers who can pay should pay; a man's duty to support his children is really a duty to the state rather than a private debt. The collection of the money, using the P.A.Y.E. system, could be modelled on the 'claw-back' for family allowances which could take into account a man's responsibilities. However, support for fatherless children is intimately bound up with support for all children. Family policy which raises, step by step, the level of living of families to that of the childless will make it more possible for absent fathers to support their children. Sidney Webb in 1909 pointed out that a minimum income was necessary for carrying out minimum social obligations:

'While it becomes more and more imperative, in the public interest, to enforce the fulfilment of personal and parental and marital responsibility on every adult it becomes more and more clear that no such responsibility can be effectively enforced without at the same time ensuring to every adult the opportunity of fulfilling them.'[1]

It is highly undesirable for any child, particularly an older child, to feel that his father has been replaced by a Post Office book entitling his mother to a small fixed maintenance allowance and that this is the full extent of the state's interest in his begetting. In Sweden[2] and Germany[3] it is thought desirable that a court of law[4] should have a responsibility for every child fatherless because he is illegitimate. Other fatherless children may be placed under guardianship if it seems in their interest. This is not the custom in the United Kingdom, but nevertheless the court should pursue and be seen to be pursuing the child's right to parental support. Because adequate machinery for collection of maintenance money is not available, the courts in the United Kingdom have quite generally failed to extract money from deserting fathers and it is

[1] Webb (1916 reprint), p. 44.
[2] Sweden (1964), Provision for Children Born out of Wedlock, Swedish Institute, Stockholm, mimeographed.
[3] Köhler (1963), pp. 30 and 34.
[4] The Swedish family court has power to appoint guardians but has not all the power of the lower courts.

at this point that the courts need the support of government. The tax authorities are specialized and experienced in the collection of money. The remedies for variation of orders and for the plea of 'other responsibilities' which are now available would remain if the P.A.Y.E. system were used to collect maintenance debts.

Many countries use tax concessions to help fatherless families. In Sweden[1] the single parent counts as a 'family taxpayer', and as such is entitled to a personal allowance double that of the single person in compiling her or his taxable income. Further, there is a lower rate of tax on taxable incomes under the 'family tax scale' than under the 'single taxpayer scale'. At the income brackets in which over half single parents (mostly, of course, single mothers) are found, the single parent pays half the percentage on his income paid by a single childless taxpayer. This is more valuable than the United Kingdom child tax allowances. Local income taxes are a major part of personal taxation in Sweden, and here earning wives with children have special tax allowances. A flat-rate family allowance worth about £62 is available for each child including the first. There is no specific child tax allowance.

In the U.S.A.[2] the lone mother or lone father (or a husband whose wife is incapacitated or institutionalized for at least ninety days), may deduct expenses paid from income up to a maximum of $600 for one dependent child under 13 years of age, and up to $900 for two or more dependants. The same deductions may be made for the cost of maintaining dependent persons of any age who are handicapped: $600 is the tax exemption for an adult or dependent child. A fatherless or motherless family thus receives up to one extra exemption for a dependent child and one and a half extra exemptions for more than one dependent child.

In France the relief from tax is provided by the income-splitting system, the 'quotient familial'. The quotient is 1·0 for the single taxpayer and 2·0 for a married couple and 0·5 for each child. The income is divided by the quotient to determine the tax payable, and the tax attributable to a single part is then multiplied by the total number of parts to give the total amount payable. The widow or widower with dependent children has a

---

[1] *Taxes in Sweden* (1963), pp. 12 and 16.
[2] United States Treasury Department, Internal Revenue Service (1965).

quotient of 2·0, as if the other spouse were still living. Any other single person who makes a home for a child before it reaches the age of 10 has a quotient of 1·5, plus, of course, the 0·5 for every child. French tax law is thus more generous to the widow than to the divorced or separated wife or unmarried mother, but makes a substantial concession to all fatherless families.

In the United Kingdom, in contrast to Sweden, France and the United States, the single mother is at a disadvantage. She is treated as a single person for tax purposes, and receives the tax-free allowance of £220 plus her earned income allowance plus the additional personal allowance for a resident housekeeper if she is working full time. A wife may earn up to £220 tax free before paying tax, her husband receives for her £120 tax-free personal allowance, and there are no conditions on the amount she works. Thus, for an earning wife a man receives tax allowances of £120 and £220, if she earns less than £283 a year, plus £220 for himself. The lone mother who works is thus more heavily taxed than the wife who works, although her needs are greater. Maintenance money is taxed as unearned income. A child's maintenance from his father is now aggregated with his mother's income for tax purposes where the court ordered it to be paid to the child. Many reforms are needed to help fatherless families, amongst them is the reclassification of maintenance money as earned income, the extension of the husband and wife personal allowance to single parents and of the wife's earned income allowance to the working single mother.

The measures needed to support the fatherless family and protect its children will differ from one country to another. Family policy is concerned with all measures to improve the viability of the family and the reduction in the number of fatherless families. In some countries with weaker marriage traditions than in Western Europe, employment preferences for legally married persons may be appropriate to increase the incentive to long-term relationships and stable families.

The final misfortune for a child is to be deprived of all parental care and of home life. This final misfortune continues to befall children whose parents are neither neglectful nor lacking in affection but who have been unable to cope with the pressures of high rents, low wages, sickness, unemployment and other

misfortunes. The mother of a fatherless family known to the
author had debts accumulated during the distress and confusion of
her marriage break-up. It was suggested to her that she should
put the children into the care of a local authority or voluntary
society and work to pay off the debts. It would have cost more to
keep the children in care than the sum of her indebtedness. She
refused, and with the help of a social worker managed to keep
her children with her. In spite of the increased 'preventive' help
to families, notably under the 1963 Children and Young Persons
Act, the number of children coming into care is still going up. In
many cases the misfortunes discussed in this chapter lie behind
the final misfortune of 'the child deprived of home life'. The
Supplementary Benefits Commission[1] should review every case of
a child going into care from parents dependent on their allowances,
and should continually review any rule which increases the
pressure of misfortune and tends to break up complete families
or fatherless or motherless families, as, for example, restrictions
on the payments by the ministry local offices of rents, debts or
mortgage repayments. If a child is taken or received into care
from parents who are not guilty of neglect or cruelty but are
victims of misfortune, the social security system must be said
to have failed.

Social security has resulted in the United Kingdom in a transfer
of resources from parents to non-parents, during the decades since
the war. But during these years the *social services* have become
more and more family centred in the United Kingdom, and the
investment content of these services is high. Children's departments of local authorities may now, under the Children and
Young Persons Act of 1963, spend money on preventive action to
keep children in their own homes, including assisting families
financially. The emphasis on social services is on support for the
family unit. Services for the mentally or physically handicapped
have moved in the same direction. The report of the Seebohm
Committee has recommended the co-ordination of all the departments of the local authorities which deal with the family.[2] The
work of these services is hampered by the social security system
of allowances and benefits which pays too little regard to family

[1] This replaced the National Assistance Board in 1966.
[2] Seebohm Report (1968).

needs. The various contribution-related schemes for unemployment, sickness and retirement pensions all make a small contribution to this problem by relieving some families from the need to support adult dependants, and by providing small children's benefits in some cases. However, these schemes make only a very modest contribution to the long-term social problems because, unlike the Local Authority services, they are biased against the family and are not family oriented. It does not, of course, follow that contribution-related schemes are unnecessary or a bad thing. It does follow that they are inadequate, more particularly because their investment content is low. It also follows that allowances for childless persons should be held steady while the allowances for children take the first step towards priority in meeting need. A first priority is the introduction of age-relation into all children's scales. The least-favoured group under flat-rate allowances is, of course, dependent young persons in their middle and later teens. The social investment content of such changes would be high.

CHAPTER TEN

Costs and Benefits of Home and School

The total resources of the United Kingdom are much less than is needed to provide a modest-but-adequate standard of living for everyone. The great majority of families with dependent children in the United Kingdom are hard-pressed, with prosperity numbers less than 2. The genuinely affluent society is a long way in the future. It follows that economic growth must remain a national goal for a long time. Economic growth depends upon producing ever greater numbers of skilled and educated work people, managers and members of the professions. The first chapter of this book began with the view of an American commission of inquiry that society will concentrate more and more in the next thirty years on investment in human capital. This investment includes expenditure on education in all forms from pre-school to higher education and vocational training. There is a considerable literature on what is called 'the economics of education', which discusses the dependence of economic growth on increasing the educational level of populations, and how this should be done from country to country according to the level of development. These concepts are becoming increasingly familiar to the general non-specialist readers.[1]

Education provides the outstanding escape route from poverty for individual men and women, and for nations. It has come to be understood that, given the right education, no man, at least in a developed country, is likely to be poor, but that poverty is the likely lot of every man or woman who receives an education that is inadequate or inappropriate to the society in which he has to live. Education has great power for good and evil quite apart from its economic consequences, but both general and vocational education

---

[1] A source book on this subject is available in paperback: Blaug (1968). See also Bowen, W. C. (1963), in Appendix 4 to Robbins Report. Other books and papers under Bell, Daniel (1968); Blaug (1966); Darras (1966); Douglas, J. W. B. (1968); Kuusi (1961); Robinson and Vaizey (1966); Vaizey (1962 and 1966); Weisbrod (1966); Zeitlin (1962).

are also essential to the wealth of nations. Education has, therefore, an economic investment quality both for the individual and for a nation. It is the argument of this chapter that 'the economics of the family' is a parallel study of 'the economics of education'. The investment in human capital is made both by the school authorities and the parents. There is a growing volume of educational research showing that a bad school can offset the influence of a good home, and that a bad home can offset the influence of a good school. There is also, however, strong evidence that good teaching in the best primary and secondary schools can partly but not wholly offset the deficiencies of parents. Indeed, the investment made by parents in the rearing of their children and the investment made in their schooling are complementary. The typical child, by the time he leaves school, has benefited from an investment in his rearing by his parents and an investment by the Government in his schooling. On the average the investment by the parents is larger than that of the Government.

Professor Douglas, in his report on the National Survey of children born in 1946, showed that most of the nation's inherited talent never reaches college or university.[1] More than half the boys of high ability born in manual working-class homes are likely to spend their lives in manual working-class occupations. This loss of talent cannot be blamed upon the schools alone, but is a consequence of the inadequacy of the total investment in these children by home and school. There is similar evidence from other countries.[2]

The literature on investment in education is largely concerned with the return on money spent on school, college and university education. There is by comparison only a very small literature concerned with the larger investment made by parents in rearing children. It is a theme of this book that the future quality of society depends upon the resources available to parents for exercising their family responsibilities. It follows that the return to individuals and society from the large sums now spent on education depends very much on the complementary expenditure by parents on their families.

[1] Douglas (1968), p. 100.
[2] Tabard (1967), Part 2, Section 2; Darras (1966), p. 384; Bourdieu, P. (1964).

H*

Outstanding social documents of post-war Britain are the Robbins, Crowther, Newsom and Plowden Reports on education.[1] The recommendations of these reports have had, and will have, many important consequences for the families of Britain, but they do not pretend to see the problems of families and of rearing children as a whole, but only in the context of school and college environments. These reports, and notably the Plowden Report, nevertheless are profoundly aware of the limitations placed by the home environment on the achievement of the educational system, but it was only within their terms of reference to examine and make recommendations about the extra-family environment of children. It was not part of their task to study ways of increasing the income of families or of relieving the present heavy taxation of the family, or to comment upon the increasing transfer of resources from parents to non-parents that has resulted from post-war social legislation.

In the United Kingdom and the U.S.A. family policy is only in embryo, and is still an unfamiliar concept except to a small minority who have studied continental experience. The great contribution of both the United Kingdom and the U.S.A. to the study of education is making it increasingly apparent that the right deployment of resources requires a family policy that will ensure not only that one public agency is not undoing the work of another, but that the parents are not so oppressed by inadequate resources, bad housing or ill-health that they cannot co-operate with the schools in the bringing up of their children. Each successive post-war United Kingdom report on education is more conscious of family problems than the last. The Plowden Report of 1966 stated:

'It has long been recognized that education is concerned with the whole man; henceforth it must be concerned with the whole family.'[2]

The national survey (1946–68) showed that high parental interest alone could not counter entirely the deficiencies of the poorest schools. The Plowden Report suggested a concentration on the educational priority areas in which

[1] See Bibliography under these titles.
[2] Plowden Report, vol. 1, p. 48.

"too many children leave school. . . . . without the knowledge to fit them for a part more intellectually demanding than their fathers or their grandfathers. . . . . they will suffer, and so will the economy; both needlessly. It should not be assumed that even the ablest children can surmount every handicap. They may suffer as much as any from adverse conditions.'[1]

These words apply equally to parents. It should not be assumed that even the most devoted and loving parent can surmount every handicap. Any step which removes strain and disappointment from parents and makes the child-rearing years of a man's or a woman's life happier and more satisfying will show dividends in the attitude of these parents to their children and to their children's education. Those who can earn their living and become respected members of the community are the successes of both the educational and family environments, and provide the return on the investment of both family and school. In the words of Pestalozzi, 'The aim of education is not to perfect scholarly knowledge but to prepare the individual to stand on his own feet'. The failures are those who fail to earn a satisfactory living or become a charge on the community. There are, of course, degrees of success and failure and there are other possible criteria of success and failure. However, the economic viability of the individual is a yard-stick that accords well with the concept of investment.

Children agree with Pestalozzi. A survey of the opinions of school leavers of 15 was conducted by the Government Social Survey for the Schools Council.[2] 'School', said the children, 'should help you to become independent and stand on your own feet.' The children wanted their schools to teach them the skills required to 'help you to get as good a job or career as possible'. These school leavers know the facts of life. Within a few years these young people will be married and have children to support, and the quality of their family life and their relationships with spouse and children will be affected by the ability of the man to support his family at a decent level of living, to compete in the labour market, and of the woman to do likewise until she has children and then to cope with the trough of the family life cycle. Even the poorest young men and women marry full of hope.

---

[1] Plowden Report, vol. 1, p. 54.
[2] Schools Council (1968), Inquiry No. 1.

The strain of living on a low wage in an ugly neighbourhood, and above all in poor housing, defeats these hopes. As children arrive, and as they grow older and more expensive, the parents come to realize that they will never leave their poor neighbourhood, never see better times while their children are in the house. An American sociologist has described the cut-off point in the hopefulness of poor parents:

"In other words there are cut-off points in parents' optimism and confidence about themselves, the future of their families, and in their belief that the future could be affected by their efforts alone. This cut-off point in parental optimism and confidence is one of the most disastrous phenomena affecting child rearing.'[1]

Alfred Marshall, over sixty years ago, described the attitude of mind which is required if the educational horizon for each generation is to enlarge:

". . . it requires the habit of distinctly realizing the future, of regarding a distant event as of nearly the same importance as if it were close at hand; this habit is at once a chief product and a chief cause of civilization.'[2]

Alfred Marshall gave the only answer to the question, how can the number of parents with this attitude of mind be increased:

'There are few practical problems in which the economist has a more direct interest than those relating to the principles on which the expense of the education of children should be divided between the state and the parents.'[3]

The 'economics of the family' is a familiar subject among continental economists and sociologists and has a long history. Dr Max Wingen, of the German Ministry of Family Affairs, who is a leading German authority on social security, has written on family policy from many angles. He places great stress on the family contribution to education as a form of social investment:

'An important role is played by this special expenditure by a family on

[1] Lewis, Hylan (1961).
[2] Marshall (1890), 1927 edition, p. 217.
[3] Marshall, op. cit., p. 216.

the education of the children which is facilitated by policies for equalising the family burden. This expenditure is, in its consequences, essentially investment rather than consumption and is a form of social investment of growing importance. . . . The growth of the whole economy and the prospects of a more satisfactory distribution of income in the future depend increasingly on this type of investment. Indeed the more economic help to the family, and family policy, are focused in such a way as to provide the children with a favourable educational environment, the more rapidly will a distribution of national income be achieved that is favourable to the economic growth of the country.'[1]

Dr Wingen is not concerned only with the economic return from a family policy, but with the well-being of the family as an end in itself, and with the family as the main social unit providing the continuity of values and attitudes from one generation to the next. The family is, however, also a main influence in promoting social and economic advance that depends upon each generation having a better education or greater skill than the last. The work opportunities for the uneducated and unskilled are diminishing in all developed and developing countries. Economic advance depends on spreading education and skill ever more widely. This will not happen fast enough unless the economic resources are made available to families.

The distribution of the costs and benefits of education can be illustrated from the decision to raise the school leaving age from 15 to 16. The direct cost of the extra year of school education,[2] including teachers' salaries and school accommodation, was estimated by the Ministry at £60 million a year for the original date, 1970.[3] Following the Weaver estimates, adjusted for increases in prices, the cost of maintaining these children at home at a modest standard during this extra year will be at least £70 million a year. Earnings forgone by these 350,000 children between 16 and 17 years old will be about £100 million.

The total cost of raising the school leaving age will therefore

---

[1] Wingen (1964), p. 257.

[2] There are two leaving dates (1968): pupils reaching 15th birthday from September to January may leave at the end of Easter term; pupils reaching 15th birthday after January and before September stay to the end of the Summer term. It is presumed at present that the same ruling will apply to pupils after 16th birthday when leaving age is raised in 1972.

[3] Communication from Department of Education and Science.

be about £160 million a year. Of this sum £60 million will be paid by the general taxpayer, at least £70 million by the parents of the 350,000 adolescents concerned, and £20 to £30 million in a reduced expenditure by the adolescents on themselves. The largest contribution to the cost of raising the school leaving age will be paid by a quite small minority of parents of about 350,000 families. About one-quarter of all children continue at school beyond the present school leaving age of 15 without any measure of compulsion. The additional 350,000 children who will have to continue at school until 16 plus after 1972 belong generally to the larger and poorer families whose children would not otherwise continue at school beyond age 15 plus. The great majority of these families are hard-pressed and a substantial minority are poor. The *costs* of raising the school leaving age are seen to be very unevenly distributed and to fall mainly on a small minority of poorer families, who have in any event, on the average, a lower standard of living than the non-parents, as we have seen.

So much for costs; how then are the benefits distributed? The official journal, *Economic Trends*, assumes, without discussion, that public expenditure on education is a 'benefit' to parents. Professor Kaim-Caudle, of Durham University, also assumes that public expenditure on schooling is an 'Aid to Parents'.[1] It is suggested, nevertheless, that the benefit to parents of raising the school leaving age will be altogether less than the cost to parents.

The Crowther Report of 1959 reaffirmed the desirability of raising the school leaving age, but not because of its benefit to parents. Indeed, the benefits of raising the school leaving age listed by the Crowther Report do not include any benefit to parents. The report placed particular stress on education as a 'nation-building' investment,[2] and upon the 'demand for more educated workers and for more deeply educated workers at almost all levels in industry'. The report expounded a case for greater

---

[1] Professor Kaim-Caudle in 1967 in a paper, 'Aid to Families', before the Annual Conference of the Institute of Municipal Treasurers and Accountants, classifies the cost of Secondary School between the ages of 11 and 16 as an 'Aid to Parents' of £140 per annum per child (par. 2). Later (par. 33) he categorizes the proposed *extra year* at school from 16 to 17 as a 'tax on parents' of £260 per child in income forgone. See also Nicholson, J. L. (1964); Central Statistical Office, *Economic Trends*, Aug. 1966 and July 1968.

[2] Crowther (1959), p. 55.

expenditure on education, 'if this country is to keep a place among the nations that are in the van of spiritual and material progress'.

The pay-off from investment in education accrues to the person educated and to the community at large.[1] The return on investment in education is also, of course, spread over a lifetime. A man's wage or salary obviously does not depend only upon his own education, but also upon the education of the community in which he works. The wages or salary that a man can earn depend, indeed, both upon the man himself and also upon his social environment that is heavily influenced by the education of other people. The wage of a carpenter or the salary of an engineer of given skill or training varies from one large community to the next. Part of the benefit of education accrues, therefore, directly to the man, so that the better his education the higher the wage or salary he can command. Another part of the benefit contributes to the raising of the standard of living of the community as a whole.

Parents certainly benefit from the rising standard of living of a community as a whole that results from a rising standard of education, but it is not apparent that they benefit on average more than non-parents. Nor is it apparent that the parents of three or four children benefit any more than the parents of one child. All people in developed countries are completely dependent in their old age on the flow of goods and services produced by other people's children. However, much of the benefit of education accrues after the parents who made the investment in their children are dead and gone.

Parents who successfully rear a family of children do, of course, enjoy psychic rewards; but they also pay heavily for such rewards. Ignoring altogether the long unpaid hours devoted to rearing a family, the material costs far exceed the material benefits, which accrue very largely to the children themselves and the community at large over long periods of years extending for a generation after the parents' death.

The costs to the community of every extension of compulsory education are no doubt fully covered by benefits in due course,[2]

---

[1] Blaug (1968), especially Part 3; Weisbrod (1966), p. 2 and Tables 2 and 3.

[2] Economic Report of the President to Congress, January 1963: 'Education is the ultimate source of much of our increased productivity . . . one of the deepest roots of economic growth.'

but only a small part of these benefits accrue to parents who have hitherto had to pay most of the costs. Parents, indeed, make a very large investment in human capital, but their children and many other people besides receive most of the dividends.

If the costs of rearing children were distributed in roughly the same way as the benefits, then the total expenditure incurred in having children, and not only the expenditure on educational services, would be spread across the community at large. The parents would certainly be required to pay some part of the cost of child-rearing, but not such a high proportion of it that the standard of living of most households with dependent children would be depressed, as at the present time, substantially below the standard of living of most childless households. The 'burden' would be 'shared', translating the language of the European Community and Scandinavia.

There has been a centuries-old tradition of helping poor scholars that has broadened and expanded in all Western countries as the world has become wealthier. Bursaries, exhibitions and scholarships recognized the need to invest in human capital a long time before the Industrial Revolution. Today there are still scholarships and exhibitions, and there are also school maintenance allowances and family allowances that are other forms of financial help to families intended to help with the rearing of children.

In pre-industrial times the United Kingdom could only afford to produce a small minority of educated people, and only required such a small minority. Today, it is accepted that the further advance of society depends upon there being a large minority of quite highly educated people and upon the steady growth of this minority. There are already communities with over one-third of all young persons proceeding after leaving school to take courses of higher education. Scholarships and exhibitions to help very small minorities of scholars are no longer appropriate. A family policy should be based upon a synoptic view of the needs of families and of ways of ensuring educational advance that includes scholarships, exhibitions, school maintenance allowances and family allowances as a whole, recognizing that they have essentially the same purpose of increasing the investment in the next generation.

Dr Douglas, in his report on the children in the National Survey, emphasizes the importance of the educational system sifting out the able pupils from all types of background to allow them to qualify for posts of responsibility. Today, a larger number of such able pupils are sifted out than ever before, but a majority of the able pupils are still not sifted out and do not make the grade. For this the educational system itself is only partly to blame and is not, indeed, the main culprit. A certain minimum investment is needed in even an able child by both home and school for it to rise out of a very humble environment. There is a threshold of parental and school care and attention that even able children need before they can take full advantage of education. The majority of able children today are below this threshold and do not get their chance. Most of the able children from working-class homes leave school too soon. Dr Douglas speaks of 'the large group of young men and women who, though potentially capable of entering one of the professions, choose manual work'.[1] The benefits accruing to the community from the investment in education are reduced by the wastage of talent. The abolition of 11 plus and other selection procedures, or of streaming, will not necessarily stop this wastage. Dr. Douglas is cautious in his conclusion:

'The fact that inequalities existed within the old selective system does not mean that they will disappear when selective examinations are abolished, and the fact that it is the pupils from poor homes who have been handicapped in the past, does not necessarily mean that they will lose these handicaps when comprehensive education becomes universal.[2]

The home environment is more to blame than the schools. There is no simple answer to the question of how to give every child the chance in life which his abilities merit. Certainly re-arrangements of the schools system alone will not suffice. A policy of help to parents is needed. Wastage of talent amongst children is one reason for a family policy.

Help to children by the provision of free education is, of course, widely regarded as an investment in the future. Help to families in rearing the same children is placed in a different category and

[1] Douglas (1968), p. 100.   [2] *Idem*, p. 65.

is subject to quite different standards inherited from the old Poor Law. There is a great variety of means tests operated by local authorities for free school meals, maintenance allowances for children over 15, entitlement to free school clothing, entitlement to help in attending colleges of further education, and university maintenance allowances.[1]

The means tests differ from one authority to the next, but are always complicated and oppressive. A description of the burden of the means-tested applications was given in a letter signed, 'Retired craftsman's wife':

'To get help with school uniform is not easy, as countless broken-down mothers, temporarily unable to work, or they would not apply, have found after filling in forms and haggling with husbands over details of earnings. Overtime, desperately undertaken to catch up after the last spell of sick pay, may well boost a man's average wage, over the period assessed, above the qualifying level, while exhausting him back to the inadequate basic and again to three days waiting and sick pay.'[2]

Most of the scales used by local authorities for these purposes are below any reasonable definition of the poverty line, with PNs of less than 0·8 and 0·7 and even lower. In 1965 the maximum maintenance allowance available for a Manchester school child of 16 was £80 a year, and then only if parents were living on less than £380 a year plus £75 a year for each child.[3] A larger family of older children at this level would have a PN of only about 0·5.

Of course, the income tax authorities impose a 'means test' on every individual, and begin to tax families only marginally above the poverty level, and sometimes even below this level. It is a sad commentary that the tax man's means test is not considered harsh enough for poor families with dependent children, and that such families are subject to a great variety of harsher means tests operated by a substantial local bureaucracy. Only parents suffer from these particular inquisitions. The income tax means test is operated by central Government, and these harsher means

---

[1] Corbett, A. (1966); Reddin (1968).
[2] *Guardian*, 26 Apr. 1967.
[3] Scheme of Maintenance Allowances, Manchester Education Committee, S3/MO/MM (June 1964).

tests oppressing only parents of dependent children are operated by local authorities. In fairness to local authorities it must be emphasized that they only have power to raise money by local rates on property, which may well be an appropriate means of raising money for refuse disposal, sewage or street lighting but is a regressive form of taxation that cannot be used to raise money from those people who could afford to pay for educational services. Help to families should be paid for by central Government, unless there is a change in the powers of taxation of local authorities.

The benefits to the community of many services to families are often very substantial even in the short term, although these do not necessarily increase the receipts from rates! The net cost to the economy of services that encourage more women to work is particularly low. For example, the cost to the community of day nurseries and nursery schools, even very good ones, is very low even in the short term, just because they enable large numbers of mothers to work who could not or would not otherwise do so. The total net cost to the country, even in the short term, of this part of the Plowden Committee's recommendations would probably be negligible. The Plowden Committee estimated that their recommendations for the extension of nursery schools might result in mothers' earnings by full-time and part-time work increasing by about £20 million. The value of output or the increase in GNP resulting from this work would, of course, be in excess of these additional earnings and might well approach the total cost estimated for the same year at £36 million. This conclusion has, of course, a wider importance for families with children of all ages. Measures in support of families, even quite expensive measures, cost on balance very little at all if they encourage more mothers to work even part-time. The extra contribution of the mothers to the GNP offsets the cost of the measures.[1]

Certainly, the short-term cost of nursery schools is very small, but any expenditure upon them also has a high human investment content. If it is inevitable that large numbers of mothers of both pre-school children and school children should work, then it must be the concern of family policy to reduce as far as possible any undesirable consequences to the children. A high priority should be the Plowden Committee recommendations for the extension of

[1] Plowden Report, Chapter 31, Annex B.

nursery school education. The Plowden Report recommends an extension of nursery schools and day nurseries in its plans for the Educational Priority Areas, advocating that between 1968 and 1972, all 4-to 5-year-olds in these areas should be offered nursery school places or day nursery places. Thereafter nursery school education should be offered to children in other areas. The report suggests that this might be accomplished by 1977. The report quotes United Kingdom studies and American experts on how:

'Nursery education can compensate for social deprivation and special handicaps. . . . The argument thus leads to the conclusion that one way in which the consequences of social deprivations can be overcome is to provide richer experience as soon as children are ready for nursery education.'[1]

The school meal service is another example where the real cost to the country is largely offset by benefits even in the short term. If, for example, the provision of school meals is exceptional, as in Holland, then there is a strong incentive for mothers to stay at home in order to provide the children with a prepared meal. The proportion of mothers of school children who work is much lower in Holland than in the United Kingdom, and the failure to provide school meals is certainly one factor discouraging Dutch mothers from working. The loss in GNP due to fewer mothers working, or working reduced hours, can offset a substantial part if not the whole cost of the school meals. Yudkin and Holme wrote:

'The school meals service is almost taken for granted these days but its importance cannot be over-estimated. As far as working mothers are concerned it is as directly responsible for enabling them to be away from home all day as any other single factor.'[2]

Even if school meals are provided, the charge made for the meals influences whether they are taken, and the higher the charge the more children will choose not to accept them and go home instead and the less the mothers will work on the average. Indeed, payment by the Government for school meals increases the GNP, and forcing the parents to pay reduces the GNP. Can the country afford to pay for school meals? is a false question. The country as

[1] Plowden Report, par. 131–77.   [2] Yudkin and Holme (1963), p. 60.

a whole benefits from the Government's paying. This is not, of course, true of many other headings of Government expenditure which consume national resources and offer no return either in the short term or at all.

No one, of course, suggests that school children should not be fed at midday. Children's meals are an essential charge against the GNP and have to be paid for. The cost is clearly one that should be spread across all taxpayers as a part of 'sharing the burden'. The strength of the childless, non-parent lobby is the only argument for the recent movements to load as much as possible of the cost of school meals on to parents who can, on average, least afford to pay.

The case for free school meals was stated by Alva Myrdal in Sweden nearly 30 years ago:

'The well-to-do parents need never feel that they are accepting a dole as they will certainly pay for these luncheons in their tax bill. . . . The school meal for children should, on the whole, be regarded neither as a commodity for which to pay, nor as a charitable gift for which to thank. It should be regarded as common co-operative house-holding on the part of all citizens.'[1]

However, no matter what the importance of school meals, the ways in which they are paid for are no more than symbolic of the much wider question of how the rearing of the next generation should be paid for as a whole. This is one thing that family policy is about.

The quality of the next generation and of life ten, twenty, thirty years hence will depend upon the total expenditure upon home and school life in this generation. The merits of various forms of direct help to families have been under debate for many years, and family allowances have emerged as the most satisfactory. Family allowances in Western Europe are summarized in Appendix 3.

Professor Alfred Sauvy addressed a conference on Social Security of the European Community about these allowances:

'The role of family allowances is, above all, a social role: thanks to these allowances children can be better nourished, better cared for (as

[1] Myrdal, A. (1945), p. 284.

for example by the "mother at home" allowance), better housed (which, is, in particular, the effect of the personal housing subsidy which is given in France by the family allowance fund). What will the consequences be for the development of the population? The effect of these allowances is seen rather in quality than in quantity. Put in another way, their influence will be felt in the state of health and in the physical and educational development of children though it will have no appreciable effect on the death rate at least in families which have already reached a certain level of income. In particular, infant morality is not now influenced by family allowances because it no longer depends directly on family income. But the height, weight and general development of children are favourably influenced. . . . Family allowances tend to increase the length of time children are at school and therefore defer their entry into the labour force; this must be considered a desirable result because it raises the quality of the employed population.'[1]

How are the costs and benefits of family allowances distributed? Family allowances are, of course, transfer payments. They do not have any direct effect on the GNP but transfer income from taxpayers in general to families with dependent children. As most taxpayers are non-parents, and income in the hands of parents results in a greater investment in human capital, family allowances result in such a greater investment. The resistance to increased family allowances is not based on considered views of the national interest, but upon the reluctance of non-parents to pay their fair share of the cost of rearing children and upon anti-natalist fears, discussed in the Epilogue. The argument that the country cannot afford higher family allowances derives from this reluctance and not from any tenable economic argument. There are, of course, £1,000 millions spent for ephemeral purposes that yield no dividends at all, in contrast to the return spreading over a long period of years that flows from the successful nurturing of a child.

The very recent but growing world literature on the economics of education, whatever its limitations, is beginning to throw light upon the costs and benefits of education, and the studies will be pursued with ever greater vigour as educational expenditure rises. To be truly fruitful these studies will, however, have to extend to examination of the total environment of children.

[1] Sauvy (1962), Communauté Économique Européenne conference (1962), vol. 2, p. 27.

The Department of Education and Science has supported this view in a series of papers on 'Education under Social Handicap':

'The problem . . . cannot be tackled by education and the schools alone, but only by the schools working as one element in a concerted attack by the social and welfare services.'[1]

Another paper in the same series quotes educational failure, often associated with poverty and an unstable social background, as 'a fundamental root of much of the malaise among certain groups of young people and probably a major cause of the present increase in delinquency'.[2]

Problem families are, however, only a small part of the canvas. The endeavour to concentrate all attention on the small minority of problem families, or upon a different, arbitrarily defined minority of poor families, is to sweep most of the problem under the carpet. The fate of most children, as Dr Douglas has shown, is severely circumscribed by the limitations of their home as well as of their school environment, and nations will gain by any removal of these limitations. The Newsom Report entitled, 'Half Our Future', recommended urgent research into the environmental handicaps of school children.[3] The evidence of the Newsom Committee showed that the central task is not to be found in small minorities of problem or poor families but is much wider. The task is to improve the chances of the average child.

These distinguished educational reports are a long way ahead of the political parties in their thinking and it is, of course, the accepted purpose of such reports to recommend the right action for the Government and local authorities, who will always take time to respond. Even the best Governments can only promote progress in steps from where we are today, and no Government can do all the things suggested as needing to be done about families. It is not, however, only the difficulty and cost of implementing the recommendations in the Plowden, Newsom and

[1] Education and Science, Department of, Reports on Education, No. 22, June 1965.

[2] Education and Science, Department of, Reports on Education, No. 20, March 1965.

[3] Newsom (1963), Principal Recommendations, No. 3, p. xvi; and see pp. 16 and 26.

Crowther Reports that is inhibiting their acceptance by Government; old and deep misconceptions and prejudices are being carried forward uncritically.

The notion that education is only a benefit to parents, and that Government educational expenditure is simply a subsidy to parents, is damaging, but persists in official documents and speeches though not in the more serious papers concerned with the economics of education. Nor is this found in the educational reports themselves. This notion cannot survive any serious study of the distribution of educational costs and benefits.

It is another misconception that social policies can be progressive, in any acceptable sense of the word, if their consequence is to transfer resources from parents to non-parents, thereby reducing the investment in the next generation. Such policies prejudice the future, instead of embodying a 'distinct realization of the future', in the words of Alfred Marshall. Such policies are wrapped in fine words and intentions, but if, for example, they persuade or compel parents to spend less money on rearing their children and to put by more money for their old age they are anti-progressive in any objective sense and basically inconsistent with the conclusions of the Plowden and Newsom Committees. Progressive policies must transfer resources from non-parents to families, and to educational services, not the reverse. Progressive policies must transfer resources from the childless to the child-rearing years of the family life cycle. Progressive policies must transfer resources from ephemeral consumption with no pay-off to the educational services.

There is, again, the notion that children are a private indulgence of parents, that babies are just another kind of consumer durable like pianos and television sets. The suggestion that parents behave within the family towards the other members like 'economic man' from purely economic motives does not merit discussion. However, this notion might be of some consequence if it were to be shown that human reproductive behaviour was economically motivated; this is discussed in an Epilogue to this book, 'Does Help to Families Affect the Birth-rate?'

CHAPTER ELEVEN

The Boundaries of Family Policy

Family policy must always be bounded by traditions and the extent of public support. Family policy, like all forward-looking policies, will always be threatened by the demands of the immediate future, by the pressures of short-term expediency, by the pressures for immediate consumption at the expense of longer term investment. There are, indeed, political difficulties to be overcome. Dr Simon, Permanent Head of the German Federal Ministry for Family Affairs, gave an inaugural address in 1955 in which he said that the redistribution of national income for the benefit of the family with dependent children is the essential task of social policy for our century; but he warned his audience:

'The man of politics will not take notice of these conclusions without great difficulties; we should have no illusions about this. The community will not benefit immediately but only in the future. We have, however, already examples in Western Europe showing that the difficulties are not insurmountable. These examples also show that a family policy can produce results of vital importance if its scope is wide enough.'[1]

Political parties are, however, learning that with no adequate vision of the future they quickly lose support in the modern world with its rising expectations and rising standards of education. The short-term payments to the voter for his support produce, at best, short-term support. More prolonged support for political parties in all countries today rests upon the continuing satisfaction of the rising expectations. There are few things more damaging today to the politician in office than a failure of the society that he leads to make the hoped-for progress, than stagnation and restriction, than the disappointment of the rising expectations.

There is no possibility of satisfying the rising expectations without economic growth, though growth alone may be no more than the foundation of acceptable policies. Dr Pekka Kuusi in his book *Social Policy for the Sixties*, one of the most important

[1] Simon, H. (1956), p. 193.

books on social policy published in Scandinavia in recent years, discusses 'the place and function of social policy in growth-oriented society' and asks:

'What then is the interrelation of growth and greater equality?[1] What is the place of greater social equality in the society striving for economic growth?'[2]

Dr Kuusi emphasizes the difficult balance that is essential between growth-oriented social policy and the needs of compassion. Dr Kuusi summarizes what he calls 'the burning question of the interrelation of income redistribution and growth, within the framework of the complex of public policies':

'If the primary criterion of choice is the probable effect on growth, the care of the sick should be given preference over the care of the permanently disabled and the improvement of the living conditions of children should be given preference over the aid to aged people. A growth-oriented society should, in fact, be more concerned about the labour force of tomorrow than about the labour force of yesterday. . . .

'It should be remembered, nevertheless, that the fundamental specific function of social policy is not the promotion of economic growth. Its task is to ensure the consumption possibilities of the weakest sections of the population. Therefore social policy measures cannot be designed only on the basis of their likely influence upon economic growth—not even in a growth-oriented society. The prime force, as well as the ultimate criterion of social policy is and will be the human being in need of support.[3]

The balance between the satisfaction of short-term needs and the longer term advantages of spending more money on the rearing of children merits scrutiny in the United Kingdom. The development of social security and taxation during the last twenty years has diverted resources away from families with dependent children to non-parents. The importance of the family is widely recognized but is not always reflected in the policies put into practice. The social policies of the United Kingdom are, indeed,

---

[1] In the English translation of Dr Kuusi's book the word 'equalization' is used. I have taken the liberty of substituting a more familiar translation.

[2] Kuusi (1961), p. 68.

[3] *Idem*, p. 92.

anti-growth oriented. In the United Kingdom at the present time there is not parity of treatment between children and adults, or between parents and non-parents, or between the young and the old, either in social security allowances or taxation. There is, in fact, so much leeway to be made up to meet only the short-term needs of children that there is not the least danger of any over-emphasis on social investment.

The value of all benefits received by families, including the cost of education, family allowances, health services, and social security benefits, is substantially less than these families as a whole pay in taxation including insurance contributions. The median income of parents with dependent children is also substantially lower than that of the $5\frac{1}{2}$ million married couples with no dependent children. (The median income of fatherless families is less than half that of childless couples.)

As already explained in Chapter 1, three-quarters of the next generation is being raised in only 22 per cent of United Kingdom households. The main social investment is being made by this minority of households. The equitable treatment of this minority and the full acknowledgment of their special contribution to economic growth and social progress are objectives of social policy that must take many years to attain, advancing from their present generally underprivileged status.

The International Union of Child Welfare has argued in favour of spending money on children in developing countries as a means of promoting economic growth:

'Rapid social acceleration can only be achieved through the child who is without preconceived attitudes and values. The adult is much more rigid and difficult to convince. If this is so, then investment in the child is economically beneficial since there is less waste from the investment and much more rapid growth.'

This is, of course, widely accepted, but the report continued:

'There is still evidence of double-thinking: the reiteration of the importance of the child as human resources to make physical investment meaningful, yet a denial of such priorities in the actual plans.'[1]

[1] Baig (1966), p. 1.

These last statements referred to developing countries and primarily to the countries of Asia. The double-thinking is, however, common to most countries.

The motto of the German Ministry for Family Affairs, 'Our Children, Our Future', is almost trite and is accepted by persons of goodwill everywhere, not least in the United Kingdom and the U.S.A. Our children, our future, are, however, a necessary part of the vision of a progressive society. The rising expectations are in large part expectations for our children and depend absolutely upon them. The German motto may be trite, but it is the realization of this vision in terms of hard, practical policies by the politician that will establish confidence in his wisdom, and not short-term measures of expediency at the expense of a country's future. Whatever abstract philosophy is preached, Government measures that are, in fact, biased against the family undermine a nation's vision of the future subtly, and often imperceptibly, and unintentionally.

During the last twelve months in the United Kingdom the income tax allowance for a married couple aged 65 and over has been increased from £643 to £665; the analogous allowances for a married couple plus two dependent children, one under and one over 11, is only £595 and has not been increased.[1] There is not only a bias against the family, two elderly persons being entitled to higher allowances than a family of four persons including two children, but the anti-family bias has been increased although, as we have seen, the actual cost of maintaining elderly persons is low compared with younger persons, apart from health services which are free. In the same period old-age pensions have been increased but the raising of the school leaving age has been deferred. Prescription charges in respect of children over 15 have been imposed on parents but elderly persons pay no prescription charges.

Further anti-family measures are threatened at the time of writing. The Government is proposing to introduce graduated contributions for social security benefits; it is not proposed that either the contributions or the benefits should be fairly related to

---

[1] Financial Statement 1968–9. A deduction in child tax allowances was compensated by an increase in family allowances as discussed in previous chapters.

family responsibilities. The proposals may, indeed, result in a further transfer of resources from parents to non-parents.

Medical care has been introduced in the U.S.A. for the elderly but not yet for families, so that medical resources have been diverted from families to the care of the aged. The new 'Medicare' will relieve much suffering, but an American social scientist wrote in the Journal of the American Medical Association:

'Instead of mounting extraordinary efforts on behalf of the oldest elements in the population, whose ills are emotionally compelling, should not more of our limited resources be deployed into the service of the newborn and of youth where the effects come to be realized over longer spans of years?'[1]

Medicare for children could have a higher social investment content. In the United Kingdom there is parity of medical treatment for children and the elderly under the National Health Service, though the cost of medical care for children is small by contrast with the cost of treatment for the elderly. It is probably inevitable that health services in Western society should become dominantly services to elderly people. It cannot, however, be right, as in the U.S.A., for medical services to be provided for the elderly at the expense of millions of children whose parents have to pay. A free medical service is, indeed, provided for the poorest children in U.S.A. but only subject to means test. Private insurance for medical care is a burden for American families of modest means and must compete with the other demands on the family budget. Moreover, one result of Medicare for the elderly has been to increase the cost of medical care, both at home and in hospital, for families. Medical fees, including those of pediatricians, have risen since the beginning of the Medicare scheme more than the general rise in prices.[2] American parents are witnessing a transfer of wealth from their children to the aged. It may be assumed that, in introducing Medicare for the aged, there was not the least intention to injure families. The probable effect on families of Medicare was overlooked or not considered or not given due weight. There is the same danger in a great number of public acts.

Public measures as they affect the conditions of the family are

[1] Cooper, J. (1966).   [2] Rice and Horowitz (1967).

the substance of family policy. Family policy is concerned with the ground rules of society as they affect the family, and with the many changes in these rules that are made in every country every year. Family policy is concerned with the law as it affects the family, notably the many ways in which the law makes it easier or more difficult for parents to make ends meet, and with the ways in which the law provides the family with protection against risks, notably the temporary or permanent loss of a father's earning power, or a mother's care. There is little legislation that does not influence the family environment in some measure. Family policy worthy of the name can only be a consequence of an attempt, however inadequate, to study all the interests of families in relation to one another.

In seven countries, of whom five are within the European Community, there are Ministers specially charged with watching the interests of the family. The departmental responsibilities of these Ministers vary widely between countries. In both Germany and France, projects for legislation or regulations affecting the family are submitted to the Minister charged with family affairs. In Belgium there is a Minister responsible for family affairs and housing, and since 1951 the Prime Minister has presided over a Ministerial Committee co-ordinating family policy. The Family Ministers have a watching brief on tax policy, social security legislation, education and all measures intended to help children or the family. An important role of these Ministers is to engage in a continuous dialogue with representative bodies concerned with the family.[1]

The Family Organizations of Europe[2] have no exact counterpart in the United Kingdom or the United States. They are movements of families themselves and act as pressure groups on family policy. Because of their size (the Belgian movement, for example, represents 'nearly one-quarter of the Belgian population'),[3] they have had great political influence and con-

[1] Communauté Economique Européenne, Exposé 1959, p. 276. This dialogue may be followed in the annual Exposé on social policy published by the Commission of the E.E.C. and in the publications of the Family Organizations.

[2] Fogarty (1957), Chapter 19; International Union of Family Organizations; Prigent (1960); Schorr (1965).

[3] International Union of Family Organizations, *Information Bulletin* No. 1 (1966), p. 8.

siderable success in winning concessions and help for families in
housing, educational grants, family allowances and tax policy.
The poorest families have benefited especially. The Family
Organizations have initiated and financed research on family
problems; the emphasis in which has been on the economic
position of the family. In France[1] the Family Organizations have
official support and finance, and represent family interests on
government bodies. The President of the Family Council of
Belgium, Professor Pierre de Bie, discussed the contrast between
the attitude to the family in Europe and in the United States
at a conference in New York in 1960:

'In old Europe, the problem of the economic foundations of family
security has for many long years been in the forefront of discussion at
congresses, conferences and commissions; it figures increasingly in the
programmes of movements and the large social organisations. The
principle of economic security for the family is penetrating slowly but
surely the policies of Governments.

'The contrast with the U.S.A. is startling; the American specialists
and research workers in family problems are above all preoccupied
with the relations between members of the family, the reciprocal
adaptation of spouses to each other or between parents and children, the
psychological processes that lead to the internalization of the roles of
the spouses, of father, mother and child within the nuclear family;
study the preparation for and phases of adaptation to married life,
analyse the contribution of socio-cultural factors on the reciprocal
adaptation, the marital happiness and stability of the family ties; in
contrast to Europe, the problem of the foundations of family security
figure only as a secondary problem or remain largely neglected.'[2]

The U.S.A. has made very great advances in social security
provisions in the last twenty years. There is now evidence of a
growing awareness in the U.S.A. of the need for more family-
oriented policies and of the possible convergence of the policies
of Europe and the U.S.A.

In the United States Alvin Schorr, of the Department of
Health, Education and Welfare, has written on 'Family Policy in
the United States'[3] and suggested that the United States 'may

---

[1] Talmy (1962); Beltrão (1957); Laroque (1961); Schorr (1965).
[2] de Bie (1960).
[3] Schorr (1962). See also Burns, E. M. (1968).

now conceivably be in the first stages of development towards having a national family policy'. In 1960 a group of social scientists was called together to advise the U.S. Commissioner of Social Security on 'priorities for sustaining and enriching family life'. 'The family', said these advisers, 'is, and will increasingly be, the one place a person is valued for himself and feels irreplaceable.' The great importance of the family in the socialization of children is stressed. However, there is not yet the same emphasis in the United States on the importance to a nation's future of its investment in the family. Although it is fully understood that some of the worst social problems are connected with failures of family life, the policy conclusions have not reached the statute book. Seen with European eyes, the American vision of the Great Society never rang quite true. The War on Poverty led by the President's Office of Economic Opportunity was to have been a step towards the Great Society. The United States official record showed that the problem of poverty in the U.S.A. is a problem of families with dependent children, but including a large component of fatherless families. The conclusion that the U.S.A. needs a family policy has, however, never been drawn. The U.S.A. is, for example, still the only advanced country without a system of family allowances.

The U.S.A. and, indeed, the people of every other country need the vision of the Great Society characterized by President Johnson as a world in which 'the meaning of man's life matches the marvels of man's labour'.[1] The central problem of the Great Society, said President Johnson, 'is to protect and restore a man's satisfaction in belonging to a community where he can find security and significance'. This fine vision of the future becomes tarnished, if in the pursuit of the Great Society it is forgotten that the well-being of the family is one of the objectives of all human activity. Man does not normally live in isolation without a father, mother, children or spouse. Man's 'satisfaction' begins, and should begin, with his satisfaction in belonging to a family.

The Times of London commented on the President's first year of office in a feature article under the heading 'Mr Johnson's chance of greatness'. This chance, said *The Times* commentator,

[1] Quoted in *A Nation Aroused*, 1st Annual Report of the Office of Economic Opportunity (1965), p. 10.

depended upon an appeal by the President to the American sense
of justice:

'This is a new note in American politics since the war—an almost
Biblical appeal beyond the frustrations and fears of uneasy affluence to a
force and a commitment which America's greatest leaders have never
been afraid to evoke—the force of moral obligation, the commitment to a
vision of justice.'[1]

The force of moral obligation is a political force but not if it
remains an abstract intention unrealized in policies that discharge
the moral obligation. The 'vision of justice' demands the gradual
correction of the many structural and legislative features of
American society that are biased against all families with dependent
children, and particularly against the poor and near-poor families.
Of 69·8 million children in the U.S.A. under 18 in 1966, the total
of poor and near-poor was 19·2 million.[2] The near-poor level
used was an income approximately one-third higher than the
poverty level for families of the same size and composition.
Roughly one-half of American families do not reach the modest-
but-adequate level with a PN of 2 as defined in a previous chapter.
Is justice for poor families not manifestly unrealizable in a society
in which the great majority of families with dependent children
are not treated with justice? Anti-family bias in a wide range of
policies does, of course, underlie the exceptional poverty and
suffering of the minority. A family policy should be in the fore-
ground of that big canvas, of which only a small part has ever
been painted, of the Great Society.

An enemy of right policies is the belief that men generally
behave while at work and play and in the polling booth for the
furtherance of their narrow personal economic interests. The
economists have invented the concept of 'economic man' who
has an economic scale of values, an economically one-track mind,
whose behaviour is determined by the values acquired in a
market-place where he has no friends and where total adaptation
to an environment of cut-throat competition is necessary for
survival.

Egotistical 'economic man' would, of course, die out if he

---

[1] *The Times*, 10 May 1966.   [2] Orshansky (1968).

I

existed. He is non-viable. It does not pay to have children in our industrial society in any narrow economic sense whatever. Parents, when rearing their children, behave quite contrary to what might be expected of 'economic man'. It does not generally *pay* a man to have a family, nor does it generally *pay* him to invest generously in his children, and it generally pays him better in narrow financial terms to purchase more pension or an annuity than to have another child or spend more on his existing family. A parent is less able to accumulate property, less able to provide for his old age, less likely to be socially mobile upwards than the non-parent. Parents' investment in their children depends upon instincts, and beliefs about right and wrong, and the pride and pleasure of having children and seeing them thrive, and very little indeed upon economic incentives which act in the contrary direction. All the many taxes on the family are taxes on these instincts and beliefs and not generally upon any economic surplus.

Who benefits from the investment in a young person? The main beneficiary is the young person himself. There is an extensive literature suggesting that the return on the investment in a young person is handsome to the young person himself and may, indeed, well exceed any likely return on a business investment. The return to the community from an investment in young people is also very substantial.[1] All those people who never have any children, for example, rely on other people's children to provide the flow of goods and services to support them in their old age.

The economic return to parents of the investment they make in their own children is, however, of diminishing importance. Children today rely increasingly on their parents having a pension or savings to support them in their old age and less and less expect to have to support their parents. Very few parents in present-day society ever receive back a fraction of the money that they spend on bringing-up their children. This has not, of course, always been so. Indeed, in many peasant societies today parents still look to their children, and their children alone, to support them in their old age.

Man survives today in industrial society in spite of egoistical instincts and those powerful economic incentives neither to have

[1] See Blaug (1968), Part 3, especially chapters by Hansen, Weisbrod and Blaug.

children nor to look after them that are built into the system. No child tax allowances or family allowances or family services in any country go more than a small way to compensate parents for the economic cost of bringing up children.

All civilized countries have, of course, already spread the cost of rearing children over the community in some degree, more particularly by the introduction of universal education. Universal education is, as we have seen, not a help to parents upon whom is thrown the cost of housing, feeding and tending children at ages at which they could be, and once were, independent. Universal education is an investment in the quality of the labour force of the future. The progress of society has depended upon the spread of wealth for the benefit of the next generation. The extent of the spread is both one test of the family orientation of a nation's policies and a determinant of the future progress of society. The most family oriented countries today are those of the Common Market and Scandinavia.

The main investment in the next generation has always been made by parents. There are official Swedish estimates that 77 per cent of the cost of rearing children is carried by parents.[1] There are rather similar German estimates.[2] The proportion of the cost of rearing children carried by parents in the United Kingdom is probably not very different. It is an illusion that the state does or will make the main investment in children. The altruistic instincts of man are strongest within the family. Parents do, however, need Government support at many points. Taxation of the family reduces the investment in the next generation.

The investment criterion provides a strong argument against limiting aid to families that are very poor. Whether a man's income is £500 or £3,000 a year, it is altogether better for a country that it should be used in rearing a family of children than in maintaining a bachelor establishment, and this should be fully reflected in taxation and social security legislation. The Government should seek to maximize the investment in the nation's future. A narrow egalitarianism related to incomes, as distinct from a philosophy of income distribution related to family needs, will not achieve this end.

[1] van Hofsten and Karlsson (1961), p. 142.
[2] See, for example, Jessen (1955).

Governments have a responsibility for the long-term future of their countries. Governments must take responsibility for a substantial part of the investment in the next generation by supporting and protecting families. A laissez-faire attitude to the family does not work. Alva Myrdal in her book entitled *Nation and Family*, published in 1940, wrote:

'It has been the thesis of this book and of the whole Swedish population programme, that economic forces tend to develop adversely to the interests of families if left to their own evolution.'[1]

Family policy proposes to influence the evolution of economic forces away from what is adverse to the family to what is beneficial to the family. Family policy proposes the redistribution of national wealth and income in favour of children, or in other words, the transfer of resources to investment in future generations. Throughout the Common Market countries family policy is similarly understood, although the emphasis on different measures implementing policy differs from country to country and differs between Scandinavia and the Common Market.

Family policy cannot be concerned only with family allowances or family income but must be concerned with all social arrangements as they affect the family. Family policy must be concerned with housing, described by the Family Organizations of Europe as 'problem No. 1 for the family'. It is unrealistic to look to the incomes of the majority of families being increased by means of family allowances or any other means to the point where they can compete in the market with the non-parents for the available housing. The discrepancies are too great. Families can only be helped by making housing more expensive to the non-parent and less expensive to the parents with dependent children by direct differential taxation of the housing and direct subsidy of the family housing. Market forces in our wage and salary economy leave the family with dependent children at a serious disadvantage in the competition for housing. As discussed in an earlier chapter, it is very largely families with children that are overcrowded and not households without children. The country ought not to be indifferent in its local tax measures as to whether a room is a

[1] Myrdal (1945), p. 219.

spare room or is occupied by a child, or whether a room is used by an adult for stamp collecting or for a child's homework.

Measures are needed that take the family cycle more into account. Young people who go out to work have a higher standard of living before marriage and for a short period after marriage until children arrive. Every encouragement should be given to young persons to save money in anticipation of their future needs, and particularly their housing needs, when they acquire a family.

There is a very wide range of social arrangements and legislation that affects the family. The emphasis upon one feature or another of family policy must depend upon a country's stage of development and upon traditions. Family policy must be concerned, for example, with all the arrangements for the employment of mothers as they affect employers, trade unions, the educational authorities and social insurance. The adaptation of working hours to school hours to meet the needs of working mothers, the adaptation of shopping hours to family needs, the extension of part-time employment opportunities for women, clauses in trade union agreements relating to working mothers including, for example, clauses counting sickness of children as a reason for absence, the adaptation of social security contributions to encourage part-time work—are all details of family policy.

There is, of course, in the community a code of social responsibility that runs counter to the egoistical instincts of economic man. The survival of the family and of the community depends upon this code. The great charity organizations reflect this code of social responsibility. The voluntary societies for parentless and deprived children, for the handicapped of all ages, for the old and for other minorities are the embodiment of the code as it was seen in times past, but they are continuing and expanding, notably in recent times into the field of housing for the homeless and the poor and the fatherless. They continue to make an essential contribution to the relief of poverty and distress.

The charities are essentially paternalistic in their philosophy, and no philosophy could be more appropriate, for example, than the attitude of society to the care of deprived children or orphans symbolized in the great charity of Dr Barnardo's. Private charity has, of course, long since been supplemented and extended by a wide range of state services, mostly under the local authorities.

These statutory services provide professional help to adults, children and families in need. They have largely imitated the paternalism of the private charities.

However, society is changing as education spreads to ever larger numbers of the population. Paternalism and compassion are still essential components of the code but are not enough in a society of rising expectations. Paternalism assumes non-participation of large numbers of recipients of help. Many of the legal and economic disabilities of the family today may be attributed to the non-participation of families, reflecting an undue introversion of many families that have closed their doors to the outside world in their troubles.

There is a distinction between parents who are good parents and parents who are good citizens. There is a distinction between the family that is a 'closed' society only interested in its own welfare and the family as part of an 'open' society where families, and especially parents, co-operate with other families for their mutual defence, mutual aid, mutual education and mutual legal protection. As parents become more educated and more socially conscious there must be increasing numbers anxious to participate. This trend is now apparent in the increasing number of growing points, though often still small, of the open society.

Chronic sickness and handicap afflict all income groups. Societies have in consequence been created to protect the interests of spastic, deaf, blind and crippled children. Much help has been given to such societies by professional parents who themselves have handicapped children. Families at all social levels have, however, both benefited and contributed to such societies united by common misfortune. Such societies amongst parents will grow with standards of education, rising standards of living and with the development of the code of social responsibility. Parents and non-parents have joined in mutual defence of the civilian sick in the Disablement Income Group.

Parent-Teacher associations and such groups as the Confederation for the Advancement of State Education are growing points of the open society. It is an essential feature of such organizations that they exist to help all parents regardless of the extent of their good fortune resulting from the chances of life or inheritance. The Advisory Centre for Education (A.C.E.) has as its aim 'to help the wise and good parent with his children, and by helping him to help all children'. A.C.E. is expressly and deliberately intended to help parents regardless of their means or education. It aims at the liberalization of education in favour of all children but, like all similar organizations, it relies on a small minority of parents, often with better education or more confident of their position in society, to provide the initiative and resources for its success. All these organizations for mutual help and to promote the benefit of children rely on a minority accepting a code of social responsibility that motivates them to devote some part of their energies and resources to help other parents and other children as well as their own.

There are in every community what have been called the 'silent classes' that include all those large numbers of people who are not vocal themselves in their own interests, and who are not adequately defended by any representative organization. Children, including older children, belong to these silent classes with inadequate representation in most countries. The majority of families in the United Kingdom belong to the silent classes and have no effective representation of their economic or political interests.

No political party in the United Kingdom has yet identified itself with the social and economic interests of the family. It is perhaps inevitable that political parties, with their difficult task of compromising between the views and interests of different representative bodies and privileged groups in society, should reflect only the patterns of thought of previous decades. There is a great inertia in large institutions. However, society is changing today faster than at any previous time, and there are dangers to society if the methods and policies of political parties and Government fall further and further behind the needs of the day.

Much social policy, involving the further transfer of wealth from families to non-parents, has been conceived by small groups of people behind closed doors. Much policy has not been the result of full and adequate consultation with representative organizations, nor the result of thorough investigation. The paternalistic philosophy has held sway. Policies of identifying arbitrary minorities of poor families have been conceived.

Arrangements have been devised based on political expediency by which poor families are to be assisted, not by the population at large or by those without the present charge of children, but by other parents, themselves not so poor but who are over-whelmingly the hard-pressed. The political parties differ in their choice of the arbitrary level dividing the poor from the not-so-poor.[1] The parties agree, however, in this essentially divisive approach which would never be supported by representative family organization and does, of course, inhibit thought in terms of the genuine needs of families. The levels chosen for dividing the poor from the not-so-poor by all parties are also not technically defensible as levels reflecting a standard of living at all. The concepts would not survive negotiation with representative family organizations employing professionally trained negotiators armed with the facts on the standard of living enjoyed by families and by childless persons.

An arbitrarily defined minority of persons called poor provides no basis for any viable social organization. The effect of labelling is to segregate, isolate, and separate the poor from the near-poor. The natural allies of parents are other parents. Parents who fall on evil times or who were born into difficult social circumstances should be able to look to other parents for guidance and help. The mutual interest of parents in the problems and risks of parenthood is the right basis of organization. Both the selectivity of the past and that now proposed by political parties has weakened and must continue to weaken the family organization needed for the health of the community.

The Government itself needs such organization. The Government and political parties have a central responsibility for advocating and defining the code of social responsibility appropriate to the times. This is not possible without continuous consultation and public discussion. Paternalistic policy made behind closed doors is less and less likely to be either right or acceptable.

---

[1] See for example: Fogarty (1966), Liberal Publications; Hayhoe (1968), Conservative Political Centre, and Howe and Lamont (1967), Bow Group; Houghton (1968) (Labour Party), published by Institute of Economic Affairs (2nd Edition). See also Child Poverty Action Group, Memorandum to the Prime Minister, Case Conference 12 No. 16, Apr. 1966; and Memorandum to the Chancellor of the Exchequer, Poverty No. 2, Spring 1967; Walley (1967) and Kaim-Caudle (1968). For Government policy see House of Commons Debate 22 and 23 May 1968, and House of Lords 21 June 1968.

The alternative to a widening gap between Government social policy and the real needs of the country is to provide for better consultation, which requires representative organization. In this discussion between Government and the people there is a missing voice, the voice of the family, a voice which can speak not of charity but of economics, which can speak for those in whose present care and charge are the future producers, the future citizens, the future parents.

CHAPTER TWELVE

Conclusions on Family Policy

Family policy proposes to influence the evolution of economic forces away from what is adverse to the family to what is beneficial to the family. Family policy proposes the redistribution of national wealth and income in favour of children, or in other words, the transfer of resources to investment in future generations. Economic forces tend to develop adversely to the interests of families if left to their own evolution; every country therefore needs a family policy. In the absence of a family policy, social forces also produce policies that are biased against the family. Social security systems in particular develop, that place an increasing burden on families. The great majority of recipients of pensions, sickpay, medical services, unemployment pay and non-contributory benefit are non-parents. Parents with dependent children have been called upon to pay ever-increasing contributions to these services much in excess of the benefits they receive *while they are parents*. The extension of these services has therefore reduced substantially the resources available to parents for bringing up the next generation at a time when the rearing of children is becoming an ever more exacting and expensive task.

Compulsory education and the prolongation of education to higher ages also place a greater burden on families. Family policy must be concerned with the extent to which the cost to families of raising the school leaving age should be offset by educational maintenance allowances, by family allowances or in some other way. The whole cost of maintaining those 15- to 16-year-olds who would not otherwise stay on at school will fall on only about 2 per cent of United Kingdom households, mostly in the poorer half of the community, and three-quarters of them will have other children to maintain as well.

Many conclusions flow from the general lack of correspondence between the size of incomes and the extent of family responsibilities. It follows that *family units which include dependent children generally enjoy a substantially lower standard of living than families without dependent children.* The evidence in this book suggests that the great majority of families with dependent children do not achieve a modest-but-adequate standard of living. The progress of communities is, in consequence, retarded by the poverty of the environment of most children even in the more advanced Western countries.

The great majority of families pay more in taxation, including social security contributions, than the value of the services they receive. Other government services apart from those to families have also to be paid for, but it is arguable that families with dependent children are much overtaxed compared with families without dependent children, who are left enjoying, after tax, a substantially higher standard of living, having started with the same basic income before tax.

Parents make the main investment in the next generation. Parents spend very much more than the state on bringing up their children, even taking fully into account the state expenditure on education. Money left in parents' hands or transferred to parents of dependent children is divided on average between all members of the family and therefore to a substantial extent is spent on the upbringing of the children. The income of parents has therefore an important social investment content. Social surveys have shown that parents' expenditure on their children increases on average with their income up to and beyond the modest-but-adequate level. There is, therefore, little justification for helping only families who are poor. The social investment content of many state services and much other state expenditure is lower than the social investment content of the expenditure of most parents with dependent children to rear.

The cost of bringing up a child is rising rapidly in Western countries, both because employment is demanding larger numbers of better qualified people and because better communication is increasing expectations, notably of young people. Expenditure on producing large numbers of better qualified people will produce a better return than expenditure on most other things. However, the quality of the next generation is not determined by educational expenditure alone; only too often the school teacher is defeated by the internal or external family environment. The Plowden Report of 1966 commented: '*It has been recognized that education is concerned with the whole man; henceforth it must be concerned with the whole family.'*

The outstanding British social documents of the post-war years have been the Robbins, Crowther, Newsom and Plowden reports on education. While family policy was not within the terms of reference of these Committees, each successive report has shown an increasing awareness of the limitations of the educational system unaided, and of the need for supplementary extra-mural support for families. The return from much educational investment can be greatly increased by improving the family environment. *It must be one purpose of a family policy to ensure that parents are not so oppressed by inadequate resources, bad housing or ill-health that they cannot co-operate with the schools in the bringing up of their children.*

All families need to be insured against the sickness of the breadwinner, usually the father, and also against the sickness of the mother, to cover the extra cost to the family that always arises if the mother is ill. Insurance against both sickness and unemployment has developed in most advanced countries. However, single persons and non-parents are in general much better insured than families. In both Europe and America the sickness and insurance benefit for both wives and children, in contrast to single persons, is very low and not enough to maintain dependants at recognized poverty levels. The prolonged sickness or unemployment of the breadwinner results in families suffering serious hardship.

This hardship is a consequence not only of the low level of allowances, but also of a failure to adapt allowances to family needs. *All allowances for children should increase with age at the rate at which the cost of maintaining children is found to increase.* In general, the allowance for a dependent child should reach that for a dependent adult at about the age of 14. Flat-rate allowances, that still exist quite widely in schemes of insurance and of family allowances, are not rational. *Special and priority consideration needs to be given to allowances for adolescents between the ages of 14 and 21.* Investigation in most countries has shown that the cost of maintaining adolescents is higher than that of maintaining persons in any other age-group. It is, however, influenced by the sex of the adolescent, by whether or not the adolescent goes to school or college and the kind of higher education attended, or if the adolescent goes to work, by the character of the work. Some of the worst poverty and hardship is in families containing dependent older children making strong demands upon a small family budget. Allowances for dependent adolescents under all schemes merit special review. *There can be no doubt that the economic pressures on families with dependent adolescents contribute to juvenile deliquency.*

There are many other factors influencing family need that should influence scales both for adults and children. The satisfaction of some needs, notably for clothing and some household necessities, can be deferred for limited periods. It is suggested that *allowances should be at least 20 per cent higher for persons dependent upon them for long periods than short-term allowances.* Children grow out of their clothes and wear them out quicker than adults, so that the allowances for families with dependent children should rise more quickly as dependence is prolonged than allowances for adults. *More study is merited of the effect of time on needs,* that is to say, the relation between needs and the duration of dependence on a low income.

In temperate climates, family needs in the winter time are substantially higher than in the summer time. *Food consumption, expenditure on clothes and on fuel all increase in the winter and all allowances for families should take the higher winter needs into account.* October may be the most expensive month for clothes in poor and hard-pressed families with children; December may be the most expensive month for food and January for fuel. The influence of the seasons on the needs of poor and hard-pressed families merits further study. There is little to be said for allowances being the same summer and winter.

At higher standards of living holidays can be afforded and the most expensive month may be July or August. The seasonal variation in family expenditure depends, therefore, on the standard of living. Poor families will not generally take holidays unless they are paid for by a charity or the state.

There are many other needs that can be taken into account. Men and women who go out to work have substantial additional costs for clothes, personal care, travelling and food compared with men and women who do not work.

The absence of one parent, either father or mother, raises

substantially the needs of the parent remaining. It generally costs money to replace the unpaid domestic services of the missing parent. *In particular, if a lone parent goes out to work then child care has to be provided; in general, child care services for working mothers are inadequate.* Not only children under school age but school children have to be safeguarded and provided for out of school hours or in the holidays where a single parent is working full-time. Fatherless children are a very substantial fraction of all the children suffering severe hardship, and the special needs of fatherless families merit much further study.

Adjustments of family allowances, school maintenance allowances, social security benefits, including non-contributory benefits, are necessary to adapt these to human needs by age, time and season. The needs of the fatherless, including those special needs that flow from the loss of a parent, and the needs of families with a disabled parent, are amongst the most urgent. *The historical relativities must be gradually abandoned in favour of relativities based upon objective assessments of real average needs.* The estimation of the relative needs of children, adolescents and adults in the present non-contributory (assistance) scale in the United Kingdom is seen not to be accurate if examined in the light of consumer survey data, nutritional requirements or estimates made in other countries. Nevertheless, this historical scale is used as the official poverty line.

The rationalization of all allowances, under either taxation or social security, requires better means of estimating the equivalent standards of living of single persons, couples and families of different sizes. *A scale for estimating approximately the standard of living of any family unit is required.* Such a scale is necessary whatever its limitations as it is in any case implied in a wide range of existing allowances, including tax allowances. The only alternative to making the best possible scale for describing the standard of living is to continue with scales that have merely historical justification and are open to continual criticism because of their basic irrationality. *Prosperity numbers* have been used in this book to present a standard of living scale; any standard of living has its prosperity number on this continuous scale. Families or individuals enjoying equivalent standards of living have the same prosperity number. *Much more elaborate techniques based on better consumer surveys need to be developed for estimating comparative standards of living.*

At the present time in the United Kingdom income tax is levied from people and families with a standard of living only immediately above the poverty level. Indeed, in some circumstances families are subject to income tax when living below the non-contributory benefit level. *Income tax therefore provides a means of adjusting the income of any person or family with a standard of living above the poverty level to take account of any benefits or allowances received.* Other kinds of means test are generally not necessary and are open to many objections. They make it necessary to employ an unproductive bureaucracy that is generally oppressive to families. The demands for elaborate form-filling and disclosure of detailed facts about family circumstances largely duplicate facts in income tax returns. *All the present means tests for school meals, school clothing, school maintenance allowances, scholarships for colleges of education and universities should be eliminated.* By making all such allowances subject to income tax, the extent to which families at any particular income level benefit can be made to follow automatically from the income tax return.

The rational basis of income tax allowances does, however, also need reconsideration. *It is suggested that it should be the aim of tax allowances to provide equality of treatment to individuals and families enjoying the same standard of living.* At the present time if comparison is made of the treatment of single persons, childless couples and families of different sizes at a given standard of living, such as the modest-but-adequate level, then the childless are seen to be more generously treated than the parents, and, at such a prescribed *standard of living,* the larger the family the more is the tax paid.

It appears to be generally agreed that the United Kingdom social security contributions, which are fixed in amount irrespective of a man's income or his family responsibilities, are inequitable and inexpedient. In most countries social security contributions are a percentage of income over a range of incomes, and not a flat-rate sum irrespective of income. *It would be a step forward in the United Kingdom if social security contributions were made a percentage of income.*

It seems very improbable that minimum wages will be established at a high enough level to eliminate the poverty of families with dependent children. Lord Beveridge's verdict is still true, that *family allowances are the only satisfactory means of supplementing the income of poor families with dependent children.* However, the elimination of poverty is no longer an adequate social objective. The achievement of a modest-but-adequate standard of living is increasingly the aim of social policy in all advanced countries.

If the objective of social policy is restricted to the elimination of poverty it is unlikely to succeed, because it must isolate the poor and fail to win the support of the majority of families, social policy should reflect the expectations of the majority of families and not only be concerned with the benevolent protection of the weak and the needy.

Family allowances are an essential means not only of eliminating child poverty but of enabling families to achieve standards of living comparable with that of non-parents with similar incomes. The standard of living of the majority of families with dependent children, even in the most advanced countries such as Sweden and the U.S.A., is still below the modest-but-adequate level. Family allowances are an essential means of raising the standards of families, but so also are school maintenance allowances and scholarships. Family allowances, maintenance allowances and scholarships should be made a part of a single system of allowances for children that should be based on objective assessments of the dependence of need upon age and the continuance of education.

Family allowances can, however, only be increased step-by-step, and it must be years before there will be any true correspondence between family incomes and family needs. In the meantime, families with dependent children will continue to be at a great disadvantage compared with non-parents in competing for housing. Seen over the short term or even over a period of a few years, the 'housing problem' can only be remedied by better distribution of existing housing. The total stock of housing can only be increased very slowly and at great cost, but there is much existing housing that is underoccupied. *Housing for families with dependent children should, therefore, be subsidized at the expense of households or individuals without dependent children.* This is being done by direct subsidy of the building of lower cost housing by local authorities. However, this has not proved to be enough, and there is a strong case for reducing the taxation of housing where it is occupied by families with dependent children and for increasing the taxation of underoccupied premises. Ways of subsidizing the rent or rates of the poorer families must be extended and include subsidy of rent in privately owned housing.

Poverty and hardship have been the lot of most of mankind throughout history. The good society can still only be achieved by further economic growth. Social policy may help or hinder this economic growth. Our future is in our children and, therefore, in our families with dependent children. The redistribution of wealth is today a feature of all advanced societies. Wealth may, however, be redistributed to promote economic growth by improving the upbringing and environment and education of the coming generations; or wealth may be redistributed in ways that retard economic growth by diverting the flow of wealth away from families with dependent children. Wealth may be used to prevent the passing on of poverty and poor education from one generation to the next within individual families or within whole communities; this is a growth promoting use of wealth. Propaganda pressure groups drawing attention to poor families and circumstances likely to perpetuate poverty through poor schools, poor housing, parental ill-health, fatherlessness, or insular poverty caused by declining industries, make an essential contribution to a growth-oriented social policy.

Alternatively, wealth may be used in subsidizing only the immediate consumption of persons without dependants, or in permitting non-parents the luxury of conspicuous expenditure that makes no contribution to economic growth.

The good of the citizen must always be the first objective of public policy, but there is a contradiction at some points between the good of the citizen today and the citizen of tomorrow. There are strong pressures supporting the static, unprogressive society that promotes immediate consumption retarding economic growth. There are strong pressures against the progressive society that insists on a high social investment content in its social policy. There are, therefore, strong forces resisting a family policy not because there is opposition to social investment or economic growth, but because of other claims on natural resources. These are not just the claims of the small minority who purchase expensive cars or houses, but include the claims of very large numbers of people in need of resources in the short term.

The balance between immediate consumption and investment in a country's future is a political matter. Every country will work out the balance in its own way. In the past, however, the balance has been achieved almost unconsciously, without full understanding of the likely consequences of this or that policy upon either the immediate or more distant future. The background of sociological knowledge and understanding today is still such that decisions on social or family policy are matters of judgement and expediency. There is a great need for more social research to support the decisions of politicians. Can it be doubted that greater under-standing by both politicians and the public must lead to more family-oriented, growth-oriented social policies? Is it all clear today which political party in the United Kingdom has the most progressive social policy or which shows most interest in the family? This must remain an important political matter for the rest of the century and may well influence the fate of political parties. The problems will certainly become more urgent as the United Kingdom inevitably becomes a more integral part of Europe. The social policies of France, Germany, Belgium, Sweden and other countries of Western Europe differ from those of the United Kingdom. Are the social policies of these European countries more progressive, more growth-promoting, more family-oriented than those of the United Kingdom, or less so? Insular policies must become increasingly difficult to pursue as the international competition for progress becomes more intense.

The time is, indeed, ripe for a review of the social policies of the United Kingdom much deeper than has been undertaken hitherto.

Does Help to Families Affect the Birth-rate?

The relief of child poverty has been connected in public discussion with the problem of population control. Poverty has been blamed both for a low and high birth-rate by different writers.[1] Men have remarked that the poor breed faster than the rich, and have considered that if the standard of living of the poor were only raised they too would, in time, limit their families. Elsewhere men, observing a falling birth-rate, have attributed this to the economic burden of child-rearing, and have hastened to recommend enriching families in the hope of increasing their children. Levasseur, a French writer on population problems, said in 1889:

'Men see, or believe that they see, a phenomenon and attribute it to institutions; and when the phenomenon persists in spite of a change of institutions, the contrary then is maintained.'[2]

The notion that raising the standard of living of families will increase their birth-rate is still advanced as a reason for not increasing family allowances or for not helping poor children. The Incorporated Association of Architects and Surveyors proposed fiscal penalties for large families, and the suggestion was condemned as 'absurd' in a *Times* leader.[3] A book about family policy cannot ignore these beliefs, which have influenced legislation in one country or another.

Both Government and private views on population policy differ widely. In one country large families are welcomed and in another they are deplored. Calamity from over-population

[1] See for example Royal Commission on Population; Hubback (1944); Myrdal (1945); Mackintosh, J. M. (1944); Hajnal and Henderson (1950), 'Evidence', vol. 5; Report of the Economics Committee (1950); and Report of the Commission. See also Beltrão (1957); Prigent (1962); Sauvy (1943) (1960) (1967); Titmuss (1942) (1961) (1968).

[2] Levasseur (1889), vol. 2, p. 177.

[3] Incorporated Association of Architects and Surveyors (1964), *Comment on the South-East Study* (mimeographed). See also *The Times*, 9 and 10 Sept. 1964.

was predicted by experts in the United Kingdom while the Government was predicting a manpower shortage; not so many years ago there was much concern about the fall in the birth-rate although unemployment was a central problem of the day. In other countries the immigration of very large numbers of foreign workmen and their families is welcomed while at the same time measures to relieve child poverty are not taken because they might lead to a serious problem of over-population.

There is no accepted measure of optimum population size, and over- and under-population are matters of opinion. It is no purpose of this book to take sides in these controversies. There are many papers suggesting that the rate of increase of population, rather than absolute numbers, should be the major cause for concern over periods of a generation or so.

There is, however, no question that in the end population must be controlled and that new means of control must be found. The population of the world cannot increase indefinitely and, within a few generations, some way must be found of limiting population growth. Whether or not it is an urgent problem in a particular country, or is believed to be urgent at the present time, fertility must eventually be matched to the human environment. The population of the world has been limited in the past by mal-nutrition, disease and war. Larger numbers of children needed to be conceived and born to compensate for high death-rates. Malnutrition, disease and war have been the traditional scourges of mankind. They are the antithesis of civilized life, and need to be replaced as factors limiting population by the conscious efforts of mankind to reduce the birth-rate to lower levels that will be needed.

Populations change slowly on a time-scale measured in genera-tions, but it may also take humanity generations to learn how to control its own numbers by civilized means. There is, therefore, probably no time to be lost in seeking the understanding that will make it possible eventually to avoid the traditional evils and enable mankind to control population size.

The purpose of this book might be served by showing that simple economic measures are likely to prove quite inadequate as a means of increasing or decreasing the birth-rate. All the evidence suggests that population can never be brought under control by the shading or elimination of tax allowances for children, or by the granting or withholding of family allowances. Moreover, as health services improve and society becomes more affluent, the problems of population control expand while the response of reproduction rates to simple fiscal and economic measures diminishes.

Population numbers will only ever be brought under control by greater understanding of human motivation and of the motivation of women in particular. Contraceptive practices will not, of themselves, produce an optimum birth-rate; though they may make it easier for parents to regulate the size of their family, if they so wish. The motivation of parents is discussed later in this chapter because the control of population and child welfare are interrelated. Ways of influencing parents that go much deeper than the decrees of the tax man or the discretions of the public assistance office are suggested. However, doubt needs to be thrown first upon the view that the reproductive behaviour of men and women follows the model of the economist's 'economic man'. The belief that population numbers can be limited by the deliberate impoverishment of large families lingers not only in men's minds but in the institutions of some advanced countries. The taxation of the family and the meagreness or absence of family allowances are defended in some countries on the grounds that more generous policies would encourage an undesirable increase in the numbers of the population as a whole or of a particular social class.[1]

An extreme example is to be found in the American State of Texas, where the regulations governing the aid to poor dependent children provided in 1963 for a maximum allowance of $54 a month for the first child and the mother, $22 for the second, $18 for the third, $13 for the fourth, and nothing for subsequent children.[2] Over 26 per cent of Texan families in receipt of Aid to Families with Dependent Children (A.F.D.C.) had, in fact, five or more children. All children's allowances for second and subsequent children are also well below the minimum estimated cost of maintenance. Texan provision must result in the progressive

[1] See House of Commons, National Health Service (Family Planning) Bill, 17 Feb. 1967. The effect of the pill on the birth-rate, the disadvantages of large families, and the burden on parents of rearing children were discussed.

[2] U.S. Dept. of Health, Education and Welfare: Money Payments to Recipients of Special Types of Public Assistance (1963), released 1964.

impoverishment of the growing family, both by making no provision beyond a low maximum for the rising cost of children as they grow older and reducing the allowance with each successive child, and by providing a low absolute ceiling that cannot be exceeded no matter how large the family. Texas has one of the world's wealthiest communities; thus the perpetuation of child destitution in Texas is in no sense attributable to shortage of resources, as it is in some other American States, but to community attitudes. It is sought to influence poor parents by economic pressure.

The concept of economic man still holds sway in the minds of the many authorities generating pro- and anti-natalist policies. Any hard evidence that taxation or children's allowances really affect birth-rates is lacking. There has been a very large number of surveys in the U.S.A. between 1936 and the present day of the views of adults about how many children they would like to have. These surveys have been summarized by Judith Blake[1] in the Journal *Population Studies*. The views of many thousands of people have been studied and analysed by income level and social class. These studies do not show that the size of family desired increases at all with size of income. The size of family desired is, indeed, almost the same in every survey over a wide range of income. In so far as there is any variation of family size desired with income, and it is very small, the relationship is inverse, i.e. the higher the income the smaller is the number of children desired, but there is very little difference even between the wishes of the really poor and the well-to-do. Thus, in a recent survey, poor women wished for 3·6 children on average and well-to-do women 3·4 children on average, the difference being within the sampling error of this survey. The climate of opinion of whole large communities is more important; these surveys show, for example, that Catholics wish for more children than non-Catholics, but the difference is quite small, amounting to an average of only about 0·2 or 0·3 children per family. These surveys suggest, indeed, that income and economic factors play a very minor part in determining the birth-rate. They indicate that

[1] Blake, J. (1968). See also for France, 'La Fécondité des Couples' (under Bastide, 1967), and 'La Fecondité en France' under France (1967). See for Belgium Julemont and Morsa (1964). See Glass (1968).

family income has little effect on numbers of children and, indeed, no effect in any way commensurate with the great effect of family income on the quality of the next generation.

Such surveys throw much light on motivation, but very little light on the numbers of unwanted pregnancies. There is certainly some implication that differential birth-rates may be due more to differences in unwanted pregnancies than to differences in parental intentions. This is no more than one possible influence.

In the Western world the time has gone when infant mortality seriously limited the rate of rise of population. Policies that simply reduce the standard of living of large, or of all, families with dependent children cannot provide an effective substitute for the once limiting effect of infant mortality. Such policies may or may not have some effect on family size in some cases, but any effects are certainly very slight.

Policies that deliberately leave children impoverished are evil in the traditional, Christian sense. Such policies are not only morally evil but do not stand up to the test of expediency. The various degrees of poverty suffered by children are not, in fact, limiting population increase in either developing or Western countries. The parent, cast in the image of economic man, is a fiction, unsupported by any correlation between reproductive rates and the economic ability to support a family, once nations rise above the depths of poverty where malnutrition and disease severely limit population increase. The notion that high birth-rates are a consequence of economic incentives is contradicted by the internal statistics of most nations. Indeed, it is not infrequently a poor and underprivileged minority that has the highest reproduction rates. In spite of all the evidence, the heresy is still abroad that parents beget and bear children for mercenary reasons.

The American negro is increasing in numbers much faster than the American of European stock, although negro upper-class families have fewer children than their white counterparts. However, in 1960 the total fertility rate for non-white mothers was 28 per cent higher than for white mothers.[1] The low-income white mothers, with a husband earning under $2,000 a year in 1959, had 3·6 children, but a non-white mother of the same age

[1] Kilagawa, E. M., and Hauser, P. M. (1964), Table 4, in Burgess and Bogue (1964).

and in the same income bracket had 5 children. Similar mothers, if their husbands earned over $5,000, averaged 2·7 children each, and there was little difference between white and non-white mothers in this higher income bracket.[1] Is this higher reproduction rate of the American negro not connected with his past and present underprivileged status? Indeed, the differential birth-rates of America and many other nations suggest that much of the earth will be inherited by the poor, in spite of economic disincentives, which if they act at all must act in the contrary sense.

In every Western country there are amongst the poorest families a small minority of so-called 'problem families', in which the parents lack the ability and stamina needed to rear children satisfactorily in difficult circumstances. Such families cannot generally base their self-respect upon income, or possessions, or upon special skills or neighbours' esteem. It is in these families in particular that the self-respect of both men and women depends in an unusual degree upon their sexual potency, their reproductive powers and their possession of children, more particularly young children. Parents who find it difficult to cope with the external environment have deep instincts to find satisfaction and self-respect within their own families. Indeed, if parents of these poor families really behaved like the economists' 'economic man' they would generally not be poor. Fred Philp, of the Family Service Units London headquarters, echoes many social investigators when he describes the experience of his own society:

'The fathers took pride in the size of their families and some spoke openly of this as an indication of their potency and superiority over others. In general the men neither took steps to limit their families nor approved of their wives doing so. . . . The women, too, were unsure of themselves. In general, worth seemed to be clearly associated with motherhood and here they seemed to find some reassurance about themselves. With the baby the mother seemed to find some reassurance that she can love and give to others and that she has something good within her. She seemed quite satisfied when she had a young child with her and any discussion of the problems created by repeated pregnancies needs to take this into account. Family limitation is unlikely to be accepted by these families until they can come to feel that they have more value in other areas of their lives, but in general they do not seem to feel this.'[2]

[1] Schorr, A. (1965), p. 28.   [2] Philp (1964), p. 278–9.

This account adds to our understanding of the higher birth-rates of certain depressed social classes and minority groups which are likely to be little affected by economic incentives. The problems of these people can only be solved by making it easier for such families to be assimilated and socialized by the community. If this is difficult for the parents, then society must find means of socializing their children. This can only be obstructed and delayed by perpetuating the poverty of the family. Problem families, and also many very poor families, have motives for excessive pro-creation which will only become more compelling if they are punished in Texan style.

In a country with a declining birth-rate, poor and under-privileged sections of the community lag behind in their cultural development and many reproduce the higher birth-rate that was prevalent twenty or thirty years previously.

Every country is wrestling with the problem of housing the poorest families, who cannot compete with the better off and the childless. An associated question is how to help poorer families purchase the household durables which make the mother's work so much lighter and contribute to the socialization of the problem family. Very little attention has been paid to this in the United Kingdom. In Europe the family organizations have pressed for government aid to families in equipping homes, and have organized self-help schemes for hire and purchase of cookers, washing machines and refrigerators. The Family Allowance Funds in France are able to use funds surplus to the allowances to help equip poorer households. Mothers of large poor families could be helped to purchase labour-saving machines and other electric equipment even if they cannot yet be rehoused in new homes.

The problem family is perhaps least influenced of all families by social pressures or public opinion; it is generally more isolated than the average citizen, and therefore tends to be less conscious of the social climate. Racial minorities often contract out of the normal community life of the racial majority. If the only civilized way of controlling population is by securing willing agreement to the standards aimed at, or by acceptance of a 'code of social responsibility', to use the words of Lord Brain,[1] the danger that

---

[1] Brain (1964), p. 229; Sauvy (1958) refers to: 'une prise de conscience collective qui s'est traduit par une reprise de la natalité', p. 511.

any substantial minority should feel themselves to be strangers within the gate or outcasts or socially unacceptable in any sense is apparent. Birth-control techniques are often unacceptable in such poor families. Human motivation can defeat all such devices. Birth control by instrumentation or pill is no more than a means of controlling births if the man or woman wishes to do so. Furthermore, if people wish to limit their reproduction rates they can do so without the techniques of birth control. The French nation limited births by common consent from the beginning of the nineteenth century without our present paraphernalia.[1] An American demographer, addressing the British Royal Society, said:

'If fertility levels were high in pre-industrial societies simply because of inadequate contraceptive technology then current programmes for reducing fertility in [underdeveloped] areas can concentrate on making modern contraceptives available. This very simple solution is no longer widely espoused because programmes for making contraceptives available in underdeveloped areas have not been very successful to date. . . . I take the position that a variety of control measures, including some forms of contraception, have been available potentially in underdeveloped areas and that past failure to use them more extensively has been a result of normative pressures for high fertility. . . . This reduced to a simple statement that couples had many children because they wanted them, not because they were ignorant of how to avoid having them.'[2]

There are, however, unwanted births, though the word 'unwanted' lacks definition and will always do so. How many children are wanted one moment and unwanted the next? How many children are wanted from one point of view and not from another? How many people change their minds? How many people

[1] A discussion of ideal family size in France and changes in the birth-rate in the last 25 years is given in Bastide, H. (1967), 'La Fécondité des couples dans la France Contemporaine.'

[2] Freedman (1962), p. 221. Freedman echoes the words of Levasseur in 1889, 'La condition sociale exerce (une influence) plus sensible . . . la cause réside dans la volonté des parents. On peut poser comme règle générale que, si dans une condition sociale telle que celle des Français du XIXe siècle le nombre des enfants est restreint, c'est que la volonté de la majorité des parents est de le restreindre. Il est inutile de chercher des raisons subtiles; le dominant est simple: Les familles en France n'ont pas beaucoup d'enfants parce qu'elles ne veulent pas en avoir beaucoup.' Book 2, p. 161.

would reveal the truth in such matters even if they really knew the truth about their own wishes? It is indeed in doubt how high a proportion of children in any country are 'unwanted'. But certainly the prevalence of abortion is sad evidence of unwanted conceptions and improvidence, but, in speaking of the United Kingdom, the Lafitte Report on Family Planning is surely right when it states that:

'Never in history have there been fewer unwanted children born, fewer unwanted or wrongly timed pregnancies, fewer marriages deprived of attainable happiness by fear of pregnancy.'[1]

Voluntary parenthood, as the Lafitte Report underlines, is now certainly 'part and parcel of our culture'. The numbers of unwanted children will diminish as more parents decide how many children to bring into the world and how they shall be spaced.[2]

A safe and effective birth-control pill will accelerate the elimination of unwanted conceptions and reinforce the principle of voluntary parenthood. The pill may also influence human motivation to an extent that cannot be foretold. It is only certain that the final result of every advance in the technique of birth control and of education in family planning must be to make the birth-rate more dependent than ever before upon human motivation, and increasingly upon the motivation of women. Birth-control techniques are only a contribution to the enabling of mankind to control his own future. Just how this new power will be used by the world's parents will depend upon very deep instincts, expectations and beliefs. The provision of easier and better means of controlling family size does not guarantee that family size will be controlled with wisdom. There must be a code of social responsibility which can provide this wisdom. The 'pill' may well have spectacular and disturbing effects on the differential birth-rate between nations and the world's races.

To be successful a code of social responsibility must reflect a wide consensus of opinion. Not only must the opinion setters be of one mind, but there must be no very substantial minorities who take no notice of the general view. A very substantial number

[1] Lafitte (1963), p. 11.
[2] Preliminary report of a more recent study of contraception in marriage, see Glass (1968), p. 55.

of families living below or around subsistence level are likely to be just such a minority that will refuse to conform. The continuance of large underprivileged minorities and real population control may well prove to be incompatible. There can be no question of compulsion or limitation of human rights of parents to have children. There is therefore no substitute for a public opinion embodying a code of social responsibility.

Before the 1939–45 war, the birth-rates of the poor in Germany were very much higher than the birth-rates of the well-to-do middle classes. Germany certainly suffered from the differential birth-rate, characteristic of most Western countries, which has been so much discussed by the eugenists. This has now all changed.[1] Professor Helga Schmucker wrote in 1961:

'A sample survey of more than 150,000 households in West Germany has recently been undertaken. In general the average household income now increases steadily with the number of children under 18 . . . The available material shows clearly that the poorest families no longer have the largest number of children.'[2]

A great change has taken place at a time when the German standard of living has been rising, and German social services for poor families have been extended beyond those available in the United Kingdom or the United States of America. In particular, Germany has supported the large poor family with increased allowances for third and subsequent children. Germany has been pursuing a pro- rather than anti-natalist policy, but it is not apparent that their children's allowances have increased the numbers of large poor families. The contrary has happened. While there are no grounds for believing in a causal connection, German experience is important. A country that pays higher allowances to children in large families has a most satisfactory relationship of birth-rate to income.

Germany has established a public opinion in these matters, and has an accepted code of social responsibility of a kind that extends to all the main social classes, and this is something new.

[1] I am indebted to Professor Hans Harmsen for drawing my attention to a publication of the German Academy for Population Science; see Deutsche Akademie für Bevölkerungswissenschaft (1965).
[2] Schmucker (1961), p. 33.

It is now generally accepted by all sections of the German population that the size of families should be limited to the number
parents can support at some undefined standard typical of a
particular social class; and now, on the average, the parents of
each social class act accordingly. A positive correlation between
income and family size was noted in Stockholm in the twenties,
and was confirmed for the whole of Sweden by a census in the
thirties. In evidence to the British Royal Commission on Population in 1945, Mrs Alva Myrdal showed that there was, nevertheless, in Sweden a group who did not take part in the general
trend, a group whom she described as 'the fringe outside any
social class, people dependent on the poor-law authorities, people
with no ambitions who, on account of lack of ambition, also have
children'.[1]

In England and Wales there has been a levelling of the birth-rate
between occupational groups, but family size is not correlated
to income, as is seen in the following table taken from the 1961
census. It will be seen that clerks have the lowest mean family
size at 84 and labourers the highest at 121 (see Table 32).

A change resulting in a rough correspondence between family
size and family income may be a step towards a more comprehensive code of social responsibility embracing population size.
But it is only a step. As German poor families become better off
they may increase the size of their family to match that of the
income bracket they are entering. Germany may be faced with
the population question which is beginning to cause despondency
amongst English anti-natalists: Will the well-to-do become trend
setters in family building? Not content with leisure and possessions,
will the affluent want a large family too?[2]

Most human decisions are a choice between alternatives. It is
increasingly the woman who decides how many children there
shall be, and it is therefore increasingly the alternatives before
women that determine the number of children.

Given a reasonable income, it is, of course, easier today to rear
a family than at any previous time. Medical knowledge and services
have reduced the anxieties of rearing children to a new low level.
Washing machines, refrigerators, motor cars and processed food

[1] Myrdal (1945), p. 9.
[2] Compare Belgium (1967), *Natalité et Famille*. See also Morsa (1963).

Table 32

MEAN FAMILY SIZE BY SOCIO-ECONOMIC GROUP

England and Wales* (1961)

Women married once only, under 45, and enumerated with their husbands; mean family size = 100; all figures standardized for age and duration of marriage.

Socio-economic Group	Mean Family Size
1. Employers and managers; large establishments	88
2. Employers and managers; small establishments	90
3. Professional workers; self-employed	104
4. Professional workers; employees	89
5. Intermediate non-manual workers	87
6. Junior non-manual workers	88
7. Personal service workers	100
8. Foreman and supervisors—manual	95
9. Skilled manual workers	101
10. Semi-skilled manual workers	106
11. Unskilled manual workers	121
12. Non-professional workers on own account	94
13. Farmers—employers and managers	118
14. Farmers on own account	109
15. Agricultural workers	116
16. Members of armed forces	108

* Census 1961. Fertility Tables: Table 14.

have greatly reduced the toil of rearing children. The pleasures of rearing a family are enhanced. The labour-saving products of technology are reinforcing the strong maternal instincts of most women. At each stage of adult life and family building, the alternatives before typical women in an affluent society must compete with the obvious attractions of increasing the family.

The attractions to the average woman's self-respect, creative instincts, and general wish for human satisfaction, of rearing four or even more children successfully are great. What are the alternatives that can persuade her to limit her family to two or three children or persuade a proportion of women to remain childless? There are few women who will not choose to be mothers in preference to doing menial or uncongenial work, and there are many women who prefer to have another child or two rather than return to work that has no great attractions, even although a much lower standard of living has to be faced.

There is much evidence that the education of women provides one outstanding means of influencing reproduction rates. For many women, when they are young, marriage and further education are alternatives. Education in the average case delays marriage and, again in the average case, the longer marriage is postponed the fewer children does a woman have.[1] The continuation of girls' education is, indeed, one certain means of reducing average birth-rates. Education is one activity that can compete successfully with family building for large numbers of girls, at least to the extent that it can postpone marriage. Table 33 shows the average age of marriage of American women according to the years of education; the most likely age at marriage is seen to increase with the years of education (see Table 33).

Later marriage of a young woman is desirable on other grounds. Later marriage and better education reduce the risk of marriage break-down, and therefore reduce the risk of children becoming fatherless or motherless. By improving women's employment opportunities, education greatly reduces the chances of women ever becoming poor even if they are so unfortunate as to become lone mothers.

There can also be little doubt that education has a greater or less effect upon the birth-rate according to its content, and that the education of women has a greater effect than the education of men. In recent years the education of girls has been frequently debated between those who wish for a special child- and home-centred education for the majority of school girls, and those who wish women to be educated largely in the same way as boys with more vocational emphasis. The demographic consequences of these two policies are generally neglected in the debate, although it is, indeed, doubtful whether population and educational policies can be usefully considered separately in isolation from each other. Sir John Newsom has been an advocate of more child- and home-centred education for girls. Education of this

---

[1] See Waldman (1967) for evidence from U.S.A. of postponement of the birth of first child by working wives.

Table 33

YEARS OF EDUCATION COMPLETED BY WIFE BY AGE AT MARRIAGE: U.S. COUPLES UNDER 35 YEARS OLD, 1960*

Years of School completed by Wife

Age of Wife at Marriage	Primary Only	High School			College		
		1 and 2 Years	*3 Years*	*4 Years*	*1 Year*	*2 and 3 Years*	*4 Years or More*
14 to 16 years	**445,293**	**620,144**	148,622	177,136	10,159	11,173	7,211
17 years	190,614	337,524	**223,690**	439,081	16,909	10,449	5,047
18 years	181,059	268,798	164,418	**1,001,603**	66,325	26,825	10,118
19 years	143,950	186,344	102,897	937,663	**125,735**	85,791	26,143
20 years	114,261	131,615	72,039	734,159	99,339	**145,304**	59,163
21 years	85,993	92,078	49,936	519,887	67,975	136,982	122,554
22 years	63,422	62,253	32,702	343,555	42,304	85,607	**140,654**
23 years	48,435	43,010	22,633	217,215	26,105	53,106	96,504
24 years	32,874	29,604	14,156	139,775	18,552	31,027	59,525
25 to 29 years	76,636	59,753	28,396	238,278	27,866	50,814	95,967
30 years and over	12,217	8,351	3,654	25,857	2,876	5,412	9,940

* United States Census of Population, 'Families' (1960), vol. PC (2) A4, Table 53, p. 401.

kind is almost certainly pro-natalist. Sir John discussed the problem in his book *Education for Girls* and more recently in the *Observer* newspaper. If a professional woman is away from work for, say, ten years to raise her family, she is lucky to get back at the same grade; she is out-of-date, and may not get back at all. He continued:

'As for the great majority of working women, it is one of the ironies of modern life that they occupy the serf jobs. You have only to look up the figures and compare the percentage of interesting jobs held by women with the percentage held by men. The huge majority of unskilled and semi-skilled jobs in our society are filled by women.'[1]

Sir John accepts that this is and will be so because girls are mainly interested in marriage. He suggests, therefore, that:

'They should be taught the domestic arts, those that can be practised in the home, e.g. creative writing, painting, drawing and modelling and making one's own music—at least up to quartet level.'

The greatest of all domestic arts, however, and the one giving the profoundest pleasure, is the bearing and raising of children.

There is, of course, a continuous spectrum of possibility from a home- and child-centred education at one extreme to purely vocational education at the other, and the ends of this scale correspond to the extreme pro- and anti-natalist educational policies. There is a wide choice of policies between these extremes. The teaching of home economics, including child management, is not in itself pro-natalist and may, indeed, raise the standards of the mother and father and incline them to have the number of children within their competence. There is a great difference between teaching boys and girls efficient home management and child care as part of a general education, and teaching girls home management to the exclusion of vocational training.

There is an even greater difference between a balanced education and open advocacy of a child-centred education of girls. Mr Martin James, a psychiatrist, asked by the *Observer* to comment on Sir John's views, did not comment on the other domestic arts but advocated a single-minded encouragement of women's

[1] *Observer*, 6 Sept. 1964. See also 11 Oct. 1964.

K

'child-centred assumptions', and added that the philoprogenitive instincts of men might also be encouraged.[1] These views might well be very appropriate to an underpopulated but wealthy country but they are not consistent with any code of social responsibility for the control of population. If girls are taught little except how to be good mothers and look after a home and if they can earn little in any other occupation, then they are indeed likely to look forward to the considerable satisfactions to be derived from rearing a family, and preferably a large family, given the health and strength. The growing automation of industry will doubtless free husbands to give more time to cultivating their philoprogenitive instincts also, and to lead a more child-centred existence in support of their wives. But we should beware of basing an educational policy on such a partial view of women's psychology, and of ignoring the demographic consequences of educational policy. It may seem a paradox to state that as more and more married women, including mothers, take paid work, the household management, child care and budgeting taught in schools increases in importance. The woman who does two jobs needs to have greater skill, efficiency and knowledge on the running of her home if her family is not to suffer. This efficiency may enable her to work and keep her family above poverty.

The vocational education of women can be expected to act as a brake on the birth-rate. Vocational education opens the door to attractive alternatives to continued maternal experience. A vocationally trained or educated woman is more likely to return to her vocation after the first, second or third child and to limit the size of her family, than her sister who has no alternative to child-rearing that appeals to her.

A study of the French census data for 1954 and 1962, published by the French National Institute of Statistics in 1964, showed that the proportion of French women working varies with educational level. French women graduates, for example, stay at work on marriage or return to work more than those who have not received an education beyond secondary school.[2] The United States Census of Population showed that the wife with one year or more of college education was more likely to go out to work than the wife

[1] *Observer*, 27 Sept. 1964.
[2] Études et Conjoncturé, Dec. 1964. See also Guelaud-Leridon (1964).

with not even high school education. The wife with the better education is more likely to wish to work and less likely to be unemployed and is much more likely to earn a higher salary. Only when a mother has children under 6 is there little difference between the tendency of the educated and uneducated woman to work; however, lone mothers with children under 6 are more often forced out to work by economic pressure. The United States Bureau of Labor commented on the educational level of women workers:

'The high correlation between the level of education and labor force participation of married women, as for other women, is strongly evidenced by the March 1962 [census] data on educational attainment of workers. . . . As the number of years of school completed increases, the likelihood of participation in the labor force increases for married women. Furthermore, comparison of data for 1959 and 1962 on the labor force participation of married women indicates a growing tendency for those with more schooling to enter the labor force while the proportion of the less well educated entering the labor force remains fairly constant.'[1]

Many studies show a strong correlation between the proportion of women who work and fertility. A study in Chicago,[2] for example, showed that as the proportion of employed women increases the gross reproduction rate decreases. It is not clear from such studies whether work is a substitute for fertility or an adjustment to biological infertility, but in this Chicago study whole neighbourhoods are shown to have low fertility and high female employment rates. The Chicago data are wholly consistent with the hypothesis that lower fertility combined with a higher than average proportion of women in employment can become part of a community's culture, or a 'cultural trait imbedded in values', in the words of the authors of the study.[3] The American demographer in the address quoted above said:

'I think the role of education and literacy is more basic. I suggest that with increased education and literacy the population becomes

[1] *Monthly Labour Review*, 87, No. 2, Feb. 1964, p. 152.
[2] Kilagawa and Hauser in Burgess and Bogue (1964), p. 59ff.
[3] *Idem*, p. 56.

involved with the ideas and institutions of a large modern culture . . .
major expenditures for education in a development programme are
justified not only for developing skills but also for their potential effect
on the fertility level if lower fertility is a social objective.'[1]

This is fully confirmed in 1968 by the American Department of
Labor:

'Women in professional occupations tend to have a longer work-life
expectancy than women in other occupations. One of the important
reasons for this difference is that women in professional occupations
tend to have fewer children than other women, and work-life expectancy
increases as the number of children decreases. The relative attractiveness
of professional work and the higher income it provides are also factors.'[2]

Professor Glass points out that the employment of married
women merits further research by demographers with support of
the census:

'The statistics for Norway, Switzerland and England and Wales show
that the economically active women constitute a very important element
in differential fertility. Indeed, in England and Wales such women
exhibit a lower fertility as a group than any of the 17 socio-economic
categories into which husband's employment is classified. This kind of
situation suggests that much more attention should be—and should
have been—given to the analysis of married women's employment in
fertility censuses.'[3]

A crux of the problem in developed countries may prove to be
the attitude of mothers of two and perhaps three children. If a
woman leaves her employment to rear a family, she may well see
no purpose in limiting her family to two or even three children,
unless she can see some more desirable alternative. If by interrupt-
ing her career for ten or fifteen years to rear a family she loses
her vocational skill and status and is offered no serious opportunity
for retraining, then her job-opportunities may well be so poor
that further child-bearing may be much more attractive and
creative. Opportunities for the further education and retraining
of married women should form part of a population policy.

[1] Freedman (1963), p. 220.
[2] Perrella, Vera (1968), p. 2.
[3] Glass, D. V. (1968), p. 120, and note 11, p. 121.

EPILOGUE 293

Many vocations, such as nursing and school-teaching, are
missing workers that they could regain if they made it easy for
women who leave work to have children to keep in touch by
classes, occasional locum work or work for a few hours a week
when their children are small. By such means the road would be
left open for many women to return to half-time work when the
youngest child goes to school, with economic and psychological
benefit to many families and to the community. The satisfactions
of such vocations combined with the enjoyment of family life
may add up to a satisfying life for many women. Such means can
be regarded as retaining devices largely replacing the need for
elaborate retraining when a married woman returns to work as
her children get older. Such schemes would be aimed at retaining
a woman's vocational interest to the extent that she did not lose
confidence in her ability to practise her vocation, and would
provide her with a little untaxed pocket money. Such schemes are,
indeed, only easy to run for those services and vocations that
women leave with regret. Unfortunately, at the present time, the
part-time work offered to women is predominantly unskilled
labour. The professions and vocations are backward in offering
women part-time work, although there are a few exceptions;
there is a great and unnecessary economic loss to the community
in consequence. An English expert on women's employment
found from studies in industry that

'Slightly more than one-half of the married women in employment have
part-time jobs . . . there are not nearly as many part-time jobs available
as there are married women wanting them.'

Part-time jobs are more likely to be unskilled than full-time jobs;
for example, there is a shortage of typists and secretaries yet:

'Among typists and secretaries the proportion of full-time to part-
time workers is eight to one. This is the occupation which seems to offer
least scope for part-time employment . . . The majority of married
women in employment, therefore, do unskilled work. . . . The return to
work by married women at a later stage of their lives has to be paid for by
a loss of occupational status.'[1]

[1] Klein (1965), p. 34. See also Klein (1960).

A tradition of high standards of child care will tend to reduce the number of large families. It is now well established that in families of modest means the children suffer in many ways as their numbers increase. This is not only due to reduced resources available per child but also to reduced parental attention to each child. The result is often a reduced standard of nutrition and health and a lower average educational performance with increase in the size of the family. High standards of child care are required not only for the children themselves, but as part of a code of social responsibility intended to limit the size of families. No mother will, however, be convinced of the community's concern by exhortation, but only be the quality of the childcare services. The community must set the example. In his address to the British Association in 1960, Professor Glass stated:

'The establishment of new demographic patterns involves the development of new incentives which press upon reproductive behaviour. Such incentives need to be imbedded in the social framework. They can be encouraged by persuasion but can hardly be created entirely or even primarily by an apparatus of symbols. Symbols are important and far too little use is at present made of them in social and economic transformation. But in countries with low levels of living, perhaps even more than elsewhere, it is necessary, so to speak, to have something material to be "symbolic about".'[1]

Professor Glass was speaking of under-developed countries, but his words apply to economically depressed classes and deprived racial minorities in the developed countries.

While the French and German Governments pursue pro-natalist policies, the British Government has avoided having any express population policy at all.[2] It might be inferred that the present population trend in the United Kingdom is regarded as satisfactory or at least causes no great concern in official circles. However, many institutions in the United Kingdom are structured to encourage a high birth-rate, whether by tradition or design. Tax allowances for persons employing child-minders or house-keepers do not help the ordinary mother to go out to work. The

[1] Glass (1960), p. 363.
[2] See, for example, Correspondence between Sir David Renton, M.P. and the Prime Minister, *Guardian*, 15 May 1967.

official ban on nursery schools by the Ministry of Education has now been lifted for the children of women intending to return to teaching, but only to help this one profession. However, the discouragement of day nurseries by the Ministry of Health continues, though some local authorities are planning new nurseries to meet the local demand. An official or unofficial *numerus clausus* is operated to control the number of women entering many professions and higher educational establishments such as the older universities.

Indeed, not only Government policy but many institutional arrangements of all kinds are such as to discourage women from whole or part-time work and encourage women to stay at home. There can be little doubt that the total effect of these pressures must be strongly pro-natalist. The fertility rates of the United Kingdom are among the lowest of any country, and it can be argued that the long-term trend is still downwards in spite of post-war bulges. It is certainly desirable for the United Kingdom to be guided increasingly by a European rather than an insular view of demographic needs. It can be argued that the very much lower reproduction rates in all the developed countries of the Western world compared with the developing countries may become a matter of serious concern during the next ten or twenty years, and that it is therefore right to have some pro-natalist bias in British institutions.

It may well be that some of the measures needed to relieve child poverty will have a pro-natalist effect. Opposition to helping poor children on anti-natalist grounds is not, however, logical in a country like the United Kingdom that retains a wide range of laws and institutions with a heavily pro-natalist bias. If, indeed, the rate of increase of the population of the United Kingdom came to be regarded as excessive and a matter for genuine public concern, a long list of measures could be taken without deliberately impoverishing children or using blunt economic weapons on the more defenceless parents of large families. The birth-rate will never be controlled by such means, but only by a much more thoroughgoing examination of our institutions and their influence upon the motivation of men and women, particularly women.

POSTSCRIPT

A Note on the White Paper Entitled National Superannuation and Social Insurance 1969 Cmnd. 3883

1. The White Paper opens with the statement: 'The Government are proposing the most fundamental changes in social security since the present national insurance scheme was introduced soon after the Second World War.'[1] The proposals in the White Paper are part of a total review of social security in the United Kingdom and 'are set out . . . for public comment and debate'.[2]

2. The Government of every developed country must have a policy on pensions. The problem of maintaining the elderly who have made inadequate provision for their old age is a serious human problem. The White Paper, in stating the problem 'for public comment and debate' is, however, less than frank. There is little reference to the cost to families of the proposals or to the transfer of resources from parents to non-parents inherent in the proposals, or to any objective assessment of the comparative needs of elderly persons and of families with children. There is no indication as to how the pension proposals are related to the total policy for social security and taxation. There has been no similar invitation to 'public comment and debate' on social security as it affects children and their parents, nor has any public document been produced on which such a debate could centre.

The evidence on which families are divided into those 'in need' and those 'not in need' has never been produced. The new policy on family allowances[3] was not placed before the public but was part of the crisis measures of the Spring of 1968. The contrast with the period of study and debate which is to be given to the White Paper is marked. Moreover, the effects on families with an earning mother of the present proposals are not spelt out, though they may be discerned by close attention to the small print.

[1] White Paper, par. 1. [2] White Paper, par. 7.
[3] Discussed on pp. 28–9, 189–92, 197–200 of this book.

3. It is central to this scheme that it would eventually guarantee a pension for all men over age 65 and all women over age 60. The pension would be related to earnings, and for a single man would amount to 60 per cent of earnings up to half national average earnings, plus 25 per cent of the balance of earnings up to one and a half times national average earnings.[1] At 1968 earnings levels, a single man who had had life earnings of half the national average earnings, or £11 a week, would have a pension of 60 per cent of his wage, and this would decline to about $36\frac{2}{3}$ per cent of his wage at the ceiling of £33 a week. The single pensioner who had earned the national average wage would have a pension equal to $42\frac{1}{2}$ per cent of his life earnings.

4. These proposals would cost over £3,000 million a year by the end of the century.[2] A variation of even one per cent in this pension of $42\frac{1}{2}$ per cent of average life earnings would cost a sum rising to more than £50 million per year.

5. Is $42\frac{1}{2}$ per cent of life earnings, for the man earning the average national earnings—up-dated as promised for the effects of inflation and changes in earnings level generally—a reasonable pension for a single man with no dependants? Let us suppose that the single pensioner who earns this pension once had a wife and three children to support. Would his standard of living be higher or lower as a pensioner than it was when he was a family man? The answer is very clear that his standard of living as a single pensioner would be very substantially higher than it was when he had a wife and three children to support. His standard of living as a pensioner would in particular be very much higher than during those years when his children were older and adolescent. We have seen in this book that such a father spends much less than $42\frac{1}{2}$ per cent of his income on himself, and much more than the balance of $57\frac{1}{2}$ per cent on his wife and children. Furthermore, the pensioner has none of the substantial costs of working of the average man, as discussed in Chapter 3. He will not, as a pensioner, need to spend as much on clothing or on food as he did in his middle age when he went to work every day. As a pensioner he will not, indeed, need or wish to spend as much on food or clothing as his wife or a single one of his adolescent children once

---

[1] White Paper, par. 64 and Table 3.
[2] White Paper, Table 6.

cost him. The average citizen, as he grows older, spends gradually less on food and clothing even while still working and well able to afford a higher expenditure. As a pensioner he will in the average case need much more medical care than he or his family needed when he was younger, but this is provided free under the Health Service. He will also need a little more money for fuel.

6. Under the scheme proposed by the White Paper, the poorer man with average life earnings of only half national average earnings would receive a pension of 60 per cent of his wage. Did such a man once spend 60 per cent of his wages on himself and only 40 per cent on his wife and three children? There are no grounds whatever for such an assumption. It will be remembered that about two-thirds of all the nation's children at any one time are in families with two or more children, and 40 per cent are in families with three or more children. The 'fundamental changes' proposed in the White Paper are general and would apply to the great majority of people. They would guarantee a standard of living to single pensioners very substantially higher than the same men and women enjoyed when they were fathers and mothers of dependent children. They would also guarantee a standard of living for the pensioner substantially higher than enjoyed by the majority of families bringing up most of the nation's children at the same point of time.

7. The comparison has so far been made between the family and the single pensioner. For a married couple, where the wife had no earnings record, the pension would be 55 per cent of his wage if the man's life earnings had been at the average national level.[1] At this level, therefore, the pension for a married couple is $1 \cdot 3$ times that of a single pensioner. One man is equated to $3 \cdot 4$ dependent wives! The standard of living of the elderly couple would be very substantially lower than that of the single pensioner, but nevertheless still substantially higher than that of the family with three children, and higher than the pensioner couple enjoyed when they were the father and mother of dependent children.

8. If the wife as well as the husband had an earnings record the pension could be higher still. The extent to which wives work depends very much upon the number of their children.

---

[1] Par. 71: husband's earnings assumed £22 (1968); pension £9 7s., wife's flat-rate pension £2 16s., Total £12 3s.

The mothers who have spent much of their life rearing families will receive lower pensions than those wives who have escaped from family responsibilities in one way or another. The more years spent in rearing a family, the lower the pension for the average woman. The larger a family is, the less the mother is able to work outside her home. The White Paper proposals would extend this penalty on parents into their old age.

9. Who would pay for these proposals? All working people would help to pay except the very poorest earning less than about £5 5s. a week.[1] The majority of the nation's families with dependent children would help to pay and would be made poorer if the proposals were implemented. The proposals would transfer substantial resources, amounting to tens of millions of pounds, from households with dependent children to households, and more particularly to pensioners, without dependent children. These 'fundamental changes' would make men and women poorer during those years when they are responsible for dependent children, but better off in their latter years when the children had left home.

10. There are between 1 · 5 and 2 million mothers with dependent children who go out to work and now opt not to contribute to national insurance at the full rate.[2] The 'fundamental changes' would remove the right of all these mothers to opt out in this way. At a wage of £8 a week, a working mother would have to contribute an additional 10s. 3d. a week.[3] From earnings of £5 5s. to £33 a week she would pay $6\frac{3}{4}$ per cent of earnings, which is an additional tax except for a small sum of 7d. a week that she pays if she opts not to contribute in full. The paper has a number of paragraphs under the heading, 'The New Deal for Women', that contain no reference to the substantial extra burden that the proposals would impose on working mothers. We have seen in earlier chapters that most of the unemployment and sick pay is received by older workers without dependent children. A mother is more likely to be off work because her children are sick rather than sick herself, and this would not entitle her to benefit.

[1] White Paper, par. 99.

[2] Out of $4\frac{1}{2}$ million married women who are gainfully employed only 1,130,000 pay the full rate. Annual Report 1967, Ministry of Social Security, Table 1, p. 71.

[3] See Note *beneath* Table 2, p. 21, of White Paper.

11. The contribution levels proposed in the White Paper pay no regard to the family circumstances of the contributor. The bachelor, the spinster, the family man with a wife and children to support, the mother of a fatherless family, or the father of a motherless family all pay the same contributions at the same earnings level. The amount of contributions would not be related to the standard of living of the contributor but to his earnings, disregarding the numbers, ages or incomes of his dependants. The White Paper has two paragraphs on fatherless or one-parent families, promising further consideration and research, but does not explain that the proposals would make large numbers of such families poorer by forcing their mothers to pay higher contributions. The increased contributions would also make it more difficult for mothers to rely on their own earnings instead of on supplementary benefit.

12. The White Paper also proposes that no regard should be paid to the standard of living of the recipients. There is to be no selectivity. The retired merchant banker and the building labourer are to receive their pensions according to the same principles. This is a contrast to the treatment of the family with dependent children. Family allowances were made selective in 1968; increases in family allowances only went to the poorest children. School meals, school clothing allowances, school maintenance allowances, scholarships, rate and rent rebates are subject to means tests. How does the standard of living at which means tests are imposed upon families compare with the standard of living that would be guaranteed to pensioners by the White Paper proposals? The reader can answer this question from previous chapters. Of course, the well-to-do pensioner will have to pay tax on his pension, but at a lower rate than families subject to means test, which are, in reality, a 100 per cent tax above an income threshold near the poverty level. Contributions will be paid by the poorest families above an income of £5 5s. a week, and benefits will go to many elderly persons enjoying investment income, occupational pensions, annuities, and other private means.

13. There is a paragraph in the White Paper stating that the general standard of living of pensioners is substantially below that of the working population.[1] This may or may not be so.

---

[1] White Paper, par. 12.

The standard of living of households with dependent children is, however, also very substantially below that of the households without dependent children, as we have seen. The report also wrongly assumes that the average cost of a child is half that of an adult. This is only true of very young children; as seen in earlier chapters, teenage children cost more than adults. It is also implied in the same paragraph of the White Paper that the cost of maintaining a pensioner is as high as that of an average adult. A pensioner needs substantially less money than a younger working adult to maintain the same standard of living.

14. The White Paper proposals are intended to be compulsory. The father of the family would not be left to choose whether he wished to spend the margin of his income upon his family or to save more for his old age when he would enjoy a higher standard of living. He would be forced to pay his contributions at the same rate in his thirties and forties, before his children left home, as in his fifties when he was enjoying a higher standard of living and his children might well have homes of their own. The proposals pay no regard to the family cycle, and would involve a transfer of resources from the minority of households containing most of the nation's children to many childless households enjoying a higher standard of living.

15. Flat-rate allowances for children are to continue to be paid both to those pensioners who still have dependent children and to widowed mothers. The pensions for childless widows, retired men and women, short- and long-term sickness benefit for adults, and unemployment benefit would all be earnings-related, but not the allowances for dependent children. Minimum subsistance allowances for children would continue, and there is no suggestion that these child allowances should even be rationalized to be age-related or that they should be related to pensions or to average earnings. The White Paper in its treatment of child allowances is, indeed, overtly biased against the family with dependent children. There are other features with the same bias against the family. Pensions are to be reviewed by law every two years to compensate for inflation. Entitlement to pensions is to be reviewed every twelve months to keep pace with rises of wages; pensions are to be 'dynamized', in the words of the White Paper. There has been no suggestion that children's allowances or family

allowances should be adjusted for inflation, or be dynamized by relating them to the rising standard of living of the community. Indeed, under 'claw-back' arrangements, the retained value of family allowances diminishes as money wages increase, in contrast to pensions. The more a family man earns, the less value he retains from family allowances but the more pension he would receive in old age.

16. The White Paper continues a trend. There has been public discussion in Sweden about the effect of the Swedish pension scheme increasing the standard of living of pensioners much above that of families with dependent children. There has been over-insurance for old age in Sweden, also to some extent at the expense of families with dependent children. The White Paper proposes compulsory over-insurance for old age in the United Kingdom at the expense of families with dependent children. The Beveridge plan of twenty-five years ago is criticized in the White Paper. Whatever the weaknesses of Beveridge's scheme, it took a balanced view of the needs of all classes of the community. The Beveridge Report said expressly:

'Better distribution of purchasing power is required among wage-earners themselves, as between times of earning and not earning, and between times of heavy family responsibilities and of light or no family responsibilities.'[1]

Provision for children was central to the Beveridge recommendations. Provision for old age is central to the White Paper's fundamental proposals.

17. The White Paper suggests that its proposals should have no adverse effect 'on future economic growth'.[2] There is no reference to an expanding world literature that discusses the dependence of economic growth upon the investment in children by both the educational system and their parents. The transfer of resources from parents proposed in the White Paper to a pay-as-you-go pension scheme will most certainly have an adverse effect on economic growth.

18. There has been no invitation to 'public comment and debate' on social security as it affects children and their parents.

[1] Beveridge Report (1942), par. 449. See also pars. 11 and 413.
[2] White Paper, par. 177.

There has been no parallel document with proposals to assist parents during their years of heaviest economic burden. The title of the White Paper is not only 'National Superannuation' but 'Social Insurance'. What has the White Paper to say about the important role of social insurance in safeguarding the standard of living of children? The public, and particularly parents who have the present care and charge of children, should challenge the narrow confines of the public debate suggested by the White Paper and should call for adequate documents on the standard of living of families, the cost of children and adolescents, and should call for the family policy of the Government and of Her Majesty's Opposition.

THE COMPARATIVE COST OF CHILDREN, YOUNG PERSONS AND ADULTS

Costs of Goods and Services by Type of Family: Food, clothing and other costs that vary with family status, age, sex and work status of individuals

	Rela-tivities[1]	Men and Boys $	Women and Girls $	Rela-tivities[1]
1. Persons living in Family Groups.				
1.1 Head of family				
1.11 Employed or seeking work				
Under 35	174	26·75	27·00	175
35–54	169	26·05	26·75	174
55–60	166	25·50	26·30	171
65 and over	159	24·45	25·25	164
1.12 Retired or not seeking work				
Under 35	118	18·20	15·50	101
35–54	114	17·50	15·25	99
55–64	110	16·95	14·80	96
65 and over	97	14·95	12·95	84
1.2 Dependants of head				
1.21 Adult: under 35	105	16·10	13·40	87[2]
35–54	100	15·40	13·15	85
55–64	96	14·85	12·70	82
65 and over	91	13·95	11·85	77
1.22 Child: under 1	38	5·80	5·80	38
1–5 (pre-school)	55	8·45	8·45	55
6–11 (elementary)	75	11·55	11·55	75
12–15 (junior high)	101	15·55	15·25	99
16–20[3]	127	19·50	17·15	111
1.3 Earners other than head (full-time job)				
1.31 Wife of head	—	—	25·80	168
1.32 Other 16–20[4]	210	32·40	30·70	199
21–34	200	30·80	29·55	192
35–54	184	28·40	24·65	160
55–64	152	23·40	24·20	157
65 and over	152	23·35	24·15	157
2.0 Persons Living Alone:				

[Continued Opposit

	Rela-tivities[1]	Men and Boys $	Women and Girls $	Rela-tivities[1]
2.1 Employed or seeking work				
Under 35	181	27·90	27·20	177
35–54	177	27·20	26·75	174
55–64	173	26·65	26·30	171
65 and over	163	25 15	25·25	164
2.2 Retired or not seeking work				
Under 35	126	19·35	15·50	101
35–54	121	18·65	15·25	99
55–64	118	18·10	14·80	96
65 and over	100	15·40	12·95	84

[1] Relativities, as used in this book, have been added by the author to this table, as have the footnotes.

[2] Non-working wife of head of family included in these adult female dependants.

[3] Non-working young persons, e.g. senior school children, students living at home.

[4] Working young persons living at home.

Taken from Table I IVa of A Family Budget Standard (1963), published by Budget Standard Service of the Research Department, Community Council of Greater New York. Costs in dollars relate to October 1962. These costs are brought up to date for current practice in the Annual Price Survey and Family Budget Costs.

LEVEL OF GROSS INCOME AT WHICH UNITED KINGDOM INCOME TAX AT REDUCED RATE AND STANDARD RATE AND SURTAX ARE FIRST PAID

Taxpayer	Income Tax first paid			Standard rate first paid			Surtax first paid
	per year	per week		per year	per week		
	£	£	s.	£	£	s.	£
Married couple	438	8	8	823	15	17	5,136
Single person	283	5	9	669	12	17	5,001
Married couple with 1 child	618	11	18	1,003	19	6	5,294
Married couple with 2 children	798	15	7	1,183	22	15	5,451
Married couple with 3 children	978	18	16	1,363	26	4	5,609
Married couple with 4 children	1,158	22	5	1,543	29	13	5,766
Married couple with 5 children	1,338	25	15	1,723	33	3	5,924
Married couple with 6 children	1,518	29	4	1,903	36	12	6,081
Elderly single taxpayer							
(a) All investment income	402	7	14	669	12	17	2,001
(b) Income all from investment except standard national retirement pension	402			669			2,049

NOTES

1. The reliefs used in arriving at these figures are those in force for income tax for the year 1967–8 and for surtax for the year 1966–7.

2. For all entries other than those for the 'elderly, single taxpayer', it is assumed that the income is all earned, that the wife is not earning, and that the child allowance is £140.

3. For the 'elderly, single taxpayer', it is assumed in (a) that all his income is investment income, and in (b) that he receives the standard national insurance retirement pension but that the remainder of his income is investment income.

4. Where the 'elderly, single taxpayer's' income is between £401 and £482, the tax charged is 9/20ths of the income in excess of £401, this being less than tax on the more usual basis.

5. Levels of gross income prior to the reduction in child tax allowances in Financial Statement 1968–9.

The following two tables compare levels of family allowances, in sterling. in 1967.[1] These tables do not include the special forms of family allowances, such as the holiday allowance in Belgium or the housing allowance in France; nor do they include the allowances for special groups, as for handicapped children, or for the further education of young persons in poor or single parent families (Germany). The allowances here given are for wage and salary earners.

[1] Levels of allowances have been increased since 1967 and extended, including those in the United Kingdom. For E.E.C. see *Tableaux Comparatifs des Régimes de Sécurité Sociale*, vol. 1. *Régime Général*, published every two years.

Table 36

FAMILY ALLOWANCES IN E.E.C., U.K. AND SWEDEN IN STERLING PER MONTH

	£	s.
BELGIUM		
1st child	4	0
2nd child	6	9
3rd and later children	8	19
Supplement: 6–10 years		18
Supplement: 10–14 years	1	11
Supplement: over 14 years	2	6
FRANCE		
2nd child	5	0
3rd and later children	7	10
Supplement: 10–15 years	2	1
Supplement: over 15 years	3	13
Supplement: single salary allowance		
couple	1	8
couple + 1 child	2	16
couple + 2 children	5	13
couple + 3 or more children	7	1
GERMANY		
2nd child (when family income not over £700 or there are 3 or more children)	2	5
3rd child	4	17
4th child	5	8
5th and later children	6	6
HOLLAND		
1st child	3	5
2nd child	3	15
3rd child	3	15

HOLLAND–(*Contd.*)	£	s.
4th child	5	1
5th child	5	1
6th child	5	9
7th child	5	9
8th and later children	6	5

ITALY		
Each child	3	6

LUXEMBOURG		
1st child	3	18
2nd child	3	18
3rd child	4	11
4th child	4	19
5th child	5	7
6th child	5	16
7th child	6	4

SWEDEN		
Each child	5	4

UNITED KINGDOM (average monthly amount)*		
2nd child	1	15
3rd and later children	2	3

* Family allowances are paid weekly in the United Kingdom, monthly in E.E.C. and Sweden. The figure given is average calendar month to nearest shilling in 1967. Increases in 1968 which benefited only families below standard rate tax level are described in Chapter 8.

Table 37

FAMILY ALLOWANCES FOR A FAMILY OF 3 CHILDREN (6, 11, 15 YEARS) IN STERLING PER MONTH

Country		Allowances in Total	
		£	s.
BELGIUM		24	3
FRANCE	Normal allowance	18	4
	With single wage allowance	25	5
GERMANY		7	2
HOLLAND		10	15
ITALY		9	18
LUXEMBOURG		12	7
SWEDEN		15	2
UNITED KINGDOM (1967)*		6	1

* See footnote to previous table.

Bibliography

For the convenience of students a number of items have been translated and others listed under the journals in which they may be found. Other entries are in the usual form.

ABEL-SMITH, D., and TOWNSEND, P. (1965), *The Poor and the Poorest*, Bell.

ABEL-SMITH, B. (1968), "Conclusion: the Need for Social Planning', *Social Services for All?*, Fabian Society.

ABRAMS, M. (1959), *Teenage Consumer Spending in 1959*, London Press Exchange, Paper No. 5.

ACHINGER, H., ARCHINAL, S., BANGERT, W. (1952) 'Reicht der Lohn für Kinder?', *Schriften des Deutschen Vereins für öffentliche und private Fürsorge*.

ACTON TRUST (1959), *Wider Shareholding*, Research Publications 858–1717.

AGRICULTURE, FISHERIES AND FOOD, MINISTRY OF, *Domestic Food Consumption and Expenditure*. (1958 to 1967), H.M.S.O.

ALLEN, R. G. D. (1942), 'Expenditure Patterns of Families of Different Sizes', *Studies in Mathematical Economics*, ed. Lange, O., Chicago University Press.

ALLEN, R. G. D. (1958), 'Movements in Retail Prices since 1953', *Economica*, Feb. 1958.

ALLEN REPORT (1965), *Report of Committee of Enquiry into the Impact of Rates on Households*, H.M.S.O.

AMSTERDAM BUREAU OF STATISTICS (1966), Amsterdam Scale of Consumption Units: personal communication.

ARETS, PAUL (1962), 'Extension du Champ d'Application de la Sécurité Sociale', *Report presented to Conférence Européenne sur la Sécurité Sociale*, Brussels, Dec. 1962, vol. 1, p. 57.

ASSOCIATION OF EDUCATION COMMITTEES (1964), *Primary Education: Evidence Submitted to the Central Advisory Council for Education (Plowden Committee)*, May 1964 (mimeographed).

AYDON, C. N. (1967), 'A New Plan for Child Poverty', *New Society*, 19th Jan. 1967.

BADEN-WÜRTTEMBERG (1963), 'Die Neuberechnung eines Preisindex für die einfache Lebenshaltung eines Kindes', *Statistische Monatshefte; Baden Württemberg*, No. 2, 1963, p. 45.

BADEN-WÜRTTEMBERG (1964), 'Die Unterhaltskosten für ein Kind von der Geburt bis zum 18 Lebensjahr', *Statistisches Landesamt*, 1963 and 1964.

BADEN-WÜRTTEMBERG (1965), Preisindex der einfachen Lebenshaltung und Unterhaltskosten eines Kindes, Sozialstatistik', *Statistisches Landesamt*, Stuttgart, Apr. 1965.

BAIG, TARA ALI (1966), *Report to Bangkok Conference on Children and Youth*, News Letter of the International Union for Child Welfare, May–Aug. 1966.

BALL, R. M. (1965), 'Is Poverty Necessary?', *Social Security Bulletin*, **28**, No. 8, Aug. 1965, U.S. Department of Health, Education and Welfare.

BALL, R. M. (1966), 'Policy Issues in Social Security', *Social Security Bulletin*, **29**, No. 6, June 1966, U.S. Department of Health, Education and Welfare.

BANGERT, W. (1964), *Die Sozialhilfe*, Bundesministerium für Arbeit und Sozialordnung.

BANKS, J. A. (1954), *Prosperity and Parenthood*, Routledge.

BARCLAYS BANK REVIEW (1966), 'Taxes and Welfare Benefits', **41**, No. 2, May 1966.

BASTIDE, H., and GIRARD, A. (1966), 'Les Tendances demographiques en France et les Attitudes de la Population', *Population*, **21**, No. 1, Jan.–Feb. 1966.

BASTIDE, H. (1967), 'La Fecondité des Couples dans la France Contemporaine.' *Documents d'Actualité*, No. 117, Feb.–Mar. 1967, No. 142, La Documentation Française.

BAVARIA (1962), *Aufwand für den Mindestunterhalt eines unehelichen Kindes von der Geburt bis zum vollendeten 18 Lebensjahr*, Staatsministerium des Innern, Oct. 1962, Feb. 1963, Mar. 1965.

BECKER, GARY S. (1960), *An Economic Analysis of Fertility in Demographic and Economic Change in Developed Countries*, National Bureau of Economic Research, Princeton University Press.

BELGIUM, *Enquête sur les Budgets des Ménages* 1961, 3 vols., Institut National de Statistique, vol. 1, No. 5, 1963; vol. 2, No. 7, 1964; vol. 3, No. 9, 1965.

BELGIUM (1963–4), *Budgets Familiaux*, vol. 2, Office Statistique Communautés Européennes, Brussels.

BELGIUM, MINISTRE DE LA SANTÉ PUBLIQUE ET DE LA FAMILLE (1965), *Les Fonctions de l'Aide Publique et Privée à la Famille et leur Coordination: Reponse Belge aux Questionnaires Préparatoires à la 7e Conférence des Ministres Chargés des Interêts Familiaux.*

BELGIUM, MINISTRE DE LA SANTÉ PUBLIQUE ET DE LA FAMILLE (1966), *Les Mésures d'Ordre Familial en Belgique.*

BELGIUM (1967), *Natalité et Famille: Chiffres et Situation*, Dossier du Centre d'Études de la Population et de la Famille. (Popular presentation of the 1967 Census and studies of Centre d'Étude de la Population et de la Famille).

BELGIUM, INSTITUT DE SOCIOLOGIE (1968), *Familles d'Aujourd'hui*, Université Libre de Bruxelles.

BELL, DANIEL (1968), 'Relevant Aspects of the Social Scene and Social Policy', in Burns, E. M. (ed.), *Children's Allowances and the Economic Welfare of Children.*

BELL, WINIFRED (1965), *Aid to Dependent Children*, Columbia University Press.

BELTRÃO, P. C. (1957), *Vers Une Politique de Bien-être Familial*, Institut de Recherches, University of Louvain.

BERGUES, H. (1967), *La Prévention des Naissances dans La Famille: ses Origines dans les Temps Modernes*, Institut National d'Études Demographiques, Travaux et Documents, No. 35, Presses Universitaires Français.

BERTHOMIEU, CLAUDE (1966), 'La Loi et les Travaux d'Engel', *Consommation*, **13**, No. 4, 1966, Centre de Recherches et Documentation sur la Consommation.

BEST, W. (ed.) (1963), *Die Forderung der Familie als Aufgabe der Gesundheitspolitik*, Report of a Conference of the Deutsche Zentrale für Volksgesundheitspflege, Frankfurt-am-Main.

BEVERIDGE, W. H. (1942), *Social Insurance and Allied Services* (Report), H.M.S.O.

BEVERIDGE, W. H. (1944), *Full Employment in a Free Society*, Allen & Unwin.

BEVERIDGE, W. H. (1944), *The Pillars of Security*, Allen & Unwin.

DE BIE, PIERRE (1960), 'Aspects Économique de la Sécurité Familiale', *Familles dans le Monde*, **13**, Nos. 2 and 3, June and Sept. 1960.

DE BIE, PIERRE (1960), *Budgets Familiaux en Belgique*, 1957–8, Nauwelaerts, Louvain.

DE BIE, PIERRE (1962), 'Niveaux de Vie, Prestations Familiales et Communauté Européenne', *Familles dans le Monde*, **15**, Nos. 3 and 4, Sept. to Dec. 1962.

DE BIE, PIERRE (1963), 'Politique Familiale et Politique Demographique', *Population et Famille*, No. 1, Oct. 1963, Ministre de la Santé Publique et de la Famille, Brussels.

DE BIE, PIERRE (1965), *Le Niveau de Vie des Ménages Belges en 1961 en Fonction du Nombre d'enfants*, Centre d'Études de la Population et de La Famille, Ministre de la Santé Publique et de la Famille, Brussels.

BLAKE, J. (1968), 'Are Babies Consumer Durables?', *Population Studies*, **22**, No. 1, Mar. 1968.

BLAUG, M. (1966), *Economics of Education: A selected annotated Bibliography*, Pergamon Press.

BLAUG, M. (ed.) (1968), *Economics of Education No. 1*, Penguin Books.

BOARDING EDUCATION, WORKING PARTY ON, see Martin Report.

BOOTH, CHARLES (1891), *Life and Labour of the People in London*, 1st Series, Part 1, Poverty'.

BOSANQUET, HELEN (1906), *The Family*, Macmillan.

BOURDIEU, P. (1964), *Les Héritiers: Les Étudiants et la Culture*, Éditions de Minuit.

BOWEN, W. C. (1963), 'Assessing the Economic Contribution of Education', Appendix 4, Part II of *Robbins Report*, H.M.S.O.

BRADY, DOROTHY (1948), *Budget Levels for Families of Different Sizes; Workers' Budgets in the United States: City Families and Single Persons 1946 and 1947*, Bulletin 927, Mar. 1948, Bureau of Labor Statistics, U.S. Department of Labor.

BRADY, DOROTHY (1951), 'Research on the Size Distribution of Income', *Studies in Income and Wealth*, **13**, National Bureau of Economic Research, N.Y.

BRAIN, LORD (1964), 'Science and Behaviour', President's address to British Association, Aug. 1964, *Advancement of Science*, Sept. 1964, p. 220.

BRILL, K., and THOMAS, R. (1964), *Children in Homes*, Gollancz.

BRITISH MEDICAL ASSOCIATION (1950), 'Summary of Daily Allowances', *Report of the Committee on Nutrition*, H.M.S.O.

BRITISH MEDICAL ASSOCIATION (1961), 'Dietary Allowances', *Manual of Nutrition*, Ministry of Agriculture, H.M.S.O.

BRITISH TRAVEL ASSOCIATION (1965), *The British on Holiday: British National Travel Survey*, prepared by Gallup Pole for British Travel Association. (mimeographed).

BRUNTZ, F. (1963), 'Les Prestations Familiales dans les Pays de la Communauté Européenne', *Pour la Vie*, June–Sept. 1963.

BUNDESMINISTERIUM FÜR FAMILIE UND JUGEND (1963), *Deutsche Politik* 1963, Reprint from Tätigkeitsbericht der Bundesregierung.

BURGESS, E. W., and BOGUE, D. S. (eds.) (1964), *Contributions to Urban Sociology*, University of Chicago Press.

BURNETT, J. (1966), *Plenty and Want: A Social History of Diet in England from 1815 to the Present Day*, Nelson.

BURNS, E. M. (1949), *American Social Security System*, Houghton Mifflin.

BURNS, E. M. (ed.) (1968), *Children's Allowances and the Economic Welfare of Children*, Conference of Citizens' Committee for Children of New York.

CANADA, *Royal Commission on Taxation* (1966), 'Taxation of the Family' Studies No. 10.

CANADA, *Royal Commission on Taxation* (1966), 'Taxation of Individuals and Families', vol. 3, Part A.

CARRÈRE, P. (1955), 'Enquête sur le Budget Familial par Carnets de Comptes Annuels à Marseille', *Bulletin de l'Institut National d'Hygiène*, **10**, July–Sept. 1955.

CARTER, H., and PLATERIS, A. (1963), 'Trends in Divorce and Family Disruption', *Health Education and Welfare Indicators*, Sept. 1963, National Vital Statistics Division, U.S. Department of Health, Education and Welfare.

CECCALDI, DOMINIQUE (1957), *Politique Française de la Famille*, Privat.

CENTRAL STATISTICAL OFFICE, *Economic Trends*, H.M.S.O., 'Family Income and Size', Feb. 1964, 'More Light on Personal Saving', Apr. 1965, 'The Incidence of Taxes and Social Service Benefits in 1963 and 1964', Aug. 1966. 'The Incidence of Taxes and Social Service Benefits Particularly among Households with Low Income', July 1968.

CENTRE FOR URBAN STUDIES (1968), *Housing—Rents Study*, Prepared for the Camden Borough Council, London, Feb. 1968 (mimeographed, to be published).

CHESTER, T. E. (1962), 'Growth, Productivity and Woman Power', *District Bank Review*, No. 143, Sept. 1962.

CHILD POVERTY ACTION GROUP, *Poverty*, Nos. 1 to 8, 1966–8.

CHILD POVERTY ACTION GROUP (1965), *Letter and Memorandum to Prime Minister*, reprinted *Case Conference*, **12**, No. 10, Apr. 1966.

CHILD POVERTY ACTION GROUP (1967), *Letter to Chancellor, Guardian*, 14th June 1967.

CHILD POVERTY ACTION GROUP (1967), *Letter to Members of Cabinet following Budget 1967, Guardian*, 13th Apr. 1967.

CHILD POVERTY ACTION GROUP (1967), *Memorandum to Chancellor*, reprinted *Poverty*, No. 2, Spring 1967.

CHILDREN'S BUREAU (1960), *Chartbook Children and Youth*, Department of Health, Education and Welfare, Children's Bureau, No. 363.

CHRONIQUE SOCIAL DE FRANCE (1958), *Famille d'Aujourd'hui: Situation et Avenir*, Librairie Gabalda.

CHURCH OF ENGLAND (1958), *The Family in Contemporary Society*, Report of a Group convened by the Archbishop of Canterbury.

CLEGG, SIR ALEC (1968), *Waste of Human Potential in Education*, Paper presented to Education Authority of West Riding, 7th May 1968 (mimeographed).

CLERC, P. (1967), *Des Millions de Jeunes*, Étude démographique, Editions Cujas.

COLLOQUES INTERNATIONAUX DU CENTRE NATIONAL DE LA RECHERCHE SCIENTIFIQUE (1963), *L'évaluation et le rôle des besoins de biens de con-*

sommation dans les divers régimes économiques, Editions du Centre National de la Recherche Scientifique.

COMMUNAUTÉ EUROPÉENNE DU CHARBON ET DE L'ACIER (1962), *Rapport sur la Comparaison du Système Britannique de Sécurité Sociale avec les Systèmes des Pays de la Communauté*, Luxembourg, 23rd July 1962.

COMMUNAUTÉ EUROPÉENNE DU CHARBON ET DE L'ACIER (1964), *Tableaux Comparatifs des Régimes de Sécurité Sociale dans les États Membres des Communautés Européennes*, vol. 1, Régime Géneral. The same (1966).

COMMUNAUTÉ ÉCONOMIQUE EUROPÉENNE, *Exposé sur l'Évolution de la Situation Sociale dans la Communauté*, 1958 to 1967, Brussels.

COMMUNAUTÉ ÉCONOMIQUE EUROPÉENNE (1962), *Étude sur la Physionomie Actuelle de la Sécurité Sociale dans les Pays de la C.E.E.*, Serie politique sociale 3, Brussels.

COMMUNAUTÉ ÉCONOMIQUE EUROPÉENNE (1962), *Étude Comparée des Prestations de Sécurité Sociale dans les Pays de la C.E.E.*, Serie politique sociale 4, Brussels.

COMMUNAUTÉ ÉCONOMIQUE EUROPÉENNE (1962), *Financement de la Sécurité Sociale dans les Pays de la C.E.E.*, Serie politique sociale 5, Brussels.

COMMUNAUTÉ ÉCONOMIQUE EUROPÉENNE (1962), *Conférence Européenne sur la Sécurité Sociale*, vols. 1 and 2, Brussels.

COMMUNAUTÉ ÉCONOMIQUE EUROPÉENNE, DIRECTION DES PROBLÈMES FISCAUX, 'DÉGRÈVEMENTS FISCAUX POUR CHARGES DE FAMILLE ET ALLOCATIONS FAMILIALES', Document prepared for *Conférence Européenne sur la Sécurité Sociale*, Brussels, Dec. 1962, vol. 2, p. 273.

COMMUNAUTÉ ÉCONOMIQUE EUROPÉENNE, COMMISSION ON SOCIAL SECURITY (1967), *Supplementary Social Security Benefits*.

COMMUNAUTÉS EUROPÉENNES, *European Social Charter*, European Treaty Series, No. 35.

COMMUNAUTÉS EUROPÉENNES OFFICE STATISTIQUE, *Budgets Familiaux* (1963–4), vol. 1 *Luxembourg;* vol. 2 *Belgium;* vol. 3 *Netherlands;* vol. 4 *Italy;* vol. 5 *Germany* (1962–3); vol. 6 *France;* vol. 7 *Results for the Community*.

COMMUNITY COUNCIL OF GREATER NEW YORK (1963), *A Family Budget Standard Service*, Research Department.

COMMUNITY COUNCIL OF GREATER NEW YORK (1964), *Annual Price Survey and Family Budget Costs*, Budget Standard Service, Research Department.

COMMUNITY COUNCIL OF GREATER NEW YORK (1967), *How to Measure Ability to Pay for Social and Health Services*.

Consommation, Journal of Centre de Recherches et de Documentation sur la Consommation

1960 Nos. 2 and 3, 'La Consommation des ménages Français en 1956'.
1962 No. 3, 'Les Conditions de Logement des Français en 1961'.
1964 No. 3, 'Comparaison Internationale des Dépenses d'Habitation'.
1964 No. 4, 'La Consommation des Français en 1963'.

CONSUMER BEHAVIOUR INC. (1965), *The Life-cycle and Consumer Behaviour* Consumer Behaviour, vol. 2.

COOPER, J. (1966), Communication to the Journal of the American Medical Association, Sept. 1966, reported in *The Times*, London, 14th Sept. 1966.

CORBETT, ANNE (1966), 'The School Meals Question', *New Society*, 21st July 1966.

CORBETT, ANNE (1966), 'Education Maintenance Grants', *New Society*, 10th Nov. 1966.

COX, P. R. (1967), *Population and Resources*, Paper read to Institute of Actuaries, 23rd Oct. 1967.

CROSSMAN, R. H. S. (1967), *Socialism and Planning*, Fabian Society.

CROWTHER REPORT (1959), 15 to 18, Report of the Central Advisory Council for Education (England), Ministry of Education, H.M.S.O.

DAEDALUS, Journal of the American Academy of Arts and Sciences (1968), *Historical Population Studies*, No. 2, Spring 1968.

DAMPIER, W. C. (1909), *The Family and the Nation: a Study in the Natural Inheritance and Social Responsibility*, London.

DARRAS (ed.) (1966), *Le Partage des Bénéfices*, Editions de Minuit.

DAVID, MARTIN (1962), *Family Composition and Consumption*, North Holland Publishing Co., Amsterdam.

DAVIES, B., and REDDIN, M. (1967), 'School Meals and Plowden', *New Society*, 11th May 1967.

DELPRÉRÉE, ALBERT (1962), *Report of the Working Party on Demography and the Family*, Ministre de la Santé Publique et de la Famille, Brussels.

DENEFFE, PETER (1955), 'Die Aufwendungen für Kinder in Arbeitnehmerhaushaltungen', *Wirtschaft und Statistik*, No. 9, 1955, p. 450. Statistisches Bundesamt, Wiesbaden.

DENMARK (1965), *Income-Expenditure Relations of Danish Wage and Salary Earners*, The Statistical Department, Copenhagen.

DENTLER, R., and WARSHAUER, M. E. (1966), 'Big City Dropouts and Illiterates', *Social Security Bulletin*, **29**, No. 7, July 1966, U.S. Department of Health Education and Welfare.

DESABIE, J. (1965), 'Premiers Résultats d'une Enquête sur l'Habillement (1963–4)', *Études et Conjoncture*, Institut National de la Statistique et des Études Économiques, Presses Universitaires de France.

DESMOTTES, GEORGES (1954), 'Le Rénouveau Familial dans les Institutions', *Rénouveau des Idées sur la Famille: Travaux et Documents*, No. 18, Institut National d'Études Démographiques.

DESMOTTES, GEORGES (1955), 'Technique de l'Assistance à la Petite Enfance en France, en Europe', *Pour la Vie: Revue d'Études Familiales*, No. 11, 1955.

DESMOTTES, G. (1959), 'Conclusions de la Conférence de Vienne', *Familles dans le Monde*, Sept. 1959.

DEUTSCHE AKADEMIE FÜR BEVÖLKERUNGSWISSENSCHAFT (1965), *Demographisch bedingte Veränderungen der Sozialstruktur—Bevölkerungswissenschaftliche Vorträge auf der Arbeitstagung Marburg 1964*, Akademie—Veröffentlichung Reihe A, Nr. 8, 1965, Hamburg.

DEUTSCHER VEREIN FÜR ÖFFENTLICHE UND PRIVATE FÜRSORGE, 'Die Stellung des Pflegekindes in der gewandelten Gesellschaft' (Report of the Council, March 1964), *Nachrichtendienst*, 44, Nr. 5, 1964, p. 193.

DOCUMENTA GEIGY (1964), 'Nutritional Values', reprinted from *Documenta Geigy Scientific Tables*, Geigy Pharmaceutical Co., Manchester.

DONNISON, D. V. (1961), 'The Movement of Households in England', *Journal of Royal Statistical Society*, Series A, 124, 60, 1961.

DONNISON, D. V. (1963), 'More Rented Houses Needed', *Guardian*, 13th Aug. 1963.

DONNISON, D. V. (1965), *Social Policy and Administration*, Allen & Unwin.

DONNISON, D. V. (1967), *The Government of Housing*, Penguin Books.

DOUGLAS, J. W. B. (1964), *The Home and the School—a Study of Ability and Attainment in the Primary School*, MacGibbon & Kee.

DOUGLAS, J. W. B., et al. (1968), *All our Future*, Peter Davies.

DRION, E. F. (1961), 'The Intercorrelations between the Nutrients consumed by a group of families in the Netherlands', *Journal of Royal Statistical Society*, Series A, 124, Part 3, 1961, p. 314.

DUBLIN, L. I., and LOTKA, A. J. (1930), *The Money Value of a Man*, Ronald, N.Y., reprinted (1947).

EDUCATION AND SCIENCE, DEPARTMENT OF (1964–5), 'Education under Social Handicap', *Reports on Education*, No. 17, Dec. 1964, No. 20, Mar. 1965, No. 22, June 1965, H.M.S.O.

EDUCATION AND SCIENCE, DEPARTMENT OF (1965), *Remission of the School Dinner Charge*, Circular 9/64.

EDUCATION AND SCIENCE, DEPARTMENT OF (1965), *Nutritional Standard of the School Dinner*, H.M.S.O.

EDUCATIONAL WELFARE OFFICERS (1968), *The High Cost of Education: A Cause of Poverty?*, Report to Annual Conference.

EIRE (1968), 'Household Budgets Inquiry: preliminary result'; *Irish Statistical Bulletin*, June 1968, Central Statistical Office, Dublin.

EMPLOYMENT AND PRODUCTIVITY, MINISTRY OF (ex Ministry of Labour) (1968), *A Report of the Cost of Living Advisory Committee*, Cmnd 3677, H.M.S.O.

ENGEL, ERNST (1857), 'Die Produktions und Konsumptionsverhältnisse des Königsreichs Sachsen', *Zeitschrift des Statistischen Bureaus des Königlichen Sächsischen Ministerium des Innern*, 8–9, Nov. 22, 1857, p. 27. Reprinted as appendix to his paper of 1895 in International Bulletin of Statistics.

ENGEL, ERNST (1895), 'Die Lebenskosten Belgischer Arbeiterfamilien, Früher und Jetzt ermittelt aus Familienhaushaltrechnungen', *International Bulletin of Statistics*, 9, p. 1–124, 1895.

EPSTEIN, L. A. (1961), 'Some effects of low income on children and their families', *Social Security Bulletin*, 24, Feb. 1961 U.S. Department of Health Education and Welfare.

EPSTEIN, L. A. (1963), 'Unmet Need in a Land of Abundance', *Social Security Bulletin*, 26, No. 5, May 1963, U.S. Department of Health, Education and Welfare.

EPSTEIN, L. A., and SKOLNIK, A. M. (1965), 'Social Security after Thirty Years', *Social Security Bulletin*, 28, No. 8, Aug. 1965, U.S. Department of Health, Education and Welfare.

ERICKSON, ANN (1968), 'Clothing the Urban American Family: How much for whom?', *Monthly Labor Review*, 91, No. 1, Jan. 1968

ERRITT, M. J., and NICHOLSON, J. L. (1958), 'The 1955 Savings Survey', *Bull Ox. Inst. Stats.*, 20, No. 2, 1958.

Études et Conjoncture, Revue Mensuelle de l'Institut National de la Statistique et des Études Economiques:
1964 May: 'Premiers Résultats d'une Enquête sur l'Habillement 1963–4'.
Dec.: 'L'Emploi Féminin en 1962 et son Évolution depuis 1954', by M. Praderie and V. Gentil.
1965 June: 'Les Vacances des Français en 1964'.
'Projection de la Consommation des Ménages en 1970' by G. Vangrevelinghe, 1. 'Transport', 2. 'Habillement'.
1965 Sept. 'Projection de la Consommation des Ménages en 1970 Les Dépenses d'Habitation', by G. Vangrevelinghe.
Dec. 'Les Revenus des Ménages en 1962', J. P. Ruault.
1966 May: 'Nouveaux Résultats des Enquêtes sur les Vacances des Français'.
July: 'Les Ressources des Ménages par Categorie Socioprofessionelle'.
Nov.: 'Étude sur les Loyers en 1963, Résultats de l'Enquete sur l'Habillement 1963–4'.
1967 Feb.: 'Une Enquête sur la Formation et la Qualification des Français en 1964'.
1968 Jan.: 'Situation démographique en 1966.'

EULER, M. (1965), 'Die Struktur des privaten Verbrauch nach vorläufigen Ergebnissen der Einkommens—und Verbrauchsstichprobe 1962–3', *Wirtschaft und Statistik*, 1965, No. 8, p. 488, Statistisches Bundesamt, Wiesbaden.

EULER, M. (1966), 'Die Einkommen von Arbeitnehmerhaushalten und von Nichterwerbstätigenhaushalten', *Wirtschaft und Statistik*, 1966, No. 2, Statistisches Bundesamt, Wiesbaden.

Familles dans le Monde, Journal of the International Union of Family Organizations, 1948–62.

Familles d'Aujurd'hui (1968), Report of a Conference, Éditions de l'Institut de Sociologie, Université Libre de Bruxelles.

FÉDERATION DES FAMILLES DE FRANCE (1961), Report of Congress at Angers.

FINANCIAL STATEMENT (1965–6) and (1968–9), H.M.S.O.

FINLAND: CENTRAL UNION FOR CHILD WELFARE (1967), *Social Facts about Children in Finland*, Publication No. 28.

FINLAND, *Consumption Investigation Towns and Market Towns 1955–56* Official Statistics, Helsinki.

FINLAND (1963), *Housing Subsidies for Families with Children*, State Housing Board (mimeograph).

FISHER, JANET (1952), 'Income spending and saving patterns of consumer units in different age groups', *Studies in Income and Wealth*, **15**, National Bureau of Economic Research.

FISHER, JANET (1955), 'Family life-cycle analysis in research on consumer behaviour', *Consumer Behaviour*, vol. 2.

FLETCHER, RONALD (1965), *Human Needs and Social Order*, Michael Joseph.

FLORENCE, P. SARGENT (1964), 'The Public Cost of Large Families', *Commonwealth Digest Supplement*, Dec. 1964.

FLOUD, J. E., and HALSEY, A. H., *et al.* (1956), *Social Class and Educational Opportunity*, Heinemann.

FOGARTY, M. P. (1957), *Christian Democracy in Western Europe*, Routledge & Kegan Paul.

FOGARTY, M. P. (1961), *The Just Wage*, Charles Birchall.

FOGARTY, M. P. (1966), *Wives, Widows and Children*, Liberal Publication Department.

FOGARTY, M. (1967), *Social Security*, Current Topics, May-June **6**, No. 5 and 6, Liberal Publication Dept.

FOOD AND AGRICULTURE ORGANISATION (1947), *Child Nutrition*, A Report prepared with World Health Organisation for the United Nations Children's Emergency Fund.

FOOD AND AGRICULTURE ORGANISATION (1953), *School Feeding: the contribution to child nutrition*, F.A.O. Nutritional Studies, No. 10.

FOOD AND AGRICULTURE ORGANISATION (1957), *Calorie Requirements*, F.A.O. Nutritional Studies, No. 15.

FOOD AND AGRICULTURE ORGANISATION (1957), *Protein Requirements*, F.A.O. Nutritional Studies, No. 16.

FOOD AND AGRICULTURE ORGANISATION AND WORLD HEALTH ORGANISA-TION (1955), *Report of a Conference on Human Protein Requirements and their fulfilment in Practice*.

FORSYTH, F. G. (1960), The Relationship between Family Size and Family Expenditure, *Journal of Royal Statistical Society*, Series A, **123**, Part 4, p. 367, 1960.

FRANCE (1960), 'Mésures en Faveur de la Famille en France', *Familles dans le Monde*, June and Sept. 1960.

FRANCE (1963–4), *Budgets Familiaux*, vol. 6, Office Statistique, Communautés Européennes, Brussels.

FRANCE (1965), 'Les Enquêtes Alimentaires de 1953 à 1965 ; Aperçu bibliographique', *Bulletin of the Institut National de la Santé et de la Récherche Médicale*, **20**, No. 3, 1965, p. 257–88.

FRANCE (1967), 'La Fécondité en France', *Informations Sociales*, Journal of Union Nationale des Caisses d'Allocations Familiales, Nos. 8 and 9, Aug.–Sept. 1967.

FRANCE, HAUTE COMITÉ DE LA POPULATION ET DE LA FAMILLE (1967), *La Régulation des Naissances*, Documentation Française.

FRANKLIN, N. N. (1967), 'The Concept and Measurement of Minimum Living Standards', *International Labour Review*, **95**, No. 4, April 1967.

FREEDMAN, RONALD (1962), 'The Sociology of Human Fertility; A Trend Report and Bibliography', *Current Sociology*, V X–XI, No. 2, 1961–2, Oxford University Press.

FREEDMAN, R. (1963), 'Normes for Family Size in Under-developed Countries', *Proc. Roy. Soc.*, Series B, **159**, No. 974, 10th Dec. 1963, pp. 120–41.

FREIER, D. (1963), 'Die berufstätigen Mütter', *Neues Beginnen*, No. 4, 1963, p. 55.

FRIEDLANDE, W. A. (1962), *Individualism and Social Welfare: an Analysis of the System of Social Security and Social Welfare in France*, Free Press of Glenco.

FRIEDMAN, M. (1952), 'A Method of Comparing Incomes of Families Differing in Composition', *Studies in Income and Wealth*, **15**, The National Bureau of Economic Research, N.Y.

GENERAL REGISTER OFFICE (1951), Census, *Housing Report, England and Wales*, H.M.S.O.

GENERAL REGISTER OFFICE (1961), Census, *Fertility Tables, England and Wales*, H.M.S.O.

GENERAL REGISTER OFFICE (1961), Census, *Household Composition Tables*, H.M.S.O.

GERIG, DANIEL S., and MYERS, ROBERT J. (1965), 'Canadian Pension Plan of 1965', *Social Security Bulletin*, 28, No. 11, Nov. 1965, Dept. of Health, Education and Welfare.

GERMANY (1932), Family Expenditure Survey 1928, *Die Lebenshaltung von 2000 Arbeiter—Angestellter—und Beamtenhaushaltungen im deutschen Reich von Jahre 1927–28*, Einzelschriften zur Statistik des Deutschen Reichs, Bearbeitet im Statistischen Reichsamt, Berlin 1932.

GERMANY, Expenditure on Children within Families, 'Die Aufwendungen für Kinder in Arbeitnehmerhaushaltungen', *Wirtschaft und Statistik*, Sept. 1955, p. 450, Statistisches Bundesamt, Wiesbaden.

GERMANY (1955), *Familie und Sozialreform*, Symposium. Gesellschaft für Sozialen Fortschritt e.v., Duncker and Humblot, Berlin.

GERMANY (1955), Proceedings of Conference, *Öffentliche Einkommenshilfe und Richtsatzpolitik*, Carl Heymanns, Berlin.

GERMANY (1961), *Social Conditions and Social Security*, Press and Information Office of Federal Government.

GERMANY (1962–3), *Budgets Familiaux vol. 5*, Office Statistique Communautés Européennes, Brussels.

GERMANY, Children per Marriage, 'Die Kinderzahlen in den Ehen nach Bevölkerungsgruppen', *Wirtschaft und Statistik*, 1964, No. 1, p. 71, Statistisches Bundesamt, Wiesbaden.

GERMANY, Employment of Women and Mothers and Child Minding, 'Die Erwerbstätigkeit von Frauen und Müttern und die Betreuung ihrer Kinder', *Wirtschaft und Statistik*, 1964, No. 8, Statistisches Bundesamt, Wiesbaden.

GERMANY (1965), *Child Support Scales*, Official subsistence scales for all the provinces of Germany including children of different ages for January 1965, *Nachrichtendienst* Nr. 3, March 1965.

GERMANY, *Sample Consumer Survey (1962–3)*, Wirtschaft und Statistik, 1965, No. 8, p. 480; 1966, No. 2, p. 106, Statistisches Bundesamt, Wiesbaden.

GESELLSCHAFT FÜR SOZIALEN FORTSCHRITT (1960), *Die ökonomischen Grundlagen der Familie in ihrer gesellschaftlichen Bedeutung*, Report of a Committee with recommendations and discussion, Duncker and Humblot Berlin.

GILLES, J. (1961), 'Le Consommateur dans le Marché Commun', *Familles dans le Monde*, Dec. 1961.

GINSBERG, ELI (1960), *Focus on Youth*, Preparatory Report to the 1960 White House Conference on Children and Youth.

GLASS, D. V. (1940), *Population Policies and Movements in Europe*, Oxford University Press. Reissue with new introduction, 1967.

GLASS, D. V. (1960), 'Population Growth, Fertility and Population Policy', Address to British Association 1960, *Advancement of Science*, **68**, Nov. 1960, pp. 353–63.

GLASS, D. V. (1968), 'Fertility Trends in Europe since the Second World War' Paper before University of Michigan *Conference on Fertility and Family Planning*, Nov. 1967, *Population Studies*, **22**, No. 1, Mar. 1968.

GLASS, D. V. (1968), Marriage Survey, reported in 'Contraception in Marriage', *Family Planning*, **17**, No. 3, Oct. 1968, p. 55.

GLASS, RUTH (1955), 'Urban Sociology in Great Britain,' *Current Sociology*, vol. IV, 1955.

GOODE, WILLIAM J. (1964), *The Family*, Prentice Hall.

GOODE, WILLIAM J. (1966), 'Family Patterns and Human Rights', *International Social Science Journal*, **18**, No. 1, 1966.

GORDON, M. S. (ed.) (1965), *Parents in America*, Proceedings of a Conference, University of California.

GRAHAM-HALL REPORT (1967), *Report of Committee on Statutory Maintenance Allowances*, Home Office Cmnd 3587, H.M.S.O.

GROOM, PHYLLIS (1967), 'A New City Worker's Family Budget', *Monthly Labour Review*, **90**, No. 11, Nov. 1967.

GROTH, SEPP (1961), *Kinder ohne Familie: Das Schicksal des unehelichen Kindes*, Juventa Verlag, München.

GUBBELS, ROBERT (1966), *La Citoyenneté Économique de la Femme*, Université Libre de Bruxelles.

GUBBELS, ROBERT (1967), *Le Travail au Féminin*, Éditions Gérard, Verviers, Belgium.

GUELAUD-LERIDON, F. (1964), *Le Travail des Femmes en France*, Institut National d'Études Démographiques, Presses Universitaires de France.

GUELAUD-LERIDON, F. (1967), *Recherches sur la Condition Féminine dans la Société d'Aujourd'hui*, Institut National d'Études Démographiques, Presses Universitaires de France.

GURNEY-DIXON REPORT (1954), *Early Leaving*, Report of the Central Advisory Council for Education (England), Ministry of Education, H.M.S.O.

HAJNAL, S., and HENDERSON, A. M. (1950), 'The Economic Position of the Family', vol. V, Memorandum to the *Royal Commission on Population*, 1950, H.M.S.O.

HALSEY, A. H., FLOUD, J., and ANDERSON, C. ARNOLD (1961), *Education Economy and Society*, Collier-Macmillan Paperback, 1965.

HARBERT, W. B. (1965), 'Who owes Rent?', *Soc. Review, University of Keele*, **13**, July 1965.

L

HARMSEN, HANS (1962), 'Ausmass der Erwerbstätigkeit von Müttern kleiner Kinder in unvollständigen Familien', *Die Heilkunst*, No. 12, Dec. 1962.

HARMSEN, HANS (1962), 'Was wissen wir über die Zahl der Kinder aus unvollständigen Familien in Westdeutschland?', *Gesundheitsfürsorge*, 12, No. 10–11, Oct.–Nov. 1962.

HEISE, BERNT (1962), 'Maladie-Maternité', Report presented to *Conférence Européenne sur la Sécurité Sociale*, Brussels, Dec. 1962, vol. 1, p. 247.

HEMMINGS, M. F. W. (1965), 'Social Security in Britain and Certain other Countries', *National Institute Economic Review*, 33, Aug. 1965.

HENDERSON, A. M. (1949), 'The Cost of Children', Part 1, *Population Studies*, 3, No. 1, 1949, pp. 130–50.

HENDERSON, A. M. (1950), 'The Cost of a Family', *Review of Economic Studies*, 17, (2), No. 43, 1949–50, pp. 127–48.

HENDERSON, A. M. (1950), 'The Cost of Children', Part 2 and 3, *Population Studies*, 4, No. 3, 1950, pp. 267–98.

HESSE (1959), *Zu der Berechnung von Mindestunterhaltskosten für uneheliche Kinder*, Statistisches Landesamt, Wiesbaden, Jan. 1959.

HESSE (1961), (1962) *Die Unterhaltskosten eines Kindes von der Geburt bis zum 16 Lebensjahr im März 1961, und März 1962*, Statistisches Landesamt, Hesse.

HESSE (1965), *Monatliche Aufwandbetrage zur Ermittlung des notwendigen Lebensunterhaltes hilfsbedürftigen Personen in April 1965*. Statistisches Landesamt, Hesse.

HILL, REUBEN (1962), 'Cross-National Family Research: Attempts and Prospects', *International Social Science Journal*, 14, No. 3, 1962.

HINRICHS, A. FORD (1948), 'The Budget in Perspective', *Worker's Budgets in the United States 1946 and 1947*, Bulletin No. 927, U.S. Department of Labor.

HOCHARD, J. (1963), *L'Institution Française des Prestations Familiale*, Union Nationale des Caisses d'Allocations Familiales.

HÖFFNER, JOSEPH (1954), *Ausgleich der Familienlasten*, Paderborn (quoted by Schmucker, 1961, p. 29).

HOFSTEN, ERLAND VAN (1955), 'The Cost of a Child: Alternative Solutions', Paper before the *World Population Conference 1954*, Conference Papers vol. VI, United Nations 1955.

HOFSTEN, ERLAND VAN (1961), 'Konsumtions-beloppets storlek som mått på Levnadsnivån', *Hushållens Konsumtion år 1958*, Sveriges Officiella Statistik.

HOFSTEN, ERLAND VAN, and KARLSSON, MAJ-BRITT (1961), 'Kostnader för barns Konsumtion vård och uppfostran åren 1958 och 1961', *Sociala*

Meddelanden, Statistik Information No. 6, 1961, pp. 129–42. (English summary).

HORDER, LORD, REDDAWAY, W. B., TITMUSS, R. M., *et al.* (1946), *Rebuilding Family Life in the Post-war World—An Enquiry with Recommendations*, Odhams Press.

HOUGHTON, D. (1967), *Paying for the Social Services*, Institute of Economic Affairs, Second edition, 1968.

HOUSE OF COMMONS DEBATES,
1964, 20th Nov.   Pensions and Benefits (Improvements), Minister's statement.
1966, 7th Feb.   National Insurance Bill.
1966, 23rd Feb.   Welfare State, Mr Douglas Houghton.
1966, 24th May   Ministry of Social Security Bill.
1966, 17th June   Ministry of Social Security Bill.
1966, 21st Dec.   Child Poverty, Dr David Owen.
1967, 17th Feb.   National Health Service (Family Planning) Bill.
1967, 24th Nov.   Minimum Income, Mr Gwilym Roberts.
1967, 29th Nov.   Family Allowances and National Insurance Bill.
1968, 16th Jan.   Public Expenditure, Prime Minister's statement.
1968, 17th Jan.   Public Expenditure, Chancellor's statement.
1968, 26th Feb.   Public Expenditure and Receipts Bill.
1968, 23rd May   Family Allowances and National Insurance (No. 2) Bill.
1968, 5th Nov.   Unmarried Mothers, Miss Joan Lester.

HOUSE OF LORDS DEBATES,
1968, 20th March   Selectivity in the Welfare Services.
1968, 21st June   Family Allowances and National Insurance (No. 2) Bill.

HOUSING AND LOCAL GOVERNMENT, MINISTRY OF (1966), *Rating Act 1966, Appendix, Rate Rebates: Working Arrangements with National Assistance Board*, Circular 23/66. *The Rating Act 1966*, RN 14, Rate Rebates, Leaflet 1968.

HOUSING AND LOCAL GOVERNMENT, MINISTRY OF (1967), *Rent Rebate Schemes*, Circular 46/67, 'Ministers urge Rent Rebate schemes to help tenants with low incomes or large families', Press notice, 30th June 1967, No. 206.

HOWE, G., and LAMONT, N. (1967), *Policies for Poverty*, Bow Group Memorandum (mimeographed).

HUMPHREY, HUBERT H. (1964), *War on Poverty*, McGraw-Hill.

HUNT, A. P. (1968), *Survey of Women's Employment*, Social Survey, H.M.S.O.

HYLAND, LEWIS (1966), 'Culture and Class in Child-rearing among Low Income Urban Negroes', *Jobs and Color*, ed. Arthur Ross, Harcourt Brothers & World.

ILERSIC, A. R. (1968), 'Future Developments in Taxation in the United Kingdom', *Proposals for change in the United Kingdom system of*
L*

Taxation, Asta House Pamphlets No. 2, Barking Regional College of Technology.

INCORPORATED ASSOCIATION OF ARCHITECTS AND SURVEYORS (1964), *Comment on the South East Study* (mimeographed). See also *The Times*, London, 9th and 10th Sept. 1964.

Informations Sociales, Revue Mensuelle de l'Union Nationale des Caisses d'Allocations Familiales. The following numbers deal with aspects of family policy:

1951, July No. 7   *Les obstacles matériel au development de la Famille Ouvrière.*
1951, No. 15   *Problèmes du Logement.*
1952, No. 3   *Politique du Logement.*
1952, No. 22   *Enfance et Famille.*
1956, No. 1   *L'École des Parents.*
1958, Jan., No. 1   *Aspects Sociaux du Logement.*
1958, Mar., No. 3   *Enquête de I.N.E.D. sur l'Action Sociale.*
1958, Dec., No. 12   *Les Jeunes au Travail, 1. Orientation et Apprentissage.*
1960, Jan., No. 1   *Les Jeunes au Travail, 2. Place des Jeunes dans le Monde du Travail.*
1960, Apr., No. 4   *La Formation Professionelle des Femmes.*
1960, Oct.–Nov.   *L'Action Sociale des Caisses d'Allocations Familiales.*
1961, Jan., No. 1   *Réussite et Échec Scolaire.*
1961, Feb., No. 2   *Réussite et Échec Scolaire.*
1961, Aug., No. 8   *Famille et Loisirs.*
1961, Sept., No. 9   *Les Mères Célibataires.*
1962, Jan., No. 1   *L'Action Sociale des Caisses d'Allocations Familiales.*
1962, Mar., No. 3   *Problèmes posés par la Limitation et la Regulation de la Fécondité Naturelle.*
1963, Dec., No. 12   *Contribution de la Sécurité Sociale a l'Action Sociale Familiale.*
1964, Jan., No. 1–2   *L'Économie Sociale Familiale.*
1965, July–Aug., Nos. 7–8   *Les Foyers de Jeunes Travailleurs.*
1966, Jan., No. 1   *Les Femmes et le Travail.*
1966, Mar., No. 3   *Les Conditions de Vie des Familles Françaises.*
1966, Sept., No. 11   *Les Vacances Familiales.*
1967, Feb.–Mar., Nos. 2 and 3   *L'Économie Sociale Familiale.*
1967, Apr., No. 4   *Regards sur la Consommation.*
1968, Jan.–Feb. No. 1 and 2   *La Mère Célibataire et son Enfant.*
1968, Apr.–May, No. 4 and 5   *Le Travail Social de Communauté.*
1968, June, No. 6   *Les Jeunes Filles.*
1968, Nov., No. 11   *Réflexions et Documents sur les Besoins.*

INLAND REVENUE, *Allowances for the Year, Notes on Allowances and Notice of coding*, for years 1966–7 and 1967–8, *PAYE Coding Guide*, 1968–9.

INLAND REVENUE, COMMISSIONERS OF, *Reports for years ended* 1963, 1964, 1965, 1966.

INSTITUT NATIONAL D'ÉTUDES DÉMOGRAPHIQUES (1954), *Renouveau des Idées sur la Famille*, Presses Universitaires de France.

INTERNATIONAL LABOUR OFFICE (1964), *Women Workers in a Changing World*, Report of a Conference, Report No. VI (1) and VI (2).

INTERNATIONAL LABOUR OFFICE (1965), *Employment of Women with Family Responsibilities*, Report No. V (1) and V (2).

INTERNATIONAL SOCIAL SERVICE REVIEW (1956), *Family and Child Welfare*, No. 1, Jan. 1956, United Nations Department of Economic and Social Affairs, New York.

INTERNATIONAL UNION OF FAMILY ORGANISATIONS, *Familles dans le Monde*, Journal of IUFO, 1948–62.

INTERNATIONAL UNION OF FAMILY ORGANISATIONS (1958), *Redécouverte de la Famille à Travers le Monde. Problèmes Familiaux dans le Monde*, Papers of World Conference, Paris 1958.

INTERNATIONAL UNION OF FAMILY ORGANISATIONS (1959), *Niveaux de Vie et Dimensions de la Famille*, Report of Commission on Family Levels of Living.

INTERNATIONAL UNION OF FAMILY ORGANISATIONS (1962), *Report to European Conference on Social Security*, vol. 2, Communauté Économique Européenne.

INTERNATIONAL UNION OF FAMILY ORGANISATIONS (1963), *Le Travail Professionel des Femmes Muriées des Milieux Populaires*.

INTERNATIONAL UNION OF FAMILY ORGANISATIONS (1966), *New Families in Society*, Report of World Conference, Quebec 1966.

INTERNATIONAL UNION OF FAMILY ORGANISATIONS, *Information Bulletin of European Secretariat*, 1966, 1967, 1968.

ISAMBERT-JAMATI, VIVIANE (1960), 'Qualification Professionelle et Adaptation au Travail', *Revue Française de Sociologie*, 1960.

ISAMBERT-JAMATI, VIVIANE (1960), *Enquête sur les écarts d'éducation entre les garçons et les filles dans la société urbaine française contemporaine*, Centre d'Études Sociologiques.

ISAMBERT-JAMATI, VIVIANE (1961), 'Le Choix du Métier', *Esprit*, May 1961.

ITALY (1960), *Indagine Statistica sui Bilanci di Famiglie non Agricole negli Anni 1953–54*, **89**, Serie VIII, vol. 2, 1960, Instituto Centrale di Statistica.

ITALY (1963–4), *Budgets Familiaux*, vol. 4, Office Statistique des Communautés Européennes, Brussels.

IYER, S. N. (1966), 'Degree of Protection under Family Allowances Schemes', *International Labour Review*, **95**, No. 5, Nov. 1966.

JACKSON, J. M. (1966), 'Poverty National Assistance and the Family', *Scottish Journal of Political Economy*, XIII, No. 2, June 1966.

JESSEN, ARND (1955), 'Der Aufwand für Kinder in der Bundesrepublik im Jahr 1954', *Familie und Sozialreform*, Symposium of Gesellschaft für Sozialen Fortschritt, Duncker und Humblot, Berlin.

JOHN, VERA P. (1964), *A Brief Survey of Research on the Characteristics of Children from Low Income Backgrounds*, Paper prepared for the U.S. Commission on Education 1964.

JONES, D. CARADOG (1949), *Social Surveys*, Hutchinson.

JONES, K. (1967), 'Immigrants and the Social Services', *National Institute Economic Review*, No. 41, Aug. 1967.

JORGENSEN, E. (1965), *Income-Expenditure Relations of Danish Wage and Salary Earners*, Statistical Department, Copenhagen.

JOSEPH, KEITH (1966), *A New Strategy for Social Security*, Conservative Political Centre.

JULEMONT, G., and MORSA, J. (1964), 'Le Nombre d'Enfants Désirés', *Population et Famille*, Dec. 1964, p. 19, Ministre de la Santé Publique et de la Famille, Brussels.

JUNKER, REINHOLD (1965–8), *Die Lage der Mütter in der Bundesrepublik Deutschland*,
Vol. 1. *Mütter in Vollfamilien.*
Part I *Belastungen und Folgen.*
Part II *Vorstellungen und Ziele.*
Vol. 2 *Mütter in Halbfamilien—Mütter in Vollfamilien.*
Vol. 3 *Ergebnisse und praktische Konsequenzen.*
Deutscher Verein für Öffentliche und Private Fürsorge, Frankfurt-am-Main.

KAIM-CAUDLE, P. R. (1967), *Aid to Families*, Address to Annual Conference of Institute of Municipal Treasurers and Accountants.

KAIM-CAUDLE, P. R. (1968), 'Selectivity in Family Allowances', *Social Services for All?* Part 1, Fabian Society.

KELSALL, R. K. (1963), *Women and Teaching*, Ministry of Education, H.M.S.O.

KEMSLEY, W. F. F. (1952), 'Estimating Individual Expenditure from Family Totals', *Applied Statistics*, 1, No. 3, 1952, pp. 192–201.

KEMSLEY, W. F. F., and NICHOLSON, J. L. (1960), 'Some Experiments in Methods of Conducting Family Expenditure Surveys', *Journal Royal Statistical Society*, Series A, Part 3, 1960, pp. 307–28.

KILAGAWA, E. M., and HAUSER, P. M. (1964), 'Trends in Differential Fertility and Mortality in a Metropolis—Chicago', *Contributions to Urban Sociology*, ed. E. W. Burgess and D. J. Bogue, University of Chicago Press.

KIRK, HAZEL (1953), *The Family in the American Economy*, University of Chicago Press.

KLEIN, L. R. (1958), 'The British Propensity to Save', *Journal of the Royal Society*, Series A, **121**, 60, 1958.

KLEIN, VIOLA (1960), *Working Wives*, Occasional Paper No. 15, Institute of Personnel Management.

KLEIN, VIOLA (1965), *Britain's Married Women Workers*, Routledge & Kegan Paul.

KÖHLER, W. (1963), *Handbuch des Unterhaltsrechts*, Franz Vahlen, Frankfurt.

KUUSI, PEKKA (1961), *60-luun Sosiaalipolitikka*, translated by Jaakko Railo as *Social Policy for the Sixties* (1964), Finnish Social Policy Association.

LABOUR, MINISTRY OF, FAMILY EXPENDITURE SURVEYS, 1963, 1964, 1965, 1966, 1967, H.M.S.O.

LABOUR, MINISTRY OF, (1964), *Method of Construction and Calculation of the Index of Retail Prices*, H.M.S.O.

LABOUR, MINISTRY OF (1964), *Sick Pay Schemes: A Report*, National Joint Advisory Council, H.M.S.O.

LABOUR PARTY (1963), *New Frontiers for Social Security*.

LABOUR PARTY (1968), *Family Allowances*, Talking Points, No. 9, July 1968.

LAFITTE, F. (1963), *Family Planning in the Sixties*, Report of the Family Planning Association Working Party (mimeographed).

LAFITTE, F. (1966), *The Future of Social Security*, Discussion Paper No. 6, Faculty of Commerce and Social Science, Birmingham University (mimeographed).

LAMALE, HELEN H. (1958), 'Changes in Concepts of Income Adequacy over the last Century', *American Economic Review*, **48**, No. 2, 1958, p. 291.

LAMALE, HELEN H. (1963), 'Workers' Wealth and Family Living Standards', *Monthly Labor Review*, **86**, No. 6, June 1963, U.S. Department of Labor.

LAMALE, HELEN H., and STOTZ, MAYNARD, S. (1960), 'The Interim City Worker's Family Budget', *Monthly Labor Review*, Aug. 1960, U.S. Department of Labor.

LANSING, J. B., and MORGAN, JAMES N. (1955), 'Consumer Finances over the Life-cycle', *Consumer Behaviour vol. 2, The Life-cycle and Consumer Behaviour*.

LAMBERT, ROYSTON (1964), *Nutrition in Britain, 1950–60*, Occasional Papers on Social Administration, Codicote Press, Welwyn.

LAROQUE, PIERRE (1958), *Réflexions sur les Prestations Familiales*, Union Nationale des Caisses d'Allocations Familiales.

LAROQUE, PIERRE (1958), 'Les Niveaux de Vie des Familles', Paper to the *World Congress on the Family*, Paris 1958, International Union of Family Organisations.

LAROQUE, P. (1959), 'Niveaux de Vie des Familles, Securité Sociale, Compensations des Charges Familiales', *Familles dans le Monde*, March 1959.

LAROQUE, PIERRE (1961), *Succès et Faiblesse de l'Effort Social Francais*, Armand Colin.

LAROQUE, PIERRE (1962), *Les Classes Sociales*, Presses Universitiares de France.

LAURENT, J. (1961), 'Le Travail Professionel de la Mère Hors du Foyer', *Familles dans le Monde*, **14**, No. 3, Sept. 1961.

LAZAR, L. (1965), 'The Economic Aspects of Family Law: The Basic Law Relating to Family Taxation', *The Accountants Journal*, Apr. 1965.

LEAGUE OF NATIONS HEALTH ORGANISATION (1935), *Report on the Physiological Bases of Nutrition*, Technical Commission.

LEBEL, R. (1960), 'Familles et Problèmes Economiques en France', *Informations Sociales*, Oct.–Nov. 1960.

LEBEL, R. (1962), 'Prestations Familiales', Report presented to *Conférence Européenne sur la Sécurité Sociale Brussels*, Dec. 1962, vol. 1, p. 377.

LEBEL, R. (1963), 'Évolution de l'Institution des Allocations Familiales en France', *Informations Sociales*, Dec. 1963.

LEES, D. (1967), 'Poor Families and Fiscal Reform', *Lloyds Bank Review*, No. 86, Oct. 1967.

LEGOUX, YVES (1962), 'Attitudes des Jeunes Filles devant une Profession Technique', *Sociologie du Travail*, July/Sept. 1962.

LEVASSEUR, E. (1889), *La Population Française*, Arthur Rousseau, Paris.

LEWIS, HYLAN (1961), 'Child Rearing Practices among Low Income Families', *Casework Papers*, 1961, pp. 79–92, Family Service Association of America.

LIDZ, THEODORE (1964), *The Family and Human Adaptation*, Hogarth Press.

Le Ligueur, weekly newspaper of the Family Organisations of Belgium.

LIVERPOOL PERSONAL SERVICE SOCIETY (1966), *Evidence to Central Housing Advisory Committee, Ministry of Housing and Local Government*, 25th Feb. 1966.

LUXEMBOURG (1963–4), *Budgets Familiaux*, vol. 1, Office Statistique Communautés Européennes, Brussels.

LYDALL, H. F. (1951), 'A Pilot Survey of Incomes and Savings', *Oxford Bulletin of Statistics*, **13**, No. 9, 1951, pp. 257–91.

LYDALL, H. F. (1955), *British Income and Savings*, Blackwell, Oxford.

LYDALL, H. F. (1955), 'The Life Cycle in Income, Savings and Asset Ownership', *Econometrica*, **23**, No. 2, Apr. 1955.

LYNES, TONY (1962), *National Assistance and National Prosperity*, Occasional Papers on Social Administration, No. 5, Codicote Press.

LYNES, TONY (1963), *Pension Rights and Wrongs*, Fabian Society.

LYNES, TONY (1968), 'Social Security Research', *Forecasting and the Social Sciences*, ed. M. Young, Heinemann.

MABIT, CHARLES (1961), 'Les Familles Nombreuses devant l'Instruction et l'Avenir de leurs Enfants', Supplementary Brochure to *Action Familiale*, Dec. 1961.

McGREGOR, O. R. (1964), 'Family, Home and Environment', *The Frontiers of Sociology*, ed. Fyvel, T. R., Cohen and West.

McGREGOR, O. R., and ROWNTREE, G. (1962), 'The Family', *Society: Problems and Methods of Study*, ed. Welford, A. T., Routledge.

MACKINTOSH, J. M. (1944), 'Population and Human Motives', Evidence to *Royal Commission on Population*, Evidence, 36.

M'GONIGLE, G. C. M., and KIRBY, J. (1963), *Poverty and Public Health*, Gollancz.

MACLURE, STUART (1968), *Learning Beyond our Means?*, Councils and Education Press.

MADGE, CHARLES (1943), *Wartime Patterns of Saving and Spending*, Oxford University Press.

MAGIERSKA, BARBARA (1961), 'Le Rôle du Milieu Familiale', *Informations Sociales*, Feb. 1961, Union Nationale des Caisses d'Allocations Familiales.

MÄKINEN-OLLINEN, AUNE (1964), 'The Employment of Women in Finland, especially that of family mothers, and the organisation to help them', Series *Finnish Features* (English), Ministry of Foreign Affairs.

MÄKINEN-OLLINEN, AUNE (1965), 'De Faderlösa Familjerna' (Fatherless Families, English Summary), *Social Tidskrift*, 1–2, 1965.

MARSHALL, ALFRED (1927), *Principles of Economics*, Macmillan (first Edition 1890).

MARTIN, YVES (1956), 'Niveau de Vie des Familles suivant le Nombre d'Enfants', *Population*, **11**, No. 3, July–Sept. 1956, p. 407.

MARTIN REPORT (1960), *Report of the Working Party on Assistance with the Cost of Boarding Education*, H.M.S.O.

MARTZ, H. (1963), 'Illegitimacy and Dependency', *Health Education and Welfare Indicators*, Sept. 1963, U.S. Department of Health, Education and Welfare.

MAYER, F. (1965), 'Zur Feststellung des Lebensbedarfs eines Kindes', Deutscher Verein für öffentliche und private Fürsorge, *Nachrichtendienst*, **45**, No. 1, 1965, p. 17, and see also **44**, p. 472, Frankfurt-am-Main.

MAYS, J. B. (1967), *The School in its Social Setting*, Longmans.

MENDER, S. (1967), 'The Problem of Measuring Poverty', *The British Journal of Sociology*, **18**, No. 1, Mar. 1967.

MERRIAM, I. (1960), 'The Social Security Status of the American People', *Social Security Bulletin*, Aug. 1960, U.S. Department of Health,Education and Welfare.

MILLER, D. S. (1966), *Scrooge in the Kitchen: The Economics of Good Nutrition* (mimeographed).

MILLER, F. J. W., *et al.* (1960), *Growing up in Newcastle-upon-Tyne*, Oxford University Press for the Nuffield Foundation.

MILLOT, MICHÈLE (1968), 'Les Besoins des Familles', *Informations Sociales*, **22**, No. 11, Nov. 1968, Union Nationale des Caisses d'Allocations Familiales.

MILNER-HOLLAND REPORT (1965), *Report of the Committee on Housing in Greater London*, Ministry of Housing and Local Government, Cmnd 2605, H.M.S.O.

MINISTRY OF SOCIAL SECURITY ACT 1966 AND EXPLANATORY MEMORANDUM TO THE BILL, Cmnd 2997.

MISSOFFE, FRANÇOIS (1967), *Jeunes d'Aujourd'hui*, Report of Ministry of Youth and Sports: a summary, Documentation Française.

MORGAN, JAMES N. (1962), 'The Anatomy of Income Distribution', *Review of Economics and Statistics*, **44**, Aug. 1962, p. 270.

MORGAN, J. N., DAVID, M. H., COHEN, W. J., BRAZER, H. E. (1962), *Income and Welfare in the United States*, McGraw-Hill.

MORSA, J. (1963), 'Tendances Récentes de la Fécondité Belge', *Population et Famille*, Oct. 1963, Ministre de la Santé Publique et de la Famille.

MORSA, J. (1967), 'Une Enquête Nationale sur la Fécondité', *Population et Famille*, No. 13, Dec. 1967, Ministre de la Santé Publique et de la Famille.

MUGGE, R. H. (1963), 'Aid to Families with Dependent Children: Initial Findings of the 1961 Report on Characteristics of Recipients', *Social Security Bulletin*, **26**, No. 3, Mar. 1963, U.S. Department of Health, Education and Welfare.

MURCIER, ALAIN (1957), 'Les Comptes Sociaux dans l'Europe des Six', *Le Monde Hebdomadaire*, 2nd Aug. 1967.

MURPHY, ARCHBISHOP (1965), Sermon to Meeting of British Medical Association, *Catholic Herald*, 16th July 1965.

MYRDAL, ALVA (1945), Evidence before United Kingdom *Royal Commission on Population*, 2nd Mar. 1945, Paper O, Evidence 15.

MYRDAL, ALVA (1945), *Nation and Family*, Kegan Paul, Published in Sweden, 1940.

MYERS, R. J., and GERIG, D. S. (1965), 'Canada Pension Plan', *Social Security Bulletin*, **28**, No. 11, Nov. 1965, U.S. Department of Health, Education and Welfare.

NATIONAL ASSISTANCE BOARD, *Reports for years ended 31st Dec., 1964 and 1965*. For report from 1st Jan. to 27th Nov. 1966, see *1st Annual Report 1966* of Ministry of Social Security.

NATIONAL BUREAU OF ECONOMIC RESEARCH, N.Y. (1960), *Demographic and Economic Change in Developed Countries*, Princeton University Press.

NATIONAL CENTER FOR HEALTH STATISTICS (1967), *Selected Family Characteristics and Health Measures*, Series 3, No. 7, U.S. Department of Health, Education and Welfare.

NATIONAL UNION OF TEACHERS (1962), *Investment for National Survival*.

NATIONAL UNION OF TEACHERS (1967), *20 Young Teachers*.

NETHERLANDS, *The Amsterdam Scale*, History and use, Personal communication, Amsterdam Bureau of Statistics.

NETHERLANDS (1954), *Household Expenditures of Lower Employees and Civil Servants*, National Family Expenditure Inquiry 1951, Series B2, No. 1, Central Bureau of Statistics.

NETHERLANDS (1955), *Family Consumption of Manual Workers according to Income and Size of Family*, National Family Expenditure Inquiry 1951, Series B1, No. 5, Central Bureau of Statistics.

NETHERLANDS (1955), *Family Consumption of Agricultural Workers according to Size of the Family*. National Family Expenditure Inquiry 1951, Series B1, No. 6, Central Bureau of Statistics.

NETHERLANDS (1962), *Expenditure of Families of Manual Agricultural and Brain Workers 4 person families*, Family Budgets 1959–60, Central Bureau of Statistics.

NETHERLANDS (1963–4), *Budgets Familiaux*, vol. 3, Office Statistique, Communautés Européennes, Brussels.

NETHERLANDS, NUTRITION COUNCIL (1965), *Recommenced Dietary Allowances*, Committee on Dietary Allowances, Sept. 1964 to Mar. 1965, Personal Communication.

NEVITT, D. (1967), 'The State of the Social Services: Housing', *New Society*, 5th Oct. 1967.

NEWSOM, JOHN (1948), *The Education of Girls*, Faber & Faber.

NEWSOM REPORT (1963), *Half our Future*, Report of the Central Advisory Council for Education (England), Ministry of Education, H.M.S.O.

NICHOLSON, J. L. (1949), 'Variations in Working Class Family Expenditure', Journal Royal Statistical Society, Series A, **112**, No. 4, 1949.

NICHOLSON, J. L. (1964), *Redistribution of Income in the United Kingdom in 1959, 1957 and 1953*, Bowes & Bowes.

NICHOLSON, R. J. (1967), 'The Distribution of Personal Income', Lloyds Bank Review, **83,** Jan. 1967.

NORDRHEIN-WESTFALEN (1958), Paper by H. Mingers, 'Die Lebenshaltung kinderreicher Familien in Nordrhein-Westfalen'. *Statistische Rundschau für das Land Nordrhein-Westfalen,* **10,** No. 11, Nov. 1958, p. 241.

NORDRHEIN-WESTFALEN (1958), *Die Lebenshaltung kinderreicher Familien in Nordrhein-Westfalen,* Statistisches Landesamt.

NORDRHEIN-WESTFALEN (1961), *Aufwand für den Mindestunterhalt eines unehelichen Kindes von der Geburt bis zum vollendeten 16 Lebensjahr in Nordrhein-Westfalen,* Arbeits und Sozialministers, Anlage zum Runderlass, 1961.

NORWAY (1960–1), *Survey of Consumer Expenditure (1960 and 1961),* 3 vols., Central Bureau of Statistics.

NORWAY (1964), *Public Relief and Municipal Social Pensions,* 1963, Central Bureau of Statistics.

OFFICE OF HEALTH ECONOMICS (1963), *Health Services in Western Europe.*

OFFICE OF HEALTH ECONOMICS (1965), *Work lost through Sickness.*

ORSHANSKY, M. (1952), 'Equivalent Levels of Living: Farm and City', *Studies in Income and Wealth,* vol. 15, 1952, National Bureau of Economic Research, N.Y.

ORSHANSKY, M. (1963), 'Children of the Poor in 1964,' *Social Security Bulletin,* **26,** No. 7, July 1963, U.S. Department of Health, Education and Welfare.

ORSHANSKY, M. (1965), 'Counting the Poor: Another Look at the Poverty Profile', *Social Security Bulletin,* **28,** No. 1, Jan. 1965, U.S. Department of Health, Education and Welfare.

ORSHANSKY, M. (1965), 'Who's Who Among the Poor: A Demographic View of Poverty', *Social Security Bulletin,* **28,** No. 7, July 1965, U.S. Department of Health, Education and Welfare.

ORSHANSKY, M. (1966), 'Recounting the Poor', *Social Security Bulletin,* **29,** No. 4, Apr. 1956, U.S. Department of Health, Education and Welfare.

ORSHANSKY, M. (1966), 'More about the Poor', *Social Security Bulletin,* **29,** No. 5, May 1966, U.S. Department of Health, Education and Welfare.

ORSHANSKY, M. (1966), 'The Poor in City and Suburbs 1964', *Social Security Bulletin,* **29,** No. 12, Dec. 1966, U.S. Department of Health, Education and Welfare.

ORSHANSKY, M. (1968), 'Shape of Poverty in 1966', (combination of two articles in Conference of Citizens' Committee for Children of New York, see Burns, E. M. (1968)), *Social Security Bulletin,* **31,** No. 3, Mar. 1968, U.S. Department of Health, Education and Welfare.

OXFORD INSTITUTE OF STATISTICS, Surveys on income and savings during 1950–6. See volumes of Bulletin for these years and Lydall, H. F.; Klein, L. R.; Errit, M. J., in this bibliography.

PAILLAT, M. P. (1960), 'Les Différences de Niveau de Vie au Sein de la Classe Ouvrière', *Population*, **15**, No. 5, Oct.–Dec. 1960, Institut National d'Études Démographiques.

PAILLAT, M. P. (1962), 'Influence du Nombre d'Enfants sur le Niveau de Vie de la Famille: Évolution de 1950 à 1961', *Population*, **17**, No. 3, Mar. 1962, Institut National d'Études Démographiques.

PALMORE, E. (1963), 'Factors Associated with School Dropouts and Juvenile Delinquency Among Lower-class Children', *Social Security Bulletin*, **26**, No. 10, Oct. 1963, U.S. Department of Health, Education and Welfare.

PALMORE, E., *et al.* (1966), *Widows with Children under Social Security*, Office of Research and Statistics, Research Report No. 16, U.S. Department of Health, Education and Welfare.

PARKER-MORRIS REPORT (1961), *Homes for Today and Tomorrow*, H.M.S.O.

PARKES, A. S. (1964), 'Biological Aspects of the Population Explosion', *Nature*, **204**, 320, 24th Oct. 1964.

PENSIONS AND NATIONAL INSURANCE, MINISTRY OF, *Annual Reports 1962–5*.

PENSIONS AND NATIONAL INSURANCE, MINISTRY OF (1966), *Sickness and Unemployment Benefit: Guide to New Earnings-related Short Term Benefits Scheme. National Insurance Act 1966*.

PEQUIGNOT, G., *et al.* (1962), 'Enquête sur l'Alimentation et le Budget Familial à Saint-Étienne, Lyon et Marseilles', *Bulletin de l'Institut National d'Hygiène*, **17**, No. 6, Nov.–Dec. 1962.

PERRELLA, VERA C. (1968), 'Women and the Labour Force', *Monthly Labour Review*, **91**, No. 2, Feb. 1968.

PERSSON, KONRAD (1961), *Social Welfare in Sweden*, Föreningen för främjande av folkpensionering och annan allmän försäkring.

PESTALOZZI, JOHN HEINRICH (1749–1827), *Pestalozzi's Educational Writings*, ed. J. A. Green, London 1912.

PHILP, A. F. (1964), *Family Failure*, Faber.

PIKE, M. (1967), *Needs Must*, Conservative Political Centre.

PILCH, M., and WOOD, V. (1964), *New Trends in Pensions*, Hutchinson.

PIRAUX, M. (1965), 'Budgets des Ménages et Charges Familiales', *Les Dossiers*, May–June 1965.

PITROU, A. (1965), 'Conditions de Logement et Insatisfaction des Ménages en 1961', *Consommation*, **12**, No. 3, July–Sept. 1965.

PLOWDEN REPORT (1966), *Children and their Primary Schools*, a Report of the Central Advisory Council for Education (England),
Vol. 1 Report (1966).
Vol. 2 Research and Surveys (1967), H.M.S.O.

POLANYI, K. (1945), *Origins of Our Time—The Great Transformation*, Gollancz.

POLITICAL AND ECONOMIC PLANNING (1952), 'Poverty Ten Years after Beveridge', *Planning*, 19, No. 344, Aug. 1952.

POLITICAL AND ECONOMIC PLANNING (1961), *Family Needs and the Social Services:* A Report of Survey, drafted by Winifred Moss.

POPULATION, ROYAL COMMISSION ON, Report (1949), Cmnd 7695, H.M.S.O.

POPULATION, ROYAL COMMISSION ON (1950), Report of The Economics Committee, H.M.S.O.

PRAIS, S. J. (1953), 'The Estimation of Equivalent Adult-scales from Family Budgets', Economic Journal, 63, No. 252, 1953.

PRAIS, S. J., and HOUTHAKKER, H. S. (1955), Analysis of Family Budgets, Cambridge University Press.

'Preisindex für die Einfache Lebenshaltung eines Kindes, Neuberechnung Eines', *Wirtschaft und Statistik*, No. 3, 1962, p. 95, Statistisches Bundesamt, Wiesbaden.

PRÉQUIÇA, SYLVIANE (1968), 'Les Jeunes Filles', *Informations Sociales*, No. 6, June 1968, Union Nationale des Caisses d'Allocations Familiales.

PRESVELOU, CLIO (1968), *Sociologie de la Consommation Familiale*, Les Éditions Vie Ouvrière, Brussels.

PRICE, D. O., and BURGESS, M. E. (1963), *An American Dependency Challenge*, American Public Welfare Association.

PRIGENT REPORT (1962), 'Rapport Général de la Commission d'Études des Problèmes de la Famille 1960–1962', Published in *C.A.F. Bulletin of Caisses d'Allocations Familiales*, No. 3, Mar. 1962.

RATHBONE, ELEANOR (1948), *The Case for Family Allowances*, Penguin Books.

RATHBONE, ELEANOR (1949), *Family Allowances*, Allen & Unwin. New edition of *The Disinherited Family* (1924), with additions by Lord Beveridge and Eva M. Hubback.

REDDIN, MICHAEL (1968), 'Local Authority Means Tested Services', *Social Services for All?*, Fabian Society.

REGISTRAR-GENERAL'S OFFICE (1966), *Statistical Review of England and Wales for the Year 1963*, Part III, Commentary, 1966, H.M.S.O.

REID, G. L., and ROBERTSON, D. J. (1965), *Fringe Benefits, Labour Costs and Social Security*. Allen & Unwin.

'RELATION OF SOCIAL SECURITY EXPENDITURES TO GROSS NATIONAL PRODUCT' (1965), *Social Security Bulletin*, **28**, No. 6, June 1965, U.S. Department of Health, Education and Welfare.

REYNOLDS, D. J. (1956), 'The Cost of Road Accidents', *Journal of Royal Statistical Society*, Series A, **119**, Part IV, 1956.

RHYS-WILLIAMS, JULIET (1965), *A New Look at Britain's Economic Policy*, Penguin Books.

RIBAS, J. J. (1967), 'Les Questions Familiales et les Services Sociaux dans la C.E.E.', *Informations Sociales*, No. 4, Apr. 1967, Union Nationale des Caisses d'Allocations Familiales.

RICE, DOROTHY P., and HOROWITZ, LOUCELE A. (1967), 'Trends in Medical Care Prices', *Social Security Bulletin*, **30**, No. 7, July 1967, U.S. Department of Health, Education and Welfare.

ROBBINS REPORT (1963), *Higher Education*, Report of Committee on Higher Education, Appendix IV, Cmnd. 2154, H.M.S.O.

ROBINSON, E. A. G., and VAIZEY, J. E. (eds.) (1966), *The Economics of Education*, Proceedings of a Conference convened by the International Economic Association, Macmillan.

ROTHBARTH, E. (1943), 'Note on a method of determining equivalent income for families of different compositions', Appendix 4, pp. 123–30; Madge, Charles, *Wartime Patterns of Spending and Saving* (1943), Cambridge University Press.

ROTTIER, GEORGE (1963), 'Consommation et Démographie', *Informations Sociales*, **17**, No. 12, Dec. 1963, Union Nationale des Caisses d'Allocations Familiales.

ROUTH, G. (1965), *Occupation and Pay in Great Britain*, Cambridge University Press.

ROWNTREE, B. SEEBOHM (1901), *Poverty: A Study of Town Life*, Macmillan.

ROWNTREE, B. SEEBOHM (1918), *Human Needs of Labour*, Longman Green. Revised 1937.

ROWNTREE, B. SEEBOHM (1941), *Poverty and Progress*, Longman Green.

ROWNTREE, B. SEEBOHM, and LAVER, G. R. (1951), *Poverty and the Welfare State*, Longman Green.

ST CHRISTOPHER'S FELLOWSHIP (late Fellowship of St Christopher), *A Place for Us?* (1966), *Nowhere to Live* (1967). See also *Daily Telegraph*, 22nd Feb. 1967, and *New Society*, 23rd Feb. 1967.

SALEMBIEN, E. (1960), 'Les Conditions du Marché du Logement et le Comportement des Ménages', *Consommation*, No. 3, 1960.

SANDFORD, C. (1967), *Taxing Inheritance and Capital Gains*, Institute of Economic Affairs.

SAUVY, ALFRED (1958), 'Réflexions sur la contribution des prestations familiales au progrès social', *C.A.F.* Aug.–Sept. 1958, Union Nationale Des Caisses d'Allocations Familiales.

SAUVY, ALFRED (1960), *Le Plan Sauvy*, Calmann-Levy.

SAUVY, ALFRED (1960), 'Évolution Récente des Idées sur le Surpeuplement', *Population*, June–July 1960.

SAUVY, ALFRED (1961), *Fertility and Survival* (Eng. trans.), Chatto & Windus.

SAUVY, ALFRED (1962), 'Démographie et Sécurité Sociale: Exposé General', Report presented to *Conférence Européenne sur la Sécurité Sociale Brussels, Dec. 1962*, vol. 2, p. 25.

SAUVY, ALFRED (1965), *Mythologie de Notre Temps*, Études et Documents, Payot.

SAUVY, ALFRED (1967), 'Cinquante Millions', *Le Monde Hebdomadaire*, 7th–13th Sept. 1967.

SAUVY, ALFRED (1967), *La Prévention des Naissances* (3rd ed.), Presses Universitaires de France.

SCHAEFER, R. J. (1965), *Die wissentschaftliche Forschung über die Kosten eines Kindes* (Conference Report), Deutscher Verein für öffentliche und private Fürsorge, Jan. 1965.

SCHLESINGER, B. (1963), *The Multi-Problem Family: Review and Annotated Bibliography*, University of Toronto Press.

SCHLESINGER, B. (1966), *Poverty in Canada and the United States: an Annotated Bibliography*, University of Toronto Press.

SCHMUCKER, HELGA (1954), 'Studie zur Frage des Familieneinkommens', *Allgemeines Statistisches Archiv*, **38**, 1954, p. 29, Carl Gerber, München.

SCHMUCKER, HELGA (1956), 'Der Lebenszyklus in Erwerbstätigkeit Einkommensbildung und Einkommensverwendung', *Allgemeines Statistisches Archiv*, **40**, 1956, p. 1, Carl Gerber, München.

SCHMUCKER, HELGA (1959), *Die ökonomischen Grundlagen der Familie in ihrer gesellschaftlichen Bedeutung*, Gesellschaft für Sozialen Fortschritt, Bonn 1959.

SCHMUCKER, HELGA (1959), 'Einfluss der Kinderzahl auf das Lebensniveau der Familien', *Allgemeines Statistisches Archiv*, **43**, 1959, p. 35, Carl Gerber, München.

SCHMUCKER, HELGA (1959), 'Einkommen und Kinderzahl in Bayern (1955),' *Zeitschrift des Bayerischen Statistischen Landesamts*, **91**, No. 3–4, 1959, München.

SCHMUCKER, HELGA (1961), *Die ökonomische Lage der Familie in der Bundesrepublik Deutschland*, Ferdinand Enke, Stuttgart.

SCHOOLS COUNCIL (1965), *Raising the School Leaving Age*, Working Paper No. 2, H.M.S.O.

SCHOOLS COUNCIL (1968), *Young School Leavers*, Schools Council, Enquiry No. 1, H.M.S.O.

SCHORR, ALVIN L. (1961), 'Aid to Dependent Children—What Direction?', *Child Welfare League of American Mid-Western Regional Conference 1961*.

SCHORR, ALVIN L. (1962), 'Family Policy in the United States', *International Social Science Journal*, 14, No. 3, 1962, p. 452.

SCHORR, ALVIN L. (1964), *Slums and Social Insecurity*, Nelson.

SCHORR, ALVIN L. (1965), *Social Security in Mid-career* (mimeographed).

SCHORR, ALVIN L. (1965), *Social Security and Social Services in France*, U.S. Department of Health, Education and Welfare.

SCHORR, ALVIN L. (1965), 'Income Maintenance and the Birth Rate', *Social Security Bulletin*, 28, No. 12, Dec. 1965, U.S. Department of Health, Education and Welfare.

SCHORR, ALVIN L. (1966), 'The Family Cycle and Income Development', *Social Security Bulletin*, 29, No. 2, Feb. 1966, U.S. Department of Health, Education and Welfare.

SCHORR, ALVIN L. (1966), *Poor Kids*, Basic Books.

SCHUBNELL, H. (1959), 'Number and Structure of Households and Families', Translation by Statistisches Bundesamt, May 1960, of article in *Wirtschaft und Statistik*, 11, New Series, vol. II, Nov. 1959, Statistisches Bundesamt, Wiesbaden.

SCHUBNELL, H. (1964), 'Die Erwerbstätigkeit von Frauen und Müttern und die Betreuung ihrer Kinder', *Wirtschaft und Statistik*, No. 8, 1964, p. 444, Statistisches Bundesamt, Wiesbaden.

SCHULTZ, THEODORE, W. (1959), 'Investment in Man', *Social Service Review*, 33, No. 2, June 1959.

SCHULTZ, TRUDY (1945–64), at Oxford Institute of Statistics, *Recosting of low cost diets*, using adult and child equivalent scales of Rowntree's early work, from 1945 to 1964. See Bulletin of the Institute to 1960, and thereafter the *'Cost of a Human Needs Diet'* was mimeographed until Autumn 1964.

SCHULTZ, TRUDY (1960), 'Nutrition at Different Income Levels', *Oxford Bulletin of Statistics*, 22, No. 143, 1960.

SCHULTZ, TRUDY (1962), 'Income, Family Structure and Food Expenditure Before and after the War', *Oxford Bulletin of Statistics*, 24, No. 447, 1962.

SCHWARZ, K. (1964), 'Die Kinderzahlen in den Ehen nach Bevölkerungsgruppen', *Wirtschaft und Statistik*, No. 2, 1964, p. 71, Statistisches Bundesamt, Wiesbaden.

SEEBOHM REPORT (1968), *Report of the Committee on Local Authority and Allied Personal Services*, Cmnd 3703, H.M.S.O.

SERVILLE, Y. (1963), 'Enquête sur l'Alimentation Familiale', *Nutrition, Bulletin de l'Institut Nationale d'Hygiène*, 18, No. 6, 1963.

SHAW, L. E. A. (1958), *A Study of Families in which Earnings are Interrupted by Illness, Injury or Death*, Department of Economics, University of Bristol. Unpublished but available in libraries and social science departments of universities.

SIMON, H. (1956), 'Un memoire du Ministre Fédéral de la Familie de Bonn sur la Compensation des Charges Familiales', 1954, *Pour La Vie*, June 1956, in number entitled *Aspects de la Famille dans le Monde*.

SIMON, H. (1963), 'Die Probleme der unvollständigen Familie', contained in Conference proceedings, ed. Best, Walter, under the title *Die Förderung der Familie als Aufgabe der Gesundheitspolitik*, 1963, Frankfurt-am-Main.

SOCIAL SECURITY, MINISTRY OF, Annual Reports (1966), Cmnd. 3338, and (1967) Cmnd 3693, H.M.S.O.

SOCIAL SECURITY, MINISTRY OF (1967), *Administration of the Wage Stop, Supplementary Benefits Commission*, H.M.S.O.

SOCIAL SECURITY, MINISTRY OF (1967), *Circumstances of Families*, H.M.S.O.

SOCIAL SECURITY, MINISTRY OF (1967), *Supplementary Allowances for People under Pension Age*, Leaflet S.I., *Supplementary Pensions (the Guaranteed Level)*, Leaflet S.P.1.

SOCIAL SURVEYS (GALLUP POLL) LTD. (1965), *The British on Holiday at Home and Abroad 1964*, A National Survey for the British Travel Association, 1 and 2, 1964 (mimeographed).

SOUTAR, M. S., et al. (1942), *Nutrition and the Size of the Family*, Report on a new housing estate prepared for Birmingham Social Survey Committee.

SPAIN (1964-5), *Encuesta de Presupuestos Familiares*, Instituto Nacional de Estadistica, Madrid.

STAMP, JOSIAH (1929), *The Fundamental Principles of Taxation in the Light of Modern Developments*, Macmillan.

STEINWENDER, K., *Das Kindergeld* (1961), A serial publication of the Bundesministerium für Arbeit und Sozialordnung, Kohlhammer, Stuttgart.

STONE, R. (1963), 'Consumer Wants and Expenditures: a Survey of British Studies since 1948', Paper before a Conference on *L'Évaluation et le Rôle des Besoins de Biens de Consommation dans les Divers Régimes Économiques*, Éditions du Centre National de la Récherche Scientifique, Paris.

STUTTGART (1961), *Die Unterhaltskosten eines Kindes von der Geburt bis zum 16 Lebensjahr*, Sozialamt der Stadt Stuttgart, Mar. 1961.

STUTTGART, Sozialamt: *Ergebnis der Untersuchung betr. das Verhältnis des Arbeitslohnes zum fürsorgerechtlichen Gesamtbedarf bei Städtischen Arbeitern mit 4 und mehr Kindern.*

SULLEROT, E. (1967), *Histoire et Sociologie de Travail Féminin*, Gonthier.

SUSSMAN, M. B. (1968), 'Current State and Perspectives of Research on the Family', *Social Sciences Information*, 7, No. 3, June 1968.

SWEDEN (1952), *Freedom and Welfare: Social Patterns in the Northern Countries of Europe*, Swedish Social Welfare Board.

SWEDEN (1957), *Ensamstående Mödrars Sociala och Ekonomiska Förhållanden ar 1955*, Sveriges Officiella Statistik.

SWEDEN (1961), *Family Expenditure Survey 1958, Hushållens Konsumtion År 1958*, Sveriges Officiella Statistik.

SWEDEN (1926), *Statistical Abstract of Sweden*, Aug. 1962, Central Bureau of Statistics.

SWEDEN (1963), *Taxes in Sweden*, Skattebetalarnas Förening, The Swedish Taxpayers' Association.

SWEDEN (1965), Swedish General Committee on Tax Revision, *A New System of Taxation*, Allmänna Skatteberedninges Betänkande (1965), Nytt Skattessystem, Statens Ofentligg Utredningar 1965: 28.

SWEDEN (1966), *Social Benefits in Sweden*, Swedish Institute.

SWITZERLAND (1964), Family Expenditure Survey, *Les Budgets Familiaux de Salariés en 1963*, Office Fédéral de l'Industries des Arts et Métiers et du Travail, *La Vie Economique*, Dec. 1964.

TABAH, F. (1951), 'Niveau de Vie des Familles suivant le Nombre d'Enfants', *Population*, 6, No. 2, Apr.–June 1951, pp. 287–305.

TABARD, N., *et al.* (1967), *Les Conditions de Vie des Familles*, Centre de Recherches et de Documentation sur la Consommation, Paris.

TALMY, R. (1962), *Histoire du Mouvement Familial en France (1896–1939)*, A sequel (1939–60) is in preparation, Union Nationale des Caisses d'Allocations Familiales.

TAXATION, ROYAL COMMISSION ON (1954), Cmnd 9109, H.M.S.O.

'TAXES AND WELFARE BENEFITS', *Barclays Bank Review*, 41, No. 2, May 1966.

TETLEY, HERBERT (1966), *The Changing Population of Great Britain*, Paper before the Insurance Institute of London.

TITMUSS, R. M. and K. (1942), *Parents Revolt, a study of the Declining Birth-rate in Acquisitive Societies*, Secker & Warburg.

TITMUSS, R. M. (1943), *Birth, Poverty and Wealth*, Hamilton.

TITMUSS, R. M. (1958), *Essays on the Welfare State*, Allen & Unwin.

TITMUSS, R. M., and ABEL-SMITH, B. (1961), *Social Policies and Population Growth in Mauritius 1961*, Cass (reprinted 1968).

TITMUSS, R. M. (1962), *Income Distribution and Social Change*, Allen & Unwin.

TITMUSS, R. M. (1968), *Commitment to Welfare*, Allen & Unwin.

TOWNSEND, PETER (1954), 'Measuring Poverty', *British Journal of Sociology*, 5, 1954, p. 130.

TOWNSEND, PETER (1962), 'The Meaning of Poverty', *British Journal of Sociology*, 13, No. 3, Sept. 1962.

TOWNSEND, PETER, et al. (1968), *Old People in Three Industrial Societies*, Routledge.

TOWNSEND, PETER (1968), *Social Services for All*, Fabian Society.

TREATY OF ROME: Treaty establishing the European Economic Community and connected Documents, Publishing Services of the European Communities.

TRÉMOLIÈRES, J., and VINIT, F. (1951), 'Enquête sur les Dépenses de Consommation dans Divers Milieux Sociaux de Marseille', *Bulletin de l'Institut National d'Hygiène*, 6, No. 1, Jan.–Mar. 1951.

TRÉMOLIÈRES, J. (1953), 'Enquête sur l'Alimentation des Familles Nombreuses à Marseille en Rapport avec le Niveau Socio-Économique', *Bulletin de l'Institut National d'Hygiène*, 8, No. 1, Jan.–Mar. 1953.

TRÉMOLIÈRES, J. (1959), 'Vues Actuelles sur l'Utilisation des Standards Nutritionnels pour Juger une Ration Alimentaire', *European Review of Nutrition and Dietetics*, 1, No. 1, 1959.

TRÉMOLIÈRES, J. (1963), 'Signification des Standards Calorico-Azotes Utilisés en France', *Voeding*, 24, No. 9, Sept. 1963.

UHR, CARL G. (1966), *Sweden's Social Security System*, Office of Research and Statistics, Research Report No. 14, U.S. Department of Health, Education and Welfare.

UNION NATIONALE DES CAISSES D'ALLOCATIONS FAMILIALES (1963), *Le Régime des Prestations Familiales*.

UNION NATIONALE DES CAISSES D'ALLOCATIONS FAMILIALES (1966), *XX^{ieme} Anniversaire des Allocations Familiales*, C.A.F., Dec. 1966.

UNITED NATIONS EDUCATIONAL SCIENTIFIC AND CULTURAL ORGANISATION (1963), 'Changes in the Family', *International Social Science Journal*, 14, No. 3, 1962.

UNITED NATIONS FOOD AND AGRICULTURE ORGANISATION, see under Food and Agriculture Organisation.

UNITED NATIONS (1954), *Report on International Definition and Measurement of Standards and Levels of Living*, 1954–IV–5.

UNITED NATIONS (1959), 'Improvement of Family Levels of Living through Social Security and Related Social Services', *International Social Service Review*, No. 5.

UNITED NATIONS (1961), *International Definition and Measurement of Levels of Living:* An Interim Article, United Nations 61–IV–7.

UNITED NATIONS (1964), *Handbook of Household Surveys: A Practical Guide for Inquiries on Levels of Living*, 64–XVII–13.

UNITED STATES (1963), *American Women:* Report of the President's Commission on the Status of Women.

UNITED STATES ADVISORY COUNCIL ON PUBLIC WELFARE (1966), *Having the Power we have the Duty:* Report to the Secretary of Health, Education and Welfare, June 1966.

UNITED STATES BUREAU OF CENSUS (1960), *Families*, vol. PC(2), Census of Population, 1960.

UNITED STATES BUREAU OF LABOR STATISTICS (1948), *Workers' Budgets in the United States: City Families and Single Persons*, 1946–7. Bulletin No. 927 from *Monthly Labor Review*, Feb. 1948, with additional data. U.S. Department of Labor.

UNITED STATES BUREAU OF LABOR STATISTICS (1960), 'The Interim City Worker's Family Budget', *Monthly Labor Review*, Aug. 1960. Reprint 2346 U.S. Department of Labor.

UNITED STATES BUREAU OF LABOR STATISTICS (1960), 'Estimating Equivalent Incomes or Budget Costs by Family Type', *Monthly Labor Review*, Nov. 1960, U.S. Department of Labor.

UNITED STATES BUREAU OF LABOR STATISTICS (1963), *Report of the Advisory Committee on Standard Budget Research*, U.S. Department of Labor.

UNITED STATES BUREAU OF LABOR STATISTICS (1964), *Consumer Expenditures and Income: Urban United States 1960–61*, Supplement 3, Part A, to B.L.S. Report Nos. 237–8, July 1964, U.S. Department of Labor.

UNITED STATES BUREAU OF LABOR STATISTICS (1965), *Consumer Expenditures and Income: Total United States. Urban and Rural 1960–61*, B.L.S. Report Nos. 237–93, U.S. Department of Labor.

UNITED STATES BUREAU OF LABOR STATISTICS (1966), *Handbook of Methods of Surveys and Studies*, Bulletin No. 1458, 1966, U.S. Department of Labor.

UNITED STATES BUREAU OF LABOR STATISTICS (1966), *City Workers' Family Budget: Pricing, Procedures, Specifications and Average Prices*, Bulletin No. 1570–3, 1966, U.S. Department of Labor.

UNITED STATES BUREAU OF LABOR STATISTICS (1967), *City Worker's Family Budget for a Moderate Living Standard*, Oct. 1967, Bulletin No. 1570–1, 1967, U.S. Department of Labor.

UNITED STATES BUREAU OF LABOR STATISTICS (1968), *City Worker's Family Budget: Retired Couples' Budget for a Moderate Living Standard*, Bulletin No. 1570–4, 1968, U.S. Department of Labor.

UNITED STATES BUREAU OF LABOR STATISTICS (1968), *Revised Equivalence Scales for Estimating Equivalent Incomes or Budget Costs by Family Size*, Bulletin No. 1570–2 (1968), U.S. Department of Labor.

UNITED STATES COMMISSIONER OF LABOR (1889), *Sixth and Seventh Annual Report 1791–92*, Part III, *Cost of Living*, 1889.

UNITED STATES COMMISSIONER OF LABOR (1903), Annual Report, U.S. Department of Labor.

UNITED STATES CONGRESS JOINT ECONOMIC COMMITTEE (1968), *Guaranteed Minimum Income Programs used by Governments of Selected Countries*, Paper No. 11, Economic Policies and Practice, 96–043.

UNITED STATES DEPARTMENT OF AGRICULTURE (1962), *Family Food Plans and Food Costs*, Home Economics Research Report No. 20, Consumer and Food Economics Research Division.

UNITED STATES DEPARTMENT OF AGRICULTURE (1964), *Family Food Plans*, Family Economics Review, Oct. 1964. Agricultural Research Service, Consumer and Food Economics Division, Nov. 1964.

UNITED STATES DEPARTMENT OF HEALTH, EDUCATION AND WELFARE (1963), *State Maximums and Other Methods of Limiting Money Payments to Recipients of Special Types of Public Assistance*, Oct. 1962, Division of Program Statistics and Analysis.

UNITED STATES DEPARTMENT OF HEALTH, EDUCATION AND WELFARE (1964), *Money Payments to Recipients of Special Types of Public Assistance*, Oct. 1963.

UNITED STATES DEPARTMENT OF HEALTH, EDUCATION AND WELFARE (1964), *Advance Release of Statistics on Public Assistance*, Oct. 1964, Bureau of Family Services: Division of Program Statistics and Analysis.

UNITED STATES DEPARTMENT OF HEALTH, EDUCATION AND WELFARE (1964), *Monthly Cost Standards for Basic Needs used by States for Specified Types of Old-Age Assistance Cases and Families Receiving aid to Families with Dependent Children*.

UNITED STATES DEPARTMENT OF HEALTH, EDUCATION AND WELFARE (1964), *Social Security Programs throughout the World*.

UNITED STATES DEPARTMENT OF HEALTH, EDUCATION AND WELFARE (1966), *Widows with Children under Social Security*, Research Report No. 16, 1966, Social Security Administration, Office of Research and Statistics.

UNITED STATES, *Economic Report of the President* (1963), Transmitted to Congress, Jan. 1963.

UNITED STATES NATIONAL BUREAU OF ECONOMIC RESEARCH (1952), 'Savings and Life Cycles', *Studies in Income and Wealth*, vol. 15, 1952.

UNITED STATES NATIONAL COMMISSION ON TECHNOLOGY, AUTOMATION AND ECONOMIC PROGRESS (1966), *Technology and the American Economy*, vol. I.

UNITED STATES NATIONAL RESEARCH COUNCIL, FOOD AND NUTRITION BOARD (1958), *Recommended Dietary Allowances* 1958, National Research Council Publication No. 589.

UNITED STATES TREASURY DEPARTMENT, INTERNAL REVENUE SERVICE (1965), *Federal Income Tax Forms for 1965* (Form 1040–ES 1965), *Instructions for Preparing your Federal Income Tax Form 1040 Individual Income Tax Rates 1965*, Pub. 465.

VAIZEY, J. (1962), *The Economics of Education*, Faber.

VEILLON, CHARLES (1962), 'Possibilités d'Harmonisation des Prestations de Sécurité Sociale', Report presented to *Conférence Européenne sur la Sécurité Sociale, Brussels, Dec. 1962*, vol. I, p. 193.

VERNHOLES, ALAIN (1967), 'Les Loyers sont souvent plus élevés en France que dans les autre pays du Marché Commun', *Le Monde Hebdomadaire*, 6th Sept. 1967.

VINIT, F. (1962), 'Enquête sur l'Alimentation et le Budget Familial à Saint-Étienne, Lyon et Marseille', *Nutrition, Bulletin de l'Institut National d'Hygiene*, **17**, No. 3, May–June 1962.

WALDMAN, ELIZABETH (1967), 'Marital and Family Characteristics of Workers: March 1966', *Monthly Labour Review*, **90**, No. 4, Apr. 1967.

WALDMAN, ELIZABETH (1968), 'Marital and Family Status of Workers', *Monthly Labour Review*, **91**, No. 4, Apr. 1968.

WALLEY, J. (1967), 'Future of Family Allowances I and II', *The Times*, 6th and 7th Apr. 1967. See also correspondence column, 4th Aug. 1967 and 8th Nov. 1968.

WALLEY, J. (1967), 'New Approach to Abolishing Child Poverty', *The Times*, 11th Dec. 1967.

WARIS, HEIKKI (1962), *Finnish Social Policy*, No. 81/62, Finnish Features Ministry of Foreign Affairs (in English).

WATTS, H. (1967), 'The ISO-prop Index: an Approach to the Determination of Differential Poverty Income Thresholds', *Journal of Human Resources*, **2**, No. 1, Winter 1967, p. 2.

WEAVER REPORT (1957), *Report of the Working Party on Educational Maintenance Allowances*, H.M.S.O.

WEBB, S. (1909), 'A Study of Social Evolution during the past three quarters of a Century', Cambridge Modern History 1909, reprinted by Fabian Society in a pamphlet 1916, *Towards Social Democracy*.

WIESBADEN, STATISTISCHES BUNDESAMT (1964), I. *Einnahmen und Ausgaben ausgewählter Arbeitnehmerhaushalte mit mittlerem Einkommen.* 2 *Einnahmen und Ausgaben ausgewählter Renter-und Sozialhilfempfängerhaushalte*, Statistisches Bundesamt, Wiesbaden, Fachserie M. Reihe 13, M. 13/I und 13/II Kohlhammer, Stuttgart.

WEISBROD, B. A. (1962), 'Education and Investment in Human Capital', *Journal of Political Economy*, **70**, No. 5, Part 2, 1962.

344   FAMILY POLICY

WEISBROD, B. A. (1966), 'Investing in Human Capital', *Journal of Human Resources*, **1**, No. 1, Summer 1966.

WICKENDEN, ELIZABETH (1964), 'The Legal Needs of the Poor', Paper to *Conference on the Extension of Legal Services to the Poor*. Washington, 12th Nov. 1964.

WICKENDEN, ELIZABETH (1965), *Social Welfare in a Changing World*, Welfare Administration Publication No. 8, U.S. Department of Health, Education and Welfare.

WICKENDEN, ELIZABETH (1966), 'Social Welfare Law, The Concept of Risk and Entitlement', *University of Detroit Law Journal*, **43**, No. 517, 1966.

WILLOUGHBY, G. (1964), 'Six or Seven', *Crucible*, July 1964.

WILLOUGHBY, G. (1966), 'Doctors and Patients in France', *New Society*, 22nd Dec. 1960.

WILSON, R. (1963), *Difficult Housing Estates*, Tavistock Publications.

WINGEN, MAX (1959), *Die Möglichkeiten zur Verbesserung der ökonomischen Lage der Familie*, Gesellschaft für Sozialen Fortschritt, Bonn, 1959.

WINGEN, MAX (1960), 'Der Betrieb als Träger von Familienpolitik', *Sozialer Fortschritt*, **9**, Part 1, Köln, Jan. 1960, p. 17.

WINGEN, MAX (1964), *Familienpolitik*, Bonifacius, Paderborn.

WISEMAN, S. (1964), *Education and Environment*, Manchester University Press.

WOODBURY, R. M. (1944), 'Economic Consumption Scales and their Uses', *Journal of American Statistical Association*, **38**, No. 43.

WÖRISHOFFER (1891), *Die soziale Lage der Fabrikarbeiter in Mannheim und dessen nächster Umgebung 1890*, Karlsruhe, 1891.

WRIGLEY, J. (1967), *Pre-surveys of Overspill Areas: Partington Cheshire* (mimeographed).

WUERMELING, F. J., et al. (1958), 'Familienpolitik, Gespräch uber den Familienlohn mit Beiträgen von Bundesminister', *Sozialer Fortschritt*, **7**, No. 5, May 1958.

WURZBACHER, G. (1960), 'Leistungen und Leistungsbehinderungen der Familie in der modernen Gesellschaft', In a Report of a Committee of the *Gesellschaft für Sozialen Fortschritt*, Duncker & Humblot, Berlin, 1960, p. 89.

WYNEN, L. (1962), 'The Financing of Social Housing', *Familles dans le Monde*, Sept. 1962.

WYNN, MARGARET (1964), *Fatherless Families*, Michael Joseph.

YOFFEE, W. M. (1967), 'New International Instruments on Invalidity, Old Age and Survivors' Pensions', *Social Security Bulletin*, **30**, No. 10, Oct. 1967, U.S. Department of Health, Education and Welfare.

YOUNG, M. (1952), 'Distribution of Income within the Family', *British Journal of Sociology*, **3**, No. 4, Dec. 1952, p. 305.

YOUNG, M. (1968) (ed.), *Forecasting and the Social Sciences*, Heinemann.

YOUNGHUSBAND, EILEEN (1965), *Social Work with Families*, Allen & Unwin.

YUDKIN, S., and HOLME, A. (1963), *Working Mothers and their Children*, Michael Joseph.

YUDKIN, S. (1967), 0–5: *A Report on the Care of Pre-school children*, National Society of Children's Nurseries.

ZEITLIN, L. (1962), *Life's Value in Cash*, Oswald Wolff.

ZELENKA, ANTOINE (1962), 'Les Tendances de la Securité Sociale dans le Monde: Exposé Général', Report presented to *Conférence Européenne sur la Securité Sociale*, Dec. 1962, Brussels, vol. 2, p. 7.

ZIMMERMANN, C. C. (1936), *Consumption and Standards of Living*, D. Van Nostrand, N.Y.

ZÖLLNER, D. (1964), *Social Legislation in the Federal Republic of Germany*, Asgard-Verlag, Bad Godesberg.

Index